Praise for *Culturally Responsive Mental Health Practice with Nonreligious Clients*

"Every therapist needs to read this book. People without traditional religious faith—atheists, agnostics, humanists, and 'nones'—make up the largest religious minority in America. Yet in a culture that treats Judeo-Christian faith as the default, many can and do experience discrimination, stigma, and misunderstanding—including in mental health settings.

As religious nationalists ramp up their attacks on nonbelievers, it's more critical than ever that mental health practitioners understand how to serve nonbelievers with compassion, acceptance, and positive regard, just as they would any person of faith. Dena M. Abbott has put together a deeply researched and vital guide that offers best practices for doing just that."

—**Fish Stark**, executive director of the American Humanist Association

"For too long, mental health resources have failed to keep pace with the rapid growth and diversity of nonreligious Americans. Too many well-intentioned professionals still assume faith is always a virtue, overlooking the reality that the secular community is as varied and complex as any religious one.

"As someone who has covered atheism in America for more than two decades, I've turned again and again to the researchers featured in this book. They understand the nuance. They know the history. And they can teach clinicians how to truly meet nonreligious clients where they are.

"Dr. Dena M. Abbott has brought together an extraordinary collection of voices and insights. The result is essential reading for any mental health professional who wants to move beyond headlines and stereotypes toward genuine understanding and empathy.

"This book will change how you think about the nonreligious—and, more importantly, how you work with them."

—**Hemant Mehta**, editor of FriendlyAtheist.com

"In what may be the first of its kind, this edited volume combines the latest academic research on nonreligious mental health with practical advice for health practitioners working with nonreligious populations. The authors provide a detailed history of the religious biases baked into much of Western psychology and they offer concrete suggestions for how to overcome those biases in diagnostic materials and recommended therapies. With chapters that focus in on issues related to specific nonreligious subgroups—such as BIPOC and LGBTQ nonreligious populations—and recommendations for secular approaches to a range of issues that nonreligious people face—such as addiction and religious trauma—this volume is sure to become a go-to resource for both scholars and health practitioners seeking to better understand and support the growing nonreligious population."

—**Jacqui Frost**, assistant professor of sociology, Purdue University

Culturally Responsive Mental Health Practice with Nonreligious Clients

Culturally Responsive Mental Health Practice with Nonreligious Clients

Edited by Dena M. Abbott

BLOOMSBURY ACADEMIC
NEW YORK • LONDON • OXFORD • NEW DELHI • SYDNEY

BLOOMSBURY ACADEMIC
Bloomsbury Publishing Inc, 1359 Broadway, New York, NY 10018, USA
Bloomsbury Publishing Plc, 50 Bedford Square, London, WC1B 3DP, UK
Bloomsbury Publishing Ireland, 29 Earlsfort Terrace, Dublin 2, D02 AY28, Ireland

BLOOMSBURY, BLOOMSBURY ACADEMIC and the Diana logo are
trademarks of Bloomsbury Publishing Plc

First published in the United States of America 2025

Cover design: Dustin Watson

A catalog record for this book is available from the Library of Congress.

ISBN: HB: 979-8-2162-7787-3
PB: 979-8-2162-7784-2
ePDF: 979-8-2162-7785-9
eBook: 979-8-2162-7786-6

Typeset by Integra Software Services Pvt. Ltd.
Printed and bound in the United States of America

For product safety related questions contact productsafety@bloomsbury.com.

To find out more about our authors and books visit www.bloomsbury.com
and sign up for our newsletters.

Contents

Figures

Boxes and Tables

Boxes

Tables

About the Editor

Dena M. Abbott, PhD (she/her) is a licensed psychologist in the state of Nebraska and an AASECT-Certified Sexuality Educator. She owns and operates an independent psychology practice, Dr. Dena M. Abbott Psychological Services and Sexuality Education (www.drdenaabbott.com), providing PSYPACT authorized telehealth services throughout the United States. Currently an associate professor in the APA-Accredited Counseling Psychology program at University of Nebraska–Lincoln, Dr. Abbott's research focuses on the impact of hegemonic Christianity and Christian nationalism on mental health and well-being, with a particular emphasis on the health of nonreligious Americans. Along with a colleague, in 2022 she was awarded over $170,000 from the Explaining Atheism program to fund "Unbelief Within Marginalized Communities" (www.explainingatheism.org), a project aimed at understanding the causal origins of nonbelief among diverse atheists. She has published over twenty-five peer-reviewed articles and book chapters related to nonreligion, sexual and reproductive health, and cultural responsiveness in mental health treatment.

About the Contributors

Carrie Bohmer, PhD, is currently a resident in psychology in the state of Virginia and is actively pursuing licensure as a psychologist. She works as an integrated psychologist at the Virginia Women's Center where she specializes in reproductive mental health, sexual health, and mental health of people with uteruses/vulvas. Her dissertation, "The Overturning of Roe v. Wade: An Intepretative Phenomenological Analysis," explored the lived experiences of people capable of pregnancy living in trigger-ban states following the *Dobbs v. Jackson Women's Health* decision. She is passionate about sexual and reproductive education and liberation and continues to engage in clinical work and research that aligns with these efforts.

Alex Borgella, PhD, is an associate professor of psychology at Fort Lewis College in Durango, Colorado, and director of the Social Perception Experimentation (SPEx) Lab. Broadly, his research program is dedicated to understanding the mental processes behind how biases form, the ways they persist, and how we talk about them. His main research interests concern how members of different social groups communicate in intergroup contexts, how implicit forms of bias can affect decision-making, and how bias affects people differently within individual social categories.

Melanie Elyse Brewster is a professor of psychology and education at Columbia University in the counseling psychology PhD program. As a New York state licensed psychologist, she holds a part-time private psychotherapy practice and has worked with a broad array of clinical issues. Her book, *Atheists in America*, was published in 2014. She was formerly editor of the journal *Secularism and Nonreligion* and an associate editor for the *Journal of Counseling Psychology*. Regarding research and scholarship, Brewster writes extensively on issues of minority stress, stigma, and discrimination, with over seventy peer-reviewed articles and book chapters.

Ryan T. Cragun is professor of empirical sociology at the University of Tampa. His research focuses on the nonreligious and Mormonism and has been published in various scholarly journals. He is also the author of several books, including *Beyond Doubt: The Secularization of Society* and *Goodbye, Religion: The Causes and Consequences of Secularization* (with Jesse M. Smith).

Luke W. Galen is a professor of psychology at Grand Valley State University. His main research areas include the study of the psychology of religious belief as well as the characteristics of atheists and agnostics. His most recent book is *A Social Cognition Perspective of the Psychology of Religion: "Why God Thinks like You."* He is also a co-author of the book *The Non-Religious: Understanding Secular People and Societies.*

Bethany Gull is assistant professor of integrated arts and sciences at Utah Tech University. Her research interests include religion/nonreligion, identity, and gender. She is the author of a number of research articles and book chapters and has been published in journals such as *Sociology of Religion, Social Compass,* and *Symbolic Interaction.*

Paige Hespe is a doctoral candidate in the APA-accredited Counseling Psychology PhD program at the University of Nebraska-Lincoln. Paige's research and clinical interests focus on issues related to personal meaning-making and existential concerns. Paige's research is centered on values identification, meaning-making processes, and reasons for living in transgender and atheist communities. In clinical practice, Paige often works with grief and with transgender and atheist clients from a narrative, values-based orientation.

Clayton Hartmann (he/him) is an assistant professor at Pacific University's School of Graduate Psychology. His research interests focus on the tension between the individual and mass culture as a way to better understand what are commonly understood as psychopathologies. His clinical interests include the theory and treatment of personality complications and substance misuse. Outside of the classroom and the consulting room, Clay enjoys the solitude of the hobby machinist's workshop and the challenge of a high-alpine scramble.

Simon Howard, PhD, is the director of the Psychology of Racism, Identity, Diversity, and Equity (PRIDE) lab and an assistant professor in the Department of Psychology at the University of Miami. He is a first-generation college graduate who completed his undergraduate degree at San Jose State University. Dr. Howard went on to earn his PhD in social psychology at Tufts University. Using experimental methods drawn from cognitive, perceptual, and social investigations his research aims to understand and address contemporary racism. To this end he has conducted research on the interpersonal and contextual influences on racially biased perception, judgment, behavior, and mental health of both historically advantaged (e.g., White people) and disadvantaged group members (e.g., Black people). His recent work can be organized in three broad themes: (1) the role of religion in maintaining racial hierarchy; (2) the influence of race on perception, judgment, and behavior; and (3) the consequences of exposure to vicarious racism for racially stigmatized groups.

Veronica Kim (they/them) is a doctoral student in counseling psychology at Teachers College, Columbia University and APA's Interdisciplinary Minority Fellow. Their research interests include minority stress, sex positivity, and individual/collective resilience among diverse minoritized communities with a focus on TGD people of color. They received a bachelor's in studio art and philosophy from New York University and a master's in clinical psychology with a concentration in spirituality mind-body practice from Teachers College, Columbia University.

Ginny Maril (she/her) is an assistant professor of practice in the Department of Educational Psychology and the director of clinical services at the Counseling and Mental Health Center at the University of Texas at Austin as well as a private practitioner. She is a licensed psychologist and a registered health service psychologist with clinical focus in trauma recovery, chronic illness, and college students.

Patrick T. Meyer (he/they) is a doctoral student in counseling psychology at the University of Nebraska-Lincoln. He received his bachelor's degree in psychology with a minor in women's and gender studies from the College of Charleston. Their scholarly interests include LGBTQIA+ mental health, psychodynamic psychotherapy, and existential psychotherapy. Currently, he is studying the lived experiences of religious trauma among transgender and gender diverse people in the United States. They have received the Othmer Fellowship from University of Nebraska-Lincoln and have presented their research at the American Psychological Association Annual Convention.

Debra Mollen (she/her) is a professor and director of the Counseling Psychology graduate programs at Texas Woman's University, a licensed psychologist, and a certified sexuality educator with the American Association of Sexuality Educators, Counselors, and Therapists (AASECT). Her research centers on sexuality, reproductive justice, multiculturalism, and training and professional issues. She is coauthor with Brian Baird of the ninth edition of *The Internship, Practicum, and Field Placement Handbook* published by Taylor & Francis (2023) and cochair, with Sharon Lamb and Lillian Comas-Díaz, of the revised American Psychological Association (APA)'s *Guidelines for Psychological Practice with Girls and Women* (2018). Debra is an associate editor for *Psychology of Women Quarterly* and tri-chair for the forthcoming APA *Guidelines for Sex-Positive Practice: Sex and Reproduction in Professional Psychology*. In 2020, Debra was named the Woman of the Year by APA Division 17 Section for the Advancement of Women. In 2022, she was named a Distinguished Leader for Women in Psychology by the APA's Committee on Women in Psychology. She is a fellow in APA Divisions 17 (Society of Counseling Psychology) and 35 (Psychology of Women).

Wei Motulsky, PhD (they/them) holds a doctorate in counseling psychology from Teachers College, Columbia University. Their research has emphasized queer minority stress and its intersections with marginalized identities including nonbelief, race, and social class, while their clinical foci include queer identity, complex personality presentations, and post-traumatic stress. When not working, you can find Wei going for a run, taking care of their menagerie of animals, or playing video games.

Millie L. Myers, MA, is a doctoral candidate in the counseling psychology program at the University of Nebraska-Lincoln. Millie received her master's in educational psychology from UNL and her BS in psychology and sociology at Texas A&M University. Her research interests center the well-being of nonreligious people, specifically how atheist women develop social safety and build affirming communities. Millie hopes to pursue a career in college athletics to work with young people and advocate from a platform of self-compassion, body liberation, and social justice.

Jacob S. Sawyer, PhD is an assistant professor of psychology at Grand Valley State University. His primary research interests include grief literacy, psychological experiences related to grief, and college student mental health.

Jesse M. Smith is associate professor of sociology at Western Michigan University. His research focuses on secularity and identity. He has published articles in a variety of journals and has coauthored and edited two books, including *Goodbye, Religion: The Causes and Consequences of Secularization* and *Secularity and Nonreligion in North America: An Introduction* (with Ryan T. Cragun).

Teagan M. Wilson (she/her) is a doctoral student at the University of Nebraska-Lincoln in counseling psychology. She received her bachelor's degree in psychology with minors in social welfare advocacy and criminal justice from Indiana University and a master's degree in clinical mental health from Ball State University. Teagan's research interests include sexual health and satisfaction as well as nonreligiousness and atheism.

Part I

Foundations

1

Introduction

Christian Hegemony and Western Approaches to Mental Health Care

Dena M. Abbott and Millie L. Myers

Chapter Outline

Culturally Responsive Mental Health Practice with Nonreligious Clients is a resource for mental health educators, clinicians, researchers, and advocates to promote their professional work with nonreligious people in the United States (US). The number of nonreligious US Americans has grown dramatically in the early twenty-first century, comprising 28 percent of the US population in 2023 (Pew Research, 2024). In fact, the nonreligious are projected to approach the majority in the United States by 2070 (Pew Research Center, 2022). Informed by a growing body of literature related to the psychology of nonreligious people and co-created by leading scholars and experts, this text (1) provides historical background and the current state of nonreligion in the United States, (2) highlights the unique strengths and challenges of living as a nonreligious person in the United States, (3) centers the intersections of race, gender, and sexuality among nonreligious people, and (4) offers concrete recommendations to adapt and expand the professional work of mental health specialists to promote equity, health, and healing among the nonreligious people they serve.

Mental health practice and the discipline of psychology are generally considered to be secularly grounded (Reber, 2006) and most psychologists are identified as nonreligious (Delaney et al., 2007). However, we argue the history of global (Stuerzenhofecker, 2020) and US-based Christian supremacy (Whitehead & Perry, 2020) has insidiously influenced Western psychology. Specifically, many common theories and practices in mental health care, even when secular in nature and execution, were influenced by Christian norms in US culture and developed when an overwhelming majority of people in the United States identified as people of faith. A critical reflection on the manner by which this may have influenced the science and practice of psychology and, in turn, the current state of mental health care is as yet unexamined. As a result, some elements of mental health education, practice, and research omit, misunderstand, or misalign with the values of nonreligious people, a critical problem to address given the rising proportion of religiously unaffiliated US Americans. Therefore, to begin this text and to inform mental health professionals' culturally responsive and affirming care for nonreligious people, we begin to unpack the ways in which religion and spirituality underpin Western psychology.

Author Positionalities and Reflections

In undertaking this work, we, the authors, recognize that our identities and experiences shape the perspectives offered. This chapter is, therefore, informed by our experiences as White, US settler, cisgender women in the discipline of counseling psychology. Dr. Abbott and Ms. Myers are faculty and doctoral student, respectively, at a large land-grant university in the midwestern United States. Both were raised in Protestant families, formerly identified as personally religious and/or spiritual, and currently identify as atheist. We acknowledge our position that Christian dominance in the United States negatively impacts the public, particularly when Christian faith is politicized and weaponized in ways that violate human rights. As psychologists, we are also keenly aware of the ways in which religion can promote health for religious people, through belongingness, meaning-making, and coping with stress, among other benefits. Therefore, our intention is not to critique personal theism when it feels valuable and healthy for individuals; rather, we hope to elucidate the ways structural hegemonic Christianity seeps into the fabric of our society and profession and has the potential to harm the people we serve, particularly those who are nonreligious.

As you read the following chapters, we encourage you to consider your own cultural positionalities and personal history with religion and spirituality. Specifically, you might foster curiosity about how your experiences are shaping your response to the content of this and other chapters in this text. Additionally, the following questions may help you to reflect on the ways in which (non)religion and (non)spirituality may unconsciously and consciously influence your clinical work:

- What beliefs do I currently hold regarding (non)religion and/or (non)spirituality? How have my formative experiences shaped my current (non)belief systems, values, and/or worldviews?
- What do I understand about the relationship between (non)religion and/or (non)spirituality and (mental) health? What, if anything, was I taught about this relationship in my formal mental health training?

- In what ways are (non)religion and/or (non)spirituality present and examined in my clinical work?
- How, if at all, do I disclose my (non)religious and/or (non)spiritual experiences and perspectives to clients? How might my clients be impacted by these disclosures?

Terminology

Throughout this chapter and text we use the term *nonreligious* to describe a broad range of worldviews and social identities marked by the absence of belief in god(s) (Bullivant, 2013). Some of the most common groups included in the nonreligious, as we conceptualize it, might be atheists, agnostics, and people who indicate believing in nothing in particular. However, there are infinite other labels that might be used by nonreligious people to more accurately describe their nonbelief (e.g., freethinkers, secular). In some studies of the nonreligious, people who retain a higher power but have exited organized forms of religion are included. We draw a distinction between belief in a higher power that is supernatural in nature and belief in god(s) specific to a faith system (e.g., a Christian god). People with the latter belief would be *religious* even if not actively engaged in institutionalized forms of religion (e.g., attending church), whereas the former would be nonreligious. The former may also sometimes be referred to as "spiritual but not religious."

Spirituality is sometimes considered a search for the sacred (Zinnbauer & Pargament, 2000) and when defined as such is an element of religiousness. Spirituality can also refer to a belief in something "bigger than oneself," moving, or simply important (Cragun et al., 2015; Hill et al., 2001). These nonsacred forms of spirituality, for the purpose of this book, we consider to be nonreligious. When inclusively referring to the expansive spectrum from theism to atheism, we use the terms (non)religious and (non)spirituality.

Christianity and the History of Psychology

The history of psychology has followed a fascinating path across various time periods in which spirituality and then religion were focalized or repudiated, leaving a haze of influence through which we are only just beginning to parse. In its earliest incarnations, psychology was situated at the inextricable crossroads of the fields of medicine and spirituality. Early traditions of prescientific psychology included mesmerism, the practice of clearing blockages in magnetic fluid flowing through the body (Fuller, 1982), which migrated to the United States in the 1830s as a cure for depression and various phobias through this period of "antebellum American psychology" (Schmit, 2005, p. 403). The trend of the infusion of spirituality into psychology continued through the spread of spiritualism, also known as spiritism, and broader psychic practices. Practitioners marketed their abilities to facilitate contact with the dead through séances, which experienced a significant resurgence in the midst of the mass casualties of World War I and the 1918 Influenza Pandemic after an initial decline into the twentieth century. The impossibility of establishing scientific proof of faith made spiritualism "thus organized for failure," a claim identified in seminal work documenting the history of the discipline (Beard, 1879, p. 66). A final representation of spiritualism in psychology was mental healing, otherwise known as the "mind cure" or "new thought" movement, which posited itself as a self-healing methodology "ground[ed] in a religious sensibility" (Schmit, 2018, p. 188).

At the turn of the twentieth century, spiritual practices faded in popularity with "the institutionalization of medicine and psychology" (Schmit, 2018, p. 202). As the ideology that psychology was the science of behavior became prevalent (Benjamin, 2019), many early psychologists espoused significant "religious antipathy" (Spilka, 2012, p. 93). Sigmund Freud, described by one historian as "a cantankerous atheist who denigrated religion and belittled believers," equated religious belief to pathological tendencies such as neuroticism and asserted the concept of an all-powerful god undermined an individual's independence (Hewitt, 2014, p. viii). B. F. Skinner, whose contributions to the discipline laid the foundation for the field of behaviorism, saw religion as a function of cultural values reinforced by society, rather than intrinsic to individual belief (Staddon, 2013). Skinner believed religion was not a benign force but rather "a non-scientific phenomenon and a tool for power and social control" (García-Alandete, 2024, p. 6). Albert Ellis, an early proponent of the cognitive-behavioral tradition who developed rational emotive behavior therapy, held particularly acerbic views on piety; he equated devout religiousness with dependence, masochism, and subservience to authority, describing religious psychotherapy as "exceptionally pernicious" and "antithetical" to mental health (Ellis, 1976, p. 4).

Despite pushback against the integration of religion in psychology by these early leaders, other prominent figures emerged as strong advocates for the psychological study of religiousness and its impact on mental health. With the early twentieth century came a "momentum" that characterized the fusion of religion within psychology in the United States (Wulff, 1997, p. 25). In 1902, William James, among the founders of the discipline of psychology, published *The Varieties of Religious Experience*, defending the value of religious experiences. Publicly, he criticized other psychologists for underappreciating the value of religious experience (Morgan, 2011). Stanley Hall played a key role in the establishment of psychology and the scientific psychological study of religion in the United States (Spilka, 2012). Alongside founding the American Psychological Association (APA) and serving as its first president, Hall established the *American Journal of Religious Psychology and Education*. In the ensuing decades, an entire subdiscipline devoted to religious belief proliferated, housed within APA's Division 36: Society for the Psychology of Religion and Spirituality, with more than a dozen peer-reviewed journals and thousands of members.

Other psychologists whose work contributed greatly to the philosophical development of the field were unequivocal in their belief in the importance of religion. Despite views that challenged the orthodox Christianity with which he was raised, Carl Jung remained a believer and suggested the absence of a connection to god resulted in a lack of purpose and joy that could lead to mental illness (Ulanov, 2008). Further, Jung posited religiously based worldviews could reduce chaos in modern society (Morgan, 2011). Jung attributed perpetual sociopolitical conflict and the resulting collective suffering with the decline in participation in religious life (Miranda, 2019), convicted that religion was "necessary" for the development of humanity (Shamdasani, 2009, p. 207). The persistent and misconstrued association between religion and a myriad of positive psychosocial outcomes was likely informed, in part, by Jung's influence.

Another branch of psychological tradition entrenched in religious and spiritual ideology is existentialism. Irvin Yalom identified the commonalities between psychotherapy and ministry: namely, the interpersonal relationship, confessional nature, role of self-evaluation, and forgiveness (Yalom, 2002). Yalom understood distress to be the result of deeply entrenched intrapsychic conflict about the four ultimate concerns of death, freedom, isolation, and meaninglessness, and thus developed existential therapy to counteract "the intrinsic despair of the human condition" (2002, p. 301). Existential theory posits that death anxiety is the precursor to the development of religions, rooted in an unconscious universal human desire to identify an "ultimate rescuer" figure that provides security. While Yalom described his foundational text as an offering of "excursions into philosophy," the influence of religious ideology into existential theory, and thereby existential therapy, is undeniable (Yalom, 1980, p. 16).

Under the umbrella of existential therapy is logotherapy, Victor Frankl's life philosophy and therapeutic treatment modality. Based on the pursuit of spiritual freedom as a reprieve from physical and psychological stress, Frankl described the theory as a bridge between religion and psychotherapy (Frankl, 1955). Rooted in his experience as a Jewish person who experienced internment in Europe during the Holocaust, central to logotherapy is the tenet that life without spiritual purpose is meaningless, and such a life fosters an existential frustration that underscores psychological pathology and dysfunction. Frankl deigned those without belief as living in "spiritual poverty," which "represents a symptom of the mass neuroses" (Wulff, 1997, p. 129). Frankl saw the processes of psychological and pastoral care as complementary in the respective pursuits of health and salvation, with unique goals of healing and saving the soul. Although some have defended Frankl's distinction between religion and psychology (e.g., García-Alandete, 2024), Frankl himself postulated that "religion provides man with a spiritual anchor and a feeling of security that he cannot find anywhere else" (1954, p. 39), a sentiment clearly unsupportive of the values and experiences of the nonreligious/nonspiritual.

Religious Influences Infused Within Psychotherapy

The aforementioned search for meaning is prevalent in humanistic and contemporary psychotherapies, from Frankl's logotherapy to the recent influence of positive psychology. Of course, culturally responsive psychotherapy includes integrating clients' (non)religious and (non)spiritual beliefs and values, if any, into treatment including acknowledging spiritually based healing practices. However, there are common practices in psychotherapy that find their roots in religion and may inadvertently convey a spiritual imperative in order to maximize health and wellness.

Religious influence is prevalent even in the most recently reimagined directions for the field. Mainstream psychology has long been criticized for advancing the interests of privileged groups through pathologizing political resistance and psychological maladjustment (Malherbe, 2022). In response, leaders within the discipline of psychology have identified liberation psychology as the framework of the future to center social justice and advocacy as core values (Singh, 2020). Paradoxically, the paradigm of liberation is rooted in religious tradition. Contemporary tenets of liberation psychology were developed from the theological work of Salvadoran priest Ignacio Martin-Baró, who launched a captivating social movement in the 1980s to raise critical consciousness and resist the socioeconomic oppression of marginalized people (Montero & Sonn, 2009). Martin-Baró recognized religion as a tool frequently weaponized for the ideological purpose of maintaining existing social, economic, and political structures (1994); however, his reimagining of religion as a tool to challenge dominant institutions perpetuates the religious and spiritual influence on contemporary psychology and the broader cultural milieu, thereby potentially reinforcing patriarchal harm.

The current movement toward liberation psychology, particularly in the authors' discipline of counseling psychology, is grounded in a spiritual nonreligious foundation that emphasizes the therapeutic goal of fostering psychospiritual healing (Anzaldúa, 2015). This "justice-oriented spirituality" centers spiritual traditions such as indigenous healing practices to affirm cultural practices (Comas-Díaz & Torres Rivera, 2020, p. 179). Indeed, it is critical to acknowledge and value that psychological knowledge outside the West may be grounded in the evidence of healing through religious traditions, rather than scientific observation (Dueck et al., 2017). However, little attention has been paid to secular, nonspiritual perspectives in the spiritual activism movement. Centering religion and spirituality as decolonial and liberatory pathways that facilitate cultural healing (Bryant, 2024) is crucial in advancing antiracist praxis, particularly for people from the Global Majority who are widely minoritized. However, careful and thoughtful application is necessary to avoid ignoring the historical legacy of religious/spiritual harm and/or neglecting the experience of nonreligious/nonspiritual people.

Another recent shift in the discipline has been the influence of strengths-oriented frameworks designed to promote well-being rather than to reduce symptomotology (Hage, 2003). Notable among this movement is positive psychology, a science in which subjective experiences including contentment, satisfaction, hope, optimism, and flourishing are proactively examined and fostered (Seligman & Csikszentmihalyi, 2000). The parallels between the values highlighted by positive psychology and those traditionally associated with Christian teachings have long been identified and even advocated by religious scholars, particularly the eudaimonic focus on virtues conducive to a Christian conceptualization of the "good life" (Nelson & Slife, 2016). Others advance the collectivist values of positive psychology as a salve against the "congenital spiritual-psychological defect" of self-interest (Charry & Kosits, 2017, p. 470). These underlying messages ingrained within positive psychology reinforce shaming narratives and emphasize the need for external support (i.e., religious/spiritual authority) in improving the human condition (Ağılkaya-Şahin, 2018; Faller, 2001).

Spiritual Influences Infused Within Psychotherapy

Western forms of mindfulness are prevalent in psychotherapy both as integrative or atheoretical interventions and as more intentional components of modalities grounded in theory. In Acceptance and Commitment Therapy (ACT), there is "notable overlap" with Christian beliefs and biblical parables (Fung, 2014, p. 573). The core processes of ACT, including defusion, acceptance, present moment, and self-as-context, also bear a striking resemblance to the Four Noble Truths of Buddhism, although there is no acknowledgment of the influence (Fung, 2014). Contrarily, the creator of ACT claims the approach is "a notable exception" to the list of common Western mindfulness therapeutic traditions that have emerged in part from Buddhist tenets (Harris, 2019, p. 82).

Not only are these practices potentially incongruent for aspiritual people, depending on the practitioner, they may also constitute cultural appropriation. Mindfulness originated as a Buddhist practice involving contemplating the body, emotions, states of mind, and experiences with the purpose of relieving suffering and achieving nirvana. Although Western forms of mindfulness exist, like the Christian contemplative practice of maintaining awareness of the presence of god, it is this Buddhist mindfulness that most psychotherapy approaches misappropriate (Sun, 2014). On the other hand, mindfulness as a secular practice and psychotherapy technique has been critiqued for the exclusion of the cultural worldview in which mindfulness practice was developed (Stratton, 2014).

Spiritual meditation has been identified as superior to secular forms of meditation in promoting health (Stratton, 2014; Wachholtz & Pargament, 2008). However, as in other R/S scholarship, these studies comprise predominantly religious and/or spiritual participants without methods of controlling for the influence of spirituality on findings. Therefore, extant scholarship may lead practitioners to favor spiritually based mindfulness though it may not be useful for nonreligious or nonspiritual clients.

Religious Influence on Survey Instruments

Many commonly used measures to assess psychological constructs contain items that assume religiousness and/or spirituality. For example, Tedeschi and Calhoun's (1996) Posttraumatic Growth Inventory (PTGI) includes a Spiritual Growth subscale consisting of two items, one of which reads "I have stronger religious faith." The Brief-COPE (Carver, 1997), often used in health research to assess coping strategies, includes a religion subscale with items about use of prayer and finding comfort in belief. Importantly, these sorts of items capture low to high religiousness or spirituality but not secularity or faith that is in transition (Speed & Hwang, 2019).

Similarly, measures of well-being often include items related to meaning in life. For example, the Depression Anxiety Stress Scale (DASS; Lovibond & Lovibond, 1995) includes the item, "I felt that life was meaningless." The greater the degree to which a person endorses this item applies to them, and in combination with other items measuring depressive symptoms, the more indicative of depression. Notably, although some nonbelievers make meaning in areligious ways (Coleman et al., 2019), others describe life as meaningless in accordance with their atheism. Importantly, meaninglessness does not necessarily reflect poor mental health. Existential meaninglessness, or the absence of meaning attributed to one's life, is negatively correlated with well-being (Schnell, 2009) and positively correlated with existential anxiety, which often catalyzes search for meaning (Yalom, 1980). However, confounds in research design and inaccurate measurement of (non)religion (see chapter 5, "Nonreligion, Well-Being, and Mental Health," for a review) lead to inaccurate generalizations of such research to all people—theists and atheists alike. Rather, it may be more likely that the positive relationship between meaninglessness, anxiety, and well-being is most consistent with the experiences of people of faith for whom meaning-making is more salient.

Religious Influence on Assessment

The integration of (non)religion into psychometrics is also poorly understood, as race and ethnicity have been more extensively investigated as cultural variables impacting assessment and interpretation (Allik et al., 2012). Despite efforts to expand the cultural and linguistic inclusivity of commonly utilized assessment measures, many, including the Minnesota Multiphasic Personality Inventory (MMPI), Personality Assessment Inventory (PAI), Rorschach, and Thematic Apperception Test (TAT) were normed on predominantly White samples, thereby limiting the validity of interpretation among other identity groups (Smith & Krishnamurthy, 2018). Recommendations have been made to gather separate norms to address the varying experiences of (non)religious populations (Bier, 1971), to little avail. For example, the recently updated MMPI-3 does not provide information about the (non)religious diversity of its normative sample (Technical Manual). Assessment measures may also overpathologize those with spiritual beliefs that deviate from the pervasive Christian values that underscored their development. Numerous studies have identified (non)spiritual insensitivity in the now outdated iterations of the MMPI. For example, culturally appropriate spiritual beliefs among Native Americans (Hill et al., 2010; Hoffmann et al., 1985), Black Americans (Reed et al., 1996), and Asian Americans (Sue et al., 1996) have been associated with elevations of the MMPI-2 scales for Hypochondriasis, Paranoia, Schizophrenia, and Hypomania. Cultural expectations of socially desirable positive adjustment may drive under-reporting of pathology in religious contexts, a phenomenon known as the traditional background hypothesis (Bagby et al., 2020). For example, Christian and Muslim individuals reported higher elevations on the Lie (L) scale of the MMPI-2, indicating effort to present excessively positive images of their psychological functioning (Bridges & Baum, 2013).

An Opportunity for Improvement

Despite movement among mental health care professionals toward a practice that centers justice, diversity (Hook et al., 2017), and liberation (Neville et al., 2021), nonreligion is an often-overlooked element of individual and cultural diversity. Importantly, pervasive and enduring anti-atheist stigma in the United States (Edgell et al., 2016) and hegemonic Christianity (Abbott & Anaya, 2022) result in structural oppression, discrimination (Brewster et al., 2016), and microaggressions (Cheng et al., 2018) that create psychological distress among nonreligious people (Abbott & Mollen, 2018). In mental health scholarship, studies of religion and spirituality have been misinterpreted to erroneously conclude nonreligious people are less happy and healthy than believers (Speed & Hwang, 2019). In fact, adopting a nonreligious worldview can be liberating (Abbott & Anaya, 2022), increase belongingness (Smith, 2013), and promote health (Galen & Kloet, 2011).

Psychologists (32 percent) are less likely than the general public (83 percent) to be religious, though most endorse some form of personal spirituality. Psychotherapists, themselves, have often navigated their own complex, sometimes abusive, history with religion and/or spirituality. This history paired with low levels of training in (non) religiousness/(non)spirituality (D'Andrea & Sprenger, 2007) may lead therapists working with nonreligious clients to encounter challenges that influence or limit their therapeutic work (Magaldi-Dopman et al., 2011). In line with dominant views of Christianity and pervasive anti-atheist bias in the United States, even nonreligious therapists demonstrate implicit negative bias toward atheist clients and associate positive client attributes with religiousness (Winkeljohn Black & Gold, 2019). Therefore, nonreligious clients may experience invalidations and harm in psychotherapy such as a therapist's expectation they construct meaning of/from an event, assumptions that they are religious or spiritual, or conceptualizations of events rooted in faith (e.g., *They're in a better place*, when a client experiences a death; Abbott, 2021).

Thus, the general public and mental health professionals may hold negative, potentially harmful biases about nonreligious people and their mental health. This text seeks to assist mental health clinicians, researchers, advocates, and educators to bring awareness to, interrogate, and dismantle such biases, explicit and implicit, about nonreligious people. As a result of such biases and limited attention paid to nonreligiousness as an aspect of individual and cultural diversity, mental health professionals may also be ill-equipped to capitalize on the unique strengths of nonreligious people in promoting their wellness, a gap in competence this text seeks to remedy.

Utilizing This Text

In part I of this book, "Foundations," contributors provide critical background for increasing knowledge and critical consciousness about nonbelievers in the United States and the Christian hegemony in which they exist. In this chapter, Millie Myers and I, the editor, begin by summarizing some of the ways Christianity, and religion and spirituality more broadly, have informed the secular practice and science of psychology. In chapter 2, Ryan T. Cragun and I discuss the trends in secularization in the United States over time and across various demographic groups, concluding with best practices for inclusion of nonreligious identities in clinical intake materials and procedures and ways to assess the nature of nonreligion or nonspirituality among clients. Bethany Gull and colleagues (chapter 3) outline similarities and differences among groups of nonbelievers including spiritual-but-not-religious people and the affirmatively secular, with a particular emphasis on religious exiters who may face the most challenges in psychotherapy related to religious change. In order to situate the experiences of nonreligious people within the sociopolitical climate of White Christian nationalism in the United States, in chapter 4, Paige Hespe reviews common stereotypes about atheists and the psychological consequences of anti-atheist stigma. One of the most prevalent and misunderstood relationships in psychology, the connection between religion and mental health, is discussed by Luke W. Galen in chapter 5. Specifically, he explains why it is not appropriate to extrapolate the religion = health literature to nonreligious people.

In part II, "Applications," we turn to integration of this foundational knowledge with data specific to subpopulations of nonbelievers (e.g., queer nonbelievers, nonbelievers of color) and/or presenting concerns that may be common among nonbelievers (e.g., religious trauma) and/or require alternative treatment approaches to those that are customary (e.g., substance use). Contributing authors focus on translating this information to clinical practice, offering suggestions and case examples to readers. In chapter 6, Simon Howard and Alex Borgella discuss the experiences of Black, Indigenous, and people of color (BIPOC) nonbelievers, highlighting how the history of Christianity and colonialism shape religious imperatives in BIPOC communities and trajectories to nonbelief. Melanie E. Brewster (chapter 7) outlines the ways in which organized religion is often harmful to queer nonbelievers and queer communities, by contrast, offer belongingness and affirmation. Likewise, transgender and gender diverse (TGD) people often face rejection rooted in transnegativity in religious communities and, in chapter 8, Wei Motulsky and colleagues provide recommendations for clinicians working with secular TGD people.

In chapter 9, Carrie Bohmer and I continue this exploration of nonbelievers' gendered experiences by exploring the ways patriarchal norms influence religious exiting among women and femmes as well as how these norms are replicated in male-dominated nonreligious communities. Debra Mollen and Ginny Maril offer background about the influence of purity culture on people of faith and broader US culture, complemented by a case example of how it may affect nonbelievers' sexual lives and suggestions for intervention. Grief, and the process of healing from grief, is an experience often associated with religious belief systems; therefore, Jacob S. Sawyer (chapter 11) highlights secular conceptualizations of death and loss and explains how grief counseling may need to be adapted to better support nonreligious clients. In chapter 12, Patrick T. Meyer reviews religious trauma as a precursor to religious exiting and offers suggestions for engaging in trauma-informed care with nonreligious clients or those experiencing religious doubt.

Teagan M. Wilson (chapter 13) articulates the incongruence between traditional 12-step-based treatment models for substance use disorders and nonreligious clients' worldviews, offering secularly and evidence-based alternatives.

I conclude with a chapter connecting the dots, so to speak, between the valuable contributions of this text's authors. I pay particular attention to future directions for this work including recommendations for engagement in efforts to create the structural change that is necessary to solve the problems experienced by nonbelievers in the United States, many of which are outlined in this text.

References

Abbott, D. M. (2021). Psychotherapy with the nonreligious: A relational cultural approach. *Professional Psychology: Research and Practice*, 52(5), 470–76. https://doi.org/10.1037/pro0000392

Abbott, D. M., & Anaya, E. J. (2022). "Breaking free": A grounded theory study of atheist women in the United States. *Psychology of Women Quarterly*, 46(4), 501–17. https://doi.org/10.1177/03616843221115338

Abbott, D. M., & Mollen, D. (2018). Atheism as a concealable stigmatized identity: Outness, anticipated stigma, and well-being. *The Counseling Psychologist*, 46(6), 685–707. https://doi.org/10.1177/0011000018792669

Ağılkaya-Şahin, Z. (2018). Bridging pastoral psychology and positive psychology. *Ilahiyat Studies*, 9(2), 183–210. https://doi.org/10.12730/13091719.2018.92.180

Allik, J., Massoudi, K., Realo, A., & Rossier, J. (2012). Personality and culture: Cross-cultural psychology at the next crossroads [Editorial]. *Swiss Journal of Psychology*, 71(1), 5–12. https://doi.org/10.1024/1421-0185/a000069

Anzaldúa, G. E. (2015). Flights of the imagination: Rereading/rewriting realities. In A. Keating (Ed.), *Light in the dark/Luz en lo oscuro: Rewriting identity, spirituality, reality*. (1st ed., pp. 23–26). Duke University Press. https://doi.org/10.2307/j.ctv1220hmq

Bagby, R. M., Onno, K. A., Mortezaei, A., & Sellbom, M. (2020). Examining the "traditional background hypothesis" for the MMPI-2-RF L-r scores in a Muslim faith-based sample. *Psychological Assessment*, 32(10), 991–95. https://doi.org/10.1037/pas0000941

Beard, G. M. (1879). The psychology of spiritism. *The North American Review*, 129(272), 65–80. http://www.jstor.org/stable/25100777

Benjamin, L. T. (2019). *A brief history of modern psychology*. John Wiley & Sons, Inc.

Bier, W. C. (1971). A modified form of the Minnesota Multiphasic Personality Inventory for religious personnel. *Theological Education*, 7, 121–34.

Brewster, M. E., Hammer, J., Sawyer, J. S., Eklund, A., & Palamar, J. (2016). Perceived experiences of atheist discrimination: Instrument development and evaluation. *Journal of Counseling Psychology*, 63(5), 557–70. https://doi.org/10.1037/cou0000156

Bridges, S. A., & Baum, L. J. (2013). An examination of MMPI-2-RF L-r scale in an outpatient Protestant sample. *Journal of Psychology and Christianity*, 32, 115–23.

Bryant, T. (2024). Lessons from decolonial and liberation psychologies for the field of trauma psychology. *American Psychologist*, 79(5), 683–96. https://doi.org/10.1037/amp0001393

Bullivant, S. (2013). Defining atheism. In S. Bullivant & M. Ruse (Eds.), *The Oxford handbook of atheism* (pp. 11–21). Oxford University Press. https://doi.org/10.1093/oxfordhb/9780199644650.001.0001

Carver C. S. (1997). You want to measure coping but your protocol's too long: Consider the Brief COPE. *International Journal of Behavioral Medicine*, 4(1), 92–100. https://doi.org/10.1207/s15327558ijbm0401_6

Charry, E. T., & Kosits, R. D. (2017). Christian theology and positive psychology: An exchange of gifts. *The Journal of Positive Psychology*, 12(5), 468–79. https://doi.org/10.1080/17439760.2016.1228010

Cheng, Z. H., Pagano, L. A., & Shariff, A. F. (2018). The development and validation of the microaggressions against non-religious individuals scale (MANRIS). *Psychology of Religion and Spirituality*, 10(3), 254–62. https://doi.org/10.1037/rel0000203

Coleman, T. J. III, Sevinç, K., Hood, R. W. Jr., & Jong, J. (2019). An atheist perspective on self-esteem and meaning making while under death awareness. *Secular Studies*, 1(2), 204–28. https://doi.org/10.1163/25892525-00102002

Comas-Díaz, L., & Torres Rivera, E. (2020). Conclusion: Liberation psychology—Crossing borders into new frontiers. In L. Comas-Díaz & E. Torres Rivera (Eds.), *Liberation psychology: Theory, method, practice, and social justice* (pp. 283–95). American Psychological Association. https://doi.org/10.1037/0000198-016

Cragun, R. T., Hammer, J. H., & Nielsen, M. (2015). The nonreligious-nonspiritual scale (NRNSS): Measuring everyone from atheists to Zionists. *Science, Religion, & Culture*, 2(3), 36–53. https://doi.org/10.17582/journal.src/2015/2.3.36.53

D'Andrea, L. M., & Sprenger, J. (2007). Atheism and nonspirituality as diversity issues in counseling. *Counseling and Values*, 51(2), 149–58. https://doi.org/10.1002/j.2161-007X.2007.tb00072.x

Delaney, H. D., Miller, W. R., & Bisonó, A. M. (2007). Religiosity and spirituality among psychologists: A survey of clinician members of the American Psychological Association. *Professional Psychology: Research and Practice*, 38(5), 538–46. https://doi.org/10.1037/0735-7028.38.5.538

Dueck, A., Ansloos, J., Johnson, A., & Fort, C. (2017). Western cultural psychology of religion: Alternatives to ideology. *Pastoral Psychology*, 66, 397–425. https://doi.org/10.1007/s11089-016-0731-3

Edgell, P., Hartmann, D., Stewart, E., & Gerteis, J. (2016). Atheists and other cultural outsiders: Moral boundaries and the non-religious in the United States. *Social Forces*, 95(2), 607–38. https://doi.org/10.1093/sf/sow063

Ellis, A. (1976). *The case against religion: A psychotherapist's view and the case against religiosity*. American Atheist Press.

Faller, G. (2001). Positive psychology: A paradigm shift. *Journal of Pastoral Counseling*, 36, 7–20.

Frankl, V. E. (1954). The concept of man in psychotherapy. *Proceedings of the Royal Society of Medicine*, 47(11), 975–80. https://doi.org/10.1177/003591575404701115

Frankl, V. E. (1955). *The doctor and the soul. An introduction to logotherapy*. A. A. Knopf.

Fuller, R. C. (1982). *Mesmerism and the American cure of souls*. University of Pennsylvania Press.

Fung, K. (2014). Acceptance and commitment therapy: Western adoption of Buddhist tenets? *Transcultural Psychiatry*, 52(4), 561–76. https://doi.org/10.1177/1363461514537544

Galen, L. W., & Kloet, J. D. (2011). Mental well-being in the religious and the non-religious: Evidence for a curvilinear relationship. *Mental Health, Religion & Culture*, 14(7), 673–89. https://doi.org/10.1080/13674676.2010.510829

García-Alandete, J. (2024). The place of religiosity and spirituality in Frankl's logotherapy: Distinguishing salvific and hygienic objectives. *Journal of Religious Health*, 63, 6–30. https://doi.org/10.1007/s10943-023-01760-4

Hage, S. M. (2003). Reaffirming the unique identity of counseling psychology: Opting for the "road less traveled by." *The Counseling Psychologist*, 31(5), 555–63. https://doi.org/10.1177/0011000003256434

Harris, R. (2019). *ACT made simple: an easy-to-read primer on acceptance and commitment therapy* (2nd ed.). New Harbinger Publications.

Hewitt, M. A. (2014). *Freud on religion* (1st ed.). Routledge. https://doi.org/10.4324/9781315729435

Hill, J. S., Pace, T. M., & Robbins, R. R. (2010). Decolonizing personality assessment and honoring indigenous voices: A critical examination of the MMPI-2. *Cultural Diversity and Ethnic Minority Psychology*, 16, 16–25. https://doi.org/10.1037/a0016110

Hill, P. C., Pargament, K. I., Hood, R. W., McCullough, M. E., Swyers, J. P., Larson, D. B., & Zinnbauer, B. J. (2001). Conceptualizing religion and spirituality: Points of commonality, points of departure. *Journal for the Theory of Social Behaviour*, 30, 51–77. http://doi.org/10.1111/1468-5914.00119

Hoffmann, T., Dana, R. H., & Bolton, B. (1985). Measured acculturation and MMPI-168 performance of Native American adults. *Journal of Cross-Cultural Psychology*, 16, 243–56. http://doi.org/10.1177/0022002185016002007

Hook, J. N., Davis, D., Owen, J., & DeBlaere, C. (2017). *Cultural humility: Engaging diverse identities in therapy*. American Psychological Association. https://doi.org/10.1037/0000037-000

Lovibond, S. H., & Lovibond, P. F. (1995). *Manual for the Depression Anxiety Stress Scales* (2nd ed.). Psychology Foundation.

Magaldi-Dopman, D., Park-Taylor, J., & Ponterotto, J. G. (2011). Psychotherapists' spiritual, religious, atheist or agnostic identity and their practice of psychotherapy: A grounded theory study. *Psychotherapy Research*, 21(3), 286–303. https://doi.org/10.1080/10503307.2011.565488

Malherbe, N. (2022). De-ideologization, liberation psychology, and the place of contradiction. *Journal for the Theory of Social Behaviour*, 52(2), 298–314. https://doi.org/10.1111/jtsb.12322

Martín-Baró, I. (1994). Writings for a liberation psychology. (A. Aron & S. Corne, Eds.). Harvard University Press.

Miranda, P. (2019). C.G. Jung and religion. *Journal of the Jungian Institute of São Paulo*, 4(1), e8. https://doi.org/10.21901/2448-3060/self-2019.vol04.0008

Montero, M., & Sonn, C. C. (Eds.). (2009). *Psychology of liberation: Theory and applications.* Springer Science + Business Media.

Morgan, J. H. (2011). Psychology of religion and the books that made it happen. *Journal for the Study of Religions and Ideologies*, 10(30), 277–98.

Nelson, J. M., & Slife, B. D. (2016). A new positive psychology: A critique of the movement based on early Christian thought. *The Journal of Positive Psychology*, 12(5), 459–67. https://doi.org/10.1080/17439760.2016.1228006

Neville, H. A., Ruedas-Gracia, N., Lee, B. A., Ogunfemi, N., Maghsoodi, A. H., Mosley, D. V., LaFromboise, T. D., & Fine, M. (2021). The public psychology for liberation training model: A call to transform the discipline. *American Psychologist*, 76(8), 1248–65. https://doi.org/10.1037/amp0000887

Pew Research Center. (2022). Modeling the future of religion in America. https://www.pewresearch.org/religion/2022/09/13/modeling-the-future-of-religion-in-america/

Pew Research Center. (2024). Religious "nones" in America: Who they are and what they believe. https://www.pewresearch.org/religion/2024/01/24/religious-nones-in-america-who-they-are-and-what-they-believe/

Reber, J. S. (2006). Secular psychology: What's the problem? *Journal of Psychology and Theology*, 34(3), 193–204. https://doi.org/10.1177/009164710603400302

Reed, M. K., Walker, B., Williams, G., McLeod, S., & Jones, S. (1996). MMPI-2 patterns in African-American females. *Journal of Clinical Psychology*, 52(4), 437–41. https://doi.org/10.1002/(SICI)1097-4679(199607)52:4<437::AID-JCLP8>3.0.CO;2-M

Schmit, D. (2005). Re-visioning antebellum American psychology: The dissemination of mesmerism, 1836–1854. *History of Psychology*, 8(4), 403–34. https://doi.org/10.1037/1093-4510.8.4.403

Schmit, D. T. (2018). Warren Felt Evans: 19th-century mystic, wounded healer, and seminal theorist-practitioner of mind cure. *History of Psychology*, 21(3), 187–207. https://doi.org/10.1037/hop0000070

Schnell, T. (2009). The sources of meaning and meaning in life questionnaire (SoMe): Relations to demographics and well-being. *The Journal of Positive Psychology*, 4(6), 483–99. https://doi.org/10.1080/17439760903271074

Seligman, M. E. P., & Csikszentmihalyi, M. (2000). Positive psychology: An introduction. *The American Psychologist*, 55(1), 5–14. https://doi.org/10.1037/0003-066X.55.1.5

Shamdasani, S. (2009). Introduction. In C. G. Jung, *The Red Book: Liber Novus*. W.W. Norton & Company.

Singh, A. (2020). Building a counseling psychology of liberation: The path behind us, under us, and before us. *The Counseling Psychologist*, 48(8), 1109–30. https://doi.org/10.1177/0011000020959007

Smith, J. M. (2013). Creating a godless community: The collective identity work of contemporary American atheists. *Journal for the Scientific Study of Religion*, 52(1), 80–99. http://doi.org/10.1111/jssr.12009

Smith, S., & Krishnamurthy, R., Eds. (2018). Diversity-sensitive personality assessment (1st ed.). Routledge. https://doi.org/10.4324/9780203551578

Speed, D., & Hwang, K. (2019). Heretic, heal thyself! Atheism, nonreligion, and health. *Psychology of Religion and Spirituality*, 11(3), 297–307. https://doi.org/10.1037/rel0000158

Spilka, B. (2012). Psychology of Religion, History of. In: Rieber, R.W. (Eds.). *Encyclopedia of the history of psychological theories*. Springer. https://doi.org/10.1007/978-1-4419-0463-8_154

Staddon J. E. (2013). Faith, fact, and behaviorism. *The Behavior Analyst*, 36(2), 229–38. https://doi.org/10.1007/BF03392309

Stratton, S. P. (2014). Mindfulness and contemplation: Secular and religious traditions in Western context. *Counseling and Values*, 60, 100–118. https://doi.org/10.1002/j.2161-007X.2015.00063.x

Stuerzenhofecker, K. (2020). Pluralising practical theology: International and multi-traditional challenges and opportunities. *Practical Theology*, 13(1–2), 123–36. https://doi.org/10.1080/1756073X.2020.1728960

Sue, S., Keefe, K., Enomoto, K., Durvasula, R. S., & Chao, R. (1996). Asian American and White college students' performance on the MMPI-2. In J. B. Butcher (Ed.), *International adaptations of the MMPI-2* (pp. 206–218). University of Minnesota Press.

Sun, J. (2014). Mindfulness in context: A historical discourse analysis. *Contemporary Buddhism*, 15(2), 394–415. https://doi.org/10.1080/14639947.2014.978088

Tedeschi, R. G. & Calhoun, L. G. (1996). The posttraumatic growth inventory: Measuring the positive legacy of trauma. *Journal of Traumatic Stress*. 9(3), 455–71. https://doi.org/10.1002/jts.2490090305

Ulanov, A. B. (2008). Jung and religion: The opposing self. In P. Young-Eisendrath & T. Dawson (Eds.), *The Cambridge companion to Jung* (2nd ed.). Cambridge University Press.

Wachholtz, A. B., & Pargament, K. I. (2008). Migraines and meditation: Does spirituality matter? *Journal of Behavioral Medicine*, 31, 351–66. https://doi.org/10.1007/s10865-008-9159-2

Whitehead, A. L., & Perry, S. L. (2020). *Taking America back for God: Christian nationalism in the United States*. Oxford University Press. https://doi.org/10.1093/oso/9780190057886.001.0001

Winkeljohn Black, S., & Gold, A. P. (2019). Trainees' cultural humility and implicit associations about clients and religious, areligious, and spiritual identities: A mixed-method investigation. *Journal of Psychology and Theology*, 47(3), 202–16. https://doi.org/10.1177/0091647119837019

Wulff, D. M. (1997). *Psychology of religion: Classic and contemporary* (2nd ed.). John Wiley & Sons.

Yalom, I. D. (1980). *Existential psychotherapy*. Basic Books.

Yalom, I. (2002). Religion and psychiatry. *American Journal of Psychotherapy*, 56(3), 301–16. https://doi.org/10.1176/appi.psychotherapy.2002.56.3.301

Zinnbauer, B. J., & Pargament, K. I. (2000). Capturing the meanings of religiousness and spirituality: One way down from a definitional Tower of Babel. *Research in the Social Scientific Study of Religion*, 13, 23–54. https://doi.org/10.1163/9789004496347_004

2

The Rise of the Religiously Unaffiliated

Ryan T. Cragun and Dena M. Abbott

Chapter Outline

Since 1990, there has been a dramatic increase in the percentage of people who report having no religious affiliation in the United States. Such individuals are referred to as "nones" (as they report "none" when asked, "What is your religion, if any?") or the "nonreligious" (Cragun & Smith, 2024; Kosmin et al., 2009). To give a sense of how rapid the growth has been, between 5 percent and 7 percent of adults in the United States identified as having no religious affiliation during the 1980s. By 2024, that number increased to roughly 30 percent, a more than quadrupling of the nonreligious population in a thirty-year window.

There are, of course, other ways to measure (non)religiousness in populations. Looking at just the percentage who report no religious affiliation hides the fact that the majority of Americans do not regularly attend religious services; less than 40 percent attend once a month or more. Similarly, just 13 percent report doing anything religious on a daily basis (see Cragun & Smith, 2024). There have also been shifts in beliefs, though these are somewhat more complicated. A smaller percentage of Americans report believing that the Bible is the literal word of a deity but belief in an afterlife has held relatively steady over the last thirty years, illustrating that those who report no religious affiliation may retain some supernatural beliefs (Wilkins-Laflamme, 2022).

In this chapter, we will focus on the rise of the nones or nonreligious. We will examine the growth of the nonreligious by age, period, and cohort, as well as by race, income, educational attainment, and region. Throughout the chapter we will draw on the General Social Survey (GSS) conducted by the National Opinion Research Center (Davern et al., 2022). The General Social Survey is a nationally representative survey fielded roughly every other year that includes a variety of questions related to (non)religiosity. We'll utilize all waves of the GSS, from 1972 through 2022, in order to show trends over time. When creating figures, we utilize a three-year[1] moving average to smooth the trend lines as results for any given year fluctuate. The three-year moving average balances out year-to-year changes and provides a clearer picture of trend data over time.

Definitions

Social scientists have had a clear understanding since the 1960s that religiosity is multidimensional (Stark & Glock, 1968). People can be religious (and/or nonreligious) in various ways. While the dimensions of religiosity proposed have varied (Hill & Hood, 1999), most scholars think about religiosity today as having at least three dimensions: what people believe, what people do, and how people identify (sometimes referred to as "belonging" but this is problematic language; see Cragun & McCaffree, 2021). In this chapter, we refer to these dimensions as belief, behavior, and identities or "BBI" (see Cragun & Smith, 2024 for a similar framing).

Understanding that religiosity is multidimensional is important because it better reflects reality. For instance, among the Catholics included in the General Social Survey since 2010, 42.4 percent were in favor of women being allowed to get an abortion for any reason, a belief that runs counter to the official position of the Catholic Church. Similarly, of the atheists who participated in the GSS since 2010, 6.2 percent reported attending religious services roughly every week and 16 percent of the individuals who reported a religious affiliation never attended religious services (roughly 50 percent attended just a couple of times a year or less). As Evans (2018) has argued, many people are not logically consistent in their beliefs, behaviors, and/or identities. Most people have probably never heard of logical consistency and put little emphasis on it. It is typically only highly trained scholars who value and emphasize concordance between beliefs and actions. Regardless, the point is that people can be (non)religious in various and even contradictory ways and it is important to reflect that by measuring the dimensions of religiosity.

Thinking about these dimensions as ranging on a continuum is also helpful, though data to capture the continuum is not always readily available. For instance, people could

[1]Technically, it is a "three-wave" rather than "three-year" moving average as the GSS is not conducted every year. But, considering that each wave encapsulates a year, referring to our figures as "three-year moving averages" is still accurate.

strongly hold religious beliefs or hold lots of orthodox religious beliefs, could hold some religious beliefs, or could reject all religious beliefs. That would reflect a continuum of belief. People could regularly attend religious services, regularly read scriptures, regularly pray, or regularly give money to their religion or they might do so infrequently or never. These measures would capture a continuum of behavior. People may consider their religious or nonreligious identity more or less salient, invoking that identity with varied frequency in a variety of situations based on the salience of that identity for the individual. This would reflect a continuum of identification. Likewise, there are people who do not believe in god(s), but identify with a religion as a part of their cultural background; for example, people may not believe or practice, but identify as culturally Catholic or Muslim. In general, individuals who are at the religious end on all three dimensions would arguably be the most religious while those who are at the nonreligious end on all three dimensions would be the most nonreligious. Importantly, there are a fair number of individuals who fall somewhere in the middle of these continua on many measures (Voas, 2009; Wilkins-Laflamme, 2022).

While scholars have made a fair amount of progress when it comes to measuring religiosity, spirituality has seen less progress for two reasons: spirituality is notoriously difficult to define and even harder to operationalize in clear ways. Broadly speaking, many scholars would consider spirituality to be akin to religiosity but outside the confines of organized institutions, though even this understanding is regularly challenged (Steensland et al., 2022). Beyond that, there are definitions of spirituality that are completely devoid of references to the supernatural (Baggett, 2019; Ecklund, 2010). There are nonreligious individuals who report not believing in anything supernatural who recount spiritual experiences when looking out over a beautiful vista or looking at the stars. Some scholars go so far as to consider yoga, exercise, and hiking a form of spirituality (Steensland et al., 2022). There are other definitions of spirituality that rely heavily on the supernatural, whether that is communicating with, channeling, or manifesting something divine or believing all humans are connected via some supernatural pathway (Cragun, et al., 2015; Zinnbauer & Pargament, 2002; Zinnbauer et al., 1997). Disturbingly, there are also some scholars who have defined and operationalized spirituality such that their spirituality scale also includes measures of mental health, and then, not surprisingly, those scholars have found that people who score high in spirituality also score high in mental health (de Jager Meezenbroek et al., 2012). In short, definitions of spirituality among scholars vary widely and there is not clear agreement.

While there is a lack of clarity among scholars as to what spirituality means, there is even less clarity among scholars regarding what lay individuals mean when they report they are spiritual. One study (Edgell et al., 2017) found that atheist women, in order to avoid discrimination, opted to identify as spiritual but not religious (i.e., "SBNR") instead of identifying as nonreligious or as atheists. Some scholars have gone so far as to consider anything that might be the functional equivalent of religiosity or spirituality to be "lived religion," which they argue encapsulates all of spirituality (Ammerman, 2021; McGuire, 2008), meaning all people are both religious and spiritual. If all people are religious and spiritual, these terms cease to be meaningful as they are effectively just describing universal human characteristics. Additionally, if everyone is religious/spiritual, then terms that reflect the absence of religiosity and spirituality (e.g., areligious or nonspiritual) are unnecessary and irrelevant as there are no such people. Recognizing that people could quite literally mean anything if/when they identify as spiritual means that clinicians and therapists must necessarily probe as to what the client means in order to better know how to adjust their counseling in line with their client's understanding of spirituality.

Related to but contrasted with religiosity and spirituality is nonreligion. Nonreligion is that which is not religious but related to it (Lee, 2012; Quack, 2014). What this means is that there are things that are not religious but are unrelated to religion (e.g., hiking boots). But there are also things that are not religious but are related to religion (e.g., atheism, humanism, agnosticism). That which is not religious but unrelated to religion is often referred to as "secular" while that which is related to religion is considered nonreligion. However, even when this term was first proposed by Lee (2012), she recognized that the term was problematic because it focused on what people are not rather than what they are, and it privileged religion as the default; everyone was defined in relation to religion. In light of this understanding, there has been a substantive turn in the study of nonreligion with a growing number of scholars focusing their research attention on what the nonreligious believe, do, and value. For instance, van Mulukom et al. (2023) explored the different manifestations of nonreligious worldviews around the world. Miller and Beaman (2024) examined how nonreligious people think about death and dying. Thurfjell et al. (2019) examined the experiences nonreligious people have in nature. Strhan and Shillitoe (2025) examined the beliefs, values, and behaviors of children raised without religion. Rejowska (2021) examined the forms of nonreligious weddings and the substantive content of the ceremonies in Poland. The substantive turn is beginning to examine who the nonreligious are, what they believe, what they value, what they do, who they spend their time with, how they develop relationships, and how they think (Cragun & Smith, 2024).

There are a number of other terms and definitions that are related to nonreligion, including the terminology that the nonreligious use to describe themselves. However, many of those are addressed in other chapters in this volume. Readers should consult those other chapters for additional definitions and terminology.

Trends in Nonreligious Identification by Demographic Characteristics

As noted above, the primary focus of this chapter is the growth of the nonreligious in the United States over time. In this section, we will explore some of these trends, showing that pretty much every demographic group has seen growth among the nonreligious over the last fifty years or so.

Quantitative researchers have attempted to unpack the differential effects of age, period, and cohort for quite some time (Glenn, 2005). The problem with these three concepts is that if you know two, the third is predetermined, leading to some analytic challenges. Luckily, in our case, we only need to examine two—age and cohort—as the period effects will be obvious in all of the other charts we examine. We will start with age. Figure 2.1 shows the shift toward nonreligion (measured as having no religious affiliation) for three different age brackets over time: 18 to 29, 30 to 50, and 51+ years. Importantly, readers should be aware that these are the people in those age brackets at the time of the survey and are not cohorts, which are shown in figure 2.2; the GSS is not a longitudinal survey but rather a cross-sectional survey. What we see in figure 2.1 is that young people have been more likely to be nonreligious throughout the period that the GSS examines (1972–2022). Even in 1972, over 10 percent of 18- to 29-year-old individuals were nonreligious. That percentage held steady until the early 1990s when there was a rapid increase in the percentage nonreligious in the United States (Kosmin et al., 2009).

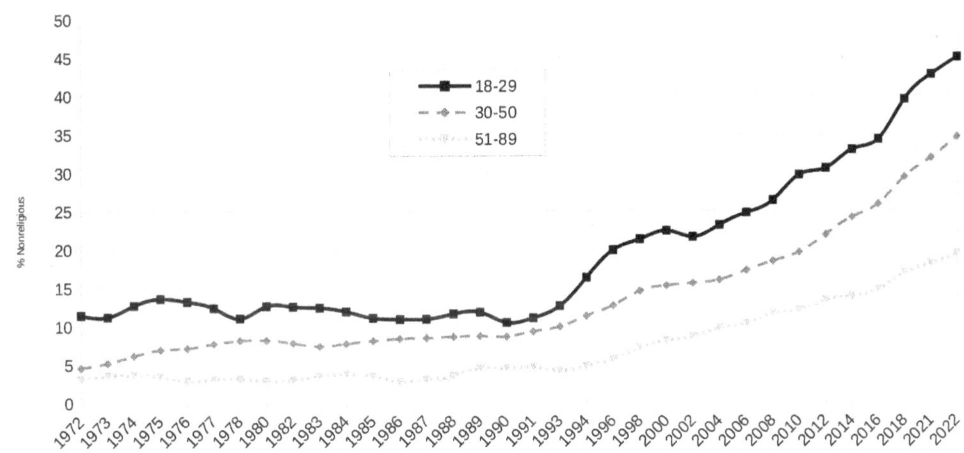

Figure 2.1 Percentage Nonreligious by Age, 3-Year Moving Average from 1972–2022.

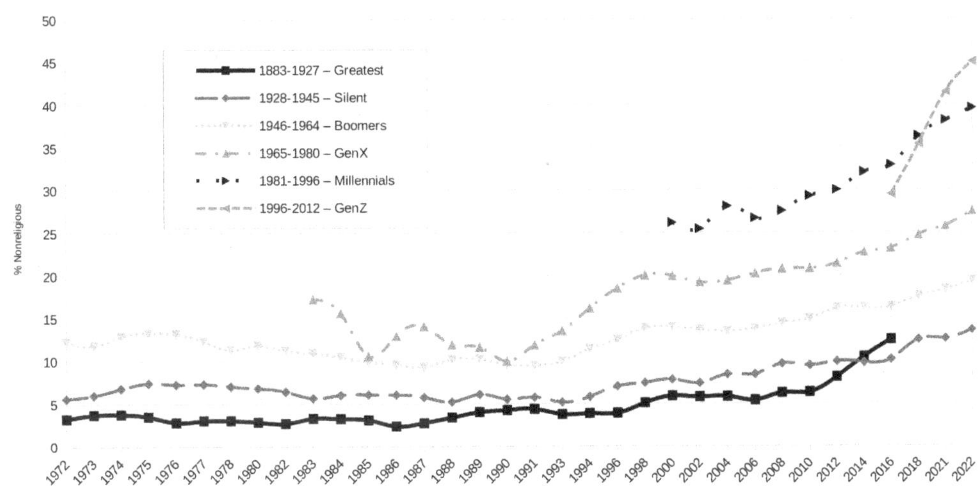

Figure 2.2 Percentage Nonreligious by Cohort, 3-Year Moving Average from 1972–2022.

As of the latest GSS data, 45 percent of 18- to 29-year-old individuals reported having no religious affiliation. All three age groups illustrate the importance of period effects as the percentage nonreligious remained relatively steady from the 1970s through the end of the 1980s, then began to grow. In the oldest age bracket, those 51 to 89 years at the time they participated in the survey, the unaffiliated increased from under 5 percent in the 1970s to nearly 20 percent by 2022. Individuals in the middle bracket, 30 to 50 years, more closely mirrored those under thirty with a steeper increase after 1990 from (around 7 percent to close to 35 percent).

Figure 2.2 is similar to figure 2.1 but plots the percentage nonreligious or unaffiliated by cohort over time. There are several important points to note about figure 2.2. First, some of the lines in the figure do not run the width of the figure. That is because some of the cohorts had not been born when the survey started (e.g., GenX, Millennials, and GenZ). One of the cohorts, the Greatest Generation, died out by 2018, resulting in that line ending. The trends in figure 2.2 are pretty clear—every subsequent cohort has been less religious than previous cohorts. The Greatest Generation was the least likely to be nonreligious, hovering below 5 percent until around 1998 and then increasing to just over 10 percent in 2016. GenZ, once they entered into the survey data, quickly outpaced even Millennials with their percentage unaffiliated, which was around 45 percent in 2022. These data illustrate quite compellingly the arguments from Kasselstrand et al. (2023) and Cragun and Smith (2024) that one of the mechanisms of secularization is parents not passing their religiosity on to their children, which both of those authors attribute to parents granting their kids greater autonomy (see also Stolz et al., 2016; Strhan & Shillitoe, 2025).

What should be clear to readers already is that the third component of the "age, period, cohort" question—period effects—is apparent in both figures 2.1 and 2.2. Period effects are changes that occur in a trend due to a specific period in time (e.g., World War II or the Great Depression). In both figure 2.1 and figure 2.2, there is a clear period effect starting around 1990. The percentage nonreligious is relatively stable until about 1990 in both of those figures then it sees a dramatic uptick starting around that time. While some scholars (Hout & Fischer, 2002) attribute this uptick to religio-political realignments, there is a growing consensus that this is better explained by the end of the Cold War and the disassociating of religiosity from nationalism (Bullivant, 2022; Cragun & Smith, 2024). In other words, during the Cold War, the United States was at war with "godless communists." Individuals who admitted they were not religious during that period often had their national loyalties questioned as well (Gunn, 2009; O'Hair, 1989). When the Cold War ended with the collapse of the Soviet Union in 1989, the link between religiosity and nationalism split. While many US Americans continue to dislike communists, attitudes toward the nonreligious have softened substantially. Likewise, if someone admits they are not religious today, it is highly unlikely that the follow-up question will be to ask them whether they are also communists. As a result, the social pressure to be religious has declined. It may very well have been the case that far more people were uninterested in religion during the Cold War than were willing to admit it and the rapid increase in the nonreligious when the Cold War ended may have been people being more willing to admit their lack of religiosity once it was safe to do so in addition to shifting attitudes toward religiosity in general, particularly in light of the many sex abuse scandals in religions that surfaced in the late 1990s and early 2000s (Shupe, 2007).

The clear period effect can also be seen when examining other demographic variables. Figure 2.3 shows the growth of nonreligion by gender over time. Note that the GSS only started asking participants whether they were transgender or nonbinary in 2021 and just twenty-four participants have identified as transgender in the 2021 and 2022 waves of the survey. As a result, we did not include them in our analyses. Thus, figure 2.3 focuses only on those individuals who were identified as a man or a woman. As a number of studies have suggested (Hadaway, 1989; Hunsberger, 2006), men have been and continue to be slightly more likely to identify as having no religious affiliation than women. The gap is not huge, about 5 percent, but it is a clear pattern. The latest data suggest the gap is shrinking and may eventually disappear altogether. But, importantly, for both male and female individuals, there has been a dramatic increase in the percentage identifying as having no religious affiliation since the 1990s with both groups now closing in on roughly 30 percent reporting no religious affiliation.

Figure 2.4 shows that White individuals are slightly more likely to identify as having no religious affiliation than are Black individuals, while individuals of other races have fluctuated more but are now closer to the 28 percent or so of White individuals who report no religious affiliation than the approximately 23 percent of Black individuals who report no religious affiliation. For all three groups, the same period effect is observable with relatively rapid growth in the nonreligious after 1990.

We also examined trends in religious affiliation by marital status, as shown in figure 2.5. Figure 2.5 is, in some ways, also a reflection of the trends in age shown above. Widowed individuals, who are much older than the other groups on average, have the lowest percentage nonreligious while never-married individuals, who are younger than all the other groups on average, have the highest percentage nonreligious. The other three groups—married, divorced, and separated individuals—are all in between them. Importantly, for all of the

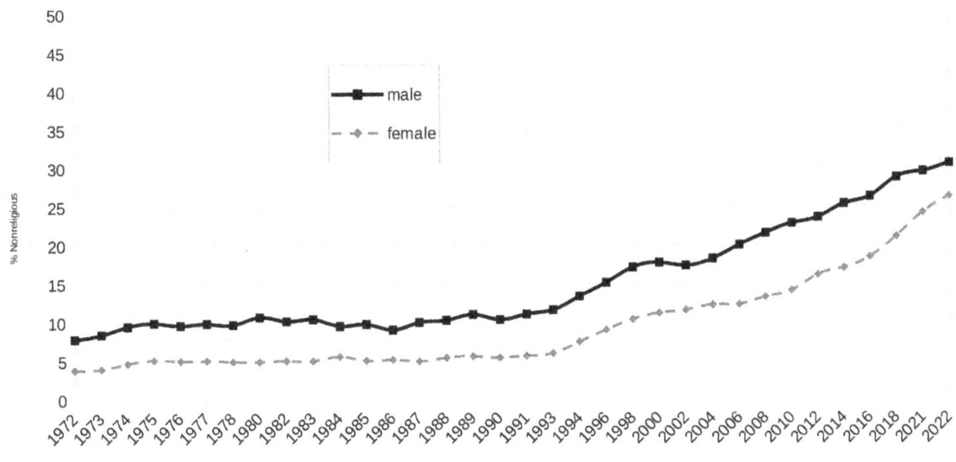

Figure 2.3 Percentage Nonreligious by Gender, 3-Year Moving Average from 1972–2022.

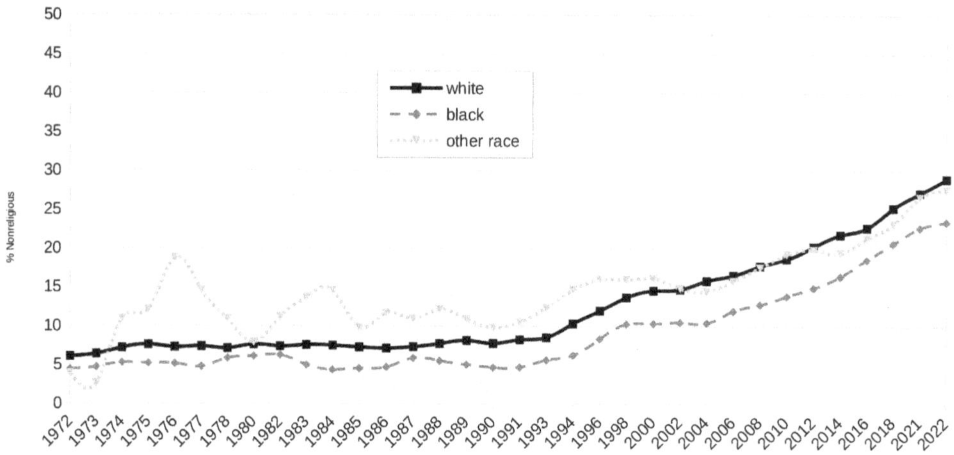

Figure 2.4 Percentage Nonreligious by Race, 3-Year Moving Average from 1972–2022.

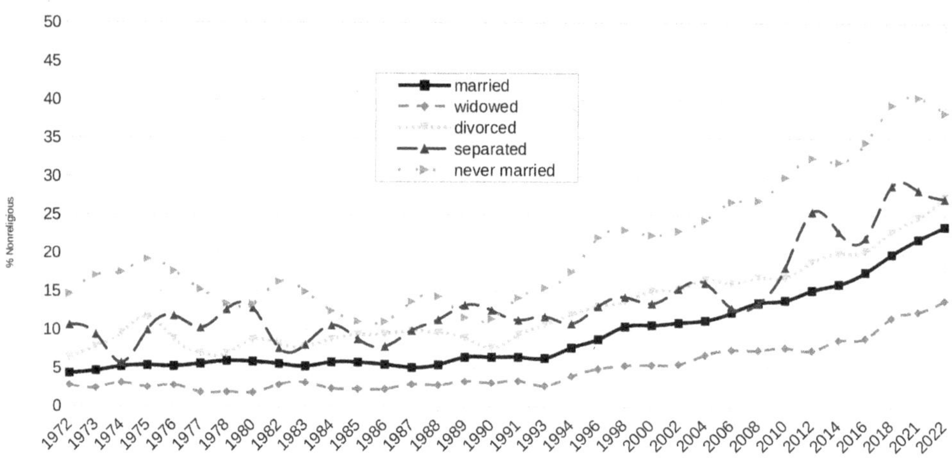

Figure 2.5 Percentage Nonreligious by Marital Status, 3-Year Moving Average from 1972–2022.

groups, the same period effect can be observed—a growth in the percentage identifying as having no religious affiliation after 1990.

We ran similar analyses for income and region. We do not include figures for these demographic variables for two reasons. First, the differences between groups were so small that it was virtually impossible to disentangle them from each other in the figures. Second, they all follow the same trend with a clear period effect beginning around 1990. For instance, both the poorest individuals (those making less than $20,000 per year in 2024 dollars) and the richest individuals (those making more than $100,000 per year in 2024 dollars) started at around 5 percent to 10 percent unaffiliated in 1975 when income was first included in the GSS. By 2022, both groups were close to 30 percent unaffiliated. People who fell into other income brackets were nearly identical. With region, there are some differences, but all show the same trend—a substantial increase in the percentage unaffiliated after 1990. The region with the lowest percentage unaffiliated, southeastern states, still saw an uptick from about 5 percent prior to 1990 to about 22 percent by 2022. In comparison, the region with the highest percentage nonreligious, the Pacific region, increased from about 8 percent to 12 percent nonreligious prior to 1990 to about 34 percent nonreligious by 2022. All of the other regions of the country fell between those two but followed a similar trend.

Similar to the analyses of income and region, the trend data on educational attainment was too fine-grained to result in a clearly interpretable figure. There were not large, meaningful gaps between groups with different levels of education. In 2022, whether someone had less than a high school education or a graduate degree did not matter—all of the groups examined (less than high school, high school diploma, some college, college degree, and graduate degree) were between 28 percent and 30 percent nonreligious. All of the groups experienced the same period effect after 1990.

Finally, the GSS has included information on an individual's sexual orientation or identity since 2008. Thus, unlike the other figures, figure 2.6 only runs from 2008 through 2022. The data are pretty clear in figure 2.6—gay, lesbian, and bisexual individuals are substantially more likely to be nonreligious than are straight individuals. In 2022, nearly 50 percent of bisexual individuals identified as nonreligious, roughly 45 percent of gay and lesbian individuals identified as nonreligious, while just 26 percent of straight individuals identified as nonreligious.

What all of the above figures and data indicate is that the nonreligious have been growing in every demographic category—age, gender, race, sexual orientation, region, income and educational brackets. Nonreligion is not exclusive to any one group and never really was. All of the figures and analyses above indicate a clear period effect beginning in 1990 with the end of the Cold War. Whether that trend will continue is unclear but the growth of the nonreligious is unmistakable at this point.

Figure 2.6 Percentage Nonreligious by Sexual Orientation, 3-Year Moving Average from 1972–2022.

Strategies for Assessing Nonreligiousness

In this final section of the chapter, we turn to something slightly different—measures of nonreligiosity. Several scholars have developed scales that are designed to measure how nonreligious people are or the various aspects of nonreligiosity. This section will discuss these measures briefly. Although these measures are designed as research instruments, therapists and clinicians who are interested in better understanding the nonreligiosity, nonspirituality, and secularity of their clients may want to consider administering the measures outlined in the following pages. Not only will these scales provide a clear sense of where these individuals are located when it comes to religiosity and spirituality but will also provide a good picture of how these individuals think and reason, and what they value.

Capturing Nonreligiousness and Nonspirituality in the Clinical Interview

Traditional clinical intake forms often collect demographic information, which offers an opportunity for clients to tell their provider about their important identities and/or social locations. However, if (non)religion is included at all, these questionnaires may only ask clients to endorse one, or more, religions with which they currently identify. Nonreligious labels are sometimes omitted and when included choices are often limited to atheist or agnostic. It is just as impossible and impractical to attempt to list all possible nonreligious orientations in a survey as it is to attempt to list every world religion. However, when necessary to use discrete categories, the (non)religions surveyed in Pew Research Center's US Landscape Survey (Pew Research, 2014) offer a good starting place based on the most common (non)religious affiliations in the US context. Most notably, in addition to atheist and agnostic, Pew Research includes "Nothing in particular" as an option that prompts a subsequent choice between "religion is important to me" or "religion is not important to me." This helps to determine whether people choose nothing in particular to mean they are not affiliated with an organized religion but likely have belief in god(s) or if they choose it to indicate nonreligiousness. We also recommend a separate question that assesses (non) religion(s) of origin, or the (non)religions with which one was raised or exposed to in their communities, in addition to items that assess current (non)religions.

These demographic survey questions provide useful information; however, nonreligious groups are not monoliths. One measure that can be used with both religious and nonreligious individuals, is designed to place them all on a continuum, and provides crucial contextual information is the Nonreligious–Nonspiritual Scale (NRNSS; see Cragun et al., 2015). In developing the scale, the authors noted that many other measures of religiosity include "one-and-a-half barreled questions" or questions that make assumptions about those taking the survey that are not valid. For instance, some measures of religiosity ask participants to indicate their agreement with items like, "I believe in a God who watches over me." Disagreeing with this statement does not mean that the participant does not believe in a god or deity only that they do not believe in a deity that watches over them. The question assumes belief in a god, which is not a valid assumption for atheists and other nonbelievers. A similarly problematic question for nonreligious individuals is this item discussed in Cragun et al. (2015), "My personal religious beliefs are very important to me." If a nonreligious person were to disagree with this statement, it does not mean they do not have personal religious beliefs only that such beliefs are not important to them. This question, again, assumes that the participants have personal religious beliefs, which is not a valid assumption for many nonreligious individuals. The NRNSS, in contrast, was developed with this consideration in mind. It includes seventeen items, eight of which focus on institutional religiosity and nine on personal spirituality. The scale can be split into two dimensions—one capturing religiosity and the other capturing spirituality—or be used as a single measure. Higher scores on the scale indicate higher degrees of nonreligiosity and nonspirituality. There are now validated versions of the scale in Greek (Polemikou et al., 2019) and Turkish (Sevinç et al., 2015).

When possible, we recommend complementing such measures with rich, descriptive qualitative accounts of clients' nonreligious stories. Take, for example, a client that identifies as atheist, notes being raised in a Christian family and community, and scores low in institutional religiousness and high in personal spirituality. There is a story beneath the survey responses about the development of a personal atheism and the rejection of the faith with which they were raised, including the messages and life experiences that informed this story. As atheism and spirituality, at face value, appear incongruous, the clinician can be curious about how the client distinguishes between the two, what they mean by the term atheism, what each offers them, and how they impact health. Given the clear period effects outlined earlier in this chapter, these stories may vary considerably based on generational cohort—with earlier cohorts more likely to have been raised nonreligious as compared to those in older cohorts.

Understanding Secular Worldviews in the Clinical Interview

As previously mentioned, atheist and agnostic labels mean different things to different people, often diverging from academic definitions, and, therefore, lack specificity. Although the aforementioned stories can help clinicians better understand how clients define terms and how they came to use the terms that currently best describe their nonreligion, it is perhaps most meaningful to understand what these terms mean about how clients make sense of the world. What, if any, responsibilities do they have to themselves, others, and the world? What is the role, if any, of meaning and/or purpose in their lives? How does their nonreligion inform their expectations for themselves and others?

Tatjana Schnell's (2015) approach to measuring nonreligiousness among nonbelievers by focusing on different aspects of belief that may be important to them can offer a snapshot of a client's worldview. Schnell developed the Dimensions of Secularity (DoS) inventory, which includes scales designed to capture agnosticism, atheism, personal responsibility, scientism, humanism, economic materialism, naturalism, and skepticism. Each of these scales includes multiple items with which respondents can indicate their (dis)agreement that have acceptable levels of inter-item reliability and have been translated into English and German. Schnell's (2015) approach is important as it captures the different ways that people can be nonreligious, similar to the work of van Mulukom and colleagues (2023).

This type of inventory begins to get at the diverse and very personal interpretations of nonreligion. Some clients may endorse a deep sense of connection to other people rooted in humanism whereas others may see life as a primarily independent and, ultimately, isolated experience. In difficult circumstances, some may use rational thinking and science to find comfort whereas others may find peace in meaninglessness. Generationally, nonreligious clients from older cohorts are more likely to have been raised with religion and, in turn, exhibit religious residue (Van Tongeren et al., 2020), or the cognitive, emotional, and behavioral processes learned in or expected by religious communities. Therefore, this line of inquiry can help spark discussions that differentiate clients' personal values from the expectations of others. Again, interviewing allows clients to expand on their worldview in illuminating ways; however, measures such as the DoS may offer language for the therapist and/or the client to begin their dialogue.

When to Assess Nonreligiousness

A common assumption among mental health professionals is that a deeper exploration of (non)religion, beyond inclusion in intake surveys and brief mention in intake interviews, is unnecessary when (non)religion is not clearly relevant to the client's presenting concerns. Given our ethical obligations to attend to individual and cultural diversity as practitioners, it is probably uncontroversial to suggest considerable integration of (non) religion is necessary when a client presents to treatment due to religious doubt or is reconciling their faith with some other aspect of identity (e.g., gender) or choice (e.g., family planning). However, many clinicians may not dedicate substantial time in therapy to learning about clients' nonreligion if they do not see the relationship between it and the client's reason(s) for seeking treatment. Likewise, clinicians are unlikely to broach (non)religion generally in secular treatment, particularly when there is not alignment between the (non)belief of the practitioner and the client (van Nieuw Amerongen-Meeuse et al., 2018).

We argue that, like other social locations, nonreligion shapes cultural positionalities, or the way people understand their place and power in the systems in which they live. As mentioned earlier in this chapter, the shift toward nonreligion in US culture is not attributable to any one cause. However, in the second author's work with nonreligious people in clinical practice and hundreds of hours of qualitative interviewing with nonreligious research participants, sociopolitical trends toward White Christian nationalism (Whitehead & Perry, 2020) are most certainly a common catalyzing factor among younger and queer cohorts of nonbelievers (see chapters 7 and 8). It is imperative to develop skills to broach and integrate clients' nonreligion into psychotherapy because nonreligious worldviews now constitute a significant proportion of the US population, but also because of the concurrent cultural shift toward Christian nationalism that nonbelievers are more likely to find incongruent with their values (Whitehead et al., 2018).

Conclusion

This chapter has several aims. First, it provides definitions of religiosity, spirituality, and nonreligion. It then shows that the percentage of Americans who are nonreligious or nones has increased dramatically since 1990. Importantly, the growth in nonreligious Americans has occurred in every demographic category—all age groups, every racial group, all marital statuses, across the income and education spectra, in every region of the country, for all sexual orientations, and for both men and women. Nonreligiosity has increased dramatically over the last thirty years across the United States. The chapter concludes with a brief discussion of ways to measure and prompt discussions of nonreligiosity and nonspirituality in psychotherapy. Therapists and clinicians should be aware of the growth and diversity of the nonreligious and, with the insights of this chapter, will have additional tools to evaluate and better understand their clients.

Code

Code for the quantitative analyses in this chapter is available here: https://osf.io/59yk3

References

Ammerman, N. T. (2021). *Studying lived religion*. NYU Press.

Baggett, J. P. (2019). *The varieties of nonreligious experience: Atheism in American culture*. NYU Press.

Bullivant, S. (2022). *Nonverts: The making of ex-Christian America*. Oxford University Press.

Cragun, R. T., Hammer, J. H., & Nielsen, M. (2015). The Nonreligious-Nonspiritual Scale (NRNSS): Measuring everyone from atheists to zionists. *Science, Religion, and Culture* 2(3), 36–53. http://doi.org/10.17582/journal.src/2015/2.3.36.53

Cragun, R. T., & McCaffree, K. J. (2021). Nothing is not something: On replacing nonreligion with identities. *Secular Studies*, 3(1), 7–26. https://doi.org/10.1163/25892525-bja10017

Cragun, R. T., & Smith, J. L. 2024. *Goodbye religion: The causes and consequences of secularization*. New York University Press.

Davern, M., Bautista, R., Freese, J., Morgan, S. L., & Smith, T. W. (2022). General Social Surveys, 1972–2022 Cross-Section.

de Jager Meezenbroek, E., Garssen, B., van den Berg, M., van Dierendonck, D., Visser, A., & Schaufeli, W. B. (2012). Measuring spirituality as a universal human experience: A review of spirituality questionnaires. *Journal of Religion and Health*, 51(2), 336–54. https://doi.org/10.1007/s10943-010-9376-1

Ecklund, E. H. (2010). *Science vs. religion: What scientists really think*. Oxford University Press.

Edgell, P., Frost, J., & Stewart, E. (2017). From existential to social understandings of risk: Examining gender differences in nonreligion. *Social Currents*, 4(6), 556–74. https://doi.org/10.1177/2329496516686619

Evans, J. H. (2018). *Morals not knowledge: Recasting the contemporary U.S. conflict between religion and science*. University of California Press.

Glenn, N. D. (2005). *Cohort analysis*. (Vol. 2). Sage Publications.

Gunn, J. T. (2009). *Spiritual weapons, the cold war, and the forging of an American national religion*. Praeger Publishers.

Hadaway, C. K. (1989). Identifying American apostates: A cluster analysis. *Journal for the Scientific Study of Religion*, 28(2), 201–15. https://doi.org/10.2307/1387059

Hill, P. C., & Hood, Jr., R. W. (Eds.). (1999). *Measures of religiosity*. Religious Education Press.

Hout, M., & Fischer, C. S. (2002). Why more Americans have no religious preference: Politics and generations. *American Sociological Review*, 67(2), 165–90. https://doi.org/10.2307/3088891

Hunsberger, B. (2006). *Atheists: A groundbreaking study of America's nonbelievers*. Prometheus Books.

Kasselstrand, I., Zuckerman, P., & Cragun, R. T. (2023). *Beyond Doubt: The Secularization of Society*. New York University Press..

Kosmin, B. A., Keysar, A., Cragun, R. T., & Navarro-Rivera, J. (2009). *American nones: The profile of the no religion population*. Institute for the Study of Secularism in Society and Culture. https://commons.trincoll.edu/aris/files/2011/08/NONES_08.pdf

Lee, L. (2012). Research note: Talking about a revolution: Terminology for the new field of non-religion studies. *Journal of Contemporary Religion*, 27(1), 129–39. https://doi.org/10.1080/13537903.2012.642742

McGuire, M. B. (2008). *Lived religion: Faith and practice in everyday life*. Oxford University Press.

Miller, C., & Beaman, L. G. (2024). Nonreligious afterlife: Emerging understandings of death and dying. *Religions*, 15(1), 104. https://doi.org/10.3390/rel15010104

O'Hair, M. M. (1989). *An atheist epic: The complete unexpurgated story of how bible and prayers were removed from the public schools of the United States*. American Atheist Press.

Pew Research Center. (2014). Religious landscape survey. https://www.pewresearch.org/religious-landscape-study/database/

Polemikou, A., Zartaloudi, E., & Polemikos, N. (2019). Estimating nonbelief: Translation, cultural adaptation, and statistical validation of the Nonreligious-Nonspiritual Scale in a nationwide Greek sample. *Archive for the Psychology of Religion*, 41(2), 105–22. https://doi.org/10.1177/0084672419878819

Quack, J. (2014). Outline of a relational approach to nonreligion. *Method & Theory in the Study of Religion*, 26(4–5), 439–69. https://doi.org/10.1163/15700682-12341327

Rejowska, A. (2021). Humanist weddings in Poland: The various motivations of couples. *Sociology of Religion*, 82(3), 281–304. https://doi.org/10.1093/socrel/sraa060

Schnell, T. (2015). Dimensions of Secularity (DoS): An open inventory to measure facets of secular identities. *The International Journal for the Psychology of Religion*, 25(4), 272–92. https://doi.org/10.1080/10508619.2014.967541

Sevinç, K., Güven, M., & Metinyurt, T. (2015). Dindar ve Spiritüel Olmama (DİSOL) Ölçeğinin Türkçe'ye Uyarlanması. *Çanakkale Onsekiz Mart Üniversitesi İlahiyat Fakültesi Dergisi* (6), 59–86. https://dergipark.org.tr/en/pub/comuifd/issue/4099/54017

Shupe, A. (2007). *Spoils of the kingdom: Clergy misconduct and religious community*. University of Illinois Press.

Stark, R., & Glock, C. Y. (1968). *American piety*. University of California Press.

Steensland, B., Kucinskas, J., & Sun, A. (Eds.). (2022). *Situating spirituality: Context, practice, and power*. Oxford University Press.

Stolz, J., Könemann, J., Purdie, M. S., Englberger, T., & Krüggeler, M. (2016). *(Un-)believing in modern society: Religion, spirituality, and religious-secular competition*. Routledge.

Strhan, A., & Shillitoe, R. (2025). *Growing up godless: Non-religious childhoods in contemporary England*. Princeton University Press.

Thurfjell, D., Rubow, C., Remmel, A., & Ohlsson, H. (2019). The relocation of transcendence: Using schutz to conceptualize the nature experiences of secular people. *Nature and Culture*, 14(2), 190–214. https://doi.org/10.3167/nc.2019.140205

van Mulukom, V., Turpin, H., Haimila, R., Purzycki, B. G., Bendixen, T., Klocová, E. K., Řezníček, D., Coleman, T. J., Sevinç, K., Maraldi, E., Schjoedt, U., Rutjens, B. T., & Farias, M. (2023). What do nonreligious nonbelievers believe in? Secular worldviews around the world. *Psychology of Religion and Spirituality*, 15(1), 143–56. https://doi.org/10.1037/rel0000480

van Nieuw Amerongen-Meeuse, J. C., Schaap-Jonker, H., Schuhmann, C., Anbeek, C., & Braam, A. W. (2018). The "religiosity gap" in a clinical setting: Experiences of mental health care consumers and professionals. *Mental Health, Religion, & Culture*, 21(7), 737–52. https://doi.org/10.1080/13674676.2018.1553029

Van Tongeren, D. R., Nathan DeWall, C., Chen, Z., Sibley, C. G., & Bulbulia, B. (2020). Religious residue: Cross-cultural evidence that religious psychology and behavior persist following deidentification. *Journal of Personality and Social* Psychology, 120(2). doi:http://dx.doi.org.esearch.ut.edu/10.1037/pspp0000288

Voas, D. (2009). The rise and fall of fuzzy fidelity in Europe. *European Sociological Review* 25(2), 155–68. https://doi.org/10.1093/esr/jcn044

Whitehead, A. L., & Perry, S. L. (2020). *Taking America back for God: Christian nationalism in the United States*. Oxford University Press.

Whitehead, A. L., Perry, S. L., & Baker, J. O. (2018). Make America Christian again: Christian Nationalism and voting for Donald Trump in the 2016 Presidential Election. *Sociology of Religion*, 79(2), 147–71. https://doi.org/10.1093/socrel/srx070

Wilkins-Laflamme, S. (2022). *Religion, spirituality and secularity among Millennials: The generation shaping American and Canadian trends*. Routledge.

Zinnbauer, B. J., & Pargament, K. I. (2002). Capturing the meanings of religiousness and spirituality: One way down from a definitional Tower of Babel. *Research in the Social Scientific Study of Religion*, 13, 23–54. https://doi.org/10.1163/9789004496347_004

Zinnbauer, B. J., Pargament, K. I., Cole, B., Rye, M. S., Butfer, E. M., Belavich, T. G., Hipp, K. M., Scott, A. B., & Kadar, J. K. (1997). Religion and spirituality: Unfuzzying the fuzzy. *Journal for the Scientific Study of Religion*, 36(4), 549–64. https://doi.org/10.2307/1387689

3

Nones and Dones

Religious Exiting in Sociological Perspective

Bethany Gull, Jesse M. Smith, and Ryan T. Cragun

Chapter Outline

We have three main goals in this chapter. The first is to describe the process of leaving religion. What does it mean for an individual to abandon a religious identity, reject formerly held religious beliefs, and/or cease to engage in religious practice? How does this process vary between different religious traditions and contexts? The second is to explain the social and demographic characteristics of the nonreligious and demonstrate the impressive diversity of this segment of society. Who are the "nones," the "dones," the spiritual but not religious, the religiously indifferent, and the affirmatively secular? What about those who were never raised with religion and therefore never left it? The third goal is to outline some of the clinical implications of interacting with nonreligious clients and underscore the value and necessity of addressing this group given that those with no religion constitute one of the fastest-growing "religious" groups in the United States and other parts of North America (Pew Research, 2024). The religiously unaffiliated also make up around 16 percent of the global population (Pew Research, 2015) so a better understanding of the diversity of groups and individuals that make up this population, and the beliefs and values they hold, should prove useful to clinicians. Although we will delve into some of the psychological consequences of religious exiting and what this might mean for clinicians, as sociologists our overall discussion and framework will be a sociological one.

We begin by defining and problematizing several of the concepts used to describe the nonreligious. There is today a robust literature on nonreligion and secularity (Bullivant and Lee, 2016; Cragun & Smith, 2024), deconversion (Gull, 2022b; Thiessen & LaFlamme, 2017; Jindra et al., 2024; Keller et al., 2024a), apostasy (Brooks, 2018; Cottee, 2015), and related topics. Although much of this scholarship has been centered on the North American and Western European contexts, there is an emerging literature focused on non-Western cultures (Eller & Khazaal, 2024; Zuckerman, 2010). We draw on this literature throughout this chapter. However, it has become increasingly important to disentangle the terminology that bears on the questions of why and how people leave religion and what this means for the lives of those who have left it. Confusing or conflating concepts, being too broad or too narrow, or leaving assumptions about terminology unchecked is unproductive, especially if we hope to understand their clinical implications and how to better support the nonreligious individuals to whom these various terms apply. To that end, we will start with the titular concepts from this chapter—the "nones" and the "dones"—suffusing these and the other groups outlined in this chapter with a discussion of how they relate to the process of leaving religion. We will then outline a few of the most significant issues with respect to the demographics of these groups before moving to discuss the clinical relevance of religious exiting and the nonreligious in general in clinical practice.

Nones, Dones, and Other Terms

The *nones*—those who claim no religious affiliation—have been the subject of much research and media attention since the latter part of the first decade of the new millennium. Many readers will be familiar with the fact that the religiously unaffiliated in the United States today make up around 30 percent of the population (Pew Research, 2024). That the nonreligious are approaching a third of society represents a massive shift in the United States, considering that in the 1970s just 6 percent of US Americans claimed no religious affiliation. Scholars, commentators, and the general public alike have been grappling with the potential consequences of this change, often coming to very different conclusions (Cragun & Smith, 2024). But as we will see throughout this chapter, the nones are far from a homogenous group, and there are important differences between, for instance, nonreligious people raised without religion and those who have left religion. Since nones are simply those who check the "none" box on surveys asking about religious affiliation, that by itself does not tell us very much about who they are and what they believe. Nones is a generic category, encompassing both those who believe in a higher power and those who do not, and those who were never religious as well as those who have exited religion. Most nones in the United States fall into the latter category; the vast majority of nones state that they were once affiliated with a religion (Bullivant, 2022).

The *dones* are a subset of the nones in that they have no religious affiliation. That they are "done" with religion tells us they were once religious, but that they have gone through some process of leaving religion. There has been no systematic attempt at quantifying through representative surveys those who self-identify as dones; rather, this subset of the nonreligious has emerged through primarily qualitative studies focused on the life narratives and the interpersonal consequences, good and bad, that people face after leaving religion (Van Tongeren, 2024). What differentiates *dones* from *nones* in these narratives, is that the former, ironically perhaps, take a greater interest in the religion they left. In some ways, they are not done with religion, because it continues to play an important role in their identities and self-narratives. Religion may be a more emotionally charged subject for them than for other nones, and certainly those who are indifferent to religion (discussed below). Still, dones are done only with organized religion; some dones maintain religious beliefs and may continue to consider themselves part of a religious tradition, but the ways in which they express their faith stands outside the parameters of conventional religious practice (Packard & Ferguson, 2019).

Nones and dones are relatively recent neologisms, having emerged from either the way scholars study religious affiliation patterns (i.e., nones), or more organically as an in vivo term, created by those who want to signal their distaste for and rejection of organized religion (i.e., dones). Another recent coinage describing those who have left religion is "nonverts," a portmanteau of nonreligious and convert (Bullivant, 2022). But historically, the process of leaving religion has been described by scholars across disciplines variably as deconversion, disaffiliation, apostasy, defection, or even religious "leave-taking" (Introvigne, 1999). Language matters and this type of framing has resulted in nonreligious individuals being labeled as deconverts, disaffiliates, apostates, defectors, and leave-takers (Cragun & Hammer, 2011). Studies of the "unchurched" (Fuller, 2001) and those who leave religion often explain the rise of the nonreligious as a consequence of the "failure to transmit" religion across generations; much of this literature implies the nonreligious are a problem in need of fixing (Perry et al., 1980). Indeed, much of the research that adopts the term "unchurched" is made up of guidelines for how and why the nonreligious need to be brought into the religious fold (Barna, 2002).

Though a term like disaffiliation has a more technical, neutral tone to it, most of the other litany of terms just outlined have quite negative, even condescending connotations. Indeed, much of the early work in this area characterized the nonreligious generally as defectors, apostates, or unchurched people who are more likely to engage in immoral and socially undesirable behaviors (Cragun & Hammer, 2011). Scholars who use this language and/or the failure-to-transmit framing (Smith & Denton, 2005) are intimating that the nonreligious could be a danger to society and that improving religious transmission from parents to children (i.e., to "successfully" transmit instead of "failing" to transmit religion) would be a boon for society. We think this way of conceptualizing how and why more people are leaving religion "fails" to understand the wider social forces shaping the (non)religious landscape and contributes to the social stigma and even discrimination some nonreligious groups face in society (Abbott & Mollen, 2018; Hammer et al., 2012). This underscores the clinical relevance and need for understanding what the social and psychological process of leaving religion might mean for nonreligious clients.

Religious Exiting

It is for the reasons outlined above that we use the phrase *religious exiting* to describe the process of leaving religion. Though it is generic and perhaps less exciting than a word like apostasy, it is precisely because of its neutrality that we find it more useful, especially in relation to the topic of mental health care for secular clients. It does not carry with it some of the negative connotations or potentially confusing aspects of other terms like defection, deconversion, or apostasy. To be sure, there are situations in which words like apostasy are appropriate (Bromley, 1998a); indeed we have written scholarly pieces on the topic (Smith, 2016). There are historical, cultural, and conceptual reasons that justify its use (among them the fact some individuals proudly adopt the apostate label; Brooks, 2018). Likewise, deconversion can be useful for describing the process by which people lose religious faith or move out of organized religion; one of us has written on it as being a stage in the exit process (Gull, 2022c). However, it also has semantic baggage and can be misleading. For instance, although conversion may well be a necessary concept, "deconversion" can implicitly privilege religion. If conversion is about *becoming* religious, then is deconversion just about losing religion, or is it about *becoming* secular—for instance, adopting affirmatively secular beliefs? This is not always clear in the literature and can lead to misunderstandings, as the notion of deconversion implicitly subscribes to the "subtraction theory" of secularity—that becoming nonreligious represents a "loss" of something. But one might argue, as some scholars do (Roberts & Yamane, 2016), that the word conversion should simply refer to *any* major transitions in beliefs, identities, and behaviors, whether these redound to a religious or a secular disposition and view of the world. In this case, the word deconversion is superfluous. And yet, nonreligious individuals themselves might take issue with the suggestion that they have "converted" to nonreligion. This is another reason to default to the phrase religious exiting.

To be clear, there is nothing intrinsically at odds with, at the descriptive level, distinguishing "religious exiting" from some of these other terms. Indeed, we rely on and cite the literature that uses other terminology. But, in addition to its neutrality, religious exiting has the advantage of functioning as a kind of umbrella term subsuming a variety of processes by which people become nonreligious. For instance, it could still be appropriate to refer to deconversion when examining individuals who were deeply committed to a specific religion but then left that religion, such that they are now outsiders looking in. When a person undergoes an intense period of doubting, followed by disengagement, and then de-fellowshipping (Gull, 2022c) from their religious community, they can arguably be said to have experienced deconversion. But for other individuals who had minimal religious commitment or who were only nominally affiliated with some religious organization in the first place but then drifted away from religion entirely, they cannot be said to have undergone deconversion. They, like our "deconverts," have exited religion, but in meaningfully different ways and with different consequences, some of which will bear on the question of mental health and well-being. "Religious exiting" covers both such cases, while also avoiding privileging any particular descriptor that may be fraught with connotations unhelpful to understanding how and why many individuals turn away from religion.

So how exactly should we define religious exiting? It is the social and psychological process of an individual's movement away from each of the primary dimensions of religiosity (Cragun & Smith, 2024). These dimensions, already mentioned above, are widely discussed in the sociological literature, and they include religious beliefs, religious behaviors, and religious identification or belonging (Cragun & McCaffree, 2021). When a person disengages from all three of these, they have exited religion. A former pastor who has spent her whole life as a devout Christian, but then comes to renounce her religious beliefs, leaves the congregation she led, stops engaging in religious rites and rituals, and now calls herself an atheist, adopting a completely secular worldview, has had a sharp break with religion and is a religious exiter.

But of course, the reality for most of the people we would categorize, sociologically, as religious exiters is not so clear cut. Many individuals leave organized religion but maintain some religious beliefs (see SBNRs below); some people value belonging to a religion but reject much or even all of its core doctrines (this is sometimes referred to as "fuzzy fidelity" or liminality; Voas, 2009; Wilkins-Laflamme, 2022). There are also those individuals who are affirmatively secular (Hwang et al., 2011). It is less clear that we should call such people, strictly speaking, religious exiters, though some may be. Two of these groups are part of the nonreligious: the *spiritual but not religious* (SBNRs) and the *affirmatively secular*. Both of these relate to religious exiting in different ways, and highlighting their differences will help illuminate the relevance for how clinicians might think about and interact with secular clients. We discuss the clinical relevance of both these groups in the final section of this chapter, but defining them here will be useful as we turn to these and other categories again in the next section.

The SBNRs have been studied for decades (Steensland et al., 2022; Wilkins-Laflamme, 2022), but they tend to be a diffuse and somewhat ambiguous group in society. Some scholars (Mercadante, 2014), in outlining their defining characteristics, suggest that SBNRs are simply those who are open and inclined to explore many different kinds of spiritual paths.[1] Some SBNRs view their lives as spiritual journeys that will take them in different directions at different moments in the life course. "Religion is not a fixed thing for them, and they fully expect to change their religious beliefs regularly" (Fuller, 2001, p. 4). SBNRs, as the name implies, are suspicious of institutional and organized religion and therefore seek and develop spiritual beliefs and practices outside conventional religion. There are individuals who unambiguously self-identify as SBNR, but most of the people to whom

[1]Of course, "spirituality" can mean many different things. For some, it involves belief in the supernatural, but others, with wholly naturalistic worldviews, may also refer to themselves as spiritual. This is part of what makes defining and measuring spirituality empirically so challenging.

this category applies do not necessarily adopt the label. Many SBNRs have left organized religion, often as a consequence of their distrust of religious institutions, so many of the elements of religious exiting discussed earlier apply. But of course not all SBNRs are religious exiters; some are cradle nones (those who were never religious). This will make a difference to clinicians as they account for the life histories and specific needs of their secular clients.

The affirmatively secular, on the other hand, are those who positively affirm nonreligious identities (Langston et al., 2015). This means they think in terms of, and hold, substantive secular beliefs. They also adopt specific identities that correspond with various secular categories. Rather than, or in addition to, being a "none" on a survey about religion, the affirmatively secular adopt labels including humanist, secularist, secular humanist, freethinker, atheist, agnostic, naturalist, nontheist, or other terms. Whereas most SBNRs would not necessarily identify with, for example, the label atheist, some affirmatively secular people, including atheists, do identify as spiritual. The meaning and relevance of all these concepts will vary from person to person, and there is gray area, but broadly speaking, it is appropriate to distinguish between SBNRs and the affirmatively secular to distinguish nonreligious groups.

What is necessary in this case is to identify at what level we are examining religious exiting. Are we focused at the most granular level of an individual's every stated or implicit religious belief or every behavior that seems to confirm or contradict these beliefs? Or are we looking at wider trends across institutions and society at large? Although religious exiting tends to focus on the micro-level aspects of secularization, the process of the individual's disengagement with religion is always embedded within broader, macro-level secularizing forces (Kasselstrand et al., 2023). Since secularization has to do with the ways in which modernization undermines religion, it is against the backdrop of changing demographics, shifts in the wider culture, and other macro-level forces of modernity that religious exiting at the micro level (i.e., individual's changing beliefs, behaviors, and to which groups they belong) takes place. In other words, it is the ways in which both macro and micro (and meso) level forces intersect that ultimately produce religious exiting.

There are many reasons people leave religion. Scholars have identified a litany of these reasons through both surveys and qualitative interviews (Zuckerman, 2011). Two of the authors of this chapter (Cragun & Smith, 2024) have summarized some of the most salient reasons, and they do this through the theoretical lens of *push and pull factors*. Borrowing from the field of migration studies where demographers examine factors pushing people out of a resident country (e.g., war, crime, lack of economic opportunity, etc.) while also pulling them toward a host country (e.g., better social safety net, educational opportunities, etc.), Cragun and Smith (2024) identified various push/pull factors encouraging religious exiting. There are political and moral push factors (e.g., abortion, homosexuality), disagreement with religious doctrines and teachings, and hypocrisy, among others. Underlying them all is value misalignment, or all the ways in which the beliefs and values of the individual are out of sync with what their religions—which they often inherited as children—promote. At the same time, there are pull factors drawing people toward a more secular life: the desire for intellectual autonomy, wanting to spend their time in other ways, not having to defend discredited religious dogmas, and the general pull of a modern worldview. Studies of exiting have tended to focus on what we are calling push factors, and most of that research converges on similar findings (see Keller et al., 2024a). Pull factors have been much less studied, but they are perhaps equally important in highly secularized and secularizing societies where the cultural norms of autonomy and, not just freedom of, but freedom from religion set the conditions for individuals to adopt beliefs and values that align with a more secular view of the world (van Mulukom et al., 2023).

Notwithstanding these common patterns of religious exiting, it is important to note, as other scholars have (Barbour, 1994), that individuals interpret their own religious exiting in different ways, and they do this, in part, through the post hoc narrativization of their experience (Smith & Halligan, 2021). People tell stories about their deconversion from religion (just as people tell stories about their conversion to religion; Gooren, 2007). These stories are not purely objective accounts of everything that has happened. They are constituent parts of the process of leaving religion itself and they tell us something important about the meaning individuals ascribe to their experience; indeed such stories can be an important source of meaning (Brooks, 2018; Gull, 2022a). Thus, to say that people tell stories about leaving religion is not the same as saying these stories are fabrications or unjustified. People make sense of their experience, in part, by talking through it, both to themselves and to others, a central activity in psychotherapy.

Context(s) of Religious Exiting

Having defined religious exiting and identified its basic features, we can now discuss other groups beyond the nones and dones, and the different contexts in which religious exiting occurs. However, there is a generic point about context that we need to address before we focus our discussion. That point is that although scholars have made inroads to the comparative and cross-cultural dimensions of nonreligion and secularity generally (see Zuckerman, 2010), there is not yet a robust literature on religious exiting per se that incorporates a cross-cultural and interdisciplinary approach. As a consequence, though we fully acknowledge the importance of and need for more work in this area, we cannot address in any detail how different cultural contexts around the globe shape religious exiting. There is, however, reason to think that, in addition to differences brought on by disparate norms and values across cultures, much about the structure, process, and core features of religious exiting that have been studied in one cultural context (e.g., the push/pull factors among exiters in the United States discussed earlier), will hold for exiters in other cultures too (see Cragun & Smith, 2024). Likewise, much of what we explain below will be broadly applicable to religious exiting across cultural contexts.

There are two central issues at play when considering the context of religious exiting: the type of religion in question, and the nature of religious socialization. But first, it is important to note that many—and in fact, possibly *most*—religious exiters simply drift away from religion, usually the religion they inherited as children, in a slow and gradual way without experiencing any obvious "break" with it (Kasselstrand et al., 2023; Quack & Schuh, 2017). This characterizes many of today's nones. The various push and pull factors outlined above may be in the background for such individuals, and they may appeal to some of them if asked directly about why they are no longer religious, but the social and psychological move away from religion is often much less pronounced, and less a part of the narrative of the individual's life. For some of these exiters, religion may never have been all that important to them, even when they identified and affiliated with a religion. These individuals may not have had a clear "experience" leaving religion, or even thought much about how they exited it. They just do not care or think much about religion. This describes what scholars refer to as *religious indifference* (Quack & Schuh, 2017), which includes those who were never religious as well as religious exiters. Therefore, in some cases, for the religiously indifferent, discussions about faith crises, trauma, social stigma, newfound intellectual freedom, liberation, sense of autonomy, and other negative and positive consequences that can attend religious exiting simply are not there. Even in the United States, where religion is held in high esteem compared to other advanced nations, given generational trends over the last half-century, where each generation has tended to be less religious than the last (Cragun & Smith, 2024), many exiters simply transition out of religion in ways they and others hardly notice.

As we have suggested, when considering the dynamics of religious exiting, context is key. One critical piece of context is the kind of religious tradition or organization an individual leaves, because this can play a significant role in the character of the exiting process (Cottee, 2015; Davidman, 2014). For example, those who come from what scholars call high-demand (or alternatively, high-cost) religions will often have a very different experience than those who come from lower-demand religions. High-demand religious groups tend to have conservative religious teachings and traditions, they are more exclusionary, have high in-group levels of commitment, and place significant demands—spiritual, practical, financial—on adherents (Keller et al., 2024a). People who leave fundamentalist religions, for example, may have more dramatic exits that take on more urgency and require greater attention and knowledge on the part of clinicians. In addition, it matters a great deal whether one resigns and leaves a religious group voluntarily, or is ejected, shunned, or excommunicated from a religion without their consent. Of course, something in between can happen as well. Some individuals voluntarily renounce a faith and leave a religion, only to then be disowned by family, rejected by friends, or become ostracized by their religious community. In either case, this is quite a different situation from the person who quietly quits a liberal religion that placed minimal demand on their time, energy, and mental life in the first place. So although someone can experience significant stress leaving any religion, those exiting high-demand groups, especially new religious movements that isolate and abuse members, are more likely to have trauma that will require clinical intervention (see chapter 12; Bromley, 1998a; Bromley, 1998b).

Contrasting two different religious exiters from opposite ends of the low/high-demand spectrum will illustrate the impact of the kind of religious socialization one undergoes and the importance of context generally. The first is Sue,[2] a woman in her forties from the West Coast of the United States. Sue was brought up in the Unitarian Church by liberal parents. She had a happy and stable home life. Both of her parents identified as Christian, and they were regular churchgoers, but Sue sometimes questioned whether either of them sincerely believed in the core claims of Christianity. Sue, though she thought of herself as a Christian, remembered being skeptical of religion from a young age. Her parents made clear early on that she could pursue her own spiritual path and that she was under no obligation to even maintain a religious identity if she did not want to. She even joked that "[because] I was raised Unitarian, I [wasn't] raised with religion." In her teenage years, Sue's church attendance thinned out, and after she moved away from home for school, she simply drifted away from religion entirely. Neither her parents nor anyone else close to her questioned Sue on her transition out of religion. She harbors no resentment toward her parents or the religious socialization she received. Now a mother herself, Sue does not think about religion much and has not felt any need to raise her own children in any religion—though she commented she would follow the tradition of her parents, giving her own children the autonomy to choose their own path, whether that included religion or not. She is now agnostic, identifies as a humanist, and has a thoroughly secular worldview. Sue described her exit from religion as "organic, and totally natural."

Compare Sue to Glen, a man in his fifties from the Midwest. Glen grew up in an independent fundamentalist Baptist church. His father was the pastor of their congregation. Both his parents were incredibly strict, he was homeschooled, and everything in Glen's world was centered on their religion. As he described it, "[W]e were pretty isolated from secular activities, such as music, television; we went to church every time the door was open, five, six, seven times a week, [and] Satan was controlling public schools." As he reflected on his early life, he acknowledged he was a "true believer" and that his religion was everything to him. "I accepted everything, you know? I mean, why would you question your parents?" This last clause is important. It underscores the power of early religious socialization. Glen simply had no reason to doubt that what his parents were telling him was true.

However, there was a critical turning point in Glen's life early on that initiated his exit from religion. When he was just fourteen, he came out as gay to his parents. Given what they believed, and what they had taught Glen to believe, they could not abide this, and they kicked him out of his home. Glen lost his family, church, and community. He spent some time homeless and moved around frequently. One might expect a sudden, hard exit from religion on Glen's part given the high-cost context he came from. But that actually was not the case. He spent more than a decade exploring different religious groups including Wicca and the Hare Krishnas. He continued to think of himself as religious for many years. But after attempting to return to Christianity once more as a young adult, he finally cast off all religion. As it happens, Glen, now middle aged, is an example of a "Done" and he self-identifies as such. He is also a humanist and a skeptic, and he has spent many years forming new relationships, finding community, and rebuilding his life.

[2]These are actual cases drawn from interviews conducted by Smith. Pseudonyms are used to protect participants' identities.

As these two cases illustrate, the intensity of one's religious socialization will often correlate with their future level of commitment to religion. For instance, some research finds greater religious "residue" among religious exiters compared to those brought up in secular families (Beider, 2022). Sue's peaceable and "totally natural" move away from religion, and her lack of interest in it now is consistent with her level of religiosity as a youth. By comparison, the fraught and distressing religious exit Glen had, and the fact he spent many years attempting to maintain a religious identity, resonates with the intensity—the "indoctrination" to use his words—of the religious training he received as a child.

Finally, it is important to consider how the life course itself can shape the nature of the exiting process. There are various elements of the life course that can precipitate or mediate leaving religion. Personal crises, health issues, divorce, the death of a loved one, along with more positively valenced events like getting married, having children, and getting a college degree, can all signal important turning points and transitional moments that influence both the likelihood and character of a religious exit (Desmond et al., 2010; Ingersoll-Dayton et al., 2002). More than a hundred years ago psychologist-philosopher William James observed that "counter-conversions" (i.e., religious exiting in our framing) are often succeeded by, "period[s] of storm and stress and inconsistency" (James, 2004, p. 159) that attend transitional moments along the life course. The implications can be far-reaching in the life of the individual. Leaving religion will not merely entail rejecting a former set of specific beliefs and practices. It may involve leaving and forming new interpersonal relationships or whole communities; social networks may change; stigma or discrimination may arise and need to be managed (Zimmerman et al., 2015), and a new set of beliefs about the world—or even a wholesale new lifestance—can emerge out of the context of having left religion (Cragun & Smith, 2024). Whatever the specific consequences may be—and they can vary dramatically from individual to individual—turning points and other components of the life course will need to be inspected closely to gain a fuller understanding of the set of factors that leads one out of religion.

Next, we turn to a more detailed discussion of the varieties of nonreligious groups, including those just discussed, by examining and comparing several of their social and demographic similarities and differences.

Demographics of the Nonreligious

We draw on the General Social Survey (GSS) to provide a demographic profile of the nonreligious. To have sufficiently large numbers for the somewhat smaller groups of the nonreligious, we aggregated three waves of the GSS: 2018, 2021, and 2022. As a result, the data may not perfectly represent the characteristics of these groups at present but do reflect these groups in recent years. To be able to provide demographic characteristics of the various types of nonreligious individuals, we had to figure out how to operationalize these groups. For some of the groups, this is fairly straightforward, but it is more challenging for others. Before describing the demographic characteristics of the groups, we first detail how we were able to disentangle the various types of nonreligious individuals.

The primary variable used in classifying individuals as nonreligious is a relatively straightforward question about religious identity or affiliation. The question asks participants what their religious affiliation is and provides "none" as one option among many religious affiliations. We recoded this variable into two groups—those who reported a religious affiliation ("Religious") and those with no religious affiliation ("Nones"). Because we also wanted to examine four additional groups, we had to develop ways to capture those groups. For "Exiters," the GSS includes a question that asks about religious affiliation at the age of sixteen. This makes for a relatively simple classification of individuals: those who reported a religious affiliation at sixteen but no religious affiliation at the time they took part in the GSS were classified as "Exiters" or individuals who had left religion. Another subset of the nonreligious are those who identify as "Spiritual But Not Religious" or SBNR. To classify individuals as SBNR we used another survey question that asked participants to indicate how religious they consider themselves to be on a four-point scale with the following options: "Very spiritual," "Moderately spiritual," "Slightly spiritual," and "Not spiritual at all." Individuals who reported no religious affiliation but rated themselves as either "Very spiritual" or "Moderately spiritual" were classified as SBNRs. Finally, for the last two groups, we used a more complicated classification system as variables that would best allow us to capture these groups (e.g., importance of your nonreligious identity) are not included in the GSS at this time. Instead, we turned to a recently published article by Blankholm et al. (2025) that noted atheist activists tend to have two characteristics in common—they do not believe there is a life after death and they are exclusive empiricists, meaning they only accept scientific methods for knowing what is real. To capture these individuals, we combined three variables: (a) we included individuals who reported they were atheists or agnostics, (b) they had to select that they consider the Bible to be a book written by humans that is a collection of myths, and (c) they had to select that they do not believe there is an afterlife. Individuals who met all of those criteria we classified as "Affirmatively Secular." It is not a perfect classification but, given data limitations, will satisfy our purposes. Finally, to capture the religiously indifferent we combined two criteria: (a) individuals had to report no religious affiliation and (b) they could not be the affirmatively secular. This classification is also problematic, but we believe it comes close to capturing the individuals described by Quack and Schuh (2017) and Kasselstrand et al. (2023) in describing where the vast majority of people who leave religion end up—they are indifferent to questions of religion.

With our operationalization of the six groups of interest in place, we now turn to their demographics. Figure 3.1 details the average ages of the groups. In line with prior research (Cragun & Smith, 2024), religious individuals are six to ten years older than all of the nonreligious groups. Nones, generally, and the religiously indifferent are the youngest groups, on average, while the affirmatively secular are the oldest nonreligious group.

Also in line with prior research, we see a clear pattern when it comes to the gender makeup of the six groups in figure 3.2. Scholars have long known that women are more religious than men in the United States (Voas et al., 2013). That still holds, with 58 percent

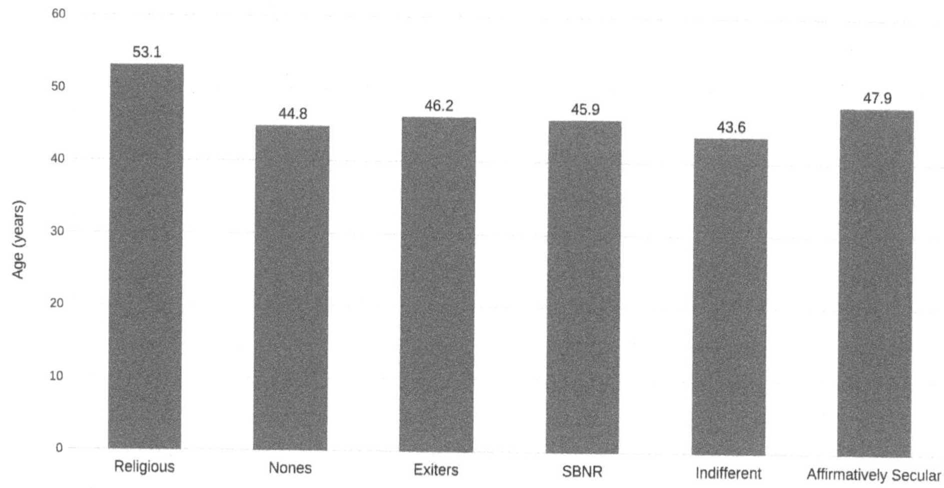

Figure 3.1 Average Age by Nonreligious Type.

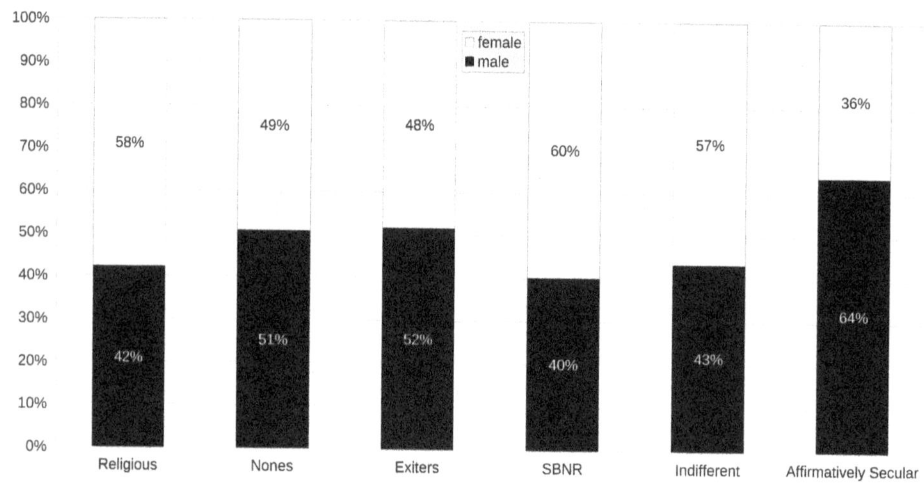

Figure 3.2 Gender by Nonreligious Category.

of the individuals categorized as religious identifying as female. For two of the nonreligious groups—nones and exiters—the gender split is nearly 50/50. There are, however, two groups that are fairly similar to the religious in their gender makeup—the SBNRs and the religiously indifferent. This aligns with prior research suggesting that women are more likely to adopt a "softer" or "milder" nonreligious identity to minimize the risks of prejudice and discrimination (Edgell et al., 2017; Wilkins-Laflamme, 2022). There is just one nonreligious group that is predominantly male—the affirmatively secular. Nearly two-thirds of the affirmatively secular (64 percent) are male; 36 percent are female. This finding aligns with a large body of literature suggesting that individuals who identify as atheists or secular activists are disproportionately likely to be male (Cragun, 2014; Hunsberger, 2006). Of note, the gender variable in the GSS is dichotomous (i.e., male/female); the researchers behind the GSS recently added an "other" gender option in a separate question but the number of people who have chosen that option is so small—below 20—therefore, analyses of so few individuals would not be statistically meaningful.

Racially, the nonreligious generally look like the rest of the US population as figure 3.3 illustrates, though there is some variation among the groups as well. Among the religious, 75 percent of Americans identified as White, 14 percent identified as Black, and 11 percent identified as some other race in the GSS. Very similar percentages were observed among Nones and Exiters, though they were slightly less diverse with a slightly higher percentage of White individuals. SBNR and religiously indifferent individuals were slightly more diverse than the religious, with 73 percent identifying as White and slight increases in the other two groups. Once again, the affirmatively secular stand out; they are the most likely to identify as White (90 percent), with just 3 percent identifying as Black and 7 percent as some other race. These findings also align with prior research on the nonreligious generally (Cragun & Smith, 2024) and atheists (Hunsberger, 2006).

The demographic characteristic where the nonreligious are the most likely to differ from the religious is marital status. Figure 3.4 shows that 50 percent of religious individuals are married and just 21 percent have never married, with the remaining 29 percent being a mix of separated, divorced, or widowed. These numbers are quite different for all of the nonreligious categories, though, intriguingly, the affirmatively secular are the most similar to the religious. For Nones, 39 percent are married and 39 percent have never married. Similar percentages are seen among Exiters—41 percent married and 37 percent never married—and the religiously indifferent—36 percent married and 41 percent never married. A slightly lower percentage of SBNR individuals were married, just 32 percent, the lowest of any of the nonreligious groups. For the affirmatively secular, 48 percent were married but a much higher percentage were never married compared to the religious, 34 percent. These data suggest that, while the affirmatively secular differ from the religious in a lot of ways (see below), they are also similar in their older ages, on average, and their higher likelihood of being married.

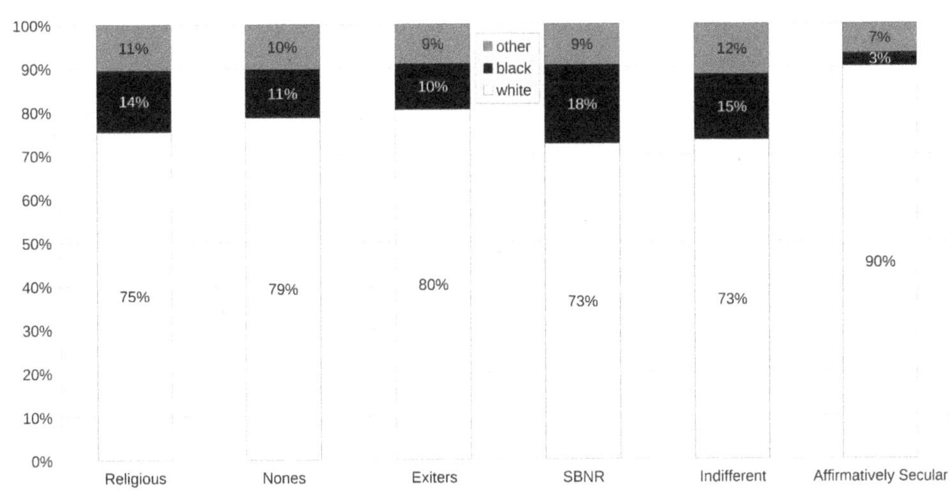

Figure 3.3 Race by Nonreligious Category.

Another area where the affirmatively secular stand out is their higher educational attainment, on average. Figure 3.5 shows the average years of education by religious group; twelve years of education is the equivalent of a high school diploma while sixteen years is the equivalent of a college degree and twenty years would be a graduate degree. The affirmatively secular individuals' average, if rounded up, would be a college degree. The differences between the other groups are quite small, averaging out to a couple of years of college after high school. There are basically negligible differences between the religious, nones, exiters, SBNRs, and the religiously indifferent.

Figure 3.6 presents the average income for the six groups in 2022 dollars. The averages are quite informative but also reflective of some of the demographic characteristics already observed. The most notable group, again, are the affirmatively secular, whose

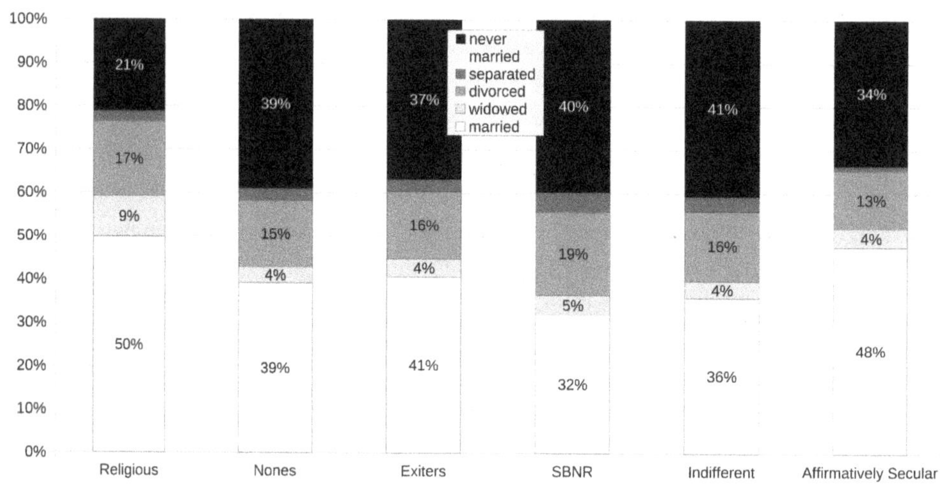

Figure 3.4 Marital Status by Nonreligious Category.

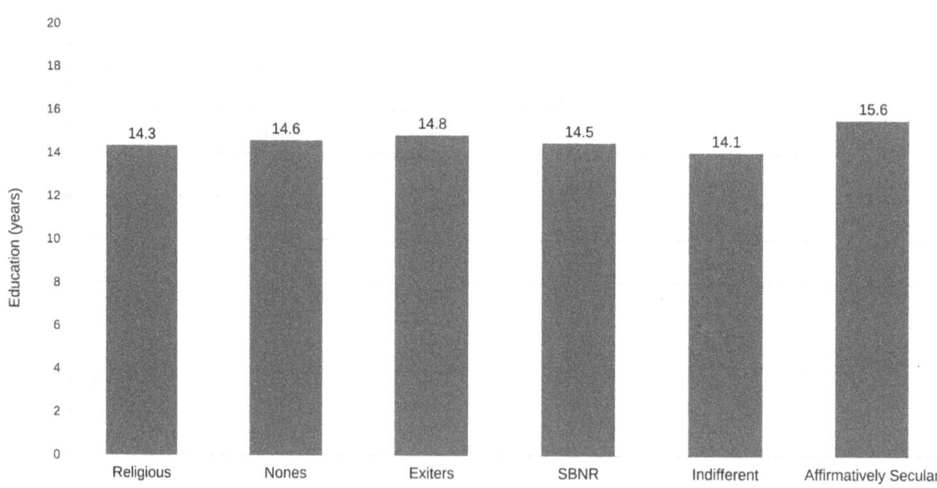

Figure 3.5 Average Educational Attainment in Years by Nonreligious Category.

average income of $63,873 is nearly twenty thousand dollars higher than the next closest group—the religious. Three groups are quite similar—the religious, nones, and exiters—are all around $45,000. Two groups stand out on the low end—SBNRs and the religiously indifferent, whose incomes are just under forty thousand dollars per year. Given the gender, racial, marital, and educational differences between these groups, these gaps make sense. Effectively, the groups that have higher proportions of racial and ethnic minorities also have lower educational attainment and incomes, on average.

The last demographic characteristic we examined is political affiliation. The question we used in the GSS for figure 3.7 includes more categories (e.g., Strong Democrat, Not a Strong Democrat, Independent but Lean Democrat, etc.). We collapsed them to make the figure easier to interpret. In line with prior research (Cragun & Smith, 2024), the religious

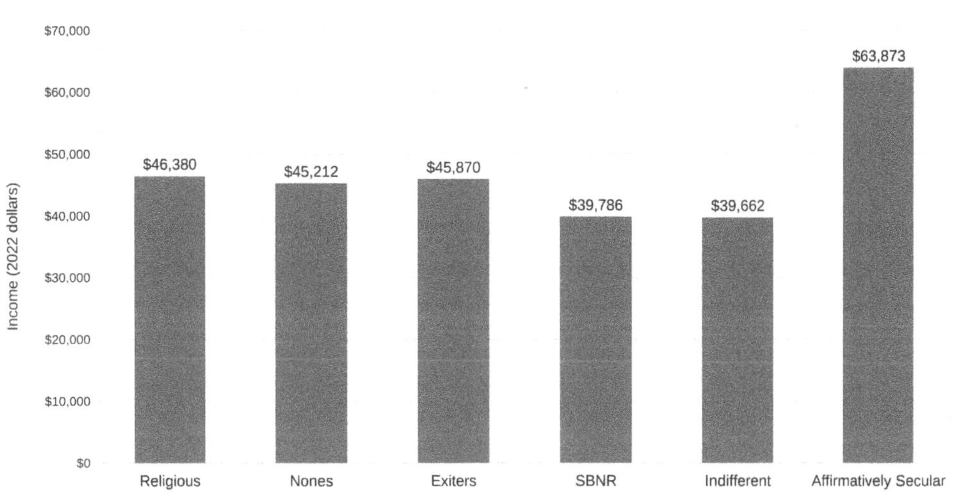

Figure 3.6 Average Income by Nonreligious Category.

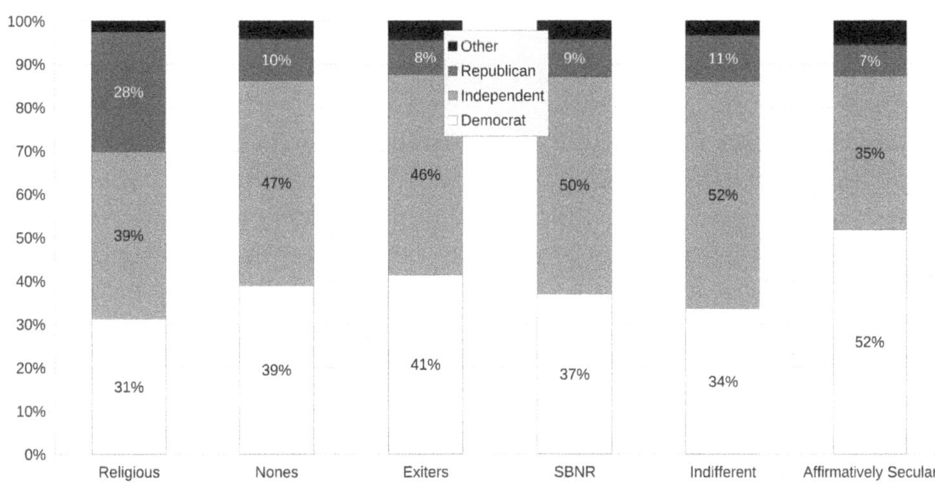

Figure 3.7 Political Party Identification by Nonreligious Category.

are the most conservative with 28 percent identifying as Republicans, 39 percent as Independents, and 31 percent as Democrats. All of the nonreligious groups lean to the left, politically, with somewhere between 34 percent and 52 percent identifying as Democrats. Nones, exiters, SBNRs, and the religiously indifferent all have close to 50 percent who identify as political independents. The affirmatively secular are the most left-leaning with just 7 percent identifying as Republicans and 35 percent as political independents.

Implications for Clinical Practice

Thus far, we have outlined the different types of nonreligious identities, highlighting the variation of belief, behavior, and identification that are often invisible when we collapse all nonreligious persons into the category of "religious nones." We have shown how they differ on a number of demographic characteristics. We have also outlined common pathways for religious exiting and the types of nonreligious identities in which those pathways are more likely to end.

We now turn to a discussion of the implications of these nonreligious identities for clinical practice, or common issues that may arise when counseling nonreligious clients. While these are not concerns found only among the nonreligious, they are those that research into this population has shown occur with relative frequency. Some of these issues are related to the experience of religious doubting and the process of religious exiting. Others are related to the social context of that exiting, such as changes in close relationships and finding community outside of religion. Others are challenges that are more likely to be found among the nonreligious more generally, whether they be indifferent, spiritual but not religious, or affirmatively secular. Issues discussed here are drawn from the authors' research as well as other relevant literature with the goal of equipping clinicians with a general understanding of common experiences among this population.

A review of the research on counseling nonreligious clients indicates that it is an understudied topic (Abbott, 2021). This is surprising for a number of reasons, two of which we will discuss here: (1) the rise in nonreligious identification has been widely cited and noted in the news, and (2) the increased comfort across mental health professions with the idea that clients' spiritual and/or religious beliefs may be ethically and effectively incorporated into the therapeutic process (Jacobs, 2010; Cook, 2020). If religious clients' worldviews can be drawn upon to assist clients, then nonreligious clients' worldviews should also be utilized in clinical practice. There is a robust body of work on general guidelines for incorporating clients' worldviews into therapy that focuses on how to do so within the therapeutic relationship. Guidance for practitioners includes practicing humility rather than certainty about clients' beliefs (Evans & Nelson, 2021; Jindra & Lee, 2021) and asking for clarification rather than assuming one knows and understands the nature of a client's beliefs. As we have indicated in this chapter, this is especially important for working with nonreligious clients as their beliefs are likely to be difficult to define within a specific, institutionalized system. Clinicians are also encouraged to explore the ways clients' spiritual beliefs or worldviews contribute to or detract from their quality of life (Evans & Nelson, 2021; Jindra & Lee, 2021). If clinicians choose to incorporate clients' worldviews—be they spiritual, religious, indifferent, or secular—into therapy, they should inquire into how these beliefs relate to the issues for which individuals are seeking therapy (Evans & Nelson, 2021).

As we proceed with this section, we will break down our discussion of the implications for clinical practice into several categories of nonreligious individuals. For the sake of simplicity, we will collapse the identities discussed above into three broad nonreligious categories: religious exiters (recent and long-term), the spiritual but not religious (SBNR), and the affirmatively secular. We begin with a discussion of issues faced by religious exiters. We believe it is particularly important to highlight the needs of recent exiters as they are most likely to have issues related to religious change emerge during therapy or have their exit be the reason they seek therapy in the first place.

Religious Exiters: Recent and Long-Term

As we have indicated throughout this chapter, the context in which religious exiting takes place has a great deal of influence on how that exit is experienced. Context includes multiple aspects, including but not limited to the type of religious organization exited, the degree of religious socialization a person experiences, family dynamics, and major life events. While we cannot touch on all of these contextual factors here, we will discuss several of the most salient. Clients who have exited a high-demand religion (defined earlier in the chapter) are likely to face different challenges in therapy than those who are simply nonreligious. For instance, there is an elevated (albeit small) risk of intrafamilial abuse when a person leaves a high-demand religion practiced by the entire family (Johnson, 2019; Parekh & Egan, 2021). Internalized powerlessness coupled with literal or simplistic interpretation of scripture may leave these exiters vulnerable to abuse and emotional manipulation. This is particularly concerning if they live with their highly religious family members (Parekh & Egan, 2021). However, most religious exiters will face less extreme issues related to transitioning from a religious identity to a nonreligious one. Examples include a need for religio-spiritual identity and worldview reconstruction, the onset or worsening of depression or anxiety (Nica, 2019, 2020, 2024), and substance abuse (Jindra & Lee, 2021).

Another issue common among recent religious exiters can be summed up by a term used frequently in sociological literature: anomie. A word of French origin, anomie roughly translates as "normlessness." It was popularized by the French sociologist Emile Durkheim (1893/1933) to describe the difficulties people often face during times of rapid social change when the norms of social behavior and expectations for beliefs and values are unclear. Exiters often experience their own form of anomie as they step away from their religious community and its worldview (Brooks, 2018; Gull et al., 2023). In many ways, a religious exit is a microcosm of a community in rapid change. A sense of normlessness may emerge as exiters realize that the ways in which they have previously patterned their lives no longer make sense in light of their religious and spiritual changes. While most religious exiters transition from their religious identity gradually and do not experience major adjustment issues, those who come from high-demand faiths, experience intense religious socialization, and/or have a sudden and jarring "deconversion" are more likely to experience the radical alteration of their worldview. High-demand faith communities have very different plausibility structures, or frameworks for understanding and interpreting the world, than secular societies (Berger & Luckmann, 1967). Plausibility structures create our reality by establishing ideas about what is right and true, allowing us to interpret our world through a particular sensemaking lens. Thus, a therapist should be ready to confront the loss of norms exiters may experience and work to help these clients build new norms based on their emerging nonreligious value system (Nica, 2020).

Religious exiters who seek therapy may also be processing the loss of a valued and/or tight-knit religious community (Nica, 2019). Particularly common for those who exit high-demand religions where intense socialization is the norm, exiters may experience community fractures all along the spectrum, from formal shunning to strained friendships (Nica, 2019; Gull et al., 2023). The social impacts of religious community have been well documented, with implications in everything from the obvious aspect of belonging and relationships to health outcomes, childrearing, and employment opportunities (Speed et al., 2020). Thus, religious exiters may not only be seeking to repair the anomie resulting from leaving a belief system and its undergirding plausibility structures; they may also be facing the loss of supportive relationships that have provided them with a solid social base and imparted many intangible benefits. Clinicians should discuss the loss of community belonging experienced by exiters and aid them in identifying and establishing new forms of community based on values, interests, identities, or hobbies.

The "loss" of a tight-knit religious community, however, may also be a source of liberation and empowerment for exiters. They may see the separation from their church as necessary to the development of their authentic selves and look forward to building their own communities based on new values and beliefs. Examples of positive reactions to shedding religious community can be found in literature on religious exiting and include experiences such as walking away from perfectionism pressures, discarding limiting gender roles, and rejecting exclusionary and judgmental treatment by former co-religionists (Gull, 2022b; Gull et al., 2023). Thus, clinicians should seek to understand their clients' feelings on the loss of their religious community and how it has impacted their well-being.

The community ties formed with fellow religionists are not the only ties that may be damaged or severed by a religious exit. Family ties may also be affected if the person has left a religion shared by their entire family (Davidman, 2014; Nica, 2019). Many high-demand faiths preach an exclusivist road to salvation and build strong in-group boundaries. This may result in exiters being viewed as damaged, dangerous, and sufficiently "other" that contact is cut or at least minimized (Hookway & Habibis, 2015). Even when formal shunning is not employed, the emergence of religious differences within a family may result in new conflicts or give additional emotional weight to old ones. Clients may face challenges including ongoing proselytizing attempts, demeaning comments on their new (non)religious identities, and expressions that something intrinsic to the person has changed in such a way that family members no longer feel comfortable around them (Cragun & Smith, 2024; Zuckerman, 2011). In addition, some exiters may have recently come out as lesbian, gay, bisexual, transgender, and/or queer (LGBTQ) and face hostile and exclusionary comments and behaviors from religious family members. Thus, clinicians should be aware of these possibilities and be ready to assist recent exiters on several fronts related to family relationships.

Long-term exiters may experience issues similar to those of recent exiters; however, they may have been dealing with these issues over an extended period (Hunsberger, 2006). Family relationships may still be strained and pressures to re-convert may be ongoing. Clinicians should inquire into whether family relationships are an ongoing source of stress for their long-term exiter clients and assist them in finding ways to address them, if desired. Learning how to establish healthy boundaries, have difficult conversations in a non-confrontational way, and communicate commitment to maintaining family ties are examples of practices that can be addressed within the clinical setting.

Although the process of developing new norms, values, and beliefs may not be as urgent, long-term exiters still may face uncertainty about the nature of their worldviews and how to build a meaningful and fulfilling life outside of their former religion (Nica, 2019). They may also face ongoing difficulties in establishing community bonds. Relationships with family and friends may still contain conflict rooted in differing religious beliefs. Unhealthy family dynamics may have developed following their religious exit. Clinicians should seek to understand how these ongoing challenges play out in their clients' lives.

Affirmatively Secular

Although the literature on working with nonreligious clients' worldviews is rather slim, research on incorporating atheists' values and beliefs into therapy is even slimmer. In a recent review of the literature on this topic, several misconceptions about secular individuals were found to be common (Bishop, 2018). These included beliefs that they are narcissistic, untrustworthy, morally repugnant, and stand as existential threats to theists' belief systems. As these are commonly held misconceptions in American society (Schmidt, 2016), and perhaps in other contexts as well, therapists should inquire about their affirmatively secular clients' value systems to help them incorporate their values into the counseling process rather than assume they have none. All people hold worldviews or lifestances based on beliefs about the nature of existence and shaped by values about what one finds important and worthwhile (van Mulukom et al., 2023). Since atheists are still stigmatized in many circles (Hammer et al., 2012), therapists should carefully assess their own biases to ensure that they do not further stigmatize these clients in therapy.

Another common misconception that may hinder the therapeutic process involves the idea that religiosity, or even "spirituality," is associated with improved mental health

(Speed & Lamont, 2023). Many studies find a positive association between multiple aspects of religiosity and mental health, including holding religious beliefs and participating in religious communities (Haney & Rollock, 2020; Schieman et al., 2013). However, a number of recent studies have challenged the idea that these associations are based on anything inherent in a religious worldview (Cragun & Speed, 2022). It is incorrect to assume that nonreligious and secular clients will have worse mental health than religious clients simply because they do not hold traditional spiritual beliefs or believe in a higher power (Brewster et al., 2014). Rather, the relationship between religiosity and well-being appears to be primarily related to two factors: the strength of belief or nonbelief (Galen & Speed, 2024), and the robustness of religious people's social networks (Speed et al., 2020). Clinicians should be alert to the possibility that affirmatively secular clients may lack the same degree of social embeddedness as the actively religious. As atheism is a highly stigmatized identity in the United States and many other countries (Gervais et al., 2017), the affirmatively secular may engage in a practice of disconnection to avoid negative interactions with religious people in their lives or in society at large. Relational-Cultural Therapy (RCT) may be helpful in instances where this occurs, as it is a relational approach to therapy and focuses on undoing damaging oppressive or discriminatory relationships or power structures (Abbott, 2021; Jordan, 2018). Deconstructing the effects of living with a stigmatized identity such as atheism may assist clients in more effectively building social ties and finding empowerment in their affirmatively secular identity. In addition, clinicians may want to encourage affirmatively secular clients to connect with others sharing their worldview through atheist or humanist organizations such as American Atheists or Sunday Assembly.

As with religious exiters, the affirmatively secular may also experience distress over their worldview. This can take several forms. Secular clients may express nihilistic ideas and find that life has no purpose or meaning since they do not believe in an afterlife (Hammer et al., 2013). While nihilism is best understood as taking the view that there is no inherent meaning, purpose, or morality to human existence, it is important to note that holding a nihilistic viewpoint does not necessarily mean that one experiences life as negative and fails to derive enjoyment from one's relationships or pursuits (Li et al, 2019). The concept of "meaning" itself is a contested one (Leontiev, 2013). Psychological literature on life meaning shows this concept to be a multifaceted one. For instance, life meaning might include dimensions such as *coherence*, feeling that one's life makes sense, *purpose*, feeling that one's life has direction, and *significance*, feeling that one's life is worth living (Martela & Steger, 2016). Thus, they may alternately state that they believe meaning and purpose in life come from the individual but they do not feel they can identify what those things are for them (Cragun & Smith, 2024). Still others may express that they have much in life that gives them a sense of purpose but they feel overwhelmed by daily demands and need assistance sorting out their priorities. Clinicians should find ways to help affirmatively secular clients develop healthy and productive worldviews by getting them to identify their values and rank them in order of salience.

Spiritual but Not Religious

We end with a discussion of the spiritual but not religious (SBNR) population because, in many ways, this group not only represents the experiences of the other types of nonreligious clients but presents an opportunity to consider how the concept of spirituality relates to that of worldview. Counseling clients who are SBNR allows both the therapist and client the opportunity to explore multiple meaning systems and worldviews for resources to improve the client's well-being. SBNR clients may not have the same issues related to belief and community loss as exiters. However, they may share a need to more clearly establish a worldview and value system.

How should we understand spirituality disconnected from organized religion? Cook (2020) references a conversation between Freud and a close friend to establish a definition of spirituality that is "oceanic," "limitless," and "unbounded." While this is not an especially helpful definition for measurement purposes, it does give a sense of just how broad a concept spirituality is (see discussion of spirituality earlier in this chapter). Spirituality can encompass experiences as varied as praying to a higher power, experiencing a sense of wonder in the natural world, or connecting with one's cultural background. Canda and Furman (2010) offered a detailed exploration of spirituality for use in clinical settings and identified twelve dimensions of spirituality that may be useful when counseling SBNR clients. While we do not have the space here to discuss all twelve dimensions, we will note that many of them focus on helping clients to develop practices that support personal growth, connection with a higher power, and cultivate well-being. In other words, spirituality is simply one way to describe one's worldview and contains many of the same elements as the worldview of an affirmatively secular person. Clearly, the exception here is the concept of connecting with a god or higher power, but the end goal is the same: the development of a healthy, forward-looking perspective based on personal values that enable the person to craft a life of meaning and purpose and respond to life's challenges with resilience. Thus, if the clinician takes a broad approach to the concept of spirituality, they can use similar resources to help religious exiters, the affirmatively secular, and the spiritual but not religious. One example of a practice rooted in spirituality but which has been adapted by many nonreligious people is mindfulness. Though it first emerged from Buddhist thought, mindfulness can be used as a tool to build resilience and well-being in spiritual as well as affirmatively secular clients (Jacobs, 2010; Kabat-Zinn, 1990).

One approach to assessing how to address spirituality in therapy is to conduct a "worldview history" with clients at the outset of treatment. A generic worldview history that is neutral and does not favor religiosity or spirituality over secularity is unlikely to result in a negative response from the affirmatively secular. But clinicians should not assume that clients are religious or spiritual and should not assume that a lack of religiosity or spirituality are "problems" that need to be addressed in therapy. Through activities such as life reviews and spiritual or worldview genealogies, the therapist and client may together identify places of conflict in need of resolution or spiritual turning points that can be discussed during therapy (Jacobs, 2010; Koenig, 2004). These practices may be particularly helpful for SBNR clients seeking to better understand their own experiences with spirituality (see Jacobs, 2010 for an excellent review of literature on this topic). However, as stated above, clinicians should be cautious when conducting assessments of this sort so as not to further stigmatize secular clients who do not see themselves as spiritual. An open discussion of the client's worldview at the outset of therapy should establish the ways in which spirituality, worldview, and associated concepts are understood by the client and identify appropriate terminology to use during therapy. Similarly, SBNR clients may also experience difficulty finding community outside of organized religion. Again, while the orientation of these clients may be different to exiters and the avowedly secular, the desire for community is not.

Conclusion

While we have spent much of this chapter decomposing the nonreligious into clearly delineated categories, the reality is that there is much overlap between them. Individuals may experience both a high-demand religious exit and the development of an affirmatively secular identity, for instance. Thus, we do not want to reify these categories by detailing the experiences common among them. Rather, we want to raise clinicians' awareness of common themes that may arise when counseling clients with these backgrounds.

Integrating discussions of worldview or spirituality into therapy requires a deft hand. The very terminology one uses can impact the therapeutic relationship, as clients may have negative experiences with words such as "religion," "spirituality," or "god." Similarly, focusing on "loss" or "deconversion" can keep the client focused on past challenges rather than moving toward a hopeful future. When bringing issues of nonreligious spirituality and secular worldviews into therapy, clinicians should assess whether they feel prepared and comfortable discussing these issues. Experienced clinicians have developed techniques for integrating these issues into therapy; newer clinicians may need to seek training before attempting to approach these topics with clients (Jacobs, 2010).

At its core, the goal of therapy is to enhance human flourishing. Clinicians would be wise to consider whether or how a focus on flourishing includes a discussion of clients' worldview/spirituality. The recognition that nonreligious and secular individuals have worldviews that enhance or detract from their ability to live healthy, productive lives and that these worldviews should be taken seriously by clinicians is a major focus of this chapter. Giving attention to how to help clients reduce anxiety, manage stress, develop resilience, and better understand their own values, beliefs, and lifestances is at the core of the therapeutic process. Developing a more nuanced understanding of the different experiences of secular and nonreligious clients can only aid in the therapeutic process.

Data and Code

The code for creating the categories of nonreligious individuals and for the tables that underlie the figures in this chapter is available here: https://www.osf.io/59yk3

References

Abbott, D. M. (2021). Psychotherapy with non-religious clients: A relational-cultural approach. *Professional Psychology: Research and Practice*, 52(5), 470–76. https://doi.org/10.1037/pro0000392

Abbott, D. M., & Mollen, D. (2018). Atheism as a concealable stigmatized identity: Outness, anticipated stigma, and well-being. *The Counseling Psychologist*, 46(6), 685–707. https://doi.org/10.1177/0011000018792669

Barbour, J. D. (1994). *Versions of deconversion: Autobiography and the loss of faith*. University Press of Virginia.

Barna, G. (2002). *Grow your church from the outside in: Understanding the unchurched and how to reach them*. Gospel Light Publications.

Beider, N. (2022). Religious residue: The impact of childhood religious socialization on the religiosity of Nones in France, Germany, Great Britain, and Sweden. *The British Journal of Sociology*, 74, 51–70. https://doi.org/10.1111/1468-4446.12982

Berger, P. L., and Luckmann, T. (1967). *The social construction of reality: A treatise in the sociology of knowledge*. Anchor.

Bishop, B. (2018). Advocating for atheist clients in the counseling profession. *Counseling and Values*, 63(1), 17–30.

Blankholm, J., Cragun, R., Hawley Suárez, A., and Stephen, S. (2025). The beliefs of nonbelievers: Exclusive empiricism and mortal finitude among atheists and agnostics. *Sociology of Religion*, 86(1), 27–49. doi:10.1093/socrel/srae003

Brewster, M. E., Robinson, M. A., Sandil, R., Esposito, J., & Geiger, E. (2014). Arrantly absent: Atheism in psychological science from 2001 to 2012. *The Counseling Psychologist*, 42(5), 628–63. https://doi.org/10.1177/0011000014528051

Bromley, D. G. (Ed.). (1998a). *The politics of religious apostasy: The role of apostates in the transformation of religious movements*. Praeger Publishers.

Bromley, D. G. (1998b). The social construction of contested exit roles: Defectors, whistleblowers, and apostates. In D. G. Bromley (Ed.), *The politics of religious apostasy: The role of apostates in the transformation of religious movements* (pp. 19–48). Praeger Publishers.

Brooks, E. M. (2018). *Disenchanted lives: Apostasy and ex-Mormonism among the Latter-Day Saints*. Rutgers University Press.

Bullivant, S. (2022). *Nonverts: The making of ex-Christian America*. Oxford University Press.

Bullivant, S., & Lee, L. (2016). Interdisciplinary studies of non-religion and secularity: The state of the union. In E. Arwekc, S. Bullivant, & L. Lee (Eds.), *Secularity and non-religion* (pp.1–9). Routledge.

Canda, E. R., & Furman, L. D. (2010). *Spiritual diversity in social work practice: The heart of helping.* (2nd ed.). Oxford University Press.

Cook, C. C. H. (2020). Spirituality, religion and mental health: Exploring the boundaries. *Mental Health, Religion & Culture*, 23(5), 363–74. https://doi.org/10.1080/13674676.2020.1774525

Cottee, S. (2015). *The apostates: When Muslims leave Islam.* Hurst.

Cragun, R. T. (2014). Who are the "New Atheists"? In L. Beamon & S. Tomlins (Eds.), *Atheist identities: Spaces and social contexts* (pp. 195–211). Springer.

Cragun, R. T., & Hammer, J. H. (2011). "One person's apostate is another person's convert": Reflections on pro-religion hegemony in the sociology of religion. *Humanity & Society*, 35(1–2), 149–75. https://doi.org/10.1177/016059761103500107

Cragun, R. T., & McCaffree, K. J. (2021). Nothing is not something: On replacing nonreligion with identities. *Secular Studies*, 3(1), 7–26. https://doi.org/10.1163/25892525-bja10017

Cragun, R. T., & Smith, J. M. (2024). *Goodbye religion: The causes and consequences of secularization.* NYU Press.

Cragun, R. T., & Speed, D. (2022). Religiosity and happiness: Much ado about nothing. In S. Sugirtharajah (Ed.), *Religious and secular perspectives on happiness and wellbeing* (pp. 167–91). Routledge.

Davidman, L. (2014). *Becoming un-Orthodox: Stories of ex-Hasidic Jews.* Oxford University Press.

Desmond, S. A., Morgan, K. H., & Kikuchi, G. (2010). Religious development: How (and why) does religiosity change from adolescence to young adulthood? *Sociological Perspectives*, 53(2), 247–70. https://doi.org/10.1525/sop.2010.53.2.247

Durkheim, E. (1933/1893). *The division of labor in society* (G. Simpson, Trans.). Macmillan.

Edgell, P., Frost, J., & Stewart, E. (2017). From existential to social understandings of risk: Examining gender differences in nonreligion. *Social Currents*, 4(6), 556–74. https://doi.org/10.1177/2329496516686619

Eller, J. D., & Khazaal, N. (Eds.). (2024). *Nonbelievers, apostates, and atheists in the Muslim world.* Routledge.

Evans, A. L., & Nelson, J. K. (2021). The value of adapting counseling to client's spirituality and religion: Evidence-based relationship factors. *Religions*, 12, 951. https://doi.org/10.3390/rel12110951

Fuller, R. C. (2001). *Spiritual, but not religious: Understanding unchurched America.* Oxford University Press.

Galen, L., & Speed, D. (2024). Testing the religion/spirituality-mental health curvilinear hypothesis using data from many-analysts religion project. *Religion, Brain & Behavior. Advance online publication.* https://doi.org/10.1080/2153599X.2024.2378992

Gervais, W. M., Xygalatas, D., McKay, R. T., van Elk, M., Buchtel, E. E., Aveyard, M., Schiavone, S. R., Dar-Nimrod, I., Svedholm-Häkkinen, A. M., Riekki, T., Kundtová Klocová, E., Ramsay, J. E., & Bulbulia, J. (2017). Global evidence of extreme intuitive moral prejudice against atheists. *Nature Human Behaviour*, 1(8), 1–6. https://doi.org/10.1038/s41562-017-0151

Gooren, H. (2007). Reassessing conventional approaches to conversion: Toward a new synthesis. *Journal for the Scientific Study of Religion*, 46(3), 337–53. https://doi.org/10.1111/j.1468-5906.2007.00362.x https://doi.org/10.1111/j.1468-5906.2007.00362.xhttps://doi.org/10.1111/j.1468-5906.2007.00362.x

Gull, B. (2022a). Becoming exvangelical: The faith journeys, identity work, and activism of former evangelicals in the digital age (Publication no. 29208258) [Doctoral dissertation, University of Utah]. ProQuest Dissertations & Theses Global.

Gull, B. (2022b). "We are the women our parents warned us against": Identity reconstruction and the re-imagining of gender after high-cost religious disaffiliation. *Symbolic Interaction*, 45(1), 97–122. https://doi.org/10.1002/symb.541

Gull, B. (2022c). When certainty cracks: Early identity-change work among women exiting high-cost religion. In J. Hardie-Bick & S. Scott (Eds.), *Ex-treme identities and transitions out of extraordinary roles* (pp. 59–80). Palgrave Macmillan. https://doi.org/10.1007/978-3-030-93608-2_4

Gull, B., Smith, J., & Cragun, R. (2023). Outcast women: Gender and authenticity in ex-Mormon women's disaffiliation narratives. *Nova Religio*, 26(3), 7–29. doi:https://doi.org/10.1525/nr.2023.26.3.7

Hammer, J. H., Cragun, R. T., Hwang, K., & Smith, J. (2012). Forms, frequency, and correlates of perceived anti-atheist discrimination. *Secularism and Nonreligion*, 1(1), 43–67. https://doi.org/10.5334/snr.ad

Hammer, J. H., Cragun, R. T., & Hwang, K. (2013). Measuring spiritual fitness: Atheist military personnel, veterans, and civilians. *Military Psychology*, 25(5), 438–51. https://doi.org/10.1037/mil0000010

Haney, A. M., & Rollock, D. (2020). A matter of faith: The role of religion, doubt, and personality in emerging adult mental health. *Psychology of Religion and Spirituality*, 12(2), 247–53. https://doi.org/10.1037/rel0000231

Hookway, N. S., & Habibis, D. (2015). Losing my religion: Managing identity in a post-Jehovah's Witness world. *Journal of Sociology*, 51(4), 843–56. https://doi.org/10.1177/1440783313476981

Hunsberger, B. (2006). *Atheists: A groundbreaking study of America's nonbelievers*. Prometheus Books.

Hwang, K., Hammer, J. H., & Cragun, R. T. (2011). Extending religion-health research to nontheistic minorities: Issues and concerns. *Journal of Religion and Health*, 50(3), 608–22. https://doi.org/10.1007/s10943-009-9296-0

Ingersoll-Dayton, B., Krause, N., & Morgan, D. (2002). Religious trajectories and transitions over the life course. *The International Journal of Aging and Human Development*, 55(1), 51–70. https://doi.org/10.2190/297q-mrmv-27te-vlfk

Introvigne, M. (1999). Defectors, ordinary leave-takers, and apostates: A quantitative study of former members of New Acropolis in France. *Nova Religio: The Journal of Alternative and Emergent Religions*, 3(1), 83–99. https://doi.org/10.1525/nr.1999.3.1.83

Jacobs, C. (2010). Exploring religion and spirituality in clinical practice. *Smith College Studies in Social Work*, 80(2–3), 98–120. https://doi.org/10.1080/00377317.2010.486358

James, W. (2004). *The varieties of religious experience*. Barnes and Noble Classics. (Original work published 1902).

Jindra, I. W., & Lee, J. (2021). Negotiating leaving religion, family relationships, and identity: The case of LDS faith transitions in therapy. *Clinical Social Work Journal*, 51(3), 1–11. doi:10.1007/s10615-021-00822-y

Jindra, I. W., Thompson, J., & Giesler, F. (2024). Gender, symbolic and social boundaries, and deconversion from the Church of Jesus Christ of Latter-Day Saints. *Sociology of Religion*, 85(3), 346–70. https://doi.org/10.1093/socrel/srad043

Johnson, E. (2019). Apostasy, human rights and hate crime in England and Wales: A mixed methods study. [Doctoral dissertation, Sheffield Hallam University].

Jordan, J. (2018). *Relational-cultural therapy* (2nd ed.). American Psychological Association. https://doi.org/10.1037/0000063-000

Kabat-Zinn, J. (1990). *Full catastrophe living: Using the wisdom of your body and mind to face stress, pain, and illness.* Dell.

Kasselstrand, I., Zuckerman, P., & Cragun, R. T. (2023). *Beyond doubt: The secularization of society.* NYU Press.

Keller, B., Bullik, R., & Streib, H. (2024a). Deconversion from high-tension religious groups. In K. Taku & T. K. Shackelford (Eds.), *The Routledge international handbook of changes in human perceptions and behaviors* (pp. 489–507). Routledge.

Koenig, H. G. (2004). Religion, spirituality, and medicine: Research findings and implications for clinical practice. *Southern Medical Journal*, 97(12), 1194–200. https://doi.org/10.1097/01.smj.0000146489.21837.ce

Langston, J. A., Hammer, J. H., & Cragun, R. T. (2015). Atheism looking in: On the goals and strategies of organized nonbelief. *Science, Religion, and Culture*, 2(3), 70–85. https://doi.org/10.17582/journal.src/2015/2.3.70.85

Leontiev, D. A. (2013). Personal meaning: A challenge for psychology. *The Journal of Positive Psychology*, 8, 459–70.

Li, P. F. J., Wong, Y. J., & Chao, R. C. L. (2019). Happiness and meaning in life: Unique, differential, and indirect associations with mental health. *Counselling Psychology Quarterly*, 32(3–4), 396–414. https://doi.org/10.1080/09515070.2019.1604493

Martela, F., & Steger, M. F. (2016). The three meanings of meaning in life: Distinguishing coherence, purpose, and significance. *The Journal of Positive Psychology*, 11(5), 531–45.

Mercadante, L. A. (2014). *Belief without borders: Inside the minds of the spiritual but not religious.* Oxford University Press.

Nica, A. A. (2019). Exiters of religious fundamentalism: Reconstruction of social support and relationships related to well-being. *Mental Health, Religion & Culture*, 22(5), 543–56. https://doi.org/10.1080/13674676.2019.1636015

Nica, A. A. (2020). Leaving my religion: How ex-fundamentalists reconstruct identity related to well-being. *Journal of Religion and Health*, 59, 2120–2134. https://doi.org/10.1007/s10943-019-00975-8

Nica, A. A. (2024). Meaning-making and well-being among exiters of religious fundamentalism. *Journal of Contemporary Religion*, 39(2), 249–69. https://doi.org/10.1080/13537903.2024.2359298

Packard, J., & Ferguson, T. W. (2019). Being done: Why people leave the church, but not their faith. *Sociological Perspectives*, 62(4), 499–517. doi:10.1177/0731121418800270

Parekh, H., & Egan, V. (2021). Apostates as a hidden population of abuse victims. *Journal of Interpersonal Violence*, 36(23–24). https://doi:10.1177/0886260519898428

Perry, E. L., Davis, J. H., Doyle, R. T., & Dyble, J. E. (1980). Toward a typology of unchurched Protestants. *Review of Religious Research*, 21, 388–404. https://doi.org/10.2307/3510680

Pew Research. (2015). *The future of world religions: Population growth projections, 2010–2050.* https://www.pewresearch.org/religion/2015/04/02/religiously-unaffiliated/

Pew Research. (2024). *Religious "Nones" in America: Who they are and what they believe.* https://www.pewresearch.org/religion/2024/01/24/religious-nones-in-america-who-they-are-and-what-they-believe/

Quack, J., & Schuh, C. (Eds.). (2017). *Religious indifference: New perspectives from studies on secularization and nonreligion*. Springer.

Roberts, K. A., & Yamane, D. (2016). *Religion in sociological perspective*. Sage Publications.

Schieman, S., Bierman, A., & Ellison, C. G. (2013). Religion and mental health. In C. S. Aneshensel, J. C. Phelan, & A. Bierman (Eds.), *Handbook of the sociology of mental health* (pp. 457–78). Springer Nature.

Schmidt, L. E. (2016). *Village atheists: How America's unbelievers made their way in a godly nation*. Princeton University Press.

Smith, C., & Denton, M. L. (2005). *Soul searching: The religious and spiritual lives of American teenagers*. Oxford University Press.

Smith, J. M. (2016). Apostasy. In P. Zuckerman (Ed.), *Beyond religion* (pp. 71–91). Macmillan Reference USA.

Smith, J. M., & Halligan, C. L. (2021). Making meaning without a maker: Secular consciousness through narrative and cultural practice. *Sociology of Religion*, 82(1), 85–110. https://doi.org/10.1093/socrel/sraa016

Speed, D., Barry, C., & Cragun, R. (2020). With a little help from my (Canadian) friends: Health differences between minimal and maximal religiosity/spirituality are partially mediated by social support. *Social Science & Medicine*, 265, 1–9. https://doi.org/10.1016/j.socscimed.2020.113387

Speed, D., & Lamont, A. (2023). (Life) satisfaction guaranteed? Subjective well-being attenuates religious attendance–life satisfaction association. *Psychology of Religion and Spirituality*, 15(4), 471–79. https://doi.org/10.1037/rel0000443

Steensland, B., Kucinskas, J., & Sun, A. (Eds.). (2022). *Situating spirituality: Context, practice, and power*. Oxford University Press.

Thiessen, J., & Wilkins-Laflamme, S. (2017). Becoming a religious none: Irreligious socialization and disaffiliation. *Journal for the Scientific Study of Religion*, 56(1), 64–82. https://doi.org/10.1111/jssr.12319

van Mulukom, V., Turpin, H., Haimila, R., Purzycki, B. G., Bendixen, T., Kundtová Klocová, E., Řezníček, D., Coleman, T. J., Sevinç, K., Maraldi, E., Schjoedt, U., Rutjens, B. T., & Farias, M. (2023). What do nonreligious nonbelievers believe in? Secular worldviews around the world. *Psychology of Religion and Spirituality*, 15(1), 143–56. https://doi.org/10.1037/rel0000480

Van Tongeren, D. R. (2024). *Done: How to flourish after leaving religion*. American Psychological Association.

Voas, D. (2009). The rise and fall of fuzzy fidelity in Europe. *European Sociological Review*, 25(2), 155–68. https://doi.org/10.1093/esr/jcn044

Voas, D., McAndrew, S., & Storm, I. (2013). Modernization and the gender gap in religiosity: Evidence from cross-national European surveys. *Kölner Zeitschrift Für Soziologie Und Sozialpsychologie*, 65(1), 259–83. https://doi.org/10.1007/s11577-013-0226-5

Wilkins-Laflamme, S. (2022). *Religion, spirituality and secularity among millennials: The generation shaping American and Canadian trends*. Routledge.

Zimmerman, K. J., Smith, J. M., Simonson, K., & Myers, W. B. (2015). Familial relationship outcomes of coming out as an atheist. *Secularism and Nonreligion*, 4(4), Art. 4. https://doi.org/10.5334/snr.aw

Zuckerman, P. (2010). *Atheism and secularity*. Praeger.

Zuckerman, P. (2011). *Faith no more: Why people reject religion*. Oxford University Press.

4

Anti-Atheist Stigma and Christian Nationalism

Paige Hespe

Chapter Outline

Atheists in the Context of Christian Nationalism

It would be a disservice to atheist and nonbelieving clients to discuss the stereotypes they face and the psychological consequences of these stereotypes without contextualizing these difficulties within the cultural assumptions made about atheists. To simply name the stigma and hardship faced by atheists, in a vacuum, inadvertently labels atheism as a default risk factor or inherently "pathological" when, in fact, nonbelievers are subject to systemic bias across several facets of American life. Anti-atheist stigma must be understood within the structural context that it emerges: Christian nationalism. This chapter will define Christian nationalism and discuss how Christian nationalist views of atheism produce anti-atheist stigma and stereotypes. The psychological consequences of these stereotypes and how to support clients experiencing anti-atheist stigma will also be explored.

What Is Christian Nationalism?

Christian nationalism is a cultural framework that fuses US American identity and Christian identity based on the belief that the United States was and is a Christian nation. Christian nationalism, therefore, argues that US American political, legal, educational, social, and other systems ought to reflect such Christian values in the country's history, policy, and symbolism (Du Mez, 2020; Gorski & Perry, 2022; Nie, 2023; Whitehead & Perry, 2020). Christian nationalism incorporates the beliefs and assumptions of several other frameworks including nativism, political conservatism, patriarchy, white supremacy, militarism and imperialism, cisnormativity, and heteronormativity (Davis & Perry, 2021; Whitehead & Perry, 2019; Whitehead & Perry, 2020). Christian nationalism and its accompanying "isms" identify a clear social hierarchy, labeling White, heterosexual, cisgender Christian Americans as superior and anyone presumed to be un-Christian (e.g., atheists, practitioners of different beliefs, queer folks) or un-American (e.g., people of color, immigrants, etc.) as inferior. This social hierarchy offers a sense of belonging and righteousness to those at the top while identifying those at the bottom (e.g., atheists) as immoral threats to the very system itself.

Beliefs that America is a country meant to serve a Christian God have been used for a myriad of social and political purposes. The intentions and purposes of Christian nationalism have been widespread: to masculinize the Christian faith, to justify imperialism, to capitalize on a Christian voting base and influence American politics, to identify and promote "traditional" and conservative values, to uphold existing racial hierarchies in the nation, and identify and target perceived enemies to Christian nationalism (Du Mez, 2020; Whitehead & Perry, 2020). To Christian nationalists, atheism represents a threat to not only Christianity, but to the nation as well.

What Isn't Christian Nationalism?

Christian nationalism is not to be confused with Christian practices or beliefs. Rather, there are notable differences in the political ideologies and moral beliefs between Christian nationalists and Christians. When asked about actions that were representative of a morally "good person," Christian nationalists were more likely to identify military service whereas practicing Christians were more likely to name caring for the sick and needy, seeking economic and social justice, and using fewer resources as moral actions (Whitehead & Perry, 2020). Additionally, while Christian nationalism argues that Christian values ("church") should influence American government ("state"), this is different from a theocracy, which argues that church *rules* the state (Du Mez, 2020). Another common myth is that evangelicalism and Christian nationalism are synonymous. This misconception is likely due to Christian nationalism, as a system, identifying and capitalizing on the fact that evangelical Christians are a particularly active voting base compared to other US adult groups (Emerson, 2024). Specifically, about 85 percent of white evangelical voters identify with or lean toward the Republican Party (Pew Research Center, 2024). But rather than assuming that this means evangelicalism and Christian nationalism are one and the same, this should be interpreted as the system of Christian nationalism recognizing and taking political advantage of this pattern. At its core, evangelical Christianity is a *theological* (rather than cultural or political) framework concerned with biblical literalism and identifying Christ as the Messiah.

Atheists as Enemies of Christian Nationalism

Woven into the fabric of Christian nationalism is the identification of heroes (white American-born Christian men) and enemies, one of the most vile being atheists and nonbelievers (Du Mez, 2020; Gorski & Perry, 2022; Whitehead & Perry, 2020). Christian nationalism, as a cultural narrative, calls on these heroes to convert or eliminate atheist enemies to restore Christian virtues to the nation and save their damned souls in the eventual Rapture. In this way, the mission of Christian nationalists—to defeat atheism and promote the word of God—is validated by the belief system itself. Throughout American history, political and religious leaders have called on the American public to "wake up" to the heinous agenda of atheists, claiming that these "infidels" are out to "remove God" from American politics, effectively replacing God's blessing to America with His wrath (Whitehead & Perry, 2020).

In fact, researchers Andrew Whitehead and Samuel Perry (2020) have identified that Americans holding especially strong Christian nationalist beliefs (who they call "ambassadors" of the system) also tend to believe that atheists are a threat to their personal liberties and physical safety. In short, there is a demonstrated pattern that those with stronger Christian nationalist beliefs are more likely to express greater anti-atheist stigma (Nie, 2023). Other groups that were significantly more likely to name atheists as a threat were those living in the Midwest and American South or other rural areas, those with politically conservative values, those who read the Bible literally (evangelicals), those with fewer years of traditional education, those in older generations, and men (Nie, 2023; Whitehead & Perry, 2020). Interestingly though, Whitehead and Perry (2020) also found that greater intolerance toward atheists was characteristic of stronger Christian nationalist beliefs but did *not* find a relationship between religious practice (e.g., prayer, reading scripture, attending religious services) and intolerance toward atheists. This, too, speaks to the important distinction between Christian nationalism and Christian beliefs, as Christian nationalism is a cultural framework built on other social systems, such as patriarchy, but is not necessarily representative of the average American Christian.

With atheists clearly identified as a perceived threat to Christian nationalism and American virtues, we can now turn toward a discussion of the discrimination, stigma, and stereotypes faced by atheist communities as a product of Christian nationalism.

Stereotypes of Atheists

What do Americans think of atheists? Christian nationalist beliefs in America's obligation to serve a Christian God and beliefs that Christians are morally superior bring with them parallel beliefs that atheists and other nonbelievers are morally inferior due to their failing to fulfill God's purpose for their lives. As mentioned previously, this results in Christian nationalism naming atheists as a primary enemy of its framework, identifying even the affiliation with atheists as morally dangerous. For these reasons, most stereotypes about atheists can be understood as by-products of dominant Christian nationalist beliefs.

Value Violation and Immorality

Perhaps the most prevalent stereotype about atheists in America is that they are value violators, meaning that their existence violates the values of Christianity and Christian nationalism (Cook et al., 2015; Moon et al., 2021). In a national survey completed by over a thousand American atheists, over 75 percent of respondents indicated that they have been told that atheism is "sinful, wrong, or immoral" (Hammer et al., 2012, p. 53). Additionally, 25 percent of American respondents to a 2023 Pew Research Center survey endorsed the belief that "it is necessary to believe in God in order to be moral and have good values" (Lipka et al., 2024). This implies that approximately a quarter of Americans would find atheists to be value violators. Sometimes, this perception that atheists violate "traditional" values evolves into a belief that atheists are simply amoral, or without moral beliefs and values (Gervais, 2014). A nationally representative survey conducted in 2014 found that 36 percent of respondents believed that atheists "lack a moral center" and 27 percent of the same sample reported that atheists do not share their morals or values (Edgell et al., 2016, p. 13).

This raises the following question: Which values are atheists perceived to be violating? In a study examining stereotypes held by both Christians and atheists toward each other, Christian participants believed that they held values of compassion, justice, loyalty, respect for authority and tradition, and sanctity to higher degrees than atheists (Simpson & Rios, 2016). It has also been suggested that religion tends to promote values of honoring tradition, social conformity, self-control, and security (Schwadel et al., 2021). One can assume, then, that the perception is that atheists do not hold these values as highly as religious people and that, perhaps, they value *opposite* virtues. In fact, stereotypes have been identified that are grounded in the idea that atheists' values oppose religious values, including that atheists value individualism, independence, rebelliousness, and being opinionated (Grove et al., 2019).

Although stereotypes identifying atheists as "opinionated" can appear harmless on the surface, stereotypes that atheists are without values and morals come with real-world consequences, particularly societal feelings of disgust and distrust toward atheists. In a study comparing perceptions toward atheists with perceptions toward other potentially value-threatening groups in the United States (e.g., gay men, Muslims, people with HIV), respondents found atheists to be a *greater* threat to values and elicited stronger feelings of moral disgust compared to people in the other groups (Cook et al., 2015). Another study found that self-identifying Christians experienced a stronger physical reaction of disgust after reading and copying an atheist text (*The God Delusion* by Richard Dawkins) than they did after reading and copying a neutral text (passage from a dictionary) (Ritter & Preston, 2011). Emotionally and physiologically, disgust is a common reaction to atheist identities and ideas.

Distrust toward atheists and the consequences of this distrust have also been well documented (Edgell et al., 2016). Typically, societal distrust toward atheists is the result of confusion about where or from whom atheists acquire their sense of morality and confusion about how atheists behave morally without the presence of religious reinforcement and punishment (Gervais, 2013). This moral distrust is nearly exclusively reserved for atheists as well; individuals who are religious, but not necessarily Christian, are generally perceived as being guided by at least *some* divine moral code. Atheists, however, are thought of as moral wildcards, thus generating an aura of distrust. This skepticism creates tangible consequences in our society, including political and legal consequences. A study investigating verdicts in a mock rape trial found that mock jurors were more likely to find perpetrators guilty when the victim in the story was Christian than when the victim was an atheist (Brown-Iannuzzi et al., 2019). Gervais (2014) found that participants reading vignettes about a variety of immoral crimes (e.g., incest, murder, cannibalism) were more likely to identify the perpetrator as an atheist than a religious person. These findings can be understood to mean that the American public finds atheist immorality to be to a degree that they are more likely to commit violent crimes or lie under oath. Another study examining the role of anti-theist stigma in political contexts found that religious participants were less trusting of and less likely to vote for a mock Christian political candidate who endorsed support for atheists, exemplifying the idea mentioned previously that even affiliation (rather than identification) with atheists can be considered morally precarious (Franks et al., 2018).

Clearly, stereotypes depicting atheists as without values and morals create feelings of disgust and distrust that negatively affect the daily lives of atheists in the United States, even in settings that appear objective on the surface such as our legal and political systems. However, the persistence of this distrust has been questioned. Some research suggests that distrust toward atheists is fairly rigid, as evidenced by the finding that atheists are considered less trustworthy than Christians, even when described according to attributes that are more stereotypically Christian (e.g., tradition-loving) (Grove et al., 2019). This may indicate the label "atheist" is more emotionally powerful than the actual stereotypes of atheists. However, there is also research supporting the idea that distrust toward atheists can be reduced in a variety of ways, including by imagining a relaxed and educational discussion with an atheist (LaBouff & Ledoux, 2016). Other ideas to increase trust in atheists include education about the prevalence of atheists, education about nonreligious ways of meaning-making (e.g., belief in evolution), and easing anxieties about atheist lawlessness by identifying government and society (rather than a God) as reinforcers of moral behavior (Gervais, 2013). Interestingly, it also appears that belief in ideals often related to Christian nationalism (e.g., right-wing authoritarianism and religious fundamentalism) is more associated with distrust toward atheists than beliefs in *Christianity* (Shen et al., 2013; Whitehead & Perry, 2020). This, again, highlights that Christian religious beliefs are not necessarily accompanied by distrust toward atheists, but the identification of atheism as an enemy of Christian nationalism is what elicits this distrust.

Importantly, these stereotypes that atheists are immoral, despite their prevalence, have been shown to be untrue. Atheists have been shown to be more likely to be supportive of women's rights and LGBTQ+ rights than religious people and less likely to support violent actions, such as the American invasion of Iraq, the death penalty, and the use of torture (Zuckerman, 2009). Additionally, atheists have been shown to demonstrate less ingroup bias and more prosociality toward members of a differing group when compared to Christians (Cowgill et al., 2017).

The Angry, Liberal, Scientific Atheist

Another common caricature is that of the angry, liberal, dogmatically scientific, and contrarian atheist. Research suggests that atheists are labeled as angrier than theists, other people in general, and even other minority groups (e.g., gay and lesbian individuals) and that this stereotype is held more often by those with a stronger belief in God, despite the debunking of the myth of the angry atheist (Meier et al., 2015). It is unclear what, specifically, drives the continued existence of this stereotype; however, as atheists have been identified as an enemy to Christian nationalism, it logically follows that this framework would name a moral enemy as "angry," perhaps as a means of justifying further stereotyping and prejudice. The identification of perceived opposition as angry may create a narrative in which stigmatizing atheists is deemed justified, citing the belief that their uncontrolled anger initiated conflict. Additionally, this stereotype may have origins in the controversial beliefs and arguments of the "four horsemen" of the New Atheism movement of the 2000s (Richard Dawkins, Daniel Dennett, Sam Harris, and Christopher Hitchens). These figureheads of the New Atheist movement are known for being particularly critical toward religion and theists. These aggressive critiques, alongside other concerns about their polarizing language and behavior, have elicited angry reactions from both theists and atheists alike, particularly atheists who do not feel represented by these "leaders" (Amarasingam & Brewster, 2016). Thus, the behavior of four atheists with power and influence may be unfairly and inaccurately generalized to *all* atheists.

Additionally, atheists are often thought of as scientifically minded and rational, even to a rigid extent (Grove et al., 2019). Specifically, it has been found that those who are more religious are more likely to identify atheists as scientific (Moon et al., 2021). This stereotype, while seemingly harmless, may also work to justify other stereotypes of atheists, such as the previously mentioned belief that atheists are "value violators." In a study examining the perceived morality of scientists, participants labeled scientists as "somewhat inhuman and obsessed enough with the pursuit of knowledge that they are perceived as capable of immoral conduct and can be potentially dangerous," even though scientists were not believed to be inherently atheist (Rutjens & Heine, 2016, p. 11). Thus, when Christian nationalism denounces the legitimacy of science and identifies science as amoral in this way (Baker et al., 2020; McLaren, 2020; Perry et al., 2021), the perception of atheists as scientific is yet another avenue of justifying the belief that they are immoral adversaries of the Christian nationalist narrative.

Another related and common stereotype of atheists is that they are more often politically liberal (Grove et al., 2019); however, this is a stereotype that has been shown to include a grain of truth. Research has shown consistently that atheists and nonbelievers are far less likely to identify as politically conservative or Republican (e.g., frequently identifying as liberal, Democratic, independent) than religious people and that politically liberal people are more likely to identify as atheist (Baker & Smith, 2009; Cragun, 2014; Kettle, 2013; Schwadel, 2020). This is an important trend to mention since, as stated previously, Christian nationalism as a framework is typically highly connected with political conservatism (Whitehead et al., 2018; Whitehead & Perry, 2020). This, again, means that conflating nonbelief with political liberalism enables Christian nationalism to name this "liberal atheist" as its enemy. And the power behind this cultural framework allows for the integration of Christian nationalist messaging into civic society (e.g., citing the Pledge of Allegiance in schools, listing "In God We Trust" on national currency, etc.). This cultural narrative, identifying America as a Christian nation, does not go unnoticed either as many atheist Americans report "distress over what they [see] as the declining wall of separation between church and state in the U.S." (Hammer et al., 2012, p. 55).

The culmination of these stereotypes then raises this question: How does anti-atheist stigma affect atheists' psychological well-being?

Psychological Consequences of Anti-Atheist Stigma

Though research on the consequences of anti-atheist stigma and discrimination is scarce, the existent findings show that the negative consequences spread across a variety of social and emotional domains. Psychologically, anti-atheist discrimination has been shown to be associated with increased depression (Cheng et al., 2018), increased feelings of loneliness (Brewster et al., 2016), and lower self-esteem (Brewster et al., 2020). Relationally and socially, it is estimated that over half of American atheists have felt socially ostracized and the process of disclosing an atheist identity to family members often results in highly negative, angry, and rejecting reactions, including being questioned by family members as to how they could raise moral children (Hammer et al., 2012; Zimmerman et al., 2015). While these findings are indeed eye-opening, a complete understanding of the consequences of anti-atheist stigma requires the recognition of atheist identity as a *concealable* stigmatized identity.

Atheism as a Concealable Stigmatized Identity

Since identifying as an atheist can be concealed or hidden from others, atheist identity can be understood as a *concealable stigmatized identity*, a concept based on Goffman's

(1963) scholarship on stigma and stigmatized identities. Thus, an atheist's psychological well-being can be understood according to exposure to positive and negative messaging about atheism, the degree to which they have internalized anti-atheist stereotypes and stigma, amount of stress about disclosure of their atheist identity, anticipation of stigma and discrimination, and the amount of importance one ascribes to their atheist identity (Quinn & Earnshaw, 2013). A study investigating the relationship between atheism as a concealable stigmatized identity and psychological well-being found that "higher levels of anticipated stigma were associated with less disclosure of atheist identity, more concealment of atheist identity, and lower psychological . . . well-being" (Abbott & Mollen, 2018, p. 699). This suggests that when atheists anticipate that disclosing their atheist identity will be met with a high degree of stigma, they are more likely to conceal their identity; this dual process of expecting a stigmatized response and concealing their identity then lowers their psychological well-being. This same study, though, found that a greater sense of community with other atheists and more positive feelings about one's atheist identity were associated with more disclosure, less concealment, and higher psychological well-being. Relatedly, while perceptions and experiences of discrimination have obvious negative consequences on psychological well-being, discriminatory experiences can result in a person feeling more strongly connected to their atheist identity which, again, can increase psychological well-being (Doane & Elliott, 2015). These findings indicate that viable strategies in counseling clients experiencing anti-atheist discrimination would be to help them identify a supportive community, decrease internalized stigma, and strengthen positive emotions toward their atheist identity. This strengthened identification can then result in a stronger sense of well-being.

It is also important to mention, though, that the comfort one feels in disclosing their atheist identity depends on the communities that surround them and whether a person holds other stigmatized identities. For example, it has been found that atheists who are also persons of color may experience *greater* discrimination after disclosing their atheist identity and the act of disclosing this identity may be associated with significant distress (Abbott et al., 2020). The compounding effects of holding multiple stigmatized identities and the traditionally strong presence of religiosity within communities of color (Pew Research Center, 2015) may explain why disclosure is not always associated with increased psychological well-being in these groups. Other cultural and identity factors, such as regionality, may also affect the disclosure of atheist identity. American Southerners, for example, may anticipate greater stigma and, as a result, be more likely to conceal their identity rather than publicly identify as atheist (Frost et al., 2022; Mackey et al., 2021). Additionally, atheists who also identify as Republican, female, and those who were raised in or still attend religious services are more likely to conceal their atheist identity (Frost et al., 2022). This means that atheists who exist in more religious (or atheist-stigmatizing) environments may be less likely to feel positively toward their atheist identity and less likely to find a supportive atheist community, resulting in decreased psychological well-being.

Psychological Well-Being of Atheists and the Importance of Community

The research comparing the mental health and psychological well-being of atheists and religious people is mixed. Some research suggests that religious people experience greater psychological well-being (e.g., greater happiness and self-esteem, lower anxiety and depression) when compared to atheists (Hayward et al., 2016). Other research demonstrates that atheists experience less religious/spiritual distress (e.g., anxieties surrounding divine punishment, feeling angry with or disappointed by a divine being) than religiously identified people (Sedlar et al., 2018). However, claims that religious *(non) belief,* specifically, causes differences in psychological well-being provide an incomplete picture. In fact, it appears that the most likely cause of differences in well-being between believers and nonbelievers has more to do with their sense of connectedness to a community, whether religious or secular, than the actual beliefs themselves (Galen, 2015; Hammer et al., 2012; Hayward et al., 2016). When separating nonbelievers into those with a confident nonbelief (e.g., atheists) as opposed to those with a less definite nonbelief (e.g., agnostics, nonbelievers with doubt) and separating believers into the devout and the doubtful, both strongly identified atheists and believers fare better psychologically than those with religious or spiritual doubts (Baker et al., 2018; Galen & Kloet, 2011; McCaffree, 2019). This emphasizes that the difference in well-being is attributable to a strong sense of identity and affiliation with community. See chapter 5 of this volume for an extended discussion of nonreligiousness and health.

Supporting Nonreligious People Experiencing Anti-Atheist Discrimination

Misconceptions and Bias from Mental Health Professionals

Although most mental health professionals do not hold a belief in god(s) (Sahker, 2016), there is still evidence that clinicians bring their (non)religious and spiritual selves into the counseling process, which can bring anti-atheist bias and stigma with it. A qualitative study with a small sample of psychologists found that clinicians' religious/spiritual beliefs "inadvertently and unavoidably" affected several aspects of the counseling process, including conceptualization of client concerns and the importance placed on religious and spiritual concerns (Magaldi-Dopman, et al., 2011, p. 293). This study also found that early-career psychologists often overlooked religious/spiritual concerns and even more experienced clinicians felt ineffective in addressing these topics with clients.

Relatedly, a small mixed methods study examining psychotherapy trainees' cultural humility in their work with nonreligious clients found that trainees were more likely to associate positive client attributes to a religious client compared to an atheist client, even when they themselves did not identify as religious (Winkeljohn Black & Gold, 2019). They also found that those who endorsed this association between positive attributes and a religious client also reported greater exposure to anti-atheist media messaging and identified that their clients appeared less comfortable discussing cultural concerns with them. This indicates that clients may be more perceptive of our biases than we are, and they likely make decisions about whether to disclose their atheist identity based on those perceptions.

A major explanation for these findings and potential solutions to the problem of bias lies in professional training. Despite the fact that many psychological training programs and counseling codes of ethics emphasize multicultural competence and cultural humility, explicit focus on (non)religion and (non)spirituality is often excluded or minimized in training, leaving many psychologists feeling under-prepared to address religious/spiritual identity and concerns with clients (Sahker, 2016). Clinicians and clients alike would certainly benefit from more intentional discussions of religious/spiritual identities (including nonbelief) in their training programs (e.g., use of religiously diverse case examples, education about diverse religious and spiritual identities in multicultural counseling courses, etc.). However, there are also strategies that counselors can utilize on their own to identify and reduce the influence of religious/spiritual bias and increase their competency in working with atheist and nonbelieving clients.

One such strategy is to become familiar with competencies intended to aid clinicians in their work with nonreligious clients. The Association for Spiritual, Ethical, and Religious Values in Counseling (ASERVIC) has put forth a set of competencies, supplemental to the American Counseling Association (ACA) ethics code, to support clinicians working with (non)religiously diverse clients (https://aservic.org/spiritual-and-religious-competencies/). The Competencies for Addressing Spiritual and Religious Issues in Counseling (ASERVIC, 2009) focus on culture and worldview, counselor self-awareness, human and spiritual development, communication, assessment, and diagnosis and treatment. These competencies state that counselors should reflect on their attitudes toward different (non)religious beliefs and constantly evaluate how these beliefs are impacting the counseling process. A similar list of competencies for clinicians has been proposed by Vieten and colleagues (2013). These "Spiritual and Religious Competencies" that the authors set forth have some overlap with the competencies proposed by ASERVIC, such as recognizing the significance of (non)belief in a client's worldview, demonstrating awareness of one's own religious/spiritual biases, and understanding that religious experiences can both hinder and help psychological functioning. However, the latter competencies also include an understanding of how (non)religious identity can change over the lifespan and state that clinicians should remain up to date on research regarding (non)religiousness (Vieten et al., 2013).

Both sets of competencies, though, identify the importance of explicitly inquiring about a client's religious or spiritual (non)belief and the significance of this has been echoed by others (Abbott, 2021; Sahker, 2016). While this may seem overly simplistic, the findings previously mentioned tell us that when we do not intentionally open the door for discussions of religion/spirituality, clients will fill in the blanks on their own and may conceal their atheist identity, perhaps assuming that their clinician is religious or holds anti-atheist beliefs. As is the case when broaching other potentially taboo or diversity-related topics, we can infer that asking a client directly about their religious or spiritual (non)belief sends the message that these are acceptable topics to discuss in counseling, and we accept whatever answer they provide. Relatedly, clinicians should be mindful of the language they use in sessions and how language that conveys a potentially religious or spiritual meaning (e.g., "blessing," "thank God," "everything happens for a reason," etc.) can be interpreted by clients as a counselor's religious bias, which may cause them to believe they should conceal their atheist identity or withhold discussions about experiences with anti-atheist stigma in sessions (Abbott, 2021; Bishop, 2018). Instead, clinicians should use language that matches the client's and, when uncertain, can explicitly ask how certain phrases and terms feel to the client. Clinicians can also advertise themselves in a way that invites nonbelieving clients; for example, on the popular directory Psychology Today, clinicians can add a "Secular and Non-Religious" filter to their profile or write directly into their biographies that they are inclusive of nonreligious clients.

Mindful use of language and self-representation as well as open discussion about nonbelief are significant actions because, as previously discussed, lower anticipated stigma and the act of disclosing an atheist identity in a safe environment work to improve psychological well-being (Abbott & Mollen, 2018). After one has asked about religious/spiritual identity, it is worth asking if the client is presenting to therapy with concerns *specific* to their religious/spiritual identity. We should not assume that an atheist-identified client is inherently struggling with religious/spiritual concerns solely because of their atheist identity. If, however, a client does state that religious/spiritual concerns are a presenting concern, then we can ask follow-up questions about the nature of the concern and the client's needs. Below is a discussion of common presenting concerns of atheist clients, ways that these concerns can be conceptualized, and intervention strategies.

Presenting Concerns and Treatment Considerations

As mentioned previously, atheist clients may frequently face family and social rejection resulting from the disclosure of their atheist identity (Hammer et al., 2012; Zimmerman et al., 2015). Additionally, even if clients have not disclosed their atheist identity to family members, they may reasonably anticipate a negative reaction and this anticipated stigma, coupled with concealment of identity, is often associated with psychological distress (Abbott & Mollen, 2018). Given this and the fact that most Americans identify as religious (Gallup, 2024), when working with atheist clients, a clinician is very likely to meet a client who is experiencing religious doubts, has recognized that they are an atheist, and/or is considering whether to disclose this to their family. This process of moving from a religious affiliation to no affiliation is commonly referred to as "deconversion," and the group of people who go through this process are frequently referred to as religious "dones." As people move through this process in diverse ways, they may spend some time feeling uncertain about their beliefs and this sense of uncertainty is associated with poorer psychological well-being (Galen & Kloet, 2011). This may inform the development of treatment goals that focus on increasing clarification of and confidence in (non)beliefs. Additionally, religious "nones" (people who have never been religiously affiliated) may not see religious "dones" as being a part of their in-group, as these "dones" are often viewed by both religious and atheist people as "in the middle" (Van Tongeren et al., 2023, p. 98). This means that individuals who are considering disaffiliating with religion due to nonbelief may be particularly at risk of psychological distress due to anticipated stigma, concealment of identity, and a lack of belongingness to either religious or nonreligious communities.

Sahker (2016) has proposed the following model (see figure 4.1) to conceptualize the identity development of religious "dones" that combines an atheist identity formation model (Smith, 2011) with a theory of intellectual and ethical development (Perry, 1970):

1. *The ubiquity of theism and dualism*: Captures the idea that the starting point for religious "dones" is being surrounded by religion and, as a result, that they have accepted *learned* (religious) morality as authority.
2. *Questioning theism and multiplicity*: Clients begin to question religion and explore personal beliefs. Clients recognize multiple truths and personal truths are arrived at by weighing the "least wrong answer" (Sahker, 2016, p. 296).
3. *Rejecting theism and relativism*: Deep evaluation of one's beliefs. In the case of atheist identity development (Smith, 2011), this evaluation of personal beliefs would result in disengagement from religion. However, this deep evaluation of beliefs may result in choosing to remain religiously affiliated and not identify as nonreligious or atheist. Either way, we know that a client's confidence in their (non)belief system has a greater effect on their psychological well-being than the (non)beliefs themselves. Therefore, the intention at this stage is the clarification and commitment of (non)beliefs.
4. *Coming out and commitment*: Knowledge from authority and self-knowledge are combined, uncertainty about (non)belief is now lowered, and client commits to a belief or nonbelief system. If theism was rejected in the previous stage, then a client may disclose their atheist identity to others (e.g., family). If theism was accepted, then the client may remain affiliated with religion, ideally with less uncertainty and psychological distress.

This model allows for the assessment and conceptualization of religious/spiritual struggles and client's needs while minimizing the influence of bias: the end goal is not that the client becomes devoutly religious or nonreligious, but that they reach a sense of commitment to their beliefs, whatever they may be. This sense of commitment serves to improve the client's psychological well-being (Galen & Kloet, 2011) and to find a community that shares these beliefs. By openly asking about religious/spiritual identity and concerns early in treatment, a client will ideally feel more comfortable sifting through these deeply personal and philosophical concerns in sessions without fear that the clinician is pushing them to hold specific beliefs.

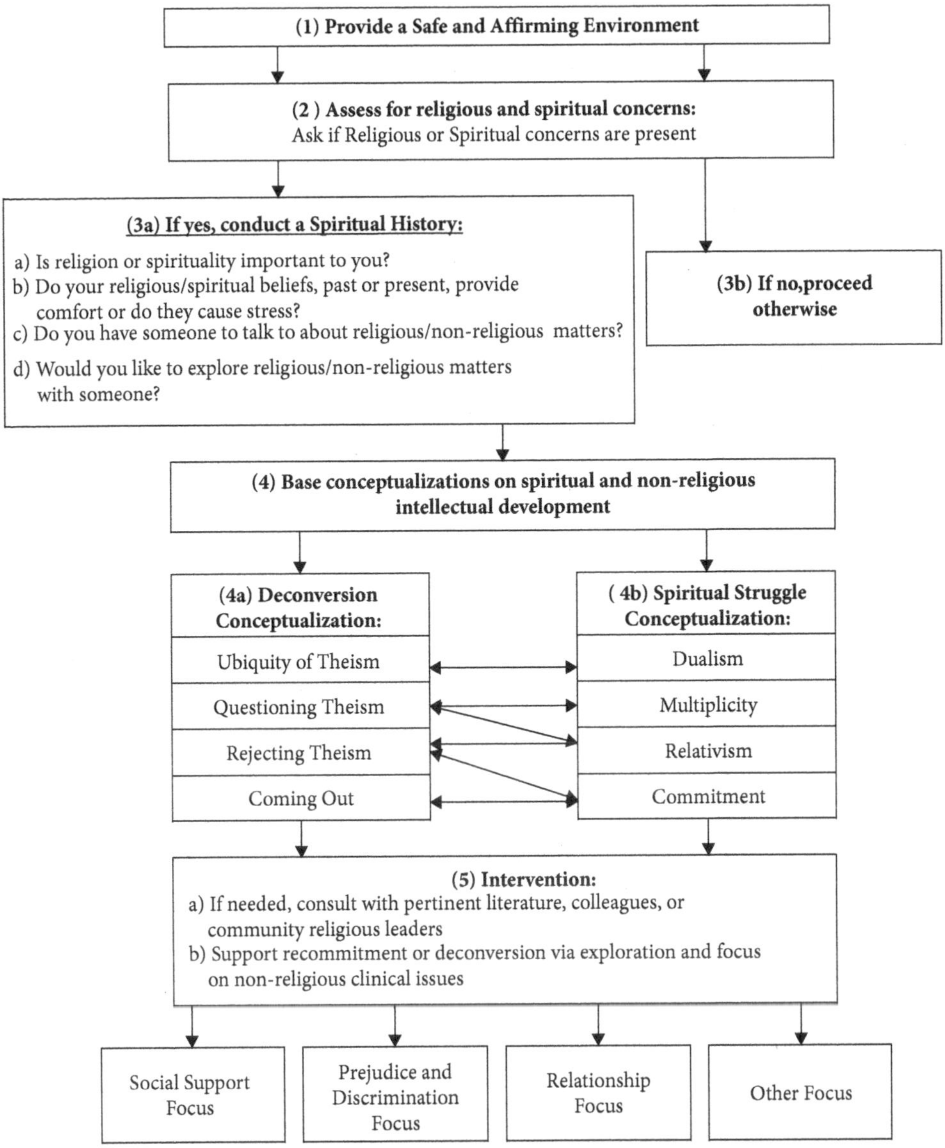

Figure 4.1 Sahker's (2016) Theoretical Model of Assessment, Conceptualization, and Intervention for Nonreligious Clients.

If a client committed to a system of nonbelief and an atheist identity, whether through a process of "deconversion" or because they were never religious, a subsequent form of assessment might be asking clients if they have desires or intentions to disclose this identity ("come out") to their families and social circles. While many clinicians hope for their clients to live as their authentic selves and may personally wish for their clients to "come out," clients are the experts on their own families and relationships so the counseling process at this stage may include discussions about the difference between "comfort zones" and "danger zones." As discussed previously, for clients of color, clients living in predominantly religious areas (e.g., the American South), and clients in potentially atheist-stigmatizing (e.g., politically conservative) communities, disclosure of atheist identity may only *increase* psychological distress (Abbott et al., 2020; Frost et al., 2022; Mackey et al., 2021). As a result, clinicians and clients would benefit from parallel conversations about strengthening assertive communication when disclosing in the "comfort zone" and finding community to increase a sense of belonging if disclosure falls within a "danger zone." When disclosure is the client's goal, interventions might include role playing disclosure from the perspective of different family members and loved ones, collaboratively writing "coming out" letters in sessions, exploring the myriad responses the client may receive, and creating a safety plan in the case that disclosure goes awry.

Given that a strong, positive self-identity as an atheist (as opposed to uncertainty) and connection to atheistic communities are well-documented protective factors for atheist clients (Abbott, 2021; Brewster et al., 2020; Galen, 2015), it can very helpful in clinical work with atheists to provide education about and help connect them to atheist organizations on a national or local level and online. American Atheists, for example, is a national organization that hosts conventions, publishes a magazine for members, and has established many chapters in cities across the nation (https://www.atheists.org/). The Secular Student Alliance functions similarly with chapters established at a variety of university campuses in the United States (https://secularstudents.org/). Clinicians can also point clients to online resources, such as Facebook groups and sub-Reddits. Many atheist organizations offer opportunities for political activism, open discussions of what a collective atheist identity means, and can provide clients with opportunities to have their nonbelief validated by others. This validation and community may be especially crucial for those who do not feel they can disclose their atheist identity to family, those who have been rejected by family for their nonbelief, and/or religious "dones" who still desire a sense of connection around (non)religious/spiritual identity (Wilkins-Laflamme & Thiessen, 2020).

Finally, there have been mixed findings on whether atheists struggle with meaning-making in their lives. Some research suggests that atheists struggle with issues of "ultimate meaning" about as much as the religious do (Sedlar et al., 2018), while other findings show that some atheists feel their life has no meaning or that the meaning they make of their life is not easily captured (Nelson et al., 2021). While beliefs in meaninglessness are not always "pathological" or accompanied by distress, if an atheist client is expressing distress or lowered psychological well-being due to a perceived lack of purpose or meaning, interventions that allow them to explore a secular interpretation of meaning may be helpful. One such intervention would be a Personal Values Card Sort (Miller et al., 2001), in which clients can rank a list of values (e.g., beauty, curiosity, independence) in terms of relative importance to each other. Values, once named so explicitly, may help a client who is struggling with meaning-making to feel a greater sense of purpose, find others with complementary values, and identify valued actions, especially through acceptance and commitment therapy (ACT) interventions.

Assessing for Discrimination

While most clinical assessment tools and questionnaires about religion/spirituality are aimed at religious respondents (Sahker, 2016), there exists a handful of assessment tools that can be utilized by clinicians to better understand the extent and severity of clients' experiences with anti-atheist discrimination. One such tool is the Measure of Atheist Discrimination Experiences (MADE), which includes twenty-four questions in which a client can indicate the frequency that they have encountered different forms of anti-atheist discrimination, including exposure to stereotypes of immorality, social rejection, dismissals of their atheist identity, and more (Brewster et al., 2016) (see box 4.1). When developing this measure, a higher overall MADE score was associated with increased loneliness and psychological distress (Brewster et al., 2016).

A similar tool is the Microaggressions Against Non-Religious Individuals Scale (MANRIS) which includes thirty-one questions in which a client can indicate the frequency that they have encountered the following microaggressions related to their atheist identity: "assumption of inferiority, denial of non-religious prejudice, assumptions of religiosity, endorsing non-religious stereotypes, and pathology of a non-religious identity" (Cheng et al., 2018, p. 254) (see box 4.2). When developing this measure, a greater overall level of exposure to these microaggressions was associated with increased depressive symptoms (Cheng et al., 2018).

Advocating for Atheist Clients

While the term "advocacy" may elicit mental images of political action taken on a macro level, acts of advocacy can also occur in the relationship between clinician and client. On this micro level, clinicians can advocate for and with clients in a variety of ways, including encouraging clients to learn more about the diversity that exists within atheist identity, conceptualizing client concerns as reactions to systemic anti-atheist bias and oppression, encouraging clients who are interested to engage in atheist-related activism, empowering clients who are willing to share their atheist identity with loved ones, and more (Bishop, 2018). Advocacy at this level, while at a smaller scale, works to educate and empower clients in light of the systemic stigma and discrimination that they may face and sends the message that their symptoms are often reactions to injustice, rather than the result of internal deficits.

On a community level, clinicians working with atheist clients may have a vantage point in recognizing shortcomings and anti-atheist discrimination embedded in community services. While explicit training on advocacy in clinical programs is still scarce, recommendations for advocacy at the community level might include public talks and presentations about anti-atheist stigma and its consequences, educating other local clinicians on ways to improve their work with atheist clients, and writing to local and regional political representatives to provide education on ways that religiously based

Box 4.1 Measure of Atheist Discrimination Experiences (MADE), Brewster et al., 2016

INSTRUCTIONS: Please rate how often the experience reflected in each of the following items has happened to you personally in the PAST YEAR. We are interested in your personal experiences as an atheist individual and realize that each experience may or may not have happened to you. To tell us about your experiences, please rate each item using the scale below:

Select 1st bubble = If this has NEVER happened to you
Select 2nd bubble = If this has happened to you ONCE IN A WHILE (less than 10% of the time)
Select 3rd bubble = If this has happened to you SOMETIMES (10%–25% of the time)
Select 4th bubble = If this has happened to you A LOT (26%–49% of the time)
Select 5th bubble = If this has happened to you MOST OF THE TIME (50%–70% of the time)
Select 6th bubble = If this has happened to you ALMOST ALL OF THE TIME (more than 70% of the time)

1. Despite my atheism, I have been asked to pretend that I am religious.
   1-2-3-4-5-6
2. I have been told that, as an atheist, I cannot be a moral person.
3. I have been told that I will "grow out of' my atheism and that it is just a phase.
4. People have denied me services because of my atheism.
5. People have told me that I am not a "good person" because of my atheism.
6. Because I am atheist, I have been asked how I can still have a purpose in life.
7. Because of my atheism, others have avoided me.
8. Because I am atheist, people have told me that I am disrespecting my loved ones.
9. People have treated me as if my atheism is just a rebellious phase in my life, not a sincere set of beliefs.
10. I have been told that I am selfish because I am atheist.
11. People have told me that my atheism is a source of humiliation for them.
12. I have been denied opportunities at work and/or in school because I am a known atheist.
13. I have been asked to pretend that I am not atheist.
14. I have been asked to go along with religious traditions to avoid "stirring up trouble."
15. People have talked about me behind my back because of my atheism.
16. Even knowing I am atheist, others have expressed that they expect me to hold/plan a religious life ceremony for myself (e.g., wedding, baptism, funeral).

17. People who know I'm atheist have asked me to attend religious services, despite my objections.
18. My property has been vandalized because I am atheist.
19. I have been warned that I must give up my atheist beliefs in order to avoid suffering in the afterlife.
20. Others have physically harmed or assaulted me because of my atheism.
21. I have been told that I am immature because of my atheist beliefs.
22. Others have treated me like I don't understand the difference between right and wrong because I am atheist.
23. People have asked me to join them in thanking God for a fortunate event (e.g., saying grace before a special meal) even though they know I am atheist.
24. I have been excluded from social gatherings and events because of my atheism.

***Responses across all 24 items are averaged to yield one total score.

Box 4.2 Microaggressions Against Non-Religious Individuals Scale (MANRIS), Cheng et al., 2018

Please indicate how often you have experienced the following in the last 6 months.
Scale: 1 = Never 2 = 1–3 times 3 = 4–6 times 4 = 7–9 times 5 = 10 or more times
Assumptions of Inferiority:

1. Others have assumed that I would be selfish because of my lack of religion.
2. Others have devalued my contributions because of my non-religious background.
3. Others have assumed that I am untrustworthy because of my lack of religion.
4. Others have assumed that I would not be helpful to another person because of my lack of religion.
5. Others have assumed I have less valuable things to say because of my lack of religion.
6. Others have dismissed my contributions because of my non-religious background.
7. Others have assumed that I would cheat on my work because of my lack of religion.
8. Others have assumed that I don't know right from wrong because of my lack of religion.
9. Others have assumed I have no morals because of my lack of religion.

Denial of Non-Religious Prejudice

1. Others have suggested that I should not complain about non-religious discrimination.
2. Others have denied that non-religious people face extra obstacles when compared to others.

3. Others have dismissed my experiences as a non-religious individual to be an overreaction.
4. Others have suggested that I am too sensitive about discrimination against nonreligious people.
5. Others have told me to not complain about my experiences as a non-religious individual.
6. Others have suggested that people do not experience non-religious discrimination anymore.
7. Others have suggested that my negative experiences as a non-religious individual do not compare to the negative experiences of religious individuals.

Assumptions of Religiosity

1. Others have assumed that I am religious.
2. Others have assumed I attend places of worship without first asking if I am religious.
3. Others have included a blessing or prayer in a public social gathering (e.g., a public business meeting).
4. Others have told me to express thanks to God or Gods for an event.
5. Others have acted surprised that I do not believe in God or Gods.

Endorsing Non-Religious Stereotypes

1. Others have assumed that all people in my non-religious group are all the same.
2. Others have acted as if all non-religious people are alike.
3. Others have suggested that non-religious people think they are better than everyone.
4. Others have suggested that non-religious people are not willing to accept others' viewpoints.
5. Others have suggested that non-religious people are self-centered.
6. Others have asked why non-religious people are intolerant.

Pathology of a Non-Religious Identity

1. Others have teased me because of my non-religious identity.
2. Others have made fun of my non-religious identity.
3. Others have made demeaning jokes about my non-religious identity.
4. Others have called me names because of my non-religious identity.

These assessments (Box 4.1 and 4.2) are relatively brief and can be used after clients disclose a nonreligious identity as a means of assessing or clarifying concerns related to discrimination or can be used throughout treatment to measure changes in discrimination-related distress. The results of these assessments can also be used to set or revisit treatment goals, reevaluate the boundary between the client's "comfort zone" and "danger zone," strengthen assertive communication, seek like-minded community, or discuss realistic coping skills to address concerns related to this discrimination (e.g., depressive symptoms, loneliness).

legislation discriminates against nonreligious citizens (Bishop, 2018; Miles & Fassinger, 2021). Additionally, clinicians may consider joining organizations such as the Freedom From Religion Foundation (FFRF), a nonprofit focused on defending the separation of church and state through legal actions against First Amendment violations and education efforts (https://ffrf.org/).

Advocacy at this level is most advantageous to the client and the cause when done in groups. Many of these community-level strategies may feel easier to broach when allying with other clinicians and psychological researchers in the area who also understand the consequences of anti-atheist stigma and discrimination. As is the case for atheist clients and all people, we do better as a community.

References

Abbott, D. M. (2021). Psychotherapy with nonreligious clients: A relational-cultural approach. *Professional Psychology: Research and Practice*, 52(5), 470–76. https://doi.org/10.1037/pro0000392

Abbott, D. M., & Mollen, D. (2018). Atheism as a concealable stigmatized identity: Outness, anticipated stigma, and well-being. *The Counseling Psychologist*, 46(6), 685–707. https://doi.org/10.1177/0011000018792669

Abbott, D. M., Ternes, M., Mercier, C., & Monceaux, C. (2020). Anti-atheist discrimination, outness, and psychological distress among atheists of colour. *Mental Health, Religion & Culture*, 23(10), 874–87. https://doi.org/10.1080/13674676.2020.1858771

Amarasingam, A., & Brewster, M. E. (2016). The rise and fall of the New Atheism: Identity politics and tensions within U.S. nonbelievers. In R. Cipriani & F. Garelli (Eds.), *Sociology of Atheism* (pp. 118–36). Brill. https://doi.org/10.1163/9789004319301_008

Association for Spiritual, Ethical, and Religious Values in Counseling. (2009). *Competencies for addressing spiritual and religious issues in counseling*. https://aservic.org/spiritual-and-religious-competencies/

Baker, J. O., Perry, S. L., & Whitehead, A. L. (2020). Crusading for moral authority: Christian nationalism and opposition to science. *Sociological Forum*, 35(3), 587–607. https://doi.org/10.1111/socf.12619

Baker, J. O., & Smith, B. G. (2009). The nones: Social characteristics of the religiously unaffiliated. *Social Forces*, 87(3), 1251–63. https://doi.org/10.1353/sof.0.0181

Baker, J. O., Stroope, S., & Walker, M. H. (2018). Secularity, religiosity, and health: Physical and mental health differences between atheists, agnostics, and nonaffiliated theists compared to religiously affiliated individuals. *Social Science Research*, 75, 44–57. https://doi.org/10.1016/j.ssresearch.2018.07.003

Bishop, B. (2018). Advocating for atheist clients in the counseling profession. *Counseling and Values*, 63(1), 17–30. https://doi.org/10.1002/cvj.12070

Brewster, M. E., Hammer, J., Sawyer, J. S., Eklund, A., & Palamar, J. (2016). Perceived experiences of atheist discrimination: Instrument development and evaluation. *Journal of Counseling Psychology*, 63(5), 557–70. https://psycnet.apa.org/doi/10.1037/cou0000156

Brewster, M. E., Velez, B. L., Geiger, E. F., & Sawyer, J. S. (2020). It's like herding cats: Atheist minority stress, group involvement, and psychological outcomes. *Journal of Counseling Psychology*, 67(1), 1–13. https://psycnet.apa.org/doi/10.1037/cou0000392

Brown-Iannuzzi, J. L., Golding, J. M., Gervais, W. M., Lynch, K. R., Wasarhaley, N. E., & Bainter, S. (2019). Will jurors believe nonbelievers? Perceptions of atheist rape victims in the courtroom. *Psychology of Religion and Spirituality*, 13(1), 119–26. http://dx.doi.org/10.1037/rel0000278

Cheng, Z. H., Pagano Jr., L. A., & Shariff, A. F. (2018). The development and validation of the Microaggressions Against Non-Religious Individuals Scale (MANRIS). *Psychology of Religion and Spirituality*, 10(3), 254–62. https://psycnet.apa.org/doi/10.1037/rel0000203

Cook, C. L., Cottrell, C. A., & Webster, G. D. (2015). No good without God: Antiatheist prejudice as a function of threats to morals and values. *Psychology of Religion and Spirituality*, 7(3), 217–26. http://dx.doi.org/10.1037/rel0000013

Cowgill, C. M., Rios, K., & Simpson, A. (2017). Generous heathens? Reputational concerns and atheists' behavior toward Christians in economic games. *Journal of Experimental Social Psychology*, 73, 169–79. http://dx.doi.org/10.1016/j.jesp.2017.06.015

Cragun, R. T. (2014). Who are the "new atheists"? In L. G. Beaman & S. Tomlins (Eds.), *Atheist identities—Social spaces and social contexts* (pp. 195–211). Springer.

Davis, J. T., & Perry, S. L. (2021). White Christian nationalism and relative political tolerance for racists. *Social Problems*, 68(3), 513–34. https://doi.org/10.1093/socpro/spaa002

Doane, M. J., & Elliott, M. (2015). Perceptions of discrimination among atheists: Consequences for atheist identification, psychological and physical well-being. *Psychology of Religion and Spirituality*, 7(2), 130–41. https://doi.org/10.1037/rel0000015

Du Mez, K. K. (2020). *Jesus and John Wayne: How White evangelicals corrupted a faith and fractured a nation*. Liveright Publishing Corporation.

Edgell, P., Hartmann, D., Stewart, E., & Gerteis, J. (2016). Atheists and other cultural outsiders: Moral boundaries and the non-religious in the United States. *Social Forces*, 95(2), 607–38. https://doi.org/10.1093/sf/sow063

Emerson, M. O. (2024, September 17). *Christian voters will play an outsized role in the US election*. Baker Institute for Public Policy. https://www.bakerinstitute.org/research/christian-voters-will-play-outsized-role-us-election

Franks, A. S., Scherr, K. C., & Gibson, B. (2018). Godless by association: Deficits in trust mediate antiatheist stigma-by-association. *Journal of Experimental Psychology: Applied*, 25(2), 303–16. http://dx.doi.org/10.1037/xap0000179

Frost, J., Scheitle, C. P., & Ecklund, E. H. (2022). Patterns of perceived hostility and identity concealment among self-identified atheists. *Social Forces*, 101(3), 1580–605. https://doi.org/10.1093/sf/soac012

Galen, L. (2015). Atheism, wellbeing, and the wager: Why not believing in God (with others) is good for you. *Science, Religion and Culture*, 2(3), 54–69. http://dx.doi.org/10.17582/journal.src/2015/2.3.54.69

Galen, L. W., & Kloet, J. D. (2011). Mental well-being in the religious and the non-religious: evidence for a curvilinear relationship. *Mental Health, Religion & Culture*, 14(7), 673–89. https://doi.org/10.1080/13674676.2010.510829

Gallup. (2024, March 29). *How religious are Americans?* https://news.gallup.com/poll/358364/religious-americans.aspx

Gervais, W. M. (2013). In godlessness we distrust: Using social psychology to solve the puzzle of anti-atheist prejudice. *Social and Personality Psychology Compass*, 7(6), 366–77. https://doi.org/10.1111/spc3.12035

Gervais, W. M. (2014). Everything is permitted? People intuitively judge immorality as representative of atheists. *PloS ONE*, 9(4), 1–9. https://doi.org/10.1371/journal.pone.0092302

Goffman, E. (1963). *Stigma: Notes on the management of spoiled identity*. Prentice-Hall.

Gorski, P. S., & Perry, S. L. (2022). *The flag and the cross: White Christian nationalism and the threat to American democracy*. Oxford University Press.

Grove, R. C., Rubenstein, A., & Terrell, H. K. (2019). Distrust persists after subverting atheist stereotypes. *Group Processes & Intergroup Relations*, 23(7), 1103–24. https://doi.org/10.1177/1368430219874103

Hammer, J. H., Cragun, R. T., Hwang, K., & Smith, J. M. (2012). Forms, frequency, and correlates of perceived anti-atheist discrimination. *Secularism and Nonreligion*, 1, 43–67. https://doi.org/10.5334/snr.ad

Hayward, R. D., Krause, N., Ironson, G., Hill, P. C., & Emmons, R. (2016). Health and well-being among the non-religious: Atheists, agnostics, and no preference compared with religious group members. *Journal of Religion and Health*, 55(1), 1024–37. https://doi.org/10.1007/s10943-015-0179-2

Kettle, S. (2013). Faithless: The politics of new atheism. *Secularism and Nonreligion*, 2(1), 61–72. https://doi.org/10.5334/snr.al

LaBouff, J. P., & Ledoux, A. M. (2016). Imagining atheists: Reducing fundamental distrust in atheist intergroup attitudes. *Psychology of Religion and Spirituality*, 8(4), 330–40. http://dx.doi.org/10.1037/rel0000066

Lipka, M., Tevington, P., & Starr, K. J. (2024, February 7). *8 facts about atheists*. Pew Research Center. https://www.pewresearch.org/short-reads/2024/02/07/8-facts-about-atheists/#:~:text=When%20we%20asked%20people%20which,moral%20and%20have%20good%20values.%E2%80%9D

Mackey, C. D., Silver, C. F., Rios, K., Cowgill, C. M., & Hood Jr, R. W. (2021). Concealment of nonreligious identity: Exploring social identity threat among atheists and other nonreligious individuals. *Group Processes & Intergroup Relations*, 24(5), 860–77. https://doi.org/10.1177/1368430220905661

Magaldi-Dopman, D., Park-Taylor, J., & Ponterotto, J. G. (2011). Psychotherapists' spiritual, religious, atheist or agnostic identity and their practice of psychotherapy: A grounded theory study. *Psychotherapy Research*, 21(3), 286–303. https://doi.org/10.1080/10503307.2011.565488

McCaffree, K. (2019). Atheism, social networks, and health: A review and theoretical model. *Secularism & Nonreligion*, 8(9), 1–18. https://doi.org/10.5334/snr.101

McLaren, P. (2020). Religious nationalism and the coronavirus pandemic: Soul-sucking evangelicals and branch covidians make America sick again. *Postdigital Science and Education*, 2(3), 700–21. https://doi.org/10.1007/s42438-020-00122-7

Meier, B. P., Fetterman, A. K., Robinson, M. D., & Lappas, C. M. (2015). The myth of the angry atheist. *The Journal of Psychology: Interdisciplinary and Applied*, 143(3), 219–38. http://dx.doi.org/10.1080/00223980.2013.866929

Miles, J. R., & Fassinger, R. E. (2021). Creating a public psychology through a scientist-practitioner-advocate training model. *American Psychologist*, 76(8), 1232–47. https://doi.org/10.1037/amp0000855

Miller, W. R., C'de Baca, J., Matthews, D. B., & Wilbourne, P. L. (2001). *Personal values card sort*. University of New Mexico.

Moon, J. W., Krems, J. A., & Cohen, A. B. (2021). Is there anything good about atheists? Exploring positive and negative stereotypes of the religious and nonreligious. *Social Psychological and Personality Science*, 12(8), 1505–16. https://doi.org/10.1177/1948550620982703

Nelson, T. A., Abeyta, A. A., & Routledge, C. (2021). What makes life meaningful for theists and atheists? *Psychology of religion and spirituality*, 13(1), 111–18. http://dx.doi.org/10.1037/rel0000282

Nie, F. (2023). In God we distrust: Christian nationalism and anti-atheist attitude. *Journal for the Scientific Study of Religion*, 63(1), 1–14. https://doi.org/10.1111/jssr.12886

Perry, S. L., Baker, J. O., & Grubbs, J. B. (2021). Ignorance or culture war? Christian nationalism and scientific illiteracy. *Public Understanding of Science*, 30(8), 930–46. https://doi.org/10.1177/09636625211006271

Perry, W. G., Jr. (1970). *Forms of intellectual and ethical development in the college years*. Holt, Rinehart & Winston.

Pew Research Center. (2015). *Chapter 4: The shifting religious identity of demographic groups*. https://www.pewresearch.org/religion/2015/05/12/chapter-4-the-shifting-religious-identity-of-demographic-groups/

Pew Research Center. (2024, April 9). *5. Party identification among religious groups and religiously unaffiliated voters*. https://www.pewresearch.org/politics/2024/04/09/party-identification-among-religious-groups-and-religiously-unaffiliated-voters/

Quinn, D. M., & Earnshaw, V. A. (2013). Concealable stigmatized identities and psychological well-being. *Social and Personality Psychology Compass*, 7(1), 40–51. https://doi.org/10.1111/spc3.12005

Ritter, R. S., & Preston, J. L. (2011). Gross gods and icky atheism: Disgust responses to rejected religious beliefs. *Journal of Experimental Social Psychology*, 47(6), 1225–30. https://doi.org/10.1016/j.jesp.2011.05.006

Rutjens, B. T., & Heine, S. J. (2016). The immoral landscape? Scientists are associated with violations of morality. *PloS one*, 11(4), e0152798. https://doi.org/10.1371/journal.pone.0152798

Sahker, E. (2016). Therapy with the nonreligious: Ethical and clinical considerations. *Professional Psychology: Research and Practice*, 47(4), 295–302. https://psycnet.apa.org/doi/10.1037/pro0000087

Schwadel, P. (2020). The politics of religious nones. *Journal for the Scientific Study of Religion*, 59(1), 180–89. https://doi.org/10.1111/jssr.12640

Schwadel, P., Hardy, S. A., Van Tongeren, D. R., & DeWall, C. N. (2021). The values of religious nones, dones, and sacralized Americans: Links between changes in religious affiliation and Schwartz values. *Journal of Personality*, 89(5), 867–82. https://doi.org/10.1111/jopy.12620

Sedlar, A. E., Stauner, N., Pargament, K. I., Exline, J. J., Grubbs, J. B., & Bradley, D. F. (2018). Spiritual struggles among atheists: Links to psychological distress and well-being. *Religions*, 9(8), 242. https://doi.org/10.3390/rel9080242

Shen, M. J., Haggard, M. C., Strassburger, D. C., & Rowatt, W. C. (2013). Testing the *love thy neighbor* hypothesis: Religiosity's association with positive attitudes toward ethnic/racial and value-violating out-groups. *Psychology of Religion and Spirituality*, 5(4), 294–303. https://psycnet.apa.org/doi/10.1037/a0033648

Simpson, A., & Rios, K. (2016). How do U.S. Christians and atheists stereotype one another's moral values? *The International Journal for the Psychology of Religion*, 26(4), 320–36. http://dx.doi.org/10.1080/10508619.2016.1167419

Smith, J. M. (2011). Becoming an atheist in America: Constructing identity and meaning from the rejection of theism. *Sociology of Religion*, 72(2), 215–37. https://doi.org/10.1093/socrel/srq082

Van Tongeren, D. R., DeWall, C. N., & Van Cappellen, P. (2023). A sheep in wolf's clothing? Toward an understanding of the religious dones. *Journal of Experimental Psychology: General*, 152(1), 98–119. https://doi.org/10.1037/xge0001269

Vieten, C., Scammell, S., Pilato, R., Ammondson, I., Pargament, K. I., & Lukoff, D. (2013). Spiritual and religious competencies for psychologists. *Psychology of Religion and Spirituality*, 5(3), 129–44. https://doi.org/10.1037/a0032699

Whitehead, A. L., & Perry, S. L. (2019). Is a "Christian American" a more patriarchal America? Religion, politics, and traditionalist gender ideology. *Canadian Review of Sociology*, 56(2), 151–77. https://doi.org/10.1111/cars.12241

Whitehead, A. L., & Perry, S. L. (2020). *Taking America back for God: Christian nationalism in the United States*. Oxford University Press.

Whitehead, A. L., Perry, S. L., & Baker, J. O. (2018). Make America Christian again: Christian nationalism and voting for Donald Trump in the 2016 presidential election. *Sociology of Religion: A Quarterly Review*, 79(2), 147–71. https://doi.org/10.1093/socrel/srx070

Wilkins-Laflamme, S., & Thiessen, J. (2020). Religious socialization and millennial involvement in organized and digital nonbelief activities. *Secularism and Nonreligion*, 9(2), 1–15. https://doi.org/10.5334/snr.126

Winkeljohn Black, S., & Gold, A. P. (2019). Trainees' cultural humility and implicit associations about clients and religious, areligious, and spiritual identities: A mixed-method investigation. *Journal of Psychology and Theology*, 47(3), 202–16. https://doi.org/10.1177/0091647119837019

Zimmerman, K. J., Smith, J. M., Simonson, K., & Myers, W. B. (2015). Familial relationship outcomes of coming out as an atheist. *Secularism and Nonreligion*, 4(4), 1–13. https://doi.org/10.5334/snr.aw

Zuckerman, P. (2009). Atheism, secularity, and well-being: How the findings of social science counter negative stereotypes and assumptions. *Sociology Compass*, 3(6), 949–71. https://doi.org/10.1111/j.1751-9020.2009.00247.x

5

Nonreligion, Well-Being, and Mental Health

Luke W. Galen

Chapter Outline

Problems with Associating Religiousness and Well-Being

A Mixed History

The scientific literature pertaining to the confluence of religion and mental health/well-being is massive, with most studies indicating generally positive associations (Koenig et al., 2024). Many scholars have further posited that the mechanism of this association is attributable to aspects of religious content—a "Belief as Benefit Effect" (BABE). Paterson and Francis (2017) suggest several ways by which religious content produces or mediates a positive influence on well-being including providing a coherent understanding of the world, assisting in coping with existential challenges, inculcating cognitive processes that promote acceptance of suffering, increasing existential certainty and a sense of meaning, and promoting optimism. Conversely, nonreligious beliefs, disaffiliation from religion, and secular worldviews are suggested to result in lower well-being. Given the substantial literature linking religion with positive outcomes, nonbelief and secularity have been said to constitute health "liabilities" (Hall et al., 2008, p. 370). Given the massive literature on the topic, the Belief as Benefit Effect would appear to be beyond debate.

Problems with Conceptualization and Measurement

However, a substantial portion of BABE literature is limited in terms of conceptualization and measurement (both of religiosity, as well as well-being). First, religion and religiosity are multifaceted constructs, with some components even operating in opposition to others. In addition to the basic dimensions of religion (e.g., the "four Bs" of believing, belonging, behaving, and bonding), there are distinct religious orientations (e.g., intrinsic, extrinsic, quest) as well as constructs consisting of distinct portions of religious content (e.g., fundamentalism, orthodoxy, spirituality). Although some of these have positive relationships with aspects of well-being, others have null, or even negative relationships (Hackney & Sanders, 2003). Generally, well-being has a more substantive relationship with social forms of religiosity than it does to individual religious and spiritual practices (e.g., prayer; Berthold & Ruch, 2014; Braam & Koenig, 2019). For instance, whereas depression is inversely associated with religious service attendance (r =—0.12), it has a weaker relationship with religious belief (r =—0.05; Smith et al., 2003).

Second, and relatedly, findings indicating that the nonreligious are less happy and more depressed than the religious are often based on methods that define the former group by low frequency of religious attendance and/or low subjective importance of belief (Myers, 2000; Newport et al., 2010). But low religious attendance is not the same thing as being nonreligious, nor does it represent the absence of belief in God. Further, religious attendance as a construct or variable represents an amalgam of religious belief and social behaviors. Positive relationships with well-being are most often obtained by using such combinations. For instance, happiness and prosociality are characteristic of religious belief combined with active group participation—so-called "engaged" or "involved religiosity" (Myers, 2012; Putnam & Campbell, 2010). Consequently, conclusions of the Belief as Benefit Effect type are based on connections drawn between positive outcomes and practices consisting of a combination of more than one construct. This represents a "fallacy of composition"—an inferred relationship with the whole, when the effect is produced by only a portion.

These limitations have several implications for the topic of well-being and nonreligion. Much of the literature has been framed using a religiously normative perspective in which research questions are based on the presumed effects of variation in degrees or levels of religion (i.e., denomination, affiliation, intrinsic orientation). Positive well-being associations with religiosity are thought to represent a contrast with those at the opposite or low end of the continuum—the "not religious." This amalgamated category (or "nones") consists mostly of the religiously unaffiliated combined with those with disparate beliefs. In a 2024 U.S. survey by the Pew Forum, 17 percent of *nones* identified as atheist, and 20 percent as agnostic, but 63 percent self-identified as "nothing in particular" (Pew Research Center, 2024). Likewise, overall, 72 percent of *nones* reported believing in God, a higher power, or a spiritual force but the remainder did not. Because of this heterogeneity, any research design comparing those who identify as religious with nones (or comparing frequent religious attenders versus nonattenders) does not represent a clean contrast between opposing worldviews or belief systems.

The diversity within nones derives mainly from substantial differences between those who are "religious but nothing in particular" (RNIPs) versus atheists and agnostics. This contrast is not merely one of religious belief but also involves fundamental identity aspects including basic demographics. Fifty-five percent of RNIPs are women compared to 36 percent of agnostics and 32 percent of atheists. In terms of ethnicity, 57 percent of the RNIP are white, versus 69 percent, and 77 percent of agnostics and atheists, respectively. Twenty-seven percent of RNIPs are college graduates compared to 48 percent of both agnostics and atheists. Thirty-one percent of RNIPs identify as politically liberal, compared to 56 percent and 65 percent of agnostics and atheists. In sum, the larger portion consisting of the nones and the RNIPs resembles the average of the general population, whereas the nonreligious portion (atheists and agnostics) tends to skew more White, male, educated, and liberal. This heterogeneity is directly relevant to conclusions drawn regarding outcome variables. For instance, in the Pew Forum survey, atheists and agnostics had equivalent social and communal involvement to the religiously affiliated, whereas the religiously unaffiliated had lower involvement than either of those groups (Pew Research Center, 2024).

A similar phenomenon affects interpretations of well-being aspects as they relate to the use of nones as a residual or contrast category in comparison to the religiously engaged. Typically, the latter has scored higher in well-being than the former. Because most studies of religion and well-being are concerned with religious variation (and because they are conducted in the United States where the nonreligious are a minority) individuals who are atheist, agnostic, secular, nothing in particular, or religiously unaffiliated are combined into a residual comparison category. For example, most of the studies in the above-mentioned Smith et al. (2003) meta-analysis of depression either specifically excluded nonreligious individuals or featured analyses unable to make distinctions of the above-mentioned type (i.e., between those who did not believe in God versus uncertain or unaffiliated believers). As a result, comparisons between the religious and nonreligious confound variance in religious belief with other fundamental differences such as demographics. When less invidious comparisons are used (e.g., controlling for demographics and other nonbelief related variables), differences in well-being as a function of religiosity are nonexistent or trivial. For example, in a comparison of church versus secular group members, Galen and Kloet (2011a) found that after controlling for demographics and group attendance, the groups were essentially equivalent. Instead, variation in affect was primarily a function of demographic and group attendance differences, not religious belief.

Often, the theory of lower well-being in the nonreligious is based on differences in the dimension of intrinsic religious orientation, defined as religiosity that is mature, internalized, and functioning as a "master motive." Koenig et al. (1998) found that patients with prolonged episodes of depression had lower intrinsic religiosity compared to those whose depression remitted more quickly. Similar patterns are observed across other studies. In the Hackney and Sanders (2003) meta-analysis, the strongest relationships between well-being outcomes were those studies operationally defining religion as "personal devotion," which included intrinsic orientation. However, the interpretation of relationships with intrinsic orientation also involves many of the same problems associated with amalgamated constructs. Items on the most frequently used intrinsic scale, the I/E Revised (Gorsuch & McPherson, 1989) include the following: "I enjoy reading about my religion," "It is important to me to spend time in private thought and prayer," "I try hard to live all my life according to my religious beliefs," and "My whole approach to life is based on my religion." As can be seen, this construct consists of religious belief combined with motivated commitment to a coherent and confidently held worldview. As such, low intrinsic scores do not solely represent the absence of religious belief. One could imagine a similar construct, but framed from a nonreligious perspective, consisting not only of the atheistic absence of belief in god/s but also featuring a commitment to a secular humanist worldview. For example, Schnell (2015) developed the Dimensions of Secularity instrument consisting of atheism, agnosticism, and other philosophical orientations. Whereas humanistic orientation (i.e., a non-supernaturally based emphasis on human welfare and dignity) is positively associated with well-being, atheism is unrelated. In sum, studies in the literature that appear to indicate a positive relationship between well-being and intrinsic religiosity (and similar constructs such as "importance of religion") are not equipped to specifically assess how well-being relates to complete secularism (e.g., atheism and agnosticism) because they often disregard the effect of stable, coherent worldviews lacking religious belief.

Curvilinearity

Studies involving religious belief and well-being are often misinterpreted in a "dose-response" manner—more is better. However, this assumption has been based on problematic conceptualizations and comparisons. Much of the religious well-being literature has been methodologically or analytically limited by grouping the nones together with agnostics and atheists or by using church attendance with "never" or "seldom" as a proxy for nonreligiousness. But when the full range of religiosity has been utilized and appropriately analyzed, non-monotonic, nonlinear relationships have often been found (Paterson & Francis, 2017; Pöhls, 2021; Speed & Lamont, 2021). It is the strength of belief, whether atheistic or religious, that is associated with greater psychological well-being (Dilmaghani, 2018; Galen & Kloet, 2011a; Park et al., 2019; Weber et al., 2012). For example, satisfaction with life appears to show a U-shaped pattern in which the highly religious as well as completely nonreligious report greater satisfaction compared to the moderately religious (Galen & Kloet, 2011b; Pöhls et al., 2020).

It must be stated that such relationships have not always been consistently obtained, possibly because of the substantial variation in sample and construct measurement. Some work indicates highly religious individuals have the highest level of well-being, whereas the least religious along with the moderately religious have similar well-being, resulting in a nonlinear "J-shaped" or "hockey stick" function (Gontijo et al., 2022; Nadal et al., 2018;

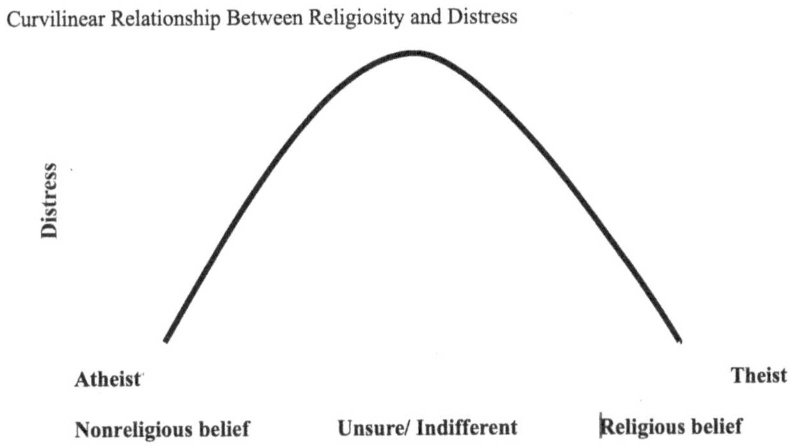

Figure 5.1 Curvilinear Relationship Between Religiosity and Distress.

Newport et al., 2010). For instance, Robbins and Longden (2024) found that the religious had greater purpose in life relative to humanists but they both had greater purpose relative to the general population. Other studies have found curvilinearity in some operationalizations of well-being (e.g., anxiety) but not others (e.g., depression; Karki et al., 2024). Therefore, such findings must be considered provisional until more extensive work including meta-analyses is conducted.

A related pattern can be seen in the trajectories of nonreligious individuals who previously have been believers and/or affiliated (the so-called *dones*) as distinct from the stable nones who have never believed in God nor been affiliated with religion. Many *dones* are recently disengaged from religion and retain religious "residue" in the form of partial beliefs or practices. McLaughlin et al. (2022) reported that those who no longer identified as being religious but who still engaged in religious practices had more mental health concerns compared to those who completely discontinued such practices. Similarly, other work has also indicated that among the nones, greater religious involvement is associated with lower well-being (Speed & Fowler, 2021). Longitudinal data have indicated that those who seriously consider leaving their religion but who maintain their institutional affiliation experience more depressive symptoms than people who completely drop out as well as the two consistent groups (i.e., stable affiliates and stable nones; May, 2018). Along with the curvilinear effects involving certainty and well-being, such findings have implications for our understanding of the mechanisms linking worldview beliefs and well-being (Malinakova et al., 2020).

Those with stable, certain worldviews and who possess an affirmative self-identity—whether religious or atheist—are better off psychologically than those who are uncertain (Moore & Leach, 2016; Pöhls, 2021; Ross, 1990; Weber et al., 2012). By contrast, weakly held beliefs and a lack of commitment produce problems associated with "fence-sitting," such as incoherence related to contradictory behaviors and beliefs (Speed & Fowler, 2021). Incompatible sets of beliefs could combine in ways that produce lower well-being. For instance, belief in a theistic and judgmental god co-occurring with belief in an afterlife featuring punishment of sinners could produce distress (e.g., "I fear going to Hell"). This can lead to phenomena such as death anxiety (discussed in greater detail below) or fears about being rejected by God (Henderson & Kent, 2022; Rybarski et al., 2023). Relatedly, dissonance could be created for people who perceive themselves as insufficiently religious or spiritual such as those with poorly internalized religious instruction or who have shallow or immature religious identities (Barry et al., 2020). Thus, many deconverts or those recently identifying as nonreligious may be experiencing distress caused not by the absence of religion per se, but because of the residue related to the process of exiting religion (e.g., familial conflict, guilt). This would also suggest that the dissonance and distress produced by challenges to doubters' identity may be subsequently reduced by completely disaffiliating establishing a new identity or role.

Distinguishing the specific source of such effects, however, is complicated in part because characteristics of the individual (e.g., cognitive uncertainty, personality traits) are confounded with factors related to the trajectory of belief change (e.g., time since disaffiliation or belief rejection). It may be that those with uncertain beliefs are in a temporal state of flux because of other ongoing existential or epistemic changes that simultaneously produce mental health challenges or an actively ongoing search for support in times of need (Malinakova et al., 2020). Consequently, in this "third variable" scenario, weakened religious beliefs, on the one hand and psychological distress on the other, could both be sequelae of the same underlying processes. This may explain why those who self-identify as spiritual but not religious or agnostic display lower well-being—because these individuals are undergoing an existential search driven by emotional distress (Paterson & Francis, 2017; King et al., 2013). These findings have implications for clinical work, such as the benefits likely to be found in encouraging and supporting clients in the exploration of their beliefs and the acquisition and development of greater confidence in their worldviews. Further suggestions are described in greater detail at the conclusion of the chapter.

Spirituality and Nonreligion

As compared to religious constructs such as institutional affiliation or belief in God, the construct of spirituality has often been suggested as enjoying a closer relationship with well-being (Braam & Koenig, 2019). But for the nonreligious, spirituality has proven to be particularly problematic, chiefly because of its amorphous conceptualization (de Jager Meezenbroek et al., 2012; Koenig, 2008). On the one hand, this breadth has been touted as maximizing inclusion and minimizing parochial divisiveness. Even metaphysical naturalists and atheists can be seen as having commonalities with theists if both groups report being spiritual. However, amorphous spirituality also creates criterion blending or "concept creep," both in terms of beliefs as well as with well-being content. Regarding the former, although the term spirituality implies transcendence (i.e., supernatural concepts), the addition of nontranscendent content, such as awe and humility, invites endorsement even by metaphysical naturalists such as atheists. However, the "spiritual experiences" of atheists typically refer to nontranscendent things like nature, science, and practices like meditation (Caldwell-Harris et al., 2011). This expansiveness of the spirituality construct is problematic from the standpoint of validity, given that any scientifically legitimate concept must specify divergent validity—in this context representing the identification of those who are not spiritual.

Conceptual blending of spirituality also involves the expansion of content to subsume elements of positive psychology, including well-being. For example, one frequently used measure, the Spiritual Transcendence Scale (Piedmont, 1999) has subscales for universality ("I feel an emotional bond to all humanity") and connectedness ("It is important to give something back to my community"). This leads to problems when used to predict well-being because similar content is shared with the predictor (Koenig, 2008). More to the present point, studies indicate that, when measures are subdivided, nontranscendent spirituality items are associated with well-being, but transcendent items are not (Schuurmans-Stekhoven, 2013).

More problematic for atheists, their rejection of the transcendent portion of content reduces their overall scores, leading to the appearance of lower overall well-being. For instance, the Religious Well-Being Scale (Ellison, 1983) includes items such as "I believe that God is concerned about my problems" that are positively endorsed by well-adjusted believers and rejected by both the nonreligious as well as depressed and hopeless believers who may believe that God does not care. Any comparison based on such items does not necessarily mean that belief in God is associated with lower depression but merely indicates the tautological (e.g., "nondepressed religious people are not depressed").

In a similar example, the Values in Action model of character strengths—as defined by Peterson (2006)—features the dimension of Spirituality/Transcendence, including facets such as "feeling spiritual" and "a sense of meaning in life." The US military has included the VIA-IS in its global assessment of comprehensive soldier fitness (CSF; Vie et al., 2016). Within the global CSF instrument, a subscale is used to generate a "spiritual fitness score." This dimension is described as universal, construing the search for sacred in a secular as well as religious sense, and the items are a mixture of transcendent and nontranscendent content ("to what extent are you united with God?," "I believe there is a purpose for my life"). When atheists reject such content, this yields feedback such as "You may lack a sense of meaning and purpose. You may not feel connected to something larger than yourself. You may question your beliefs, principles, and values" because the scoring algorithm interprets rejection of the metaphysical content as also a rejection of the well-being content. Not only does research utilizing this model not establish that nonreligiosity itself is indicative of low well-being, it has also led to the underestimation of atheists' fitness (Hammer et al., 2013).

The Efficacy of Nonreligious Treatments

Outcome studies of treatments involving putative "spiritual" components are subject to misinterpretation because of effects similar to those described above. For instance, there is a massive literature on meditation and mindfulness practices based on historically spiritual traditions. As a result, the mechanism of effect of practices such as transcendental meditation are framed in spiritual terms despite the efficacious components being essentially secular, such as controlled breathing, muscle relaxation, and cognitive distancing/present focus. When different versions of such treatments are compared, secular and transcendent forms have equivalent effectiveness on outcomes such as the alleviation of depression or the increase in pain tolerance (Feuille & Pargament, 2015; Koenig et al., 2015). Likewise, the most common methods of substance use treatment—12-step programs—are thought to have a quasi-spiritual basis, largely due to history and content (e.g., references to a Higher Power). But in Alcoholics Anonymous, success is attributable to secular mechanisms—the encouragement of regular attendance, opportunities for frequent meetings, and the provision of social support—rather than spirituality per se (Kelly, 2017). Interestingly, even though spiritual content of 12-step programs has the potential to alienate some nonreligious practitioners, atheists can nonetheless have positive outcomes because the efficacious components consist of essentially secular mechanisms (Tonigan et al., 2002). In cases where nonreligious clients perceive an irreconcilable incompatibility between their beliefs and the spiritual content of the treatment, there are also secular alternatives to 12-step programs (see chapter 13 of this volume pertaining to treatment of substance use disorders).

What Promotes Well-Being in the Nonreligious?

In contrast to the preceding material, which focused on erroneous ideas pertaining to the mental well-being of the nonreligious, the remaining material will discuss things that support well-being for the nonreligious.

Socially Valued Secularism

Religiously predominant social milieus can be particularly conducive to negative stereotypes regarding secularism and well-being. In the United States, there is a general belief that atheists are less moral, less trustworthy, and more disagreeable than the religious (Galen et al., 2014; Gervais et al., 2011). Although endorsed to a greater extent by the highly religious, these (self-)stereotypes may even be internalized by some nonreligious people. In this way, the relative normativity or social value of religiosity versus secularism interacts with the well-being of the nonreligious individuals in a given milieu. This is illustrative of a "culture fit" matching effect. Worldviews, whether religious or secular, that are normative within the surrounding culture are associated with greater well-being relative to non-normative ones (Stavrova et al., 2013). Cross-national and regional comparisons indicate that, while the nonreligious display lower well-being in religiously dominant areas, this is not the case in secular milieus (Gebauer et al., 2017; Stavrova, 2015).

In religiously predominant environments, internalized negative stereotypes may increase the tendency for the nonreligious to assume that their worldviews are inherently deficient, leading to self-fulfilling responses such as passivity or nihilism. Although it has often been assumed that traits such as disagreeableness or lower sociability are attributable to qualities intrinsic to the "atheist personality," culture-fit effects point to something more resembling an interactive relationship between the personal and the contextual. Individualistic and nonconforming people may gravitate toward, or be more willing to consider, non-normative worldviews such as atheism. Equally, in the other causal direction, consciousness of an outsider status or social rejection may potentiate these traits. Atheists often report being informed or pressured that they need to "get religion" to increase their well-being, or conversely that any negative feelings must be the inevitable result of lacking religious beliefs. Clinicians with nonreligious clients who report such existential difficulties may wish to explore the extent to which these feelings derive from unsatisfactory or inchoate worldviews as opposed to being products of erroneous stereotypes internalized from their surroundings.

As with the broader sociocultural matching effects, a similar phenomenon is operative at the level of the family. For reasons mentioned above, nonreligiosity in youth has been implicated as a mental health liability, but there is evidence that this is contingent upon the children having differing religious views from their parents (Kugelmass & Garcia, 2015). This again suggests that lower well-being is not produced by the absence of religious beliefs per se, but rather that nonreligious children of religious parents may incur lower mental health due to familial mismatch. Relatedly, for nonreligious clients who come from religious families and who are attempting to "come out," the relative success of this process is contingent upon healthy communication, family cohesion, adaptability, and the ability to remain close despite differences in beliefs (Zimmerman et al., 2015). Viewed differently, such contextual effects can also be useful in the enhancement of well-being in nonreligious clients such as providing the impetus to increase meaningful social engagement with a supportive community.

Social Engagement and Networking

Social relationships are among the influences most conducive to personal happiness and well-being. Consistent with the findings presented above, well-being is greater for those—whether religious or secular—who have formed coherent worldviews that can be socially shared and consensually validated. This can occur via close friends, by engaging in activities with a social network, and by involvement in civic-minded groups. Having a strong nonreligious identification coupled with sharing social connections can increase self-esteem and protect against the harmful effects of marginalization (Brewster et al., 2020; Doane & Elliott, 2015). Participation in secular groups, social networks, and communities can provide a sense of meaning (Smith, 2017). As mentioned above, engaged religious individuals tend to report greater well-being than the unaffiliated, but members of secular humanist groups have equivalent well-being with church members (Galen & Kloet, 2011b).

The benefits of group participation—for believers and nonbelievers alike—are attributable to multiple mechanisms (Shor & Roelfs, 2013). Members of the secular Sunday Assembly report increased well-being primarily due to informal socializing (Price & Launay, 2018). Shared secular rituals can play a role similar to religious ones in fostering feelings of social connection (Charles et al., 2021). Thus, clinicians may wish to explore ways of improving the social engagement of their nonreligious clients and, if possible, finding specifically secular groups with shared worldviews.

Existential Issues

When facing existential problems, a crucial function of individuals' worldviews is assistance in maintaining self-esteem. Perhaps the greatest of these challenges is confronting the inevitability of death. Most (although not all) nonreligious individuals believe that the cessation of life is accompanied by the annihilation of personal consciousness without the continuity of a personal afterlife (Haimila & Muraja, 2023). One method of preserving self-esteem in the face of such annihilation is to reframe the end of life as a process of symbolic or impersonal continuity (Lifton, 1979). This includes construing the physical body as being recycled, anticipating a merging with universal consciousness, or surviving vicariously via children or leaving a legacy. Given the central role played by concepts of the literal transcendence of death (i.e., personal immortality) for religious worldviews, it is often assumed that any belief system lacking this component should leave individuals vulnerable to personal distress such as pessimism. However, there is little evidence that belief in the cessation of personal consciousness necessarily implies a sense of despair for atheists. A meta-analysis by Jong et al. (2018) pointed to a very weak overall association between religion and death anxiety ($r = .06$), with most studies producing a null association.

Complementing general fears regarding death, attitudes regarding the end of life are often reflected in preferences within the context of medical treatment options such as advance care planning directives and euthanasia. Research indicates that, compared to the religious, the nonreligious are less likely to desire aggressive or extraordinary life extending measures when they would be futile (Cicirelli, 1997; Shinall et al., 2014). Thus, despite any reassurance of immortality, those lowest in religiosity show less desire compared to the religious (who seek and receive more aggressive care) to prolong their lives if their quality of living is not acceptable.

These findings offer little evidence that religious worldviews are demonstrably superior to nonreligious ones in reducing existential anxiety. Rather, studies suggest that many ways of coping with end of life are essentially secular at their core, including devoting time to family, finding joy in the present, and connecting with friends (Manning, 2023). Likewise, nontranscendent, symbolic ways of "immortality striving" and leaving a legacy exist, such as dedication to sociopolitical movements or to institutions such as government, education, patriotism, business, art, science, or sports (Vail et al., 2020).

The symbolic provision of existential support provided by secular worldviews points to a phenomenon similar to that mentioned above: those with strong, coherent belief systems—whether religious or nonreligious—are equally well-positioned in addressing existential concerns. By contrast, it is those with inchoate or incoherent beliefs that are least equipped to confront existential anxiety. Agnostics, the unsure, and spiritual-but-not-religious individuals show greater death anxiety and avoidance compared to atheists (Rybarski et al., 2023; Spitzenstätter & Schnell, 2020; 2023). Likewise, in Jong et al.'s (2018) meta-analytic review of death anxiety (mentioned above), of the eleven studies capable of testing such a relationship, eight found a curvilinear pattern. The authors suggested that other studies could also have found a similar pattern, but most did not analyze the data in a manner that could even detect a quadratic relationship. More recent studies have similarly indicated that uncertain beliefs are associated with greater death anxiety relative to firm nonbelief (Haimila & Muraja, 2023; Sawyer et al., 2021). Although the limited number of available studies renders this conclusion provisional, supportive evidence continues to accumulate that the formation of strong, coherent worldviews constitutes a valuable existential resource.

Meaning and Purpose

One existential pattern that does appear to markedly differ as a function of religiosity is that atheists report a lower degree of objective meaningfulness in life (Schnell & Keenan, 2011). In the past, this has traditionally been interpreted as reflective of the deficiency of the worldview itself, such that secular sources of meaning are less "existentially satisfactory" than religious ones (Park & McNamara, 2006). However, it is more accurate to attribute this pattern to differences in the dispositional need for, and desire to search for meaning as well as diverse ways in which individuals construe the concept of meaning itself. Whereas strong religious believers experiencing low levels of objective meaning in life tend to have lower well-being (Galek et al., 2015), atheists lacking objective life meaning or feeling cosmically insignificant do not experience a crisis of meaning, as manifested by negative affect, fatalism, nihilism, or despair (Schnell & Keenan, 2011; Speed et al., 2018). Atheists also report feeling a lower need to search for meaning relative to theists (Abeyta & Routledge, 2018; Nelson et al., 2021). Further, whereas religious individuals primarily derive meaning from sources they believe are exogenous (i.e., extrinsically produced, transcendent), atheists tend to conceptualize meaning as being endogenous (individually provided; Speed et al., 2018). Taken in the aggregate, these findings imply that the nonreligious construe a lack of objective meaning very different from the religious.

Despite these differences, the sources from which meaning is derived are largely similar regardless of personal religiosity. In a series of Pew Research Center surveys (2018a, 2018b), the aspect of life reported as being most meaningful for the religious and nonreligious alike was spending time with family. Other sources of meaning showed similarly high overlap, including relationships with friends, good health, stability, and travel. By contrast, stated life values do differ more substantially as a function of religious belief. The nonreligious tend to prioritize self-direction, autonomy, stimulation, and achievement (Schwartz & Huismans, 1995). Science plays an important role in nonreligious value systems (van Mulukom et al.,

2023). Therefore, clinicians should be cognizant that their nonreligious clients may desire greater engagement with these sources of meaning and value in their lives.

As distinct from experiencing a sense of meaning in life, having purpose in one's life refers to that which makes existence significant and leads to productive engagement with the broader world. In accordance with the general pattern of findings in this chapter, those in the general population without particularly strong beliefs either way tend to report lower purpose in life. However, Robbins and Longden (2024) found that secular humanists (as with religionists) reported significantly higher purpose in life than those in the general population. Likewise, those with a particular commitment to secular humanist worldviews also feel little need to search for additional exogenous meaning and purpose (Schnell & Keenan, 2011). Such findings imply that the constellation of beliefs held by many nonreligious individuals have the potential to provide a sense of self-esteem, meaning, and value, provided that these views are formulated coherently and lead to active engagement with others in a supportive community.

Clinical Implications

In addition to the above-mentioned recommendation of finding and engaging with a supportive community, perhaps an even more basic component of establishing a coherent sense of identity for the nonreligious is simply recognizing the centrality and importance of their identity and how this can be shared with others. As described by Smith (2011), a strong sense of secular identity is acquired not merely passively, but via an active process that defines both what the nonbeliever is, and is not. This can be enacted by taking the "bridge burning" step of coming out socially.

Because nonreligious individuals tend to have a lower sense of global or cosmic meaning and purpose, some forms of existential psychotherapy, as articulated by Yalom (1980), can be useful for enhancing these life domains. According to Yalom, engagement in a direct search for general meaning can paradoxically lead to frustration and self-absorption. Rather, clients must understand that meaning is constructed in an ongoing manner by fully engaging with life—whether with social relationships, long-range goals, important causes, and creative interests. Therapists can utilize simple exercises to elicit patterns of meaning that may have been previously unarticulated. For example, in a values clarification exercise, clients can identify or rank expressed values or priorities. Questions evocative of expressed values include the following: "What accomplishments are you most proud of?" "If you had only one year to live, how would you want to use your time?" "What do you view as your three most important values?" Answers to these can then be compared or contrasted with manifest values—how clients actually allocate their time and live their lives. For example, "Describe a typical day, week, or month in your life." or "If someone didn't know you, what would they think is important to you?" Then therapists can focus on removing obstacles to full engagement by asking questions such as "What prevents you from living more fully?"

In general, therapies tend to be more efficacious, with lower rates of attrition and greater treatment adherence, when clients are matched with preferred methods (Delevry & Le, 2019). This principle has often served as a rationale for the use of religion-adapted psychotherapy for religious clients such as Religious Cognitive Behavior Therapy (de Abreu Costa & Moreira-Almeida, 2022). However, the original versions of social learning-based methods, most notably cognitive behavioral therapies (i.e., CBT [cognitive behavioral therapy], REBT [rational emotive behavioral therapy], ACT [acceptance and commitment therapy], DBT [dialectical behavior therapy], etc.) are secular in content. Therefore, it is in many ways advantageous that the techniques and mechanisms of such methods may be particularly suited to those with secular worldviews. In fact, these treatments have historically included some critique of those aspects of religion that can promote non-evidence-based, dogmatic, or absolutist ways of thinking (Nielsen, 1994). The emphasis on rationality and evidence-based disputation of distorted or irrational thinking in cognitive-behavioral methods is likely to accord with the tendency for the nonreligious to value analytic thought, logic, and science (Yilmaz, 2021). Aside from any specifically secular methods of treatment, however, as can be seen from these findings, the most effective general clinical approach may be to simply encourage clients to view their secular and nonreligious worldviews as valuable in and of themselves, and to seek out ways to affirm, develop, and consensually validate these beliefs.

References

Abeyta, A. A., & Routledge, C. (2018). The need for meaning and religiosity: An individual differences approach to assessing existential needs and the relation with religious commitment, beliefs, and experiences. *Personality and Individual Differences*, 123, 6–13. https://doi.org/10.1016/j.paid.2017.10.038

Barry, C. M., Christofferson, J. L., Boorman, E. P., & Nelson, L. J. (2020). Profiles of religiousness, spirituality, and psychological adjustment in emerging adults. *Journal of Adult Development*, 27, 201–211. https://doi.org/10.1007/s10804-019-09334-z

Berthold, A., & Ruch, W. (2014). Satisfaction with life and character strengths of non-religious and religious people: It's practicing one's religion that makes the difference. *Frontiers in Psychology*, 5, 876. http://doi.org/10.3389/fpsyg.2014.00876

Braam, A. W., & Koenig, H. G. (2019). Religion, spirituality and depression in prospective studies: A systematic review. *Journal of Affective Disorders*, 257, 428–38. https://doi.org/10.1016/j.jad.2019.06.063

Brewster, M. E., Velez, B. L., Geiger, E. F., & Sawyer, J. S. (2020). It's like herding cats: Atheist minority stress, group involvement, and psychological outcomes. *Journal of Counseling Psychology*, 67(1), 1–13. https://doi.org/10.1037/cou0000392

Caldwell-Harris, C. L., Wilson, A. L., LoTempio, E., & Beit-Hallahmi, B. (2011). Exploring the atheist personality: Well-being, awe, and magical thinking in atheists, Buddhists, and Christians. *Mental Health, Religion & Culture*, 14(7), 659–72. http://doi.org/10.1080/13674676.2010.509847

Charles, S. J., van Mulukom, V., Brown, J. E., Watts, F., Dunbar, R. I., & Farias, M. (2021). United on Sunday: The effects of secular rituals on social bonding and affect. *PLoS One*, 16(1), e0242546. https://doi.org/10.1371/journal.pone.0242546

Cicirelli, V. G. (1997). Elders' end-of-life decisions: Implications for hospice care. *The Hospice Journal*, 12(1), 57–72. https://doi.org/10.1080/0742-969X.1997.11882843

de Abreu Costa, M., & Moreira-Almeida, A. (2022). Religion-adapted cognitive behavioral therapy: A review and description of techniques. *Journal of Religion and Health*, 61(1), 443–66. https://doi.org/10.1007/s10943-021-01345-z

de Jager Meezenbroek, E., Garssen, B., van den Berg, M., van Dierendonck, D., Visser, A., & Schaufeli, W. B. (2012). Measuring spirituality as a universal human experience: A review of spirituality questionnaires. *Journal of Religion and Health*, 51, 336–54. http://dx.doi.org/10.1007/s10943-010-9376-1

Delevry, D., & Le, Q. A. (2019). Effect of treatment preference in randomized controlled trials: systematic review of the literature and meta-analysis. *The Patient-Patient-Centered Outcomes Research*, 12(6), 593–609. https://doi.org/10.1007/s40271-019-00379-6

Dilmaghani, M. (2018). Importance of religion or spirituality and mental health in Canada. *Journal of Religion and Health*, 57, 120–35. https://doi.org/10.1007/s10943-017-0385-1

Doane, M. J., & Elliott, M. (2015). Perceptions of discrimination among atheists: Consequences for atheist identification, psychological and physical well-being. *Psychology of Religion and Spirituality*, 7(2), 130–41. https://doi.org/10.1037/rel0000015

Ellison, C. W. (1983). Spiritual well-being: Conceptualization and measurement. *Journal of Psychology and Theology*, 11(4), 330–40. https://doi.org/10.1177/009164718301100406

Feuille, M., & Pargament, K. (2015). Pain, mindfulness, and spirituality: A randomized controlled trial comparing effects of mindfulness and relaxation on pain-related outcomes in migraineurs. *Journal of Health Psychology*, 20(8), 1090–106. http://doi.org/10.1177/1359105313508459

Galek, K., Flannelly, K. J., Ellison, C. G., Silton, N. R., & Jankowski, K. R. B. (2015). Religion, meaning and purpose, and mental health. *Psychology of Religion and Spirituality*, 7(1), 1–12. http://doi.org/10.1037/a0037887

Galen, L. W., & Kloet, J. (2011a). Personality and social integration factors distinguishing non-religious from religious groups: The importance of controlling for attendance and demographics. *Archive for the Psychology of Religion*, 33(2), 205–28. http://doi.org/10.1163/157361211X570047

Galen, L. W., & Kloet, J. (2011b). Mental well-being in the religious and the non-religious: Evidence for a curvilinear relationship. *Mental Health, Religion & Culture*, 14(7), 673–89. http://doi.org/10.1080/13674676.2010.510829

Galen, L. W., Williams, T. J., & Ver Wey, A. L. (2014). Personality ratings are influenced by religious stereotype and ingroup bias. *The International Journal for the Psychology of Religion*, 24(4), 282–97. https://doi.org/10.1080/10508619.2013.837658

Gebauer, J. E., Sedikides, C., Schönbrodt, F. D., Bleidorn, W., Rentfrow, P. J., Potter, J., & Gosling, S. D. (2017). The religiosity as social value hypothesis: A multi-method replication and extension across 65 countries and three levels of spatial aggregation. *Journal of Personality and Social Psychology*, 113(3), e18–e39. http://doi.org/10.1037/pspp0000104

Gervais, W. M., Shariff, A. F., & Norenzayan, A. (2011). Do you believe in atheists? Distrust is central to anti-atheist prejudice. *Journal of Personality and Social Psychology*, 101(6), 1189–206. https://doi.org/10.1037/a0025882

Gontijo, D. F., Silva, D. M. R., & Damásio, B. F. (2022). Religiosity/spirituality and mental health: Evidence of curvilinear relationships in a sample of religious people, spirituals, atheists, and agnostics. *Archive for the Psychology of Religion*, 44(2), 69–90. https://journals.sagepub.com/doi/10.1177/00846724221102195

Gorsuch, R. L., & McPherson, S. E. (1989). Intrinsic/extrinsic measurement: I/E-revised and single-item scales. *Journal for the Scientific study of Religion*, 28(3), 348–54. https://www.jstor.org/stable/1386745

Hackney, C. H., & Sanders, G. S. (2003). Religiosity and mental health: A meta–analysis of recent studies. *Journal for the Scientific Study of Religion*, 42(1), 43–55. https://doi.org/10.1111/jssr.2003.42.issue-1

Haimila, R., & Muraja, E. (2023). A sense of continuity in mortality? Exploring science-oriented Finns' views on afterdeath. *OMEGA-journal of Death and Dying*, 88(1), 38–65. https://journals.sagepub.com/doi/10.1177/00302228211038820

Hall, D. E., Meador, K. G., & Koenig, H. G. (2008). Measuring religiousness in health research: Review and critique. *Journal of Religion and Health*, 47(2), 134–63. https://doi.org/10.1007/s10943-008-9165-2

Hammer, J. H., Cragun, R. T., & Hwang, K. (2013). Measuring spiritual fitness: Atheist military personnel, veterans, and civilians. *Military Psychology*, 25(5), 438–51. https://doi.org/10.1037/mil0000010

Henderson, W. M., & Kent, B. V. (2022). Attachment to God and psychological distress: Evidence of a curvilinear relationship. *Journal for the Scientific Study of Religion*, 61(1), 161–77. https://doi.org/10.1111/jssr.12767

Jong, J., Ross, R., Philip, T., Chang, S. H., Simons, N., & Halberstadt, J. (2018). The religious correlates of death anxiety: A systematic review and meta-analysis. *Religion, Brain & Behavior*, 8(1), 4–20. https://doi.org/10.1080/2153599X.2016.1238844

Karki, N., Warlick, C. A., Baimel, A., & Jong, J. (2024). Religiosity, spirituality, and mental health in eight countries. *Psychology of Religion and Spirituality*. Advance online publication. https://doi.org/10.1037/rel0000521

Kelly, J. F. (2017). Is Alcoholics Anonymous religious, spiritual, neither? Findings from 25 years of mechanisms of behavior change research. *Addiction*, 112(6), 929–36. http://doi.org/10.1111/add.13590

King, M., Marston, L., McManus, S., Brugha, T., Meltzer, H., & Bebbington, P. (2013). Religion, spirituality and mental health: results from a national study of English households. *The British Journal of Psychiatry* 202(1), 68–73. http://doi.org/10.1192/bjp.bp.112.112003

Koenig, H. G. (2008). Concerns about measuring "spirituality" in research. *Journal of Nervous and Mental Disease*, 196(5), 349–55. http://doi.org/10.1097/NMD.0b013e31816ff796

Koenig, H. G., George, L. K., & Peterson, B. L. (1998). Religiosity and remission of depression in medically ill older patients. *American Journal of Psychiatry*, 155(4), 536–42. https://doi.org/10.1176/ajp.155.4.536

Koenig, H. G., Pearce, M. J., Nelson, B., Shaw, S. F., Robins, C. J., Daher, N. S., Cohen, H. J., Berk, L. S., Bellinger, D. L., Pargament, K. I., Rosmarin, D. H., Vasegh, S., Kristeller, J., Juthani, N., Nies, D., & King, M. B. (2015). Religious vs. conventional cognitive behavioral therapy for major depression in persons with chronic medical illness: A pilot randomized trial. *Journal of Nervous and Mental Disease*, 203(4), 243–51. http://doi.org/10.1097/NMD.0000000000000273

Koenig, H. G., VanderWeele, T., Peteet, J. R. (2024). *Handbook of Religion and Health* (3rd ed.) Oxford University Press. https://doi.org/10.1093/oso/9780190088859.001.0001

Kugelmass, H., & Garcia, A. (2015). Mental disorder among nonreligious adolescents. *Mental Health, Religion & Culture*, 18(5), 368–79. http://dx.doi.org/10.1080/13674676.2015.1063044

Lifton, R. J. (1979). *The Broken Connection.* Simon & Schuster.

Malinakova, K., Tavel, P., Meier, Z., van Dijk, J. P., & Reijneveld, S. A. (2020). Religiosity and mental health: A contribution to understanding the heterogeneity of research findings. *International Journal of Environmental Research and Public Health*, 17(2), 494. https://doi.org/10.3390/ijerph17020494

Manning, C. (2023). Facing death without religion: how non-religious elders imagine death and how that shapes their lives. *Journal of Religion, Spirituality & Aging.* Advance online publication. https://doi.org/10.1080/15528030.2023.2243855

May, M. (2018). Should I stay or should I go? Religious (dis) affiliation and depressive symptomatology. *Society and Mental Health*, 8(3), 214–30. https://doi.org/10.1177/2156869317748713

McLaughlin, A. T., Van Tongeren, D. R., Teahan, K., Davis, D. E., Rice, K. G., & DeWall, C. N. (2022). Who are the religious "dones?": A cross-cultural latent profile analysis of formerly religious individuals. *Psychology of Religion and Spirituality*, 14(4), 512–24. https://doi.org/10.1037/rel0000376

Moore, J. T., & Leach, M. M. (2016). Dogmatism and mental health: A comparison of the religious and secular. *Psychology of Religion and Spirituality*, 8(1), 54–64. http://doi.org/10.1037/rel0000027

Myers, D. G. (2000). The funds, friends, and faith of happy people. *American Psychologist*, 55(1), 56–67. https://doi.org/10.1037/0003-066X.55.1.56

Myers, D. G. (2012). Reflections on religious belief and prosociality: Comment on Galen (2012). *Psychological Bulletin*, 138(5), 913–17. http://doi.org/10.1037/a0029009

Nadal, A. R. C., Hardy, S. A., & Barry, C. M. (2018). Understanding the roles of religiosity and spirituality in emerging adults in the United States. *Psychology of Religion and Spirituality*, 10(1), 30–43. https://doi.org/10.1037/rel0000104

Nelson, T. A., Abeyta, A. A., & Routledge, C. (2021). What makes life meaningful for theists and atheists? *Psychology of Religion and Spirituality*, 13(1), 111–18. https://doi.org/10.1037/rel0000282

Newport, F., Agrawal, S., & Witters, D. (2010, December 1). Very religious Americans report less depression, worry. http://www.gallup.com/poll/144980/Religious-Americans-Report-Less-Depression-Worry.aspx

Nielsen, S. L. (1994). A discussion with Albert Ellis: Reason, emotion and religion. *Journal of Psychology and Christianity*, 13(4), 327–41. https://psycnet.apa.org/record/1995-37966-001

Park, C., & McNamara, P. (2006). Religion, meaning, and the brain. In P. McNamara (Ed.), *Where God and science meet: How brain and evolutionary studies alter our understanding of religion* (pp. 67–89). Praeger.

Park, H. N., Cook, K., LePine, S. E., & Steininger, C. (2019). Do nonreligious individuals have the same mental health and well-being benefits as religious individuals? *Journal of Psychology & Christianity*, 38(2), 81–99. https://psycnet.apa.org/record/2019-62253-002

Paterson, J., & Francis, A. J. P. (2017). Influence of religiosity on self-reported response to psychological therapies. *Mental Health, Religion & Culture*, 20(5), 428–48. https://doi.org/10.1080/13674676.2017.1355898

Peterson, C. (2006). The Values in Action (VIA) classification of strengths: The un-DSM and the real DSM. In M. Csikszentmihalyi & I. Csikszentmihalyi (Eds.), *A life worth living: contributions to positive psychology* (pp. 29–48). Oxford University Press.

Pew Research Center. (Aug. 29, 2018a). The religious typology. https://www.pewresearch.org/religion/2018/08/29/the-religious-typology/

Pew Research Center. (Nov. 20, 2018b). Where Americans find meaning in life. https://www.pewresearch.org/religion/2018/11/20/where-americans-find-meaning-in-life/

Pew Research Center (January, 2024). Religious 'nones' in America: Who They are and what they believe. https://www.pewresearch.org/religion/2024/01/24/religious-nones-in-america-who-they-are-and-what-they-believe/

Piedmont, R. L. (1999). Does spirituality represent the sixth factor of personality? Spiritual transcendence and the five-factor model. *Journal of Personality*, 67(6), 985–1013. https://doi.org/10.1111/1467-6494.00080

Pöhls, K. (2021). A complex simplicity: The relationship of religiosity and nonreligiosity to life satisfaction. *Journal for the Scientific Study of Religion*, 60(3), 465–81. https://doi.org/10.1111/jssr.12723

Pöhls, K., Schlösser, T., & Fetchenhauer, D. (2020). Non-religious identities and life satisfaction: Questioning the universality of a linear link between religiosity and well-being. *Journal of Happiness Studies*, 21(7), 2327–53. https://doi.org/10.1007/s10902-019-00175-x

Price, M. E., & Launay, J. (2018). Increased wellbeing from social interaction in a secular congregation. *Secularism and Nonreligion*, 7, 1–9. https://doi.org/10.5334/snr.102

Putnam, R. D., & Campbell, D. E. (2010). *American grace: How religion divides and unites us.* Simon & Schuster. https://psycnet.apa.org/record/2010-25800-000

Robbins, M., & Longden, G. (2024). Purpose in life: a comparison between communities of the non-religious and the religious. *Journal of Empirical Theology*, 37(2), 157–87. https://doi.org/10.1163/15709256-20240003

Ross, C. E. (1990). Religion and psychological distress. *Journal for the Scientific Study of Religion*, 29(2), 236–45. https://doi.org/10.2307/1387431

Rybarski, R., Bartczuk, R. P., Śliwak, J., & Zarzycka, B. (2023). Religiosity and death anxiety among cancer patients: the mediating role of religious comfort and struggle. *International Journal of Occupational Medicine and Environmental Health*, 36(4), 450–64. https://doi.org/10.13075/ijomeh.1896.02094

Sawyer, J. S., Brewster, M. E., & Ertl, M. M. (2021). Death anxiety and death acceptance in atheists and other nonbelievers. *Death Studies*, 45(6), 459–68. https://doi.org/10.1080/07481187.2019.1648339

Schnell, T. (2015). Dimensions of Secularity (DoS): An open inventory to measure facets of secular identities. *The International Journal for the Psychology of Religion*, 25(4), 272–92. https://doi.org/10.1080/10508619.2014.967541

Schnell, T., & Keenan, W. J. (2011). Meaning-making in an atheist world. *Archive for the Psychology of Religion*, 33(1), 55–78. https://doi.org/10.1163/157361211X564611

Schuurmans-Stekhoven, J. B. (2013). "As a shepherd divideth his sheep from the goats": Does the Daily Spiritual Experiences Scale encapsulate separable theistic and civility components? *Social Indicators Research*, 110, 131–46. http://doi.org/10.1007/s11205-011-9920-8

Schwartz, S. H., & Huismans, S. (1995). Value priorities and religiosity in four Western religions. *Social Psychology Quarterly*, 58(2), 88–107. https://doi.org/10.2307/2787148

Shinall Jr., M. C., Ehrenfeld, J. M., & Guillamondegui, O. D. (2014). Religiously affiliated intensive care unit patients receive more aggressive end-of-life care. *Journal of Surgical Research*, 190(2), 623–27. https://doi.org/10.1016/j.jss.2014.05.074

Shor, E., & Roelfs, D. J. (2013). The longevity effects of religious and nonreligious participation: A meta-analysis and meta-regression. *Journal for the Scientific Study of Religion*, 52(1), 120–45. http://doi.org/10.1111/jssr.12006

Smith, J. M. (2011). Becoming an atheist in America: Constructing identity and meaning from the rejection of theism. *Sociology of Religion*, 72(2), 215–37. http://doi.org/10.1093/socrel/srq082

Smith, J. M. (2017). Communal secularity: Congregational work at the Sunday Assembly. In R. T. Cragun, C. Manning, & L. Fazzino (Eds.), *Organized Secularism* (pp. 151–70). De Gruyter Press.

Smith, T. B., McCullough, M. E., & Poll, J. (2003). Religiousness and depression: Evidence for a main effect and the moderating influence of stressful life events. *Psychological Bulletin*, 129(4), 614–36. https://doi.org/10.1037/0033-2909.129.4.614

Speed, D., Coleman III, T. J., & Langston, J. (2018). What do you mean, "What does it all mean?" Atheism, nonreligion, and life meaning. *Sage Open*, 8(1). https://doi.org/10.1177/2158244017754238

Speed, D., & Fowler, K. (2021). One size doesn't fit all: Religious/spiritual identities moderate salutary effects of religion. *Mental Health, Religion & Culture*, 24(2), 111–27. https://doi.org/10.1080/13674676.2020.1863934

Speed, D., & Lamont, A. (2021). (Life) satisfaction guaranteed? Subjective well-being attenuates religious attendance–life satisfaction association. *Psychology of Religion and Spirituality*, 15(4), 471–79. https://doi.org/10.1037/rel0000443

Spitzenstätter, D., & Schnell, T. (2020). The existential dimension of the pandemic: Death attitudes, personal worldview, and coronavirus anxiety. *Death Studies*, 46(5), 1031–41. https://doi.org/10.1080/07481187.2020.1848944

Spitzenstätter, D., & Schnell, T. (2023). The uncertain certainty: A mixed methods exploration of personal meanings of death and preliminary insights into their relationship with worldview. *OMEGA-Journal of Death and Dying*, 00302228231157135. Advance online publication. https://doi.org/10.1177/00302228231157135

Stavrova, O. (2015). Religion, self-rated health, and mortality: Whether religiosity delays death depends on the cultural context. *Social Psychological and Personality Science*, 6(8), 911–22. http://doi.org/10.1177/1948550615593149

Stavrova, O., Fetchenhauer, D., & Schlösser, T. (2013). Why are religious people happy? The effect of the social norm of religiosity across countries. *Social Science Research*, 42(1), 90–105. http://doi.org/10.1016/j.ssresearch.2012.07.002

Tonigan, J. S., Miller, W. R., & Schermer, C. (2002). Atheists, agnostics and Alcoholics Anonymous. *Journal of Studies on Alcohol and Drugs*, 63(5), 534–41. http://doi.org/10.15288/jsa.2002.63.534

Vail III, K. E., Soenke, M., Waggoner, B., & Mavropoulou, I. (2020). Natural, but not supernatural, literal immortality affirmation attenuates mortality salience effects on worldview defense in atheists. *Personality and Social Psychology Bulletin*, 46(2), 312–26. https://doi.org/10.1177/0146167219855051

van Mulukom, V., Turpin, H., Haimila, R., Purzycki, B. G., Bendixen, T., Kundtová Klocová, E., Řezníček, D., Coleman, T. J. III, Sevinç, K., Maraldi, E., Schjoedt, U., Rutjens, B. T., & Farias, M. (2023). What do nonreligious nonbelievers believe in? Secular worldviews around the world. *Psychology of Religion and Spirituality*, 15(1), 143–56. https://doi.org/10.1037/rel0000480

Vie, L. L., Scheier, L. M., Lester, P. B., & Seligman, M. E. (2016). Initial validation of the US Army global assessment tool. *Military Psychology*, 28(6), 468–87. http://doi.org/10.1037/mil0000141

Weber, S. R., Pargament, K. I., Kunik, M. E., Lomax, James W., II, & Stanley, M. A. (2012). Psychological distress among religious nonbelievers: A systematic review. *Journal of Religion and Health*, 51(1), 72–86. https://doi.org/10.1007/s10943-011-9541-1

Yalom, I. D. (1980). *Existential psychotherapy*. Basic Books.

Yilmaz, O. (2021). Cognitive styles and religion. *Current Opinion in Psychology*, 40, 150–54. https://doi.org/10.1016/j.copsyc.2020.09.014

Zimmerman, K. J., Smith, J. M., Simonson, K., & Myers, W. B. (2015). Familial relationship outcomes of coming out as an atheist. *Secularism and Nonreligion*, 4, 4–4. https://doi.org/10.5334/snr.aw

Part II

Applications

6

Race, Resistance, and Rejecting Religion

What Draws People of Color to Nonbelief in the United States?

Simon Howard and Alex Borgella

Chapter Outline

"If you're a Black Christian, you have a real short memory."—Chris Rock

Christianity has played a multifaceted and often contradictory role in the history of racism in the United States. Although this history has been marked with many moments of profound moral clarity (e.g., White Christian abolitionists denouncing slavery as a sin and against Christian ideals; Finney 1835; Oshatz, 2011), there have also been many moments of significant moral failings, particularly concerning conceptions of (and commentary on) the humanity of Black, Indigenous, and people of color (BIPOC). From the period of colonization through the era of chattel slavery to contemporary manifestations of racial prejudice and discrimination, Christianity has been used as a tool for oppression and justification of the inhumane treatment of BIPOC (e.g., Cone, 2011; Lum, 2022).

Whether as a consequence of experiencing religious justification for oppression (directly or vicariously), gaining an understanding of the historical trauma associated with religious oppression of one's own racial or ethnic group (e.g., Heart & Horse, 2007; Kirmayer et al., 2014), or another set of reasons altogether, BIPOC in the United States often have unique catalysts for their nonbelief. Likewise, BIPOC from religious backgrounds may also face unique challenges relative to their White counterparts in navigating the transition to nonbelief (e.g., Abbott et al., 2020a). This chapter aims to shed light on these experiences by summarizing historical and contemporary connections between White supremacy[1] and Christianity in the United States, exploring the impact of these connections on prejudice and discrimination toward various minority racial and ethnic groups, identifying factors that draws BIPOC to nonbelief and challenges faced by BIPOC nonbelievers,[2] and providing both suggestions and resources for mental health activism and clinical practice with nonbelievers of color.

The Historical Impact of Religious-Based Racism on BIPOC in the United States

Native Americans and Alaska Natives

The arrival of European settlers in the Americas was driven by a combination of economic ambitions and religious motivations. Christianity, particularly in its Catholic and Protestant forms, was instrumental in the colonization process (e.g., Heart & Horse, 2007). European colonizers, believing in their divine mandate to spread Christianity, often viewed Indigenous peoples as heathens in need of salvation (Lum, 2022; Martin & Nicholas, 2010). This perspective justified the brutal conquest and subjugation of Native American populations. The *Doctrine of Discovery*, a principle originating from papal bulls (a type of public decree, letters patent, or charter issued by a pope of the Catholic Church) issued in the fifteenth century, played a critical role in legitimizing European claims to the New World (Greenburg, 2016; Miller, 2019). This doctrine asserted that lands not inhabited by Christians were available for discovery, exploitation, and conversion. Consequently, the forced conversion of Native Americans was often accompanied by violence, displacement, and cultural erasure. Missionary efforts, while framed as "saving" souls, frequently disregarded the autonomy and humanity of Indigenous peoples, reinforcing ideological

[1]This term refers to a political, economic, and cultural system in which Whites overwhelmingly control power and material resources. Conscious and unconscious ideas of White superiority and entitlement are widespread, and relations of White dominance and non-White subordination are daily reenacted across a broad array of institutions and social settings (Ansley, 1989, p. 1024).

[2]Throughout this chapter, we refer to those without religious affiliations in several ways, including "those without religious affiliations," "the religiously unaffiliated," "nonbelievers," and "religious nones." We note there are occasionally subtle but often philosophically meaningful differences between the content represented by each of these labels, but we believe they are practically similar enough to warrant their interchangeable use in the present context.

White supremacy (i.e., racial hierarchy that deemed White Europeans superior to any other people; Lum, 2022).

Over the centuries, many Native Americans have challenged Christian beliefs and the idea of Jesus, not only due to the historical brutality inflicted upon them by White Europeans but also as part of a broader struggle for cultural survival and self-determination (Heise, 2017; Rollings, 2002). They often resisted conversion efforts, recognizing the imposition of Christianity as part of a broader strategy of colonization and control. For example, the Pueblo Revolt of 1680, led by the Tewa Pueblo leader from the Ohkay Owingeh (San Juan Pueblo) Po'pay, is one of the most notable instances of Native American resistance to Christianization. The Pueblo people of present-day New Mexico revolted against Spanish colonizers, destroying churches and driving the Spanish out of their territory for over a decade (Knaut, 2015; Ortiz, 2009). This revolt was fueled by a desire to reclaim Indigenous religious practices that had been suppressed by the Spanish mission system. Other forms of resistance included the syncretism of Indigenous and Christian practices, where Native Americans adopted certain elements of Christianity while maintaining core aspects of their traditional beliefs (Madsen, 1967; Martin & Nicholas, 2010; Lum 2022). This blending of religious traditions allowed Indigenous communities to navigate the pressures of colonization while preserving their cultural identity. The brutality inflicted upon Native Americans by White Europeans in the name of Christianity has led many Indigenous people to critique Christian theology and the figure of Jesus. These critiques often focus on the hypocrisy and contradictions inherent in the colonizers' use of Christian doctrine to justify violence and oppression (Heise, 2017; Lum, 2022).

Latine/Hispanic Americans

Similar to their Indigenous counterparts, the roots of anti-Latine racism intertwined with Christianity can be traced back to the period of Spanish colonization and the subsequent expansion of the United States (Fredrickson, 2016; Pindi & De La Garza, 2018). The Spanish colonizers, driven by a mission to spread Catholicism, often justified their conquest and subjugation of Indigenous peoples in Latin America under the guise of religious conversion. This legacy of religious imperialism laid the groundwork for future racial and cultural discrimination. In the nineteenth century, as the United States expanded westward, the annexation of territories with significant Latine populations, such as Texas, California, and New Mexico, brought Latines into direct contact with a predominantly Protestant Anglo-American society. The Treaty of Guadalupe Hidalgo in 1848, which ended the Mexican American War, promised to protect the rights of Mexican citizens in the newly acquired territories (Miguel & Valencia, 1998). However, these promises were often ignored, and Latines faced discrimination and marginalization. The Protestant White American settlers often viewed Catholicism, the dominant religion among Latines, with suspicion and disdain, further exacerbating racial and cultural tensions (Griswold del Castillo, 1998).

Racism directed toward Latines also manifests contemporarily as well. As mentioned above, Latine culture is deeply intertwined with Catholicism, and as such often faces marginalization within the broader Christian landscape of the United States (Jenkins, 2003). Protestant Christianity, particularly Evangelicalism, has been dominant in shaping American religious identity. This dominance has sometimes led to the marginalization of Latine religious practices and traditions, which are viewed as "other" or "lesser" (Fitzgerald, 2017). Such cultural marginalization reinforces stereotypes and undermines the legitimacy of Latine religious and cultural expressions. Additionally, Christian rhetoric has frequently been employed in debates over immigration, often to the detriment of Latine communities (O'Leary, 2016). Certain segments of the Christian population, particularly within conservative circles, have supported restrictive immigration policies and used Christian language to justify these positions (Harris & Steiner, 2018; O'Leary, 2016; Weidinger, 2017). For example, appeals to "law and order" and the protection of "American values" are sometimes couched in Christian terms, implicitly or explicitly targeting Latine immigrants as threats to the nation's moral and social fabric (Harris & Steiner, 2018).

Black/African Americans

The roots of racism against Black Americans within the context of Christianity can be linked to the colonial era and the institution of slavery (Amponsah, 2013; Lum, 2022). Again, driven by economic interests and a belief in their racial superiority, White European settlers enslaved millions of Africans, forcibly bringing them to the Americas. Christianity played a significant role in justifying this brutal system. Slaveholders and pro-slavery theologians often invoked the Bible to legitimize slavery, selectively citing passages that appeared to endorse the practice (Blum & Harvey, 2012; Lum, 2022). For example, *The Curse of Ham*, a story from the Book of Genesis, was frequently used to suggest that Black people were divinely ordained to be servants (Fredrickson, 2016; Park, 2021). Additionally, New Testament verses such as Ephesians 6:5–9 that explicitly instructed "slaves to obey your earthly masters with respect and fear, and with sincerity of heart, just as you would obey Christ" were used to support the institution of slavery (Fredrickson, 2016). Within this framework, the Christianity practiced by slaveholders dehumanized Black people, depicting them as inferior and destined for servitude (Amponsah, 2013; Lum, 2022). This religious justification for slavery reinforced and perpetuated racist attitudes, embedding them deeply in American society.

Recent research suggests the legacy of these religiously informed negative attitudes toward Black and African Americans is still felt today, often in subtle ways. For example, Christian imagery itself has been demonstrated to be a source of anti-Black racism (Howard & Sommers, 2015; Howard & Sommers, 2019; Howard et al., 2022; Roberts et al., 2022). During the Renaissance, European artists like Leonardo da Vinci and Michelangelo created iconic images of biblical figures that reflected their own racial and cultural context (Blum & Harvey, 2012). These images, characterized by European features and fair skin, became the standard representation of Christian figures, and when European colonizers brought Christianity to the Americas, they also brought these visual representations. Historically and currently, in the United States and far too many other countries to list, depictions of both Jesus and God as White are ubiquitous (Blum & Harvey, 2012). These portrayals are deeply embedded in the cultural and religious landscape in the United States, and they have far-reaching implications for racial attitudes and the perpetuation and maintenance of anti-Black racism and ideological White supremacy (Howard & Sommers, 2017, 2019; Howard et al., 2023; Roberts et al., 2022).

The colonizers' belief in their racial superiority was bolstered by religious imagery that depicted sacred figures in their own likeness. This fusion of racial and religious identity laid the groundwork for a cultural narrative that equated Whiteness with divinity and moral superiority (Blum & Harvey, 2012). White portrayals of Jesus and God not only reinforce ideological White supremacy explicitly, but can also reinforce implicit biases (i.e., unconscious attitudes and stereotypes) among people as well (Howard & Sommers, 2017, 2019). When individuals are constantly exposed to religious imagery that aligns Godliness with Whiteness, it can strengthen unconscious associations between superiority and White people and inferiority of non-Whites.

Asian Americans/Pacific Islanders

The arrival of Chinese immigrants during the California Gold Rush in the mid-nineteenth century marked the beginning of significant Asian immigration to the United States. Many Chinese immigrants faced severe discrimination and violence, justified by the dominant Christian culture's perception of them as "heathens" and "pagans" (Lum, 2022). Christian missionaries, while sometimes offering aid and education to Chinese communities, often reinforced cultural superiority by aiming to convert them to Christianity, viewing their own religion as inherently superior (Yang, 1998). The 1882 Chinese Exclusion Act, the first significant law restricting immigration into the United States, was supported by many Christian leaders who framed the Chinese as morally and spiritually inferior (Calavita, 2000). This legislation was rooted in a broader cultural context where Christianity was used to define and maintain racial hierarchies.

The internment of Japanese Americans during World War II is another example of how Christian influences intersected with racial policies. After the attack on Pearl Harbor, over 120,000 Japanese Americans were forcibly relocated to internment camps. This action was supported by a significant portion of the American public, including many Christian leaders who saw it as a necessary measure for national security (Goldstone, 2023). Christian rhetoric was used to justify the internment, portraying Japanese Americans as potential threats to the Christian nation. Reverend Gerald L. K. Smith, a prominent Christian nationalist, explicitly linked national security with the preservation of a Christian America, reinforcing the racialization of Japanese Americans as "other" and inherently untrustworthy.

In the post–World War II era, the "model minority" myth emerged, casting Asian Americans as a group that, through hard work and adherence to American (often implicitly Christian) values, had achieved success (Chou & Feagin, 2015). While this stereotype appears positive, it has been used to uphold White supremacy by creating a racial wedge between Asian Americans and other minority groups, particularly Black

Americans (Shu, 2024; Yi et al., 2020). Christian organizations and leaders have sometimes propagated this myth, celebrating the perceived success of Asian Americans as proof of the benefits of a Protestant work ethic and moral lifestyle. This narrative ignores the diversity and struggles within Asian American communities and is used to undermine the demands for racial justice by other marginalized groups.

The Vietnam War and the subsequent influx of Southeast Asian refugees in the 1970s and 1980s brought another wave of Asian immigrants to the United States. Many Christian organizations were involved in resettling these refugees, offering crucial support and services (Horstmann & Jung, 2015). However, this involvement was not without its complications. Christian groups often expected refugees to convert to Christianity as part of their assimilation process, viewing their conversion as a sign of successful integration into American society. This expectation placed additional pressure on refugees to conform to Christian norms and values, further marginalizing their cultural and religious identities. The implicit message was that acceptance into American society required abandoning their own traditions and embracing Christianity, reinforcing the notion of cultural and religious superiority.

In recent years, the COVID-19 pandemic has exacerbated anti-Asian racism, with Asian Americans facing increased violence and discrimination. Some Christian leaders and communities have responded with solidarity and support, condemning racism and advocating for justice. However, others have perpetuated harmful stereotypes and conspiracy theories, sometimes rooted in apocalyptic and nationalist interpretations of Christianity that cast China and Chinese people as enemies (Perry et al., 2021). For example, some evangelical leaders have linked the pandemic to divine punishment and framed it within a narrative of Christian nationalism that scapegoats Asian Americans (Perry et al., 2021). This rhetoric not only fuels racial animosity but also aligns with broader xenophobic and nationalist agendas.

The Current State of Nonbelief Among BIPOC in the United States

Categories and Correlates of Nonbelief

Various methods of categorizing people without any specific religious affiliation have existed for several decades, but more contemporary labels have emerged due to an increase in the number of nonreligious people generally, rising from 16 percent to 28 percent of US adults between 2007 and 2024 (DeRose, 2024; Pew Research Center, 2024). Three broad subgroups of nonbelievers are currently referenced in Pew Research survey data: *Atheists* (those who do not believe in a god or gods), *Agnostics* (those who believe it is impossible to know whether or not there is a god or gods), and a third category representing those who describe their religious affiliation as "nothing in particular" (*NPs*), with this lattermost group now comprising 63 percent of all those without religious affiliations (Pew Research

Center, 2021a). Collectively, these groups are referred to as "the religiously unaffiliated" or, more recently, simply as "Nones" (Pew Research Center, 2024).[3]

A significant amount of survey data published from Pew Research Center's *American Trends Panel* (Pew Research Center, 2024) have provided insight into the many reasons why the religiously unaffiliated are not attracted toward (or actively step away from) religion and religious institutions in the United States. First, conflating those who self-describe as "religiously unaffiliated" and those who self-describe as "nonbelievers" appears somewhat inappropriate. Indeed, 70 percent of Nones indicate they believe in "a higher power" of some sort (including about 13 percent who reference they believe in god "as described in the Bible"), 67 percent believe that humans possess both a physical body and a "soul" of some sort, and 63 percent indicate they believe there is "something spiritual" beyond the natural world (Pew Research Center, 2024). Additionally, the frequency these beliefs are mentioned depends on the subcategory of Nones being examined—for example, most NPs and Agnostics (83 percent and 67 percent respectively) say they believe in a "higher power" relative to only 22 percent of Atheists. Importantly, this belief in a higher power is much more common among religiously unaffiliated Blacks (90 percent) and Hispanics/Latines (81 percent) relative to Whites and Asians (64 percent respectively; Pew Research Center, 2024).

Though the religiously unaffiliated share some similar demographics as their religious counterparts, some notable exceptions exist in these data. For example, they tend to be younger, with 69 percent of nonbelievers under the age of fifty relative to only 53 percent of Christians in the United States (Pew Research Center, 2024). Many of the exceptions exist among Atheists and Agnostics specifically. For example, while there are relatively equal proportions of men and women among both religious (47 percent and 52 percent, respectively) and nonreligious groups (51 percent and 47 percent, respectively), Atheist and Agnostic men outnumber Atheist and Agnostic women three to one. Similarly, the religious and nonreligious share similar levels of education, with roughly equal proportions indicating they have high school diplomas (35 percent and 34 percent respectively), have completed some college (30 percent and 31 percent respectively), and have earned college diplomas (34 percent and 35 percent respectively). However, those who identify as Atheists or Agnostics are more likely to have graduated from college (each at 48 percent) than NPs (27 percent; Pew Research Center, 2024).

Racial Demographics of Nonbelievers

When examining the current racial demographics of the religiously unaffiliated, patterns are observed that may provide more insight into understanding racial disparities in nonbelief. Namely, although Whites comprise a majority (63 percent) of all those who identify as religiously unaffiliated in the United States, a larger proportion of Atheists (77 percent)

[3] We recognize there are also many unique subtypes of nonbelief within each of the subgroups listed here (e.g., *apatheism, ignosticism, secular humanism, naturalism*), but many of these either share features or core ideas that overlap between categories, with some even reflecting this overlap in their names (e.g., *agnostic atheism*).

or Agnostics (69 percent) are White relative to NPs (57 percent). This pattern is the exact opposite among BIPOC; for example, 17 percent and 9 percent of the religiously unaffiliated are Hispanic and Black respectively, but they are most likely to be Nones (19 percent and 12 percent respectively), relative to Atheists (9 percent and 2 percent respectively) or Agnostics (16 percent and 4 percent respectively; Pew Research Center, 2024).

Many theories have been offered to explain these and other potential racial disparities, specifically concentrating on why nonbelief is a predominantly White phenomenon. Historically, ideals associated with the Enlightenment (e.g., valuing scientific inquiry over other ways of knowing) have been more prevalent and accepted in European societies, and researchers have argued this backdrop has led to White populations adopting nonreligious identities at a higher rate (see Pigliucci, 2013 for a review). Research has also highlighted reasons why BIPOC remain mostly religiously affiliated, highlighting the ability of religious institutions to provide community, identity, stability, and unity, especially in locations and circumstances where members face prejudice and discrimination (Taylor et al., 2004).

Further, some have pointed to the role of religious institutions in providing support for (or otherwise being associated with) social and political movements promoting civil rights, social justice, racial equality, and other efforts affecting those from BIPOC communities (e.g., Bullivant & Ruse, 2013). For example, cultural associations between predominantly Black religious institutions and the ideals of the Civil Rights Movement helped its leaders craft, frame, and disseminate their messages.[4] The role of the Black church in helping organize newer social movements relating to racial inequality (e.g., Black Lives Matter) has been similar, although growing discontent with the church's views toward other policy issues among younger people (e.g., LGBTQ rights) has led to a significant decrease in its influence (Turner, 2021).

Given these trends, it is clear that those from racial minority groups could face familial, social, and other interpersonal repercussions (e.g., isolation) from becoming or remaining religiously unaffiliated. If this is the case, it is crucial to understand the reasons why BIPOC choose to abandon religious belief, the specific potential consequences they face for doing so, and how those consequences impact mental health and well-being.

What Draws BIPOC in the United States to Nonbelief

There are many common factors that lead people to nonbelief such as intellectual curiosity, reason, and inquiry (e.g., believing there is no reasonable evidence for the existence of a god or gods), contradictions in interpretations of holy texts and modern scientific understanding of natural phenomena (e.g., disagreements between biblical literalists and

[4] Some scholars have argued Black religious institutions' role in the Civil Rights Movement was not crucial to its ultimate success, but the vast majority agree progress would have slowed significantly without the financial, organizational, and social support they provided (see Calhoun-Brown, 2000 for a review).

geoscientists about the Earth's age, or the storied history of Christian denial of evolution in lieu of creationism; e.g., Downie et al., 2018; Braterman, 2021), philosophical arguments against specific attributes of god (e.g., theodicy), the gradual secularization of US society (outlined in the section above), or criticism and apoplexy toward religious institutions on moral grounds (e.g., Christianity and staunch views against abortion and homosexuality; e.g., Adamczyk, 2022). However, given the sociocultural and historical context of religion—particularly Christianity—in the United States, BIPOC have several other factors that may uniquely contribute to their decision to be nonbelievers compared to their White counterparts.

Keeping this context in mind, below we review the literature on why BIPOC may become drawn to nonbelief. Prior to this, it is important to note that neither BIPOC nor the individual racial and ethnic categories that make up this acronym are monolithic groups. Diverse experiences—both positive and negative—can lead every individual down a different path to reconsider, change, or abandon their religious affiliation. However, although each racial and ethnic group member's journey is unique, there are some commonalities in the factors that can contribute to BIPOC becoming nonbelievers, typically (though not exclusively) relating to shared experiences with stereotyping, prejudice, discrimination, and stigma.

Historical Trauma and Colonialism

The brutal history of colonization, forced conversion, and cultural genocide inflicted by European settlers under the banner of Christianity has left deep scars among BIPOC. As outlined briefly at the outset of this chapter, BIPOC throughout history have faced significant oppression and suffering, often justified (or at least exacerbated) by religious doctrines (Lum, 2022). Thus, for some, nonbelief can represent a form of resistance to a religious system that has been used to justify discrimination and inequality (Lackey, 2007). Many BIPOC nonbelievers, particularly Native, Latinc, and Black Americans, view the imposition of Christianity and the accompanying violence as a betrayal and a profound injustice. This historical trauma can lead to either skepticism or outright rejection of the religion associated with these events. They often probe the question, "Why would they, through their own volition, adopt the religion of their former colonizers and slave owners?" especially when their ancestors were practicing their own religions pre-European contact (Blum & Harvey, 2012).

The Epicurean Paradox

The Epicurean Paradox, also known as *The Problem of Evil*, poses a challenge to theistic beliefs by questioning how an all-powerful, all-knowing, and all-good deity can coexist with the existence of evil and suffering. It is often framed as follows: If God is omnipotent (all-powerful), He can prevent evil. If God is omniscient (all-knowing), He knows about evil. If God is omnibenevolent (all-good), He would want to prevent evil. From these premises, it follows that if an all-powerful, all-knowing, and all-good deity exists, evil should not exist; however, evil in the world still exists. The Epicurean Paradox, when applied to systemic racism, can highlight the perceived inadequacies of traditional theistic responses to suffering. For some BIPOC, this becomes particularly resonant when they confront persistent and systemic racial oppression (Harrison, 1917). Consequently, the perceived failure of a benevolent deity to intervene or address such profound suffering related to the historical marginalization and dehumanization of BIPOC, often in the name of Christianity, might lead to BIPOC questioning the existence or nature of such a deity.

Religion Is System Justifying

System Justification Theory (SJT) is a theory in social psychology that posits that people possess a motivated tendency to justify and defend existing social, economic, and political systems, even when those systems are unjust or put them at a disadvantage (for reviews see, Jost & van der Toorn, 2012; Jost et al. 2004; Osborne et al., 2019). System justifying beliefs are psychologically palliative for people, particularly those who have been historically disadvantaged and marginalized in society because it helps them avoid the psychological threat and anxiety produced by acknowledging that the systems they are embedded in are corrupt and/or oppressive (Jost et al., 2004; Osborne et al., 2019).

Behavioral scientists and some BIPOC nonbelievers argue that religion is system justifying and that one of its functions is to provide its adherents ideological justification for the existing social order (Jost et al., 2004; Harrison, 1917). For example, Hubert Harrison, a Black West Indian American writer, orator, educator, and political activist wrote, "Show me a population that is deeply religious, and I will show you a servile population, content with whips and chains, . . . content to eat the bread of sorrow and drink the waters of affliction" (Harrison, 1917, p. 44). Thus, instead of influencing individuals to rebel against oppressive systems (e.g., institutional White supremacy), religion can sometimes influence individuals to obey and preserve these systems (Jost et al., 2014). Thus, related to the question of theodicy (i.e., the vindication of divine goodness and providence in view of the existence of evil) and the Epicurean Paradox, one way to reduce the dissonance induced from these questions, is the afterlife (e.g., concepts of Heaven and Hell).

Ideas surrounding the afterlife reduce dissonance because injustices or wrongdoings on earth ultimately get settled. In other words, those who have engaged in horrendous acts (e.g., colonizing Indigenous Americans and enslaving Africans) will meet their judgment in the afterlife and those who have been virtuous and endured their suffering on earth will be compensated during the afterlife (Harrison, 1917). Thus, some Black nonbelievers argue that Christianity reinforces passivity. For example, Hubert Harrison argued that Christian doctrines emphasizing the virtues of suffering and forgiveness were sometimes used to encourage Black individuals to endure racial oppression within a system of White supremacy without seeking to dismantle said system. The idea of "turning the other cheek," from the Bible's Matthew 5:39, was used to discourage resistance and challenges to racial injustices (Wilson, 1988). As a result, some BIPOC turn to secular or humanistic philosophies that emphasize social responsibility, justice, and ethical living without reliance on religious explanations. For them, secularism and humanism can provide a coherent framework for addressing and combating racial injustice.

In sum, the journey of BIPOC nonbelievers is often intertwined with complex historical, cultural, and personal factors. The legacy of colonization and forced conversion, combined with individual experiences and reflections, shapes their religious or nonreligious identities. Understanding these reasons highlights the diversity of thought within BIPOC communities.

Challenges for Nonbelievers of Color

Racial Divisions Between BIPOC and White Nonbelief Communities

While the nonbeliever movement often emphasizes rationality, secularism, and skepticism, its members are not immune to the same stereotypes and systemic biases that affect people in other societal arenas. Racism within the nonbelief community is a significant and complex issue, reflecting broader societal problems of racial prejudice and discrimination. As highlighted earlier in this chapter, there is a significant lack of diversity within the nonbelief community (e.g., Scheitle et al., 2019; Pew Research Center, 2024). The majority of the nonbeliever community—and thus most of its most prominent figures and leaders—are White, which has the potential to marginalize the voices and experiences of BIPOC nonbelievers (Swann, 2020). Some BIPOC nonbelievers, like Greta Christina, suggest that the reason atheist, nonreligious, and humanist movements continue to be dominated by White men in America is because the movement itself has been subject to unconscious bias against diversity (Christina, 2009). Several prominent Black atheists have also highlighted the different agendas that White atheists have in comparison to Black atheists (and other POC; Hutchinson, 2014; Swann, 2020).

One of these Black atheists, Sikivu Hutchinson (2014), wrote an article in the *Washington Post* titled "Atheism Has a Big Race Problem That No One Is Talking About" in which several key differences between White atheists and Black atheists were discussed. She highlighted that on average, White atheists are very privileged in comparison to their Black counterparts and thus they often ignore issues concerning racial justice and equity. When issues related to racism and social justice are explicitly raised, Black atheists are often met with contempt or silenced (Swann, 2020). Hutchinson (2014) further argued that "ultimately, if people of color don't see atheists and humanists stepping up on issues that directly affect their communities, atheists proselytizing about the evils of organized religion will be dismissed as empty paternalism." The division on matters of racial and social justice is challenging for BIPOC nonbelievers because nonbeliever communities can be a source of refuge and social connection (Abbott et al., 2020b) and this division can become an obstacle that impedes that connection.

Social and Cultural Identity Threats

Research spanning across social, cognitive, counseling, health, and several other subdisciplines of psychological science overwhelmingly suggests that people who possess stigmatized social identities (e.g., racial minority group members) will appraise their environments—sometimes chronically—for threats to those identities (e.g., Steele et al., 2002, Purdie-Greenaway et al., 2008). The degree to which an individual anticipates receiving feedback about a stigmatized identity is commonly referred to as *stigma consciousness* (Pinel, 1999), and the degree to which any individual possesses this trait is closely linked to their experiences with prejudice and discrimination related to their stigmatized identity (e.g., Pinel, 2004). However, the average amount of prejudice one will anticipate receiving largely depends on characteristics of the stigmatized identity involved, namely its overall centrality (i.e., its appraised importance in one's life) and whether or not it is made salient in the present context (Quinn & Chaudoir, 2009; Quinn & Earnshaw, 2013).

One of the most common identity threats likely faced by BIPOC nonbelievers is identity denial, a threat that occurs when members of a group are not prototypical and are perceived as being weakly identified (or not at all identified) with the ingroup (e.g., Huynh, 2013). Due to atheism and nonbelief being less common among BIPOC than White individuals in the United States (e.g., Scheitle et al., 2019; Pew Research Center, 2024), atheism is sometimes explicitly associated with White people within BIPOC communities (i.e., atheism is considered to be a "White phenomenon"; Abbott et al., 2020a; Swann, 2020; Howard et al., 2022). Consequently, BIPOC who identify as atheists or as nonbelievers may be viewed as "aligning" themselves with the White community, leading to stigmatization within their own communities. Specifically, when a BIPOC individual identifies as an atheist or nonbeliever, their racial or cultural identity may be questioned and/or outright denied (Abbott et al., 2020a; Howard et al., 2021; Swann, 2020), and they could be subjected to accusations that they are "turning their back" on their culture and race (Abbott et al., 2020a; Swann, 2020). Further, these targets of identity threat often self-report experiences of exclusion, lacking a sense of belonging, loneliness, lower life satisfaction, higher levels of stress and depressive symptoms, and worse overall physical health (e.g., Albuja et al., 2019; Slepian & Jacoby-Senghor, 2021).

Coping with a Concealable Stigmatized Identity

In any social context, the salience of one's stigmatized identity depends largely on whether it is visible and/or readily detectable (e.g., race, gender, visible physical deformities, or weight status) or invisible and/or concealable (e.g., sexual orientation, mental illness and neurodivergence, having had an abortion, or having coverable tattoos). Research on this latter group—those with *concealable stigmatized identities* (CSIs)—has documented unique mental health- and physical health-related outcomes involved with balancing the decision to disclose these identities (e.g., chronic stress and quality of life perceptions; Quinn et al., 2017). The decision to not disclose a CSI can be a self-protective strategy adopted to avoid negative experiences associated with identity threats (e.g., identity denial or exclusion by ingroup members; e.g., Chaudoir & Fisher, 2010). For example, some research has reported improvements in mood and self-esteem when those with CSIs relating to sexual orientation, socioeconomic status, or eating disorders are supported by similar ingroup members (Frable et. al., 1998). Similarly, those with multiple sclerosis (a sometimes-concealable chronic illness) who decide to not disclose their illness show decreases in the amount of prejudice and discrimination they report experiencing (though this effect appears to be limited to those in earlier stages of the illness in which mobility is less affected; Cook et al., 2017).

In spite of its purported benefits, concealment can also have deleterious effects on both mental and physical health (see Camacho et al., 2020, for a review). For example, research has shown that gay and bisexual men's decisions to conceal their sexual orientations leads to increased social stress and diminished psychological well-being (Scrimshaw et al., 2013; Bry et al., 2017), with some work calling into question whether this concealment helps with prejudice reduction at all (e.g., Goh et al., 2019). Further, some researchers note that any purported benefits of ingroup support among those with CSIs is diminished simply because these groups are less likely to form due to the concealable nature of the stigma itself (e.g., Crocker & Major, 1989; Camacho et al., 2020).

To avoid the stigma associated with nonbelief within BIPOC communities, some may simply choose to not disclose their identity as atheists or otherwise religiously unaffiliated. Recent psychological evidence has supported this claim, both about nonbelievers in general and about BIPOC nonbelievers specifically. For example, quantitative analyses of atheists in the United States suggest strong associations between atheists' identity centrality, their levels of self-reported physical and psychological well-being, and their "outness" as nonreligious (Abbott & Mollen, 2018). Further, in an investigation on atheists living in the Southern United States (a region encompassing the "Bible Belt," one of the most religious areas of the United States), Mackey et al. (2020) manipulated perceived threats to atheists' identities, finding those who experience these threats are significantly more likely to conceal their identities (Mackey et al., 2020). These findings are supplemented by qualitative analyses from accounts of BIPOC atheists specifically (e.g., Abbott et al., 2020a; Swann, 2020), many of whom echo the aforementioned reasons behind the identity concealment outlined above.

The Weight of Multiple Stigmatized Identities

The intersection of race and nonbelief often creates a unique set of challenges for BIPOC nonbelievers in the US. Members of this group simultaneously hold multiple stigmatized identities, wherein the social stigmas associated with both their racial and nonreligious identities intersect and either (1) increase the severity of their stigma consciousness and typical experiences with discrimination or, perhaps worse, (2) compound, resulting in novel experiences of stigma and discrimination all together (i.e., intersectionality; Crenshaw 1989). Additionally, some work suggests that these effects take an even greater toll on both physical and mental health when CSIs are actively concealed alongside either visible stigmatized identities or other CSIs (Reinka et al., 2020). Intersectionality, with its focus on understanding how race and racism intersect with other forms of social stratification (e.g., class, gender, sexual orientation, and religion), provides a robust framework for analyzing these experiences.

For example, Black American women make up the most religious demographic in the United States, and thus when Black women identify as nonbelievers, they are likely to be excluded from some cultural social circles (Abbott et al., 2020b; Miller, 2013). Although Black men and women both run the risk of negatively impacting their social status and reputation when openly expressing their atheism, Black women are more likely to become estranged from their religious families (Miller, 2013). In the Black community there are often expectations for Black women to be active in the church and to socialize their children in the church, thus when Black women openly express their nonbelief it can be perceived as turning away from their duties, their culture, and the religious reproduction of future generations (Abbott et al., 2020a; Hutchinson, 2014; Miller 2013). Some of these same concerns are shared across women in the Latine community as well (Abbott et al., 2020b), however White women believers do not often face those same challenges.

LGBTQ BIPOC nonbelievers also face unique challenges resulting in novel experiences of prejudice. Being both nonbelieving and a member of the LGBTQ community in BIPOC communities can be perceived as being doubly negative and immoral. For example, acceptance of members of the LGBTQ community is low and in many Black churches some openly oppose homosexuality. As mentioned earlier, atheism is sometimes seen as synonymous with existing without a moral barometer (Swann, 2020); thus, BIPOC LGBTQ nonbelievers may have a particularly difficult time navigating spaces in which they feel that they do not belong with little social support (Swann, 2020).

Lack of Social Support

A common challenge repeatedly mentioned among BIPOC nonbelievers is their loss of social support either because they are not involved in religious communities or because they are rejected by their BIPOC peers (Abbott et al., 2020; Christina, 2014; Swann, 2020). Because in some BIPOC communities religion is a centerpiece for community activities and socializing, BIPOC nonbelievers who do not participate in these activities or community building run the risk of losing social support, which can be related to negative mental health outcomes (Abbott et al., 2020; Swann, 2020). Additionally, BIPOC members are rejected by their family members and their peers for their nonbelief (Abbott et al., 2020). As mentioned above, BIPOC may also experience identity denial, which is related to experiences of exclusion, lacking a sense of belonging, loneliness, lower life satisfaction, higher levels of stress and depressive symptoms, and worse overall physical health (e.g., Albuja et al., 2019; Slepian & Jacoby-Senghor, 2021).

Recommendations for Mental Health Practitioners Working with Nonbelieving BIPOC

Working with BIPOC clients who are nonbelievers involves a nuanced understanding of their unique experiences and perspectives, much of what has been detailed above. Below, we have compiled some recommendations, strategies, and helpful resources for clinicians who find themselves interacting with representatives of this population followed by a table of additional related tools and resources:

1 **Cultural Humility:**
   a **Educate Yourself:** Learn about the cultural backgrounds and experiences of your clients. Understanding their cultural context can help you provide more relevant and respectful care.
   b **Avoid Assumptions:** Do not assume that those who identify as atheist (or any other belief system) are homogeneous. As we articulate in this chapter, there may be similarities in nonbelief across racial and ethnic groups, but it is paramount to remember that each person's experience is shaped by their unique cultural, social, and personal context.

2 **Respect for Atheism:**
   c **Validate Their Beliefs:** Respect and validate your clients' atheism as a legitimate worldview. Avoid making assumptions that they need religious or spiritual guidance.
   d **Avoid Religious Bias:** Ensure that your approach does not inadvertently reflect religious bias. Be mindful of your own beliefs and how they might influence your interactions.

3 **Cultural Sensitivity:**
   e **Acknowledge Diversity:** Recognize the intersectionality of race, ethnicity, gender, class, sexual orientation, and atheism. Each client's identities can influence their experiences and perspectives.
   f **Use Culturally Relevant Approaches:** Incorporate culturally sensitive practices and interventions that are respectful of their cultural identity *and* atheistic beliefs.

4 **Build Trust and Rapport:**
   g **Listen Actively:** Allow clients to share their experiences and perspectives without interruption or judgment. Active listening helps build a strong therapeutic alliance.

h **Show Empathy:** Demonstrate understanding and empathy for the unique challenges they might face, including potential discrimination or marginalization.

5 **Addressing Discrimination:**

i **Recognize Systemic Issues:** Increase your awareness of the potential systemic and structural issues related to both atheism and racial/ethnic identity (as well as other stigmatized social identities), including how those from these groups might experience discrimination or bias.

j **Provide Support:** Offer support in navigating challenges related to clients' identities, including helping them develop coping strategies for dealing with discrimination or stigma.

6 **Collaborative Approach:**

k **Empower Clients:** Involve clients in setting goals and creating treatment plans that align with their values and preferences.

l **Cultural Adaptation:** Be open to adapting therapeutic approaches to better fit their cultural context and individual needs.

7 **Continual Learning:**

m **Seek Feedback:** Regularly ask for feedback from your clients about how well you're meeting their needs and if there are areas where you could improve.

n **Ongoing Education:** Engage in continuous learning about cultural competence and diversity to better serve clients from various backgrounds.

8 **Self-reflection:**

o **Examine Your own Biases:** Reflect on your own beliefs and biases. Understand how they might affect your therapeutic practice and work actively to mitigate any negative impacts.

p **Technical Self-evaluation:** Approach each client as an individual with a unique story. Be open to learning from them and adapting your approach as needed.

By applying these strategies, clinicians can provide more effective and respectful care to atheists of color, honoring both their nonreligious beliefs and their cultural identities.

Conclusion: The Strength and Utility of Religious Nonbelief Among BIPOC

Throughout this chapter, we have argued that the experiences of BIPOC in the United States reveal complex personal and cultural motivations that draw them toward nonbelief, often reflecting a rejection of religious doctrines that have historically marginalized their communities. The intersection of race and nonbelief challenges conventional narratives and highlights the diversity within nonbelief, emphasizing that BIPOC atheists are not a monolithic group, but individuals with varied and nuanced reasons for their secular

Table 6.1 Tools/Resources to Support Mental Health Practitioners Working with Nonbelieving BIPOC

Recommendation	Tool/Resource
Cultural Humility	**Book:** *Cultural Humility: Engaging Diverse Identities in Therapy* (This book describes how therapists can combine multicultural theory with their own lived experience to meaningfully engage clients in issues of culture. See Hook et al., 2025.) **Podcast:** *Cultural Humility Podcast* by Dr. Miguel Gallardo available on his personal website https://drgallardo.com/, Spotify, and Apple Podcasts.
Respect for Atheism	**Podcast:** *The Atheist Experience* is a long-running podcast that features discussions on atheism, secularism, and the intersection of religion and society, with the purpose of presenting a diverse perspective on atheism and opening the discussion of mutual respect and open-mindedness. It can be found on most platforms, including YouTube, Spotify, Apple Podcasts, Google Podcasts, etc.
Cultural Sensitivity	**Book:** *Addressing Cultural Complexities in Counseling and Clinical Practice: An Intersectional Approach* (This book by Pamela B. Hays proposes a framework for cultural sensitivity to address and validate multiple different identities, including diverse religious and spiritual groups. See Hays, 2022). **Podcast:** *What About Us?* by Afsana Faheem and Dr. Kate Cooper, available on Apple Podcasts and Spotify For further information on cultural sensitivity, visit this link: https://www.secularsurvey.org/black-nonreligious-americans
Build Trust and Rapport	**Book:** *Empathic Counseling: Building Skills to Empower Change* (This book by Slattery and Park [2020] published by the American Psychological Association outlines a framework for empathic therapeutic and counseling approaches, with an emphasis on diverse clientele.) **Podcast:** *Talk Less, Listen More* by Sara Walker. This particular segment features guest Marisa Schwartz, senior regional medical director for St. Luke's University Health Network, to discuss the importance of active listening and impact on patient care outcomes. Find episode here: https://cxleaderpodcast.com/talk-less-listen-more/ See the NIH's guidelines and recommendations for active listening, a cornerstone of building trust and rapport, here: https://www.ncbi.nlm.nih.gov/books/NBK442015/
Addressing Discrimination	**Book:** *Eliminating Race-Based Mental Health Disparities: Promoting Equity and Culturally Responsive Care Across Settings* by Monica T. Williams, Daniel C. Rosen, Johnathan W. Kanter, and Patricia Arredondo (2019). This book explores the urgent problem of race inequalities and biases that prevent people of color from seeking, or receiving poor, mental health treatment. **Podcast:** *The Praxis* by Edwin Lindo, JD aims to directly address and explore effects of racism and other forms of marginalization so that we can collectively achieve health justice. It can be found on Spotify and Apple Podcasts.

Table 6.1 (continued)

Recommendation	Tool/Resource
Collaborative Approach	**Book:** *The Therapist's Ultimate Solution Book: Essential Strategies, Tips and Tools to Empower Your Clients* (This book by Judith Belmont includes concrete examples, exercises, and approaches that can be implemented in clinical spaces to help clients feel empowered and understood. See Belmont, 2015). **Podcast:** *Talk Less, Listen More* by Sara Walker. This particular segment features guest Marisa Schwartz, senior regional medical director for St. Luke's University Health Network, to discuss the importance of active listening and impact on patient care outcomes. Find episode here: https://cxleaderpodcast.com/talk-less-listen-more/
Continual Learning	**Book:** *Better Patient Feedback, Better Healthcare* by Dr. Taher Mahmud focuses on the newfound importance of patient feedback in alignment with the improvement of health care services. (See Mahmud, 2012). **Podcast:** *Therapy Chat: Decolonizing Mental Health* with Dr. Shawna Murray-Browne (ep. 433)—this specific episode focuses on counseling and collective religious and racial trauma. It can be accessed through Apple Podcasts.
Self-Reflection	**Book:** *Counseling the Culturally Diverse: Theory and Practice* by Derald Wing Sue, David Sue, Helen A. Neville, and Laura Smith [2021] examines the concept of "cultural humility," roles of white allies in social justice counseling, and the concept of "minority stress" and its implications in work with minority populations. **Podcast:** *Clinical Conversations*, "Cognitive Bias and Clinical Decision Making" by Dr. Anda Bulgara (interviews Dr. Eoin O'Sullivan about cognitive bias and how it impacts on clinical decision making). Spotify Link: https://open.spotify.com/episode/0KFJDJ8SrXkXJIL7goyKIV?si=Bp3q4HdHQkSF2WolKeRayw&nd=1&dlsi=efe4b82c8e6d46dd

stances. Despite these nuances, it seems BIPOC nonbelievers frequently encounter a dual burden: like White nonbelievers, they must cope with the alienation and prejudice associated with secularism in a predominantly religious society, but they must do this while simultaneously grappling with racial discrimination from outgroup members *and* culturally bound religious expectations from ingroup members.

These challenges illuminate the ways in which religious and racial identities intertwine, influencing both personal experiences and public perceptions. The unique struggles of BIPOC atheists—from managing familial and community expectations to addressing systemic biases within secular spaces—underscore the need for a broader understanding of atheism that acknowledges and respects these intersections of identity. It is crucial to recognize and address these specific barriers to foster environments that genuinely support and embrace diverse secular identities. As we move forward, a deeper engagement with the experiences of BIPOC atheists can facilitate more equitable discourse and policies, ultimately contributing to a richer, more inclusive dialogue about belief and identity. Acknowledging and addressing these intersectional challenges not only enriches the conversation about nonbelief but also promotes broader social justice goals and understanding.

While we have acknowledged many challenges faced by nonreligious BIPOC in this paper, it is important to not misconstrue this identity as existing in a pure deficiency model. Though not the explicit focus of this chapter, it would be inappropriate to not include the numerous documented potential benefits and strengths of religious nonbelief among members of racial minority group members, including a greater sense of one's own identity and agency (e.g., Small & Bowman, 2012; Brewster et al., 2020; Abbott & Anaya, 2022), improvements in critical thinking (e.g., higher rates of system II vs. system I processing; Gervais & Norenzayan, 2012), buffers against threats to psychological well-being (e.g., Abbott et al., 2020b), an improved sense of psychological resilience (e.g., Doane & Elliot, 2015; Abbott et al., 2020b), and establishing or joining new communities of similar-minded people with similar identities (e.g., Brewster et al., 2020; Van Mulukom et al., 2023). Though nonbelievers who identify as BIPOC may face unique challenges relative to nonbelievers from majority racial groups, overcoming those challenges is certainly aided—or at least not hindered—by these benefits.

References

Abbott, D., & Mollen, D. (2018). Atheism as a concealable stigmatized identity: Outness, anticipated stigma, and well-being. *The Counseling Psychologist* 46(6), 685–707. https://doi.org/10.1177/0011000018792669

Abbott, D. M., & Anaya, E. J. (2022). "Breaking free": A grounded theory study of atheist women in the United States. *Psychology of Women Quarterly*, 46(4), 136–55. https://doi.org/10.1177/03616843221115338

Abbott, D. M., Mollen, D., Mercier, C., Anaya, E. J., & Rukus, V. A. (2020a). "Isn't atheism a White thing?": Centering the voices of atheists of color. *Journal of Counseling Psychology*, 67(3), 275–87. https://doi.org/10.1037/cou0000399

Abbott, D. M., Ternes, M., Mercier, C., & Monceaux, C. (2020b). Anti-atheist discrimination, outness, and psychological distress among atheists of colour. *Mental Health, Religion & Culture*, 23(10), 874–87. https://doi.org/10.1080/13674676.2020.1858771

Adamczyk, A. (2022). Religion as a micro and macro property: Investigating the multilevel relationship between religion and abortion attitudes across the globe. *European Sociological Review*, 38(5), 816–31. https://doi.org/10.1093/esr/jcac017

Albuja, A. F., Sanchez, D. T., & Gaither, S. E. (2019). Identity questioning: Antecedents and consequences of prejudice attributions. *Journal of Social Issues*, 75(2), 515–37. https://doi.org/10.1111/josi.12326

Amponsah, D. K. (2013). Christian slavery, colonialism, and violence: The life and writings of an African ex-slave, 1717–1747. *Journal of Africana Religions*, 1(4), 431–57. https://doi.org/10.5325/jafrireli.1.4.0431

Ansley, F. L. (1989). Stirring the ashes: Race class and the future of civil rights scholarship. *Cornell Law Review*, 74(6), 993–1077. https://scholarship.law.cornell.edu/clr/vol74/iss6/1

Belmont, J. A. (2015). *The therapist's ultimate solution book: Essential strategies, tips and tools to empower your clients*. W. W. Norton & Company.

Blum, E. J., & Harvey, P. (2012). *The color of Christ: The son of God and the saga of race in America*. UNC Press Books.

Braterman, P. S. (2021). *Why creationism bears all the hallmarks of a conspiracy theory*. The Conversation. https://theconversation.com/why-creationism-bears-all-the-hallmarks-of-a-conspiracy-theory-153831

Brewster, M. E., Velez, B. L., & Geiger, E. F. (2020). It's like herding cats: Atheist minority stress, group involvement, and psychological outcomes. *Journal of Counseling Psychology*, 67(1), 10–20. https://doi.org/10.1037/cou0000392

Brown, J. E., van Mulukom, V., Charles, S. J., & Farias, M. (2023). Do you need religion to enjoy the benefits of church services? Social bonding, morality, and quality of life among religious and secular congregations. *Psychology of Religion and Spirituality*, 15(2), 308–18. https://doi.org/10.1037/rel0000447

Bry, L. J., Mustanski, B., Garofalo, R., & Burns, M. N. (2016). Management of a concealable stigmatized identity: A qualitative study of concealment, disclosure, and role flexing among young, resilient sexual and gender minority individuals. *Journal of Homosexuality*, 64(6), 745–69. https://doi.org/10.1080/00918369.2016.1236574

Bullivant, S., & Ruse, M. (2013). *The Oxford handbook of atheism*. Oxford University Press. https://doi.org/10.1093/oxfordhb/9780199644650.001.0001

Calavita, K. (2000). The paradoxes of race, class, identity, and "passing": Enforcing the Chinese Exclusion Acts, 1882–1910. *Law & Social Inquiry*, 25(1), 1–40. https://doi.org/10.1111/j.1747-4469.2000.tb00149.x

Calhoun-Brown, A. (2000). Upon this rock: The black church, nonviolence, and the Civil Rights Movement. *PS: Political Science and Politics*, 33(2), 169–74. https://doi.org/10.2307/420886

Camacho, G., Reinka, M. A., & Quinn, D. M. (2020). Disclosure and concealment of stigmatized identities. *Current Opinion in Psychology*, 31, 28–32. https://doi.org/10.1016/j.copsyc.2019.07.031

Chaudoir, S. R., & Fisher, J. D. (2010). The disclosure processes model: Understanding disclosure decision making and post-disclosure outcomes among people living with a concealable stigmatized identity. *Psychological Bulletin*, 136(2), 236–56. https://doi.org/10.1037/a0018193

Chou, R. S., & Feagin, J. R. (2015). *Myth of the model minority: Asian Americans facing racism*. Routledge. https://doi.org/10.4324/9781315636313

Christina, G. (2009, September 10). Race, gender, and atheism, Part 2: What we need to do—and why. *Greta Christina's Blog*. https://gretachristina.typepad.com/greta_christinas_weblog/2009/09/race-sex-atheism-2.html

Christina, G. (2014). *Coming out atheist: How to do it, how to help each other, and why*. Pitchstone Publishing.

Cone, J. H. (2011). *The cross and the lynching tree*. Orbis Books.

Cook, J. E., Salter, A., & Stadler, G. (2017). Identity concealment and chronic illness: A strategic choice. *Journal of Social Issues*, 73(2), 359–78. https://doi.org/10.1111/josi.12221

Crenshaw, K. (1989). Demarginalizing the intersection of race and sex: A black feminist critique of antidiscrimination doctrine, feminist theory and antiracist politics. *University of Chicago Legal Forum*, 140, 139–67.

Crocker J., & Major B. M. (1989). Social stigma and self-esteem: The self-protective properties of stigma. *Psychological Review*, 96(4), 608–30. https://doi.org/10.1037/0033-295X.96.4.608

DeRose, J. (2024, January 24). *Religious "nones" are now the largest single religious group in the US*. National Public Radio. https://www.npr.org/2024/01/24/1226371734/religious-nones-are-now-the-largest-single-group-in-the-u-s

Doane, M. J., & Elliott, M. (2015). Perceptions of discrimination among atheists: Consequences for atheist identification and well-being. *Psychology of Religion and Spirituality*, 7(2), 130–41. https://doi.org/10.1037/rel0000015

Downie, J. R., Southcott, R., Braterman, P. S., & Barron, N. J. (2018). Evolution education and evolution denial in Scotland. In H. Deniz & L. A. Borgerding (Eds.), *Evolution education around the globe* (pp. 169–94). Springer. https://doi.org/10.1007/978-3-319-90939-4_10

Finney, C. G. (1835). *Lectures on revivals of religion*. Leavitt, Lord & Company.

Fitzgerald, F. (2017). *The evangelicals: The struggle to shape America*. Simon & Schuster.

Frable, D. E. S., Platt, L., & Hoey, S. (1998). Concealable stigmas and positive self-perceptions: Feeling better around similar others. *Journal of Personality and Social Psychology*, 74(4), 909–22. https://doi.org/10.1037//0022-3514.74.4.909

Fredrickson, G. M. (2016). Religion and the invention of racism. In S. Elliott & M. Waggoner (Eds.), *Readings in the Theory of Religion* (pp. 88–106). Routledge. https://doi.org/10.1515/9781400873678-004

Gervais, W. M., & Norenzayan, A. (2012). Analytic thinking promotes religious disbelief. *Science*, 336(6080), 493–96. https://doi.org/10.1126/science.1215647

Goh, J. X., Kort, D. N., Thurston, A. M., Benson, L. R., & Kaiser, C. R. (2019). Does concealing a sexual minority identity prevent exposure to prejudice? *Social Psychological and Personality Science*, 10(8), 1056–64. https://doi.org/10.1177/1948550619829065

Goldstone, L. (2023). *Not white enough: The long, shameful road to Japanese American internment*. Scholastic Focus.

Greenberg, J. H. (2016). The doctrine of discovery as a doctrine of domination. *Journal for the Study of Religion, Nature and Culture*, 10(2), 236–44. https://doi.org/10.1558/jsrnc.v10i2.28942

Griswold Del Castillo, R. (1998). Manifest destiny: The Mexican-American War and the Treaty of Guadalupe Hidalgo. *Southwestern Journal of Law and Trade in the Americas*, 5, 31–43.

Harris, T. M., & Steiner, R. J. (2018). Beyond the veil: A critique of white Christian rhetoric and racism in the age of Trump. *Journal of Communication & Religion*, 41(1), 33–44. https://doi.org/10.5840/jcr20184114

Harrison, H. H. (1917). *The Negro and the nation*. Cosmo-Advocate Publishing Co.

Hays, P. A. (2022). *Addressing cultural complexities in counseling and clinical practice: An intersectional approach* (4th ed.). American Psychological Association.

Heart, B., & Horse, M. Y. (2007). The impact of historical trauma: The example of the native community. In M Bussey & J. Bula Wise (Eds.), *Trauma transformed: An empowerment response* (pp. 176–93). Columbia University Press.

Heise, T. (2017). Religion and Native American assimilation, resistance, and survival. In *Oxford Research Encyclopedia of Religion*. https://doi.org/10.1093/acrefore/9780199340378.013.394

Hook, J. N., Davis, D. E., Owen, J., & DeBlaere, C. (2025). *Cultural humility: Engaging diverse identities in therapy* (2nd ed.). American Psychological Association.

Horstmann, A., & Jung, J. H. (2015). Introduction: Refugees and religion. In A. Horstmann & J. H. Jung (Eds.). *Building Noah's ark for migrants, refugees, and religious*

communities: Contemporary anthropology of religion (pp. 1–20). Palgrave Macmillan. https://link.springer.com/book/10.1057/9781137496300
Howard, S., Kennedy, K. C., & Vine, K. T. (2023). "You don't believe in God? You ain't Black": Identifying as atheist elicits identity denial from Black ingroup members. *Cultural Diversity and Ethnic Minority Psychology*, 29(2), 202–7. https://doi.org/10.1037/cdp0000397
Howard, S., & Sommers, S. R. (2015). Exploring the enigmatic link between religion and anti-Black attitudes. *Social and Personality Psychology Compass*, 9(9), 495–510. https://doi.org/10.1111/spc3.12195
Howard, S., & Sommers, S. R. (2017). Exposure to White religious iconography influences Black individuals' intragroup and intergroup attitudes. *Cultural Diversity and Ethnic Minority Psychology*, 23(4), 508–15. https://doi.org/10.1037/cdp0000152
Howard, S., & Sommers, S. R. (2019). White religious iconography increases anti-Black attitudes. *Psychology of Religion and Spirituality*, 11(4), 382–91. https://doi.org/10.1037/rel0000144
Howard, S., Vine, K. T. & Kennedy, K. C. (2022). "Jesus was a White man too!": The relationship between beliefs about Jesus's race, racial attitudes, and ideologies that maintain racial hierarchies. *Psychology of Religion and Spirituality*, 14(4), 615–24. https://doi.org/10.1037/rel0000374
Hutchinson, S. (2014). White picket fences, white innocence. *Journal of Religious Ethics*, 42(4), 612–39. https://doi.org/10.1111/jore.12075
Huynh, Q. L. (2013). Identity denial. In K. D. Keith (Ed.), *The encyclopedia of cross-cultural psychology* (pp. 658–60). Wiley.
Jenkins, P. (2003). *The new anti-Catholicism: The last acceptable prejudice*. Oxford University Press. https://doi.org/10.1093/oso/9780195154801.001.0001
Jost, J. T., Banaji, M. R., & Nosek, B. A. (2004). A decade of system justification theory: Accumulated evidence of conscious and unconscious bolstering of the status quo. *Political Psychology*, 25(6), 881–919. https://doi.org/10.1111/j.1467-9221.2004.00402.x
Jost, J. T., & Van der Toorn, J. (2012). System justification theory. In P. A. M. Van Lange, T. E. Higgins, & A. W. Kruglanski (Eds.), *Handbook of Theories of Social Psychology* (2nd ed; pp. 313–43). Sage Publishing. https://doi.org/10.4135/9781446249222.n42
Kirmayer, L. J., Gone, J. P., & Moses, J. (2014). Rethinking historical trauma. *Transcultural Psychiatry*, 51(3), 299–319. https://doi.org/10.1177/1363461514536358
Knaut, A. L. (2015). *The Pueblo revolt of 1680: Conquest and resistance in seventeenth-century New Mexico*. University of Oklahoma Press.
Lackey, M. (2007). *African American atheists and political liberation: A study of the sociocultural dynamics of faith*. University Press of Florida. https://doi.org/10.5744/florida/9780813030357.001.0001
Lum, K. G. (2022). *Heathen: Religion and race in American history*. Harvard University Press. https://doi.org/10.1017/S0009640723000872
Mackey, C. D., Silver, C. F., Rios, K., Cowgill, C. M., & Hood Jr., R. W. (2020). Concealment of nonreligious identity: Exploring social identity threat among atheists and other nonreligious individuals. *Group Processes & Intergroup Relations*, 24(5), 860–77. https://doi.org/10.1177/1368430220905661
Madsen, W. (1967). Religious syncretism. In R. Wauchope & M. Nash (Eds.), *Handbook of Middle American Indians, Volume 6: Social Anthropology* (pp. 369–91). University of Texas Press. https://doi.org/10.7560/736665-020
Mahmud, T. (2012). *Better patient feedback, better healthcare*. M&K Update Ltd.

Martin, J. W., & Nicholas, M. A. (Eds.). (2010). *Native Americans, Christianity, and the reshaping of the American religious landscape*. University of North Carolina Press. https://doi.org/10.5149/9780807899663_martin

Marx, G. (1967). *Protest and prejudice: A study of belief in the Black community*. Harper Torchbooks.

Miguel, Jr., G. S., & Valencia, R. (1998). From the Treaty of Guadalupe Hidalgo to Hopwood: The educational plight and struggle of Mexican Americans in the Southwest. *Harvard Educational Review*, 68(3), 353–413. https://doi.org/10.17763/haer.68.3.k01tu242340242u1

Miller, A. F. (2013). The non-religious patriarchy: Why losing religion HAS NOT meant losing white male dominance. *CrossCurrents*, 63(2), 211–26. https://doi.org/10.1111/cros.12025

Miller, R. J. (2019). The doctrine of discovery. *The Indigenous Peoples' Journal of Law, Culture, & Resistance*, 5, 35–42. https://doi.org/10.2139/ssrn.3541299

O'Leary, R. T. (2016). From Anglo-Saxon nativism to executive order: Civil religion and anti-immigration rhetoric. *Politics and Religion*, 9(4), 771–93. https://doi.org/10.1017/S1755048316000389

Ortiz, A. (2009). Popay's leadership: A Pueblo perspective on the 1680 revolt. In M. Weigle, F. Levine, & L. Stiver (Eds.), *Telling New Mexico: A new history* (pp. 107–14). Museum of New Mexico Press.

Osborne, D., Sengupta, N. K., & Sibley, C. G. (2019). System justification theory at 25: Evaluating a paradigm shift in psychology and looking towards the future. *British Journal of Social Psychology*, 58(2), 340–61. https://doi.org/10.1111/bjso.12302

Oshatz, M. (2011). *Slavery and sin: The fight against slavery and the rise of liberal Protestantism*. Oxford University Press. https://doi.org/10.1093/acprof:oso/9780199751686.001.0001

Pachankis, J. E. (2007). The psychological implications of concealing a stigma: A cognitive-affective-behavioral model. *Psychological Bulletin*, 133(2), 328–45. https://doi.org/10.1037/0033-2909.133.2.328

Park, W. (2021). The blessing of Whiteness in the curse of Ham: Reading Gen 9: 18–29 in the Antebellum South. *Religions*, 12(11), 1–18. https://doi.org/10.3390/rel12110928

Perry, S. L., Whitehead, A. L., & Grubbs, J. B. (2021). Prejudice and pandemic in the promised land: how white Christian nationalism shapes Americans' racist and xenophobic views of COVID-19. In J. Solomos (Ed.), *Race and ethnicity in pandemic times* (pp. 41–54). Routledge. https://doi.org/10.1080/01419870.2020.1839114

Pew Research Center. (2012). "Nones" On the rise: New report finds one-in-five adults have no religious affiliation. Pew Research Center's Religion & Public Life Project. https://www.pewresearch.org/religion/2012/10/09/nones-on-the-rise/

Pew Research Center. (2015). America's Changing Religious Landscape. https://www.pewforum.org/2015/05/12/americas-changing-religious-landscape/

Pew Research Center. (2020). In U.S., decline of Christianity continues at rapid pace. https://www.pewresearch.org/religion/2019/10/17/in-u-s-decline-of-christianity-continues-at-rapid-pace/

Pew Research Center. (2021a). Religion and Education Around the World. https://www.pewresearch.org/religion/2016/12/13/religion-and-education-around-the-world/

Pew Research Center. (2021b). Faith among Black Americans. https://www.pewresearch.org/religion/2021/02/16/faith-among-black-americans/

Pew Research Center. (2024). Religious "nones" in America: Who they are and what they believe. https://www.pewresearch.org/religion/2024/01/24/religious-nones-in-america-who-they-are-and-what-they-believe/

Pigliucci, M. (2013). New Atheism and the scientistic turn in the atheism movement. *Midwest Studies in Philosophy*, 37(1), 142–53. https://doi.org/10.1111/misp.12006

Pindi, G. N., & De La Garza, A. T. (2018). "The colonial Jesus": Deconstructing White Christianity. In D. M. D. McIntosh, D. G. Moon, & T. K. Nakayama (Eds.) *Interrogating the communicative power of whiteness* (pp. 218–38). Routledge. https://doi.org/10.4324/9780203730003-12

Pinel, E. C. (1999). Stigma consciousness: The psychological legacy of social stereotypes. *Journal of Personality and Social Psychology*, 76(1), 114–28. https://doi.org/10.1037/0022-3514.76.1.114

Pinel, E. C. (2004). You're just saying that because I'm a woman: Stigma consciousness and attributions to discrimination. *Self and Identity*, 3(1), 39–51. https://doi.org/10.1080/13576500342000031

Purdie-Greenaway V., Steele C. M., Davies P. G., Ditlmann R., Crosby J. R. (2008). Social identity contingencies: How diversity cues signal threat or safety for African Americans in mainstream institutions. *Journal of Personality and Social Psychology*, 94(4), 615–30. https://doi.org/10.1037/0022-3514.94.4.615

Quinn, D. M., & Chaudoir, S. R. (2009). Living with a concealable stigmatized identity: The impact of anticipated stigma, centrality, salience, and cultural stigma on psychological distress and health. *Journal of Personality and Social Psychology*, 97(4), 634–51. https://doi.org/10.1037/a0015815

Quinn, D. M., & Earnshaw, V. A. (2013). Concealable stigmatized identities and psychological well-being. *Social and Personality Psychology Compass*, 7(1), 40–51. https://doi.org/10.1111/spc3.12005

Quinn, D. M., Weisz, B. M., & Lawner, E. K. (2017). Impact of active concealment of stigmatized identities on physical and psychological quality of life. *Social Science and Medicine*, 192, 14–17. https://doi.org/10.1016/j.socscimed.2017.09.024

Reinka, M. A., Pan-Weisz, B. M., Lawner, E. K., & Quinn, D. M. (2020). Cumulative consequences of stigma: Possessing multiple concealable stigmatized identities is associated with worse quality of life. *Journal of Applied Social Psychology*, 50(4), 253–61. https://doi.org/10.1111/jasp.12656

Roberts, S. O., Weisman, K., Lane, J. D., Williams, A., Camp, N. P., Wang, M., Robison, M., Sanchez, K., & Griffiths, C. (2020). God as a White man: A psychological barrier to conceptualizing Black people and women as leadership worthy. *Journal of Personality and Social Psychology*, 119(6), 1290–315. https://doi.org/10.1037/pspi0000233

Rollings, W. H. (2002). Indians and Christianity. In P. J. Deloria & N. Salisbury (Eds.), *A companion to American Indian history* (pp. 121–38). Blackwell Publishers. https://doi.org/10.1002/9780470996461.ch8

Scheitle, C. P., Corcoran, K. E., & Hudnall, E. B. (2019). Adopting a stigmatized label: Social determinants of identifying as an atheist beyond disbelief. *Social Forces*, 97(4), 1731–56. https://doi.org/10.1093/sf/soy084

Schrimshaw, E. W., Siegel, K., Downing, M. J., & Parsons, J. T. (2013). Disclosure and concealment of sexual orientation and the mental health of non-gay-identified, behaviorally bisexual men. *Journal of Consulting and Clinical Psychology*, 81(1), 141–53. https://doi.org/10.1037/a0031272

Shu, H. (2024). Deconstructing Chinese international students' silence: Critical race theory, white supremacy, and modern minority myth. In A. Kempf & H. Watts (Eds.) *Critical perspectives on white supremacy and racism in Canadian education*. Routledge. https://doi.org/10.4324/9781003399360-18

Slattery, J. M., & Park, C. L. (2020). *Empathic counseling: Building skills to empower change* (2nd ed.). American Psychological Association.

Slepian, M. L., & Jacoby-Senghor, D. S. (2021). Identity threats in everyday life: Distinguishing belonging from inclusion. *Social Psychological and Personality Science*, 12(3), 392–406. https://doi.org/10.1177/1948550619895008

Steele, C. M., Spencer, S. J., & Aronson, J. (2002). Contending with group image: The psychological impact of stereotype and social identity threat. *Advances in Experimental Social Psychology*, 34, 379–440. https://doi.org/10.1016/S0065-2601(02)80009-0

Sue, D. W., Sue, D., Neville, H. A., & Smith, L. (2022). *Counseling the culturally diverse: Theory and practice* (9th ed.). Wiley.

Swann, D. (2020). *A qualitative study of Black atheists: Don't tell me you're one of those!* Lexington Books. https://doi.org/10.5771/9781498592406

Taylor, R. J., Chatters, L. M., & Levin, J. (2004). *Religion in the lives of African Americans: Social, psychological, and health perspectives*. SAGE Publications. https://doi.org/10.4135/9781452229782

Turner, C. (2021, March 30). *Where does the Black church fit in today's Black Lives Matter movement?* PBS. https://www.pbs.org/newshour/nation/where-does-the-black-church-fit-in-todays-black-lives-matter-movement

Van Mulukom, V., Charles, S. J., Brown, J. E., & Farias, M. (2023). Do you need religion to enjoy the benefits of church services? Social bonding, morality and quality of life among religious and secular congregations. *Psychology of Religion and Spirituality*, 15(2), 308–18. https://doi.org/10.1037/rel0000480

Weidinger, B. (2017). Equal before God, and God alone: Cultural fundamentalism, (anti-) egalitarianism, and Christian rhetoric in nativist discourse from Austria and the United States. *Journal of Austrian-American History*, 1(1), 40–68. https://doi.org/10.5325/jaustamerhist.1.1.0040

Williams, M. T., Rosen, D. C., & Kanter, J. W. (Eds.). (2019). *Eliminating race-based mental health disparities: Promoting equity and culturally responsive care across settings*. Context Press.

Wilson, B. R. (1988). The functions of religion: A reappraisal. *Religion*, 18(3), 199–216. https://doi.org/10.1016/S0048-721X(88)80025-3

Yang, F. (1998). Chinese conversion to evangelical Christianity: The importance of social and cultural contexts. *Sociology of Religion*, 59(3), 237–57. https://doi.org/10.2307/3711910

Yi, V., Mac, J., Na, V. S., Venturanza, R. J., Museus, S. D., Pendakur, S. L. (2020). Toward an anti-imperialistic critical race analysis of the model minority myth. *Review of Educational Research*, 90(4), 542–79. https://doi.org/10.3102/0034654320933532

7

Secular Sexual Minorities

Melanie E. Brewster

Chapter Outline

Most individuals in the United States report believing in a God/gods and/or are affiliated with an organized religion (Pew Research Center [PRC], 2024a). While the proportion of nonreligious individuals has grown dramatically since the turn of the twenty-first century—to nearly 30 percent of the populace—the likelihood of being born or socialized into a family that adheres to an organized religion remains high. Family socialization into religion may be rapidly changing though, as the most nonreligious and nonbelieving segments of the US population are quite young; specifically, 69 percent of religious "nones" are under fifty years old (PRC, 2024b).

Demographically, the composition of the United States is shifting in other unexpected ways. Across most age groups, but particularly younger generations, people are openly identifying with minoritized sexualities or genders at higher rates; Gallup reports that 7.6 percent of the population now identifies as lesbian, gay, bisexual, transgender, or queer (LGBTQ+), up from 5.6 percent in 2020 and 3.5 percent in 2012 (Jones, 2024). With more than one in five members of the Generation Z (people born between 1997 and 2012) cohort identifying as LGBTQ+, it seems likely that gains in secularity for these same generations may be related. A primary reason for moving away from religious beliefs is a concern for social justice causes, such as heterosexism in organized religion (Hunsberger & Altemeyer, 2006; Zuckerman, 2012). Indeed, "a flight from religious intolerance is a central aspect of personal 'coming out' stories" for many queer and/or sexual minority people (O'Brien, 2004, p. 184). Many nonreligious, queer clients that you encounter in therapy will have a deconstruction or deconversion journey to share, but some may have been raised in fully secular households.

Religions, particularly the "big three" monotheistic faiths (Christianity, Islam, Judaism), can be paradoxical sites of both harm and connection for sexual minority people (Wilkinson & Johnson, 2020). Moreover, the disproportionately large sociopolitical role of religion in our day-to-day lives means that even those who are intentionally unaffiliated with a faith group are subject to its rule. Secular sexual minority people may feel especially disempowered, isolated, and surveilled in our highly religious nation. That said, secular people—regardless of their own sexual orientations—are consistently among the most affirming of LGBTQ+ groups and issues in the United States (Cimino & Smith, 2007; Hunsberger & Altemeyer, 2006; Linneman & Clendenen, 2009); 85 percent of religiously unaffiliated Americans and 96 percent of atheists support the legality of same-sex marriage (Gubbala et al., 2023). Thus, secular LGBTQ+ clients who can connect with other *nones* or nonbelievers are likely to find a supportive community.

Who "Counts" as a Sexual Minority?

In this chapter, sexual minority (SM) is used as an umbrella term for anyone who does not hold a heterosexual or "straight" sexual orientation, or who engages in practices that go against the expected relational norms in the United States. This could include people who use terms such as gay, lesbian, or bisexual, as well as other labels like pansexual, queer, allosexual, omnisexual, asexual, gray ace, or fluid to describe how they choose to connect with, love or be in relation with others. I am not focusing on the experiences of transgender and gender diverse (TGD) individuals, as this content is discussed in chapter 8 of this volume. While there are often significant overlaps in identity development experiences of SM and TGD communities, there are also nuanced differences that deserve unpacking—in light of the unique constructions of sexuality and gender norms by different faith-based groups in the United States.

That said, as a psychologist, taking a broader lens to the concept of SM has felt useful in my clinical work. Particularly for younger generations, a fluid and experimental orientation to sexuality is common. Clients often present their sexuality as a dynamic constellation of queerness, intended to subvert "traditional" relationship norms (Hammack et al., 2019). Building on this, some argue that individuals who engage in consensual or ethical forms of nonmonogamy (i.e., polyamory, swinging, or open relationships) should be categorized under a queer and/or SM category (Schippers, 2019). Others have posited that participation in kink (i.e., BDSM) or other "nonprocreative" forms of sexual expression should be accounted for in SM discourse (Simula, 2021). It is beyond the scope of this chapter to tease apart what each of these terms mean to those who use them or firmly dictate who is (or is not) minoritized for their sexuality in the United States.

Heterosexism in Organized Religions

Historically, religious doctrine has castigated same-sex behavior, marking those who engage in such practices as sinful abominations. It should come as no surprise that "religions in general, and Christianity in particular, are often perceived as anathema" to holding a SM identity (O'Brien, 2004, p. 180). Innumerable studies have laid out how heterosexist policies and attitudes permeate faiths including fundamentalist Christian sects (Barton, 2010), Catholicism (Buchanan et al., 2001), conservative and orthodox Jewish sects (Kahn, 1989), the Church of Jesus Christ of Latter-day Saints or Mormon church (Skidmore et al., 2023), and some Islamic sects (Ali, 2023). The Human Rights Campaign (HRC) maintains a website that compiles position statements on sexual orientation and gender diversity across various faith groups that can be a useful resource to share with SM clients who may wonder how church or temple leaders may react to them (HRC, n.d.).

Harmful comparisons of SM people to other deviant or "sinful" groups have been widely noted in scholarship across fields; for example, a lesbian study participant reflected that as a youth, the Pentecostal preacher would discuss SM people alongside "the so-called perverts, you know, like child molesters and just awful people" (Barton, 2010, p. 472). Discussed elsewhere in the handbook (see chapter 12), experiences of *religious trauma* are common for SM populations (Jones et al., 2022).

Individual-Level, Religiously Rooted Heterosexism

The process of internalizing negative societal attitudes about SM people is often referred to as internalized homophobia or internalized heterosexism; research supports that this process of internalization can lead to deleterious mental health outcomes such as substance use, depression, anxiety, and suicidality (Newcomb & Mustanski, 2010). Within families who hold religious beliefs that are heterosexist, SM family members may internalize this negativity, incurring stress and poor mental health outcomes (Gibbs & Goldbach, 2015; Mattingly et al., 2016).

In reaction to being told that being gay is evil and a one-way ticket to hell, it is not uncommon for SM people to report trying to "pray away" being gay. Norris (2014), for example, shared the following of his attempted journey to heterosexuality:

> In hopes that the female form was an appreciation I could eventually acquire, like a taste for food or music, I tried to force myself to have sexual thoughts about women. These were sad, half-formed, half-hearted fantasies that inevitably became male focused, ending in the routine of despair, self-loathing and falling asleep pleading for God to deliver me from the demon of homosexuality.

Though they have long been condemned by the American Psychological Association (APA) and other similar medical, counseling, and psychiatric governing bodies (i.e., AMA, ACA, APA), mental health interventions that allege to "fix" homosexuality have been touted by religious organizations and therapists as humane options for bringing SM congregants back in alignment with church doctrine. Generally rooted in evangelical Christianity, these "reparative" or "conversion" therapies do not have empirical support and have been compared to torture (Forsythe et al., 2022). Methods of aversive behavioral modification such as electric shocks, violent imagery, and nausea-induction are often paired with homoerotic imagery to "prevent" or "rewire" arousal. Research has indicated that survivors of these programs have higher rates of psychological symptomatology and suicidal ideation compared to SM people who have not been in conversion therapy (Przeworski et al., 2021).

Two Closets

The process of becoming nonreligious or a nonbeliever for those from religious backgrounds has long been described as a "coming out" process that is similar to disclosing one's sexual orientation to friends and family (Abbott & Mollen, 2018; Brewster, 2013; Brewster, 2014). Within secularism literature, hiding an atheist identity is jokingly referred to as *the other closet*, as it may garner similarly oppressive social repercussions when revealed (Brewster, 2014). Many SM people may (accurately) fear that they will not be welcome or accepted into religious communities if they are out. Some secular SM people may find that they prefer to stay closeted or quiet about their sexual orientation and/or nonbelief if they can retain access to the network, friendships, and activities the religious organization offers. Research support on the mental health outcomes of identity management is mixed. Some studies find that it is psychologically harmful to keep secrets about one's identity and strains personal relationships, whereas others find that it is riskier to be "out" in environments that are unsupportive and disclosure may trigger interpersonal or professional consequences (for a review, see Pachankis et al., 2020). Thus, secular SM people may need to strategically decide which disclosures are risks worth taking. In a personal essay, Mills (2014) reflected on the parallel process of coming out as gay versus atheist, noting,

> When I sat my parents down to tell them I was gay, my mother thought I'd called the family meeting to tell them I was an atheist. Perhaps this false expectation caused my coming out as a gay man to go a bit smoother. . . . Atheists were rare in my hometown. Not as rare as gays, but rare (p. 95).

For Mills, the lack of role models in his town complicated and slowed both coming out processes; he continued, "My struggle with my sexuality and sudden departure from attending church were linked in my head, but I wasn't quite ready to give up on the whole God thing. One closet at a time."

Particularly when coming out as a SM, support from family members is a predictor of mental health outcomes (Al-Khouja et al., 2021; Reyes et al., 2023). In families with religiously fundamentalist views, there is generally lower acceptance for SM family members (Heiden-Rootes et al., 2019). As expected, high levels of family religiosity also tend to relate to higher levels of internalized homophobia and lower levels of family support for SM young adults (Shilo & Savaya, 2012).

In a personal narrative, after sharing his nonbelief and sexuality, one gay atheist man reported that his mother exclaimed, "I curse the day I had you. You are dead to me. Get thee behind me Satan" (Adams, 2014, p. 144). Such an example illustrates the potentiality for "double the rejection" faced by secular SM people from religious loved ones. This may not always be the case though; for some the act of eschewing a religion is more jarring than coming out as SM. Notably, a qualitative research participant from a 2019 study shared that his Latter-day Saints (LDS) family had more conflict arise from his decision to leave LDS faith and explore Wicca, than to come out as gay (Goodrich & Luke, 2019).

Unfortunately, there are very few studies with participants who are both nonreligious/ nonbelievers *and* SM. One notable exception is Brewster and colleagues (2021) which found that for SM atheists, family religiosity was related to poorer mental health outcomes; however, the longer someone identified as an atheist, the better their mental health outcomes were. This may suggest that just like coming out as SM, with time, "it gets better" for atheists too.

Institutional-Levels of Heterosexism

Beyond individual-level heterosexist and homophobic encounters, harmful positions by religious institutions in the United States shape legal and educational systems as well as structures of care (i.e., hospitals, social services). Rooted in Christianity, anti-sodomy or "buggery" laws from England were transplanted to the United States via settlers in the 1600s and rapidly spread such norms throughout the newly established colonies. Although such laws were rarely enforced in the early days of the United States, they became the backbone of the McCarthyist homosexual-panic of the midcentury—known as the *Lavender Scare*—fueling hundreds of arrests and dismissals of allegedly SM workers from government and university positions (Johnson, 2023). These state laws were embedded in our legal system until they were finally overturned by the US Supreme Court in 2003 with *Lawrence v. Texas* (539 US 558); with this case, the court reaffirmed that consensual sexual behavior between adults cannot be sanctioned as it would violate a right to privacy.

With their explicit condemnation of same-sex sexual behavior, religious groups in the United States have spearheaded campaigns against equal employment, housing, and healthcare protections, marriage rights, and the ability to adopt children or create families via reproductive technologies for SM populations (Karol, 2023; Kazyak et al., 2023). In particular, the Catholic Church is faulted for its demonization of SM people and subsequent complicity in the spread of HIV/AIDS across the world; by preaching against same-sex sexual activity, barring the distribution of condoms, and pushing abstinence/ fidelity as the only "safe sex" options, the virus spread (Kinkel, 2013). Collective action by queer advocacy groups such as ACT UP in the 1980s–1990s called the church to task, with performative "die ins" during mass at St. Patrick's Cathedral in New York City to protest the misinformation spread by the church. Worldwide, over 40.4 million people have died from AIDS and over 85.6 million people were infected with the virus; presently, 39 million people are living with HIV (World Health Organization, 2024). To the present day, Christian groups in the United States and abroad have been at the forefront of blocking efforts to provide adequate sex education in schools, provide condoms and contraceptives, and increase access to PEP/PrEP for vulnerable populations (Schulzke, 2013).

Diverse Perspectives and Positions Among Secular Sexual Minority Populations

For some SM people, there may be benefits to staying within a religious or spiritual network even if they are nonbelievers. For example, within Black communities the Church has been a bulwark against racism and a key place for organizing against White supremacy (Penningroth, 2021). A chance to safely hold space with others around these important issues may outweigh hearing the occasional heterosexist remark from church leadership. Similarly, concepts of being "culturally Catholic" (Turpin, 2022) or an "atheist Jew" (Gutkowski, 2021; Langton, 2024) are ways for people to stay connected to rituals, holidays, and other uniting events within a faith group without necessarily being held to the same standards of belief or attendance. Access to the social support that churches, temples, and synagogues provide is also critical for many people—particularly those who may live in more rural areas. Indeed, religious institutions can be sites of leisure, joy, and important volunteer opportunities—for example, singing in a chorus, bowling, helping with Sunday school, or volunteering with elderly or incarcerated populations.

Remaking Faiths, Finding Spiritualities

Considering there is no real consensus of what it means to be nonreligious or a nonbeliever, some SM people who fall broadly into this group may still engage with spiritual or loosely religious practices in ways that feel appropriate to them. A growing body of research suggests that some SM people undergo a solo journey to repair harms from religious trauma and reengage with a new, more accepting version of their former beliefs (Haldeman, 2004; O'Brien, 2004). Openly LGBTQ+ affirming religious groups such as the Metropolitan Community Church, Episcopal Church, Unitarian Universalist, or Reform Judaism may be options for SM secular people who want to be involved with a faith community or feel inclined to maintain ties for loved ones. Some cities may also have specific religious networks developed to serve gay communities, for example, Toronto's Unity Mosque and Berlin's Ibn Rushd-Goethe (Toesland, 2019).

Other nonreligious SM people may opt to explore expressions of spirituality that have not been affiliated historically with oppression such as paganism, Buddhism, Wiccan, and some indigenous- or earth-based traditions (Buchanan et al., 2001). For individuals whose former religion was tied to their race or cultural system, keeping up a practice may have even more importance. For Asian communities, Buddhist ideology is generally tolerant of diverse sexual orientations, while Hinduism has not always offered a clear stance on LGBTQ+ issues (Gleig, 2012; Upadhyay, 2020). Of course, many SM people do not feel that religion is important to maintain in their lives, are fulfilled without formal ties to an organized belief system, and/or become atheist or agnostic (Kolysh, 2017). Compared to heterosexual people, SM individuals are three times more likely to be atheist or agnostic (Linneman & Clendenen, 2009).

Building New Communities

Unlike other marginalized groups (i.e., racial/ethnic minorities) who may find solace in churches and temples, for many SM people, these institutions are sites of pain and rejection. The rise of explicitly secular "churches" such as Sunday Assembly or the Oasis Network offer options for SM people who would like the ritual and feel of attending a religious meeting, without the dogmatic scripture or belief system. Furthermore, some cities may have a branch of one of the longest standing secular groups—Ethical Society—which was founded in 1876 by Dr. Felix Adler and hosts Sunday talks, social justice action networks, and educational programming, as well as providing nonreligious celebrants for weddings, births, and funerals.

However, the long-standing heterosexist exclusion of SM people from traditional places of worship and other community centers gave rise to countercultural spaces (i.e., nightclubs) and arts organizations where the queer world could flourish. As a result, many of the community spaces for SM populations are inherently secular, or even aggressively anti-religious. Gay artists from the late Andy Warhol to Lil Nas X have taken sacred imagery, particularly icons from Catholicism, and imbued this iconography with campy and/or pornographic overtones. Such work draws upon Sontag's (2001) description of camp as a "solvent of morality" that "neutralizes moral indignation, sponsors playfulness" (p. 290). For SM people who have faced harm from religious structures, seeing them in a satirical or playful format is a way to reclaim power and retell a previously shameful narrative. Many metropolitan regions of the United States have bars and restaurants that host Drag Brunch on Sundays during the hours wherein many Americans are in church. Mills (2014) reflects on his experience at such an event, after being out as both atheist and gay for many years:

> Now on Sundays, I often find myself in gay club in Florida, where I live with my partner. We sit there with friends and drinks, and we watch a [B]lack drag queen in a church dress and a big hat lip-synch to a gospel number. This has become my church. My sanctuary. It has nothing to do with God, but there are rituals here. Patterns . . . A dance to my favorite song in the moment with the man I love. His hand on my back. His fingers skipping just below my waistband. Men all around. Different men. Different ages. Different skin tones and sizes. There together, dancing, drinking, and imagining all the possibilities this world holds. This is my religion.

Secular, Queer, Space and Time

Disentangling the role that Christianity had on solidifying marriage and monogamy into secular culture by the late nineteenth century (TallBear et al., 2018; Willey, 2016) can be particularly liberating for clients who feel drawn toward open or nonmonogamous practices. Providing reading and psychoeducation on the roots of heterosexual marriage as a pillar of settler-colonialism, nation-building, patriarchy, property rights, and Christian morality may feel liberating to secular SM clients who feel a malaise about "traditional" family building. *Queer space* is a concept that can be used to create a discourse frame to explore non-normative logics and transcend heteronormative ideas of stable couples and reproductive families (Carlström & Andersson, 2019; Halberstam, 2005). Indeed, the systems to affirm and legitimize love in the United States were not made with queer people in mind—normalizing feelings of misfit or dread that can arise for some clients when working within these systems may help them feel seen.

The very act of going against our well-trodden, heterosexist scripts in the United States takes an enormous amount of defiance and a commitment to liberatory practice. The relational and sexual scripts within US culture largely present as follows: (1) an expectation that after completing formal education, individuals will find one romantic partner of the "other-sex"[1] to commit to under the watchful eye of God and the US legal system, (2) once married, the heterosexual couple will begin to produce offspring with their spouse, and (3) the couple will be tasked to raise these children with moral fortitude, such that their kids will be equipped with resources and discipline to successfully complete this reproductive imperative when the time comes. Freeman (2010, p. 3) and others have referred to this cycle as "*chrononormativity*, or the use of time to organize individual human bodies toward maximum productivity." Concepts such as a "biological clock" that ticks for women or expectations that those unmarried by forty are broken and immature all speak to this concept.

Religiosity and Chrononormativity

Within the religious landscape of the United States, there are several sects that center the need to create large families to spread their faith, notably LDS/Mormons, Muslim, Amish, and orthodox Jewish communities (Burge, 2021; Stone, 2023)—all of whom enter heterosexual marriages earlier and have higher birth rates than the general population. For SM people who are not interested in or able to participate in a "traditional" family structure set forth by their religion or culture, leaving one's faith may be the only option. However, the dominance of these rigid systems also limits the ability to see a future or know how to create a life worth living when outside their bounds (i.e., SM and/or childfree by choice individuals).

Feminist and queer scholars have called attention to this pernicious cycle for decades, but its explicit connection to religion is often left unnamed. Adrienne Rich (1980/2003) described *compulsory heterosexuality* as an expectation that women will obediently participate in systems of patriarchy and capitalism by having children with men. She described that women who intentionally opted out of this system were villainized (i.e., witches, sluts), belittled (i.e., crones, spinsters), or even institutionalized

[1]The phrases "other-sex" and "same-sex" are inherently reductive and typically used within religious/political contexts to describe sexual activity between "two men" or "two women." This unnuanced wording does not leave space to acknowledge the role of gender diversity (i.e., nonbinary, fluid, or transgender individuals) within sexual encounters and experiences.

(i.e., involuntary hospitalizations of lesbian women). Referencing systems of femicide in the United States with Protestant-driven witch-hunts of the colonial era and abroad with the historic practice of sati for widows in some Hindu cultures, Rich (2003) sweepingly argues that there is an overt mandate for women to satisfy men and reproduce; a woman who does not fulfill this duty no longer has value or purpose, with queer women posing a particular threat to the patriarchal system.

The early 2000s was an era rich in theorizing issues of queer temporalities. Lee Edelman (2004) set forth a radical new ethical system for queer populations that intentionally shuns reproductive futurism. Rather than prioritizing children and unborn "next generations," Edelman urges SM people to seize the present moment and embody narcissism, *jouissance*, and the negation of the future. Refusing the current social, political, and religious orders is a way for SM people to stop acceding to and accommodating prescriptive heterosexist narratives. In a clinical context, drawing from therapeutic techniques that make use of here-and-now, relational interventions rather than prioritizing a future-focused push toward productivity may feel healing for some secular SM clients.

Going further, Jack Halberstam (2005) explored the idea of *queer time* as a counterpoint to the traditional heterosexual teleology of life—partner, career, house, kids, repeat. Queer time is marked by existential uncertainty. Some of this uncertainty, particularly for older generations followed the AIDS/HIV epidemic; many SM communities were decimated by illness and premature death, with their sense of time truncated. It was unclear who would get a full life or reach those traditional markers of adulthood. Beyond the epidemic, SM people have historically been plagued by uncertainties *beyond* the usual growing pains of young adulthood. Common questions that arise when working with secular SM clients can include the following: *If I don't want to get married, how can my relationship be valid? How will I ever feel safe when I know my parents would disown me if they knew I was gay? How can I have kids when I can't easily adopt or afford reproductive technologies? How will I accrue wealth when I can be fired from my job at any point? How will I find another queer person to love me in this small town? If I don't have children, will my life be meaningless?*

Halberstam (2005) argues that when SM people do not partake in institutions of religion, patriarchy, heterosexuality, family, capital, and easy methods of reproduction, it leads to "strange temporalities, imaginative life schedules, and eccentric economic practices" (p. 1). Indeed, queerness disrupts traditional narratives of lineage and inheritance; without the presumption of a biological heir, SM people are freed from the compulsion to create nest-eggs, college funds, and generational wealth. This lack of chrononormativity, starting in youth, allows SM people to consider alternative paths and unconventional methods of creating family. The possibility of expansive non-nuclear family structures, polyamorous relationships, and nomadic lifestyles are no longer "irresponsible" or "immature"; markers of age-appropriate behaviors no longer apply, because time moves differently (Jaffe, 2018). SM people are "figures for and bearers of new corporeal sensations, including those of a certain counterpoint between now and then, and of occasional disruptions to the sped-up and hyperregulated time of industry" (Freeman, 2010, p. 7).

Clinical Interventions for the Unmoored

Helping secular SM clients situate themselves in a lineage of queer trailblazers, rather than prioritizing a narrative that they are "missing out" on a traditionally scripted life is essential. Some of this can be done with cognitive-behavioral approaches such as *reframing*—for example, "rather than focusing on it being unfair that you cannot get married in the same church your parents did, is there a way to see it as less constricting or even more liberating?" Bibliotherapy is a key aspect of my work with intellectually curious clients and can facilitate cognitive-behavioral interventions by providing a counternarrative to self-blame and shame. When my clients take the time to engage with books between our sessions, it offers a chance for them to engage in our work at a deeper level. Books such as *The Tragedy of Heterosexuality* (Ward, 2022) and *The Queer Art of Failure* (Halberstam, 2020) illustrate the ways in which SM people operate outside of traditional systems, but also show that this is a gift.

Core tenets of existential therapy arise frequently in work with secular clients. Working with the duality of (1) having vast freedom to determine one's own life-path is wonderful, while (2) recognizing that too many choices can feel disorienting is at the heart of effective counseling with a secular SM person. The concept of *meaning vertigo* may feel salient to some SM clients. Loosely defined as the perception of an unsettling emptiness at the level of social meaning that threatens our ability to interact and communicate, Melo Lopes (2019, p. 2530) provides a clear example:

> [O]ur social practices of greeting are undergirded by culturally-specific meanings of gestures, arranged in broader schemas or scripts of interaction. Because we share these meanings, we find greeting fairly uneventful. We understand what others mean and expect when they hug rather than shake hands. All of this breaks down, of course, when you meet someone from an unfamiliar culture. Then you may receive a shockingly familiar, although politely intended, kiss on the cheek, prompting awkwardness and discomfort. Indeed, social life without social meanings would be like an unimaginable sequence of disorienting encounters with strangers and artifacts from faraway lands. Social meanings are necessary for *meaningful* and *fluid* social action, interaction and coordination.

Living outside of the confines of religious scripts *and* heteronormative scripts can leave secular SM clients feeling unmoored and unsure. Frequently, clients express that they want someone to tell them what to do, paralyzed by the yawning void of choice without the threat of an afterlife. I often have clients share that they both love and resent being able to chart their own course in life. Living without a compass or a roadmap has its benefits, but always relying on oneself to make meaning can be fatiguing. Helping clients to notice these conflicting emotions rather than push them down is a first step toward a more authentic existence.

Aspects of Dialectical Behavior Therapy can offer important perspectives for fully living in the tension of an ambiguous life-path, particularly using behavioral modification strategies such as radical acceptance and distress tolerance. Clients may (accurately) assume that loved ones will reject them because of their secularism and/or SM-identity.

How can they hold this sadness while also acknowledging that not everyone will feel this way? Grief and uncomfortable transitions are often parts of both secular and SM "coming out" narratives. Working with clients to develop personalized toolkits for managing their distress may seem like a basic recommendation, but for clients who have recently left a religious practice where they relied on prayer to self-soothe, this may be quite novel.

Pulling from both feminist therapy and queer theory, I find that introducing expansive ways to think through family structures outside of a religious framework is meaningful for some clients. SM clients are more likely to have conflicted or tense relationships with biological family members compared to heterosexual clients. When accounting for differences in religious beliefs or practices with family members for secular SM clients, this gulf may further widen. Here, bibliotherapy (or links to video lectures) may again be helpful (resources are included in appendix A). Connecting clients to local or online communities and methods of collective action is essential for working with this population. *Cruising Utopia: The Then and There of Queer Futurity* (Muñoz, 2019) is a provocative and joyful text that helps imagine the ways in which SM people can actively co-create a utopian future. The text offers ways to confront nihilism arguing that "we must dream and enact new and better pleasures, other ways of being in the world, and ultimately new worlds" (p. 1). Finally, core feminist texts such as *Staying with the Trouble: Making Kin in the Chthulucene* (Haraway, 2016) speak to the need to take an expansive lens when it comes to kinship and creating communities of care. Kin is not just for blood relatives but can also include animal companions, friends, the natural world, and more. Secular SM clients can intentionally blur and play with the boundaries of kinship without relying on religious doctrines to create places of refuge and comradery.

Recommended Further Reading

- Leaving Faith or Deconstruction/Reconstruction
  - Brewster, M. E. (Ed.). (2014). *Atheists in America*. Columbia University Press.
- Kinship/Relationship Models
  - Haraway, D. J. (2016). *Staying with the Trouble: Making Kin in the Chthulucene*. Duke University Press.
  - Muñoz, J. E. (2019). *Cruising Utopia: The Then and There of Queer Futurity*. In *Cruising Utopia*, 10th Anniversary Edition. NYU Press.
  - Ward, J. (2022). *The Tragedy of Heterosexuality* (Vol. 56). NYU Press.
- Rethinking Queerness
  - Edelman, L. (2004). *No Future: Queer Theory and the Death Drive*. Duke University Press.
  - Freeman, E. (2010). *Time Binds: Queer Temporalities, Queer Histories*. Duke University Press.
  - Halberstam, J. (2005). *In a Queer Time and Place: Transgender Bodies, Subcultural Lives* (Vol. 3). NYU Press.
  - Halberstam, J. (2020). *The Queer Art of Failure*. Duke University Press.

Podcasts

- *Queerology*
- *Two Feminists Annotate the Bible*
- *The Deconstructionists*
- *Kitchen Table Cult*
- *Deconversion Therapy*

References

Abbott, D. M., & Mollen, D. (2018). Atheism as a concealable stigmatized identity: Outness, anticipated stigma, and well-being. *The Counseling Psychologist*, 46(6), 685–707. http://doi.org/10.1177/0011000018792669

Adams, R. (2014). Dinner with Grandma. In M. Brewster (Ed.), *Atheists in America*, (pp. 143–47). Columbia University Press.

Ali, S. H. (2023). American Muslims' attitudes toward homosexuality: Exploring the effects of gender, religiosity, and income inequality. *Journal of Homosexuality*, 70(13), 2997–3023. https://doi.org/10.1080/00918369.2022.2086748

Al-Khouja, M., Weinstein, N., & Legate, N. (2021). Long-term mental health correlates of social supportive relationships in a lesbian, gay, and bisexual sample. *Psychology & Sexuality*, 12(3), 180–92. https://doi.org/10.1080/19419899.2019.1687580

Barton, B. (2010). "Abomination"—Life as a Bible Belt gay. *Journal of Homosexuality*, 57(4), 465–84. https://doi.org/10.1080/00918361003608558

Brewster, M. E. (Ed.). (2014). *Atheists in America*. Columbia University Press.

Brewster, M. E. (2013). Atheism, Gender, and Sexuality. In S. Bullivant & M. Ruse (Eds.), *The Oxford Handbook of Atheism*, 511–25. Oxford: Oxford University Press. https://doi.org/10.1093/oxfordhb/9780199644650.013.006

Brewster, M., Velez, B., Sawyer, J., Motulsky, W., Chan, A., & Kim, V. (2021). Family religiosity, support, and psychological well-being for sexual minority atheist individuals. *Psychology of Religion and Spirituality*, 13(3), 266–75. https://doi.org/10.1037/rel0000356

Buchanan, M., Dzelme, K., Harris, D., & Hecker, L. (2001). Challenges of being simultaneously gay or lesbian and spiritual and/or religious: A narrative perspective. *American Journal of Family Therapy*, 29(5), 435–49.

Burge, R. (2021). The future Of American religion: Birth rates show who's having more kids. *Religion Unplugged*. https://religionunplugged.com/news/2021/10/4/the-future-of-american-religion-birth-rates-show-whos-having-more-kids

Carlström, C., & Andersson, C. (2019). The queer spaces of BDSM and non-monogamy. *Journal of Positive Sexuality*, 5(1), 14–19. http://doi.org/10.51681/1.513

Cimino, R., & Smith, C. (2007). Secular humanism and atheism beyond progressive secularism. *Sociology of Religion*, 68(4), 407–24. https://www.jstor.org/stable/20453183

Edelman, L. (2004). *No Future: Queer Theory and the Death Drive*. Duke University Press.

Forsythe, A., Pick, C., Tremblay, G., Malaviya, S., Green, A., & Sandman, K. (2022). Humanistic and economic burden of conversion therapy among LGBTQ youths in the United States. *JAMA Pediatrics*, 176(5), 493–501. https://doi.org/10.1001/jamapediatrics.2022.0042

Freeman, E. (2010). *Time Binds: Queer Temporalities, Queer Histories*. Duke University Press.

Gibbs, J. J., & Goldbach, J. (2015). Religious conflict, sexual identity, and suicidal behaviors among LGBT young adults. *Archives of Suicide Research*, 19(4), 472–88. https://doi.org/10.1080/13811118.2015.1004476

Gleig, A. (2012). Queering Buddhism or Buddhist de-queering? Reflecting on differences amongst Western LGBTQI Buddhists and the limits of liberal convert Buddhism. *Theology & Sexuality*, 18(3), 198–214. https://doi.org/10.1179/1355835813Z.00000000015

Goodrich, K. M., & Luke, M. (2019). Consensual qualitative research of LGB persons' counseling experiences addressing religious/spiritual foci. *Journal of Counseling Sexology & Sexual Wellness: Research, Practice, and Education*, 1(1), 5.

Gubbala, S., Poushter, J., & Huang, C. (2023). How people around the world view same-sex marriage. *Pew Research Center*. https://www.pewresearch.org/short-reads/2023/11/27/how-people-around-the-world-view-same-sex-marriage/

Gutkowski, S. (2021). Secular feelings, settler feelings: The case of Palestine/Israel. *Religion, State & Society*, 49(1), 41–60. https://doi.org/10.1080/09637494.2021.1890971

Halberstam, J. (2005). *In a queer time and place: Transgender bodies, subcultural lives* (Vol. 3). NYU Press.

Halberstam, J. (2020). *The queer art of failure*. Duke University Press.

Haldeman, D. C. (2004). When sexual and religious orientation collide: Considerations in working with conflicted same-sex attracted male clients. *The Counseling Psychologist*, 32(5), 691–715. https://doi.org/10.1177/0011000004267560

Hammack, P. L., Frost, D. M., & Hughes, S. D. (2019). Queer intimacies: A new paradigm for the study of relationship diversity. *The Journal of Sex Research*, 56(4–5), 556–92. https://doi.org/10.1080/00224499.2018.1531281

Haraway, D. J. (2016). *Staying with the trouble: Making kin in the Chthulucene*. Duke University Press.

Heiden-Rootes, K., Wiegand, A., & Bono, D. (2019). Sexual minority adults: A national survey on depression, religious fundamentalism, parent relationship quality and acceptance. *Journal of Marital and Family Therapy*, 45(1), 106–19. https://doi.org/10.1111/jmft.12323

Human Rights Campaign (n.d.). Faith Positions. https://www.hrc.org/resources/faith-positions

Hunsberger, B. E. & Altemeyer, B. (2006). *Atheists: A groundbreaking study of America's nonbelievers*. Prometheus Books.

Jaffe, S. (2018). Queer time: The alternative to "adulting." *JSTOR Daily: Arts & Culture*. https://daily.jstor.org/queer-time-the-alternative-to-adulting/

Johnson, D. K. (2023). *The lavender scare: The Cold War persecution of gays and lesbians in the federal government*. University of Chicago Press.

Jones, J. M. (2024). LGBTQ+ Identification in U.S. Now at 7.6%. https://news.gallup.com/poll/611864/lgbtq-identification.aspx

Jones, T. W., Power, J., & Jones, T. M. (2022). Religious trauma and moral injury from LGBTQA+ conversion practices. *Social Science & Medicine*, 305, 115040. https://doi.org/10.1016/j.socscimed.2022.115040

Kahn, R. Y. H. (1989). Judaism and homosexuality: The traditionalist/progressive debate. *Homosexuality and Religion*, 18(3–4) 47–82. http://doi.org/10.1300/J082v18n03_03

Karol, D. (2023). How does party position change happen? The case of LGBT rights in the US. *Political Research Quarterly*, 76(4), 1736–50. https://doi.org/10.1177/10659129231176212
Kazyak, E., Burke, K., Behrendt, M., & Oliver, M. (2023). Religious exemption, LGBT rights, and the social construction of harm and freedom. *Law & Social Inquiry*, 49(2), 1–24. https://doi.org/10.1017/lsi.2023.5
Kinkel, R. J. (2013). *Papal Paralysis: How the Vatican Dealt with the AIDS Crisis.* Lexington Books.
Kolysh, S. (2017). Straight gods, white devils: Exploring paths to non-religion in the lives of black LGBTQ people. *Secularism and Nonreligion*, *6(4)*, 1–13. https://doi.org/10.5334/snr.83
Langton, D. R. (2024). The non-believing Jew: A historical survey of Judaism's engagement with atheism. *International Journal for the Study of Skepticism*, 14(2), 89–107. https://doi.org/10.1163/22105700-bja10081
Linneman, T. J., & Clendenen, M. A. (2009). Sexuality and the secular. In P. Zuckerman (Ed.), *Atheism and secularity* (pp. 89–112). Praeger.
Lopes, F. M. (2019). Perpetuating the patriarchy: misogyny and (post-)feminist backlash. *Philosophical Studies: An International Journal for Philosophy in the Analytic Tradition*, 176(9), 2517–38. http://www.jstor.org/stable/45211664
Mattingly, M. S., Galliher, R. V., Dehlin, J. P., Crowell, K. A., & Bradshaw, W. S. (2016). A mixed methods analysis of the family support experiences of GLBQ Latter-day Saints. *Journal of GLBT Family Studies*, 12(4), 386–409.
Mills, S. S. (2014). A tale of two closets. In M. Brewster (Ed.), *Atheists in America* (pp. 95–100). Columbia University Press.
Muñoz, J. E. (2019). *Cruising utopia: The then and there of queer futurity, 10th Anniversary Edition*. New York University Press.
Newcomb, M. E., & Mustanski, B. (2010). Internalized homophobia and internalizing mental health problems: A meta-analytic review. *Clinical Psychology Review*, 30(8), 1019–29. https://doi.org/10.1016/j.cpr.2010.07.003
Norris, P. D. (2014). Far from home. In M. Brewster (Ed.), *Atheists in America*, (pp. 108–16). Columbia University Press.
O'Brien, J. (2004). Wrestling the angel of contradiction: Queer Christian identities. *Culture and Religion*, 5(2), 179–202. https://doi.org/10.1080/143830042000225420
Pachankis, J. E., Mahon, C. P., Jackson, S. D., Fetzner, B. K., & Bränström, R. (2020). Sexual orientation concealment and mental health: A conceptual and meta-analytic review. *Psychological Bulletin*, 146(10), 831.
Penningroth, D. C. (2021). Everyday use: A history of civil rights in black churches. *Journal of American History*, 107(4), 871–98. https://doi.org/10.1093/jahist/jaaa462
Pew Research Center (2024a). Religion and religious affiliation. https://www.pewresearch.org/methods/2024/02/07/religion-and-religious-affiliation/
Pew Research Center (2024b). Religious "nones" in America: Who they are and what they believe. https://www.pewresearch.org/religion/2024/01/24/religious-nones-in-america-who-they-are-and-what-they-believe/
Przeworski, A., Peterson, E., & Piedra, A. (2021). A systematic review of the efficacy, harmful effects, and ethical issues related to sexual orientation change efforts. *Clinical Psychology: Science and Practice*, 28(1), 81–100. https://doi-org.tc.idm.oclc.org/10.1111/cpsp.12377
Reyes, M. E. S., Bautista, N. B., Betos, G. R. A., Martin, K. I. S., Sapio, S. T. N., Pacquing, M. C. T., & Kliatchko, J. M. R. (2023). In/out of the closet: Perceived social support and outness

among LGB youth. *Sexuality & Culture: An Interdisciplinary Quarterly*, 27(1), 290–309. https://doi.org/10.1007/s12119-022-10013-7

Rich, A. C. (2003). Compulsory heterosexuality and lesbian existence (1980). *Journal of Women's History*, 15(3), 11–48. https://doi.org/10.1353/jowh.2003.0079.

Schippers, M. (2019). Polyamory and a queer orientation to the world. In B. L. Simula, J. E., Sumerau, & A. Miller (Eds.), *Expanding the rainbow* (pp. 71–80). Brill.

Schulzke, M. (2013). The politics of new atheism. *Politics and Religion*, 6(4), 778–99. https://doi.org/10.1017/S1755048313000217

Shilo, G., & Savaya, R. (2012). Mental health of lesbian, gay, and bisexual youth and young adults: Differential effects of age, gender, religiosity, and sexual orientation. *Journal of Research on Adolescence*, 22(2), 310–25. https://doi.org/10.1111/j.1532-7795.2011.00772.x

Simula, B. L. (2021). Introduction to the special issue: BDSM Studies. *Sexualities*, 24(5–6), 699–707. https://doi.org/10.1177/1363460721993039

Skidmore, S. J., Lefevor, G. T., Larsen, E. R., Golightly, R. M., & Abreu, R. L. (2023). "We are scared of being kicked out of our religion!": Common challenges and benefits for sexual minority latter-day saints. *Psychology of Sexual Orientation and Gender Diversity*, 10(4), 663–74. https://doi.org/10.1037/sgd0000571

Sontag, S. (2001). *Against interpretation: And other essays*. Macmillan.

Stone, L. (2023). Ultra-Orthodox fertility and marriage in the United States. *Demographic Research*, 49, 769–82. https://www.jstor.org/stable/48754924

TallBear, K., Clarke, A. E., & Haraway, D. J. (2018). Making love and relations beyond settler sex and family. In S. Rayter & L. Halpern Zisman (Eds). *Queerly Canadian: An Introductory Reader in Sexuality Studies*, (pp. 18–28). Canadian Scholar.

Toesland, F. (2019). Affirming mosques help gay Muslims reconcile faith, sexuality. *NBC News*. https://www.nbcnews.com/feature/nbc-out/affirming-mosques-help-gay-muslims-reconcile-faith-sexuality-n988151

Turpin, H. (2022). *Unholy Catholic Ireland: Religious hypocrisy, secular morality, and Irish irreligion*. Stanford University Press.

Upadhyay, N. (2020). Hindu Nation and its queers: Caste, Islamophobia, and de/coloniality in India. *Interventions*, 22(4), 464–80. https://doi.org/10.1080/1369801X.2020.1749709

Ward, J. (2022). *The tragedy of heterosexuality* (Vol. 56). NYU Press.

Wilkinson, D. J., & Johnson, A. (2020). A systematic review of qualitative studies capturing the subjective experiences of gay and lesbian individuals' of faith or religious affiliation. *Mental Health, Religion & Culture*, 23(1), 80–95. https://doi.org/10.1080/13674676.2020.1724919

Willey, A. (2016). *Undoing monogamy: The politics of science and the possibilities of biology*. Duke University Press.

World Health Organization (2024). HIV. https://www.who.int/data/gho/data/themes/hiv-aids

Zuckerman, P. (2012). Contrasting irreligious orientation: atheism and secularity in the USA and Scandinavia. *Approaching Religion*, 2(1), 8–20. https://doi.org/10.30664/ar.67488

8

Living in the Margins

Transgender and Gender-Diverse Nonbelievers

Wei Motulsky, Veronica Kim,

and Clayton Hartmann

Chapter Outline

Transnegativity in Organized Religion

The Current Sociopolitical Landscape in the United States

In 2023 alone, state legislatures passed a staggering eighty-five bills—up from twenty-six in 2022—designed to further marginalize transgender and gender-diverse (TGD) people (Trans Legislation Tracker, 2024). In Oklahoma, health professionals can lose their license for providing referrals for gender-affirming care to anyone under twenty-six years old (OK SB129, 2023); in Wyoming, providing gender-affirming care to individuals under eighteen years old (regardless of whether parental consent was given) constitutes the felony of child abuse and is punishable by up to ten years in prison (WY SF0111, 2023); and in Arizona, books that discuss the topics of gender identity and pronoun use are banned and must be submitted to Arizona's Department of Education (AZ HB1700, 2023). Many of these and other bills reflect a growing religious movement spearheaded by Christian organizations such as the Alliance Defending Freedom, the Family Research Council, the Liberty Council, and the American Principles Project and backed by conservative lawmakers (e.g., Parks, 2024; Alliance Defending Freedom, 2024; Family Research Council, 2016).

These pieces of legislation—and the organizations that lobby for them—often use nonreligious language as justifications for their necessity; for instance, the Stop the Sexualization of Children Act, initially proposed in 2022, purports that books and lessons "involving gender identity, gender dysphoria, transgenderism, sexual orientation, or related subjects" (Stop the Sexualization of Children Act, 2022, para. 2) harmfully sexualize young children. Yet private correspondences between key lawmakers suggest a religious motivation. A leak of emails between Republican Representative Fred Deutch, Idaho Representative Julianne Young, and other anti-TGD lobbyists included the phrases "the Devil never sleeps" and "Know that you are HIS [God's] representative today" regarding how to pass additional anti-TGD legislation (Zoledziowski, 2023).

The aforementioned bills reflect a long-standing, religiously moored transnegativity. Rhetoric accusing TGD people of "promoting pedophilia" (Geonzon, 2021) is the latest strategy by religious conservatives to restrict TGD peoples' access to healthcare. Similarly, while the volume of transphobic bills in 2023 was unprecedented, many religiously conservative organizations have been pushing for anti-TGD legislation for decades and have only begun to garner mainstream support (Kindy, 2022). One noteworthy example is that of the Alliance Defending Freedom, which has publicly defended parents' rights to force their TGD children to undergo conversion therapy, treatment designed to "cure" queerness, despite a vast body of research concluding that conversion therapy has severe negative psychological impacts (e.g., Kindy, 2022; Trispiotis & Purshouse, 2022). These impacts can include, and are not limited to, increased levels of depression, anxiety, and suicidality (Goodyear et al., 2022).

These bills and the beliefs of those supporting them reflect a shifting and increasingly divided political landscape. As an example, one study by the Pew Research Center found that 66 percent of surveyed Republicans believe that society has gone "too far" in accepting TGD people, while only 15 percent of their Democratic counterparts hold this opinion (Parker et al., 2022). These numbers are divided not only according to party lines, but also by religious identity, with one meta-analysis finding that nonreligious and Jewish people reported lower levels of transnegativity and more positive attitudes toward TGD people compared to Muslim and Christian respondents (Campbell et al., 2019).

Of the aforementioned religions, it is particularly important to pay attention to trends within Christianity given that, as of 2020, a staggering 70 percent of those living in the United States (US) identified with one sect of Christianity (PRRI, 2021). Within those sects, 75 percent of Protestants and 62 percent of Catholics believe that sex at birth determines gender identity, up from 71 percent and 52 percent respectively, in 2021. In contrast, only 24 percent of atheists hold these views compared to 20 percent in 2021 (Lipka & Tevington, 2022). Despite overwhelming evidence suggesting that affirming one's gender identity and receiving support for it tends to significantly reduce suicidal ideation and attempts, depression, and anxiety (American Psychiatric Association, 2025; Hughto et al., 2020;

Tordoff et al., 2022), conservative religious groups continue to pour money and resources into restricting TGD peoples' access to health care and reducing public acceptance of TGD people. This push is only one of and the most public of campaigns by the Christian right, also known as the religious right.

Looking Back at the Religious Right

The religious right is a relatively new presence in American politics. Despite the widespread belief that it began with *Roe v. Wade*, the religious right was conceived in response to 1954's *Brown v. Board of Education*, the landmark Supreme Court Case ruling racial segregation in school as unconstitutional (*Brown v. Board*, 1954). When Christian universities were denied federal funding for discriminating on the basis of race, conservative leaders such as Paul Weyrich, cofounder of the conservative think tank the Heritage Foundation, saw their opportunity to galvanize millions of evangelical voters behind specific conservative causes. These causes include, but are not limited to, defending racial segregation, banning abortion, and winnowing down TGD people's rights (Balmer, 2021).

Decades later, by the time Donald Trump was elected president of the United States, the religious right had snowballed from a fringe movement to a core political identity for Christians—the majority of whom identify as evangelical—of all ages (Dias & Graham, 2023). This surge in religious conservatism can be tied to a number of factors, including widening socioeconomic inequality, a global pandemic that underscored a mistrust in secular science, and social media's ability to spread (mis)information at breakneck speeds (Jones, 2023, Stewart, 2022). In turn, these factors intersect and further heighten the tension between religion and TGD rights.

The religious right has adopted TGD issues as one of its core political agendas by leaning on several different arguments. When asked to explain the reasoning behind their beliefs, those identifying with the religious right stated unfair athletic advantages in sports, while others cited concern over impressionable children in classrooms and doctors' offices (Meckler & Clement, 2023). Christian rights groups also argue that the Christian God determines biological sex and gender identity (Anderson, 2017), that identifying as TGD rejects the natural order (Walker, 2022), and that supporting TGD people means they are more likely to be depressed, misuse substances, and die by suicide (Alliance Defending Freedom, 2022).

Religiously based transnegative arguments often call upon specific passages in various holy texts; for example, the Christian right asserts that gender is binary, immutable, and predetermined by God based on a simplified and literal interpretation of Genesis 1 (Stuart & Nichols, 2020). It is not only Evangelical Christians who overlook other interpretations of the scripture that suggest gender diversity and erase TGD identities (HRC Foundation, n.d.; Roughgarden, 2013); the Catholic Church states that gender confirmation surgery cannot change one's God-given sex, referring to one's sex assigned at birth (Norton, 2011). Pope Francis, moreover, pointed to "gender ideology" as the "worst danger" in the modern era (Shine, 2024). Similarly, the Southern Baptist Convention rejects gender confirmation surgery and argues that gender is determined by one's chromosomes and external genitalia (Helminiak, 2018). Gender affirmation surgery is also forbidden in Orthodox Judaism based on *Leviticus* 22:24, which prohibits the sexual mutilation of animals, and *Deuteronomy* 22:5, which condemns cross-dressing (Helminiak, 2018). Transnegative interpretations of religious texts negatively impact TGD Muslims as well, whose identities are considered as "rebellion against the created order . . . [that is] sinful" by Islamic conservatives despite alternative interpretations of the Quran (Zaharin et al., 2020, p. 235).

History of Gender-Based Religious Oppression

The religiously rooted criminalization of gender diversity traces back to settler colonialism when European migrants imposed Christian morality on Indigenous communities (Morgensen, 2010). Despite the long-standing tradition of gender fluidity within Indigenous cultures, individuals who deviated from Western gender norms were derogatorily labeled as *berdache*, which originates from the Arabic word for slave and is French for "kept boy" or "male prostitute" (Thomas & Jacobs, 1999; Smithers, 2022). Under the civilizing mission, Indigenous people were forced to assimilate and conform to Christian and Eurocentric understandings of gender and sexuality (Delatolla, 2020). Notably, Indigenous children were violently relocated to government-funded, church-run residential boarding schools, where their Indigenous heritage was systematically suppressed and Christian values, including cisnormative and binary gender roles, were enforced through emotional and physical abuse (Wesley, 2015). These colonial practices have critically altered Indigenous understandings of gender and sexuality, exposing the current generation of TGD and/or Two-Spirit Indigenous people to cumulative discrimination and higher rates of mental health challenges (DeChants et al., 2023).

Framed within the backdrop of the cultural genocide of Indigenous communities, religious justification for gender-based oppression is not new (see Avishai et al., 2015, for women's experiences in religions); rather, the anti-TGD campaign is only one cause taken up by religious conservatives (Robinson & Spivey, 2019). Not all religious sects have equal involvement in these efforts, however. While progressive religious sects such as the Episcopal Church and the Presbyterian Church have expressed political support for transgender rights (Schjonberg, 2017), the Evangelical Church—a global pan-Protestant movement—has been at the forefront of spreading anti-lesbian, gay, bisexual, transgender, and queer (LGBTQ) campaigns nationally and globally. Indeed, data suggest that the US Christian right spent nearly $300 million between 2008 and 2019 on anti-gay and anti-TGD messaging in countries such as Uganda, Hungary, and Poland with the goal of creating an international precedent for legislation in the United States (Perkins, 2023). These efforts culminated in evangelical US American organizations establishing a prominent visible presence in Uganda, which in 2023 passed some of the harshest anti-LGBTQ legislation in history despite its pre-colonial stance of sexual and gender diversity (Oliver, 2013; Namubiru & Wepukhulu, 2020). Put differently, despite the increase in nonbelievers in the United States, the US Christian right continues to have a neocolonial influence over international gender and sexual identity politics (Oliver, 2013).

This type of discrimination is concerning given that individuals with multiple minoritized identities, such as non-believing TGD people of color, may experience cumulative discrimination in that they may be subjected to transphobia from their racial/ethnic community and racism from their TGD community if that community is predominantly White (Abbott et al., 2020; Cyrus, 2017). The identity management of TGD people of color may be further complicated by their prior or current religious memberships, which can serve as a significant source of community connection to racial/ethnic minority groups; for example, despite the critical role the Black church has had in providing emotional, political, and social support for Black and African American individuals, the invisibility of and/or violence against TGD Black and African American individuals in the church has led this population to feel ostracized or hide their identities to avoid discrimination (Chaney & Patrick, 2011).

The link between transnegativity and religion is especially important for people of color who have recently migrated to the United States. Indeed, spirituality can be a source of resilience among Latine immigrants, but connecting to spirituality for TGD Latine individuals can be a complicated and emotionally taxing journey due to transprejudice in traditional religious spaces, notably Christian or Catholic mass (Caraves, 2021). Similarly, Christian moral values have been braided into secular family values in some Christian Chinese communities, who have been vocal about their anti-LGBTQ stances (Leung, 2017). Transnegativity is also not exclusive to Christian spaces. In TGD people with a Jewish Orthodox background, strict binary gender norms that are enforced in religious practices can further exacerbate the minority stress of TGD people of color (Darwin, 2020). Similarly, some TGD Muslims who were exposed to transphobia in mainstream Muslim culture have chosen to establish their own LGBTQ Muslim groups (Golriz, 2022).

Paths to Nonbelief Among Transgender and Gender-Diverse People

When faced with transnegativity, not all religious TGD people choose to stay in their belief communities. Transnegativity within organized religions drives many TGD individuals toward nonbelief, whether through leaving their faith or never identifying with a religious affiliation in the first place. A 2020 national survey revealed that younger TGD adults are more likely to identify as nonbelievers, with approximately 60 percent of TGD adults aged eighteen to thirty-four identifying as such (Conron et al., 2020). This trend aligns with another national survey capturing a rising rate of religiously unaffiliated adults regardless of gender identity (Smith et al., 2024). Given the significant proportion of TGD adults who identify as nonbelievers, it is important to understand their paths to nonbelief. A previous study involving TGD nonbelievers found that 58 percent of the sample left traditional monotheistic religions, whereas 24.6 percent of the sample reported never having been religious (Exline et al., 2021). This section describes various reasons and struggles that propel TGD people to denounce religion, as well as the identity integration processes that follow.

It is first important to note that clinicians, both religious and secular, may have their own biases and lack nuance in understanding faith practices and even spirituality, consequently viewing them as cultural monoliths or existing in complete binaries. The first step in understanding a TGD client's transition out of a previously held faith identity is to understand and respect the diversity of approaches that various religious communities have taken in position with or in opposition to the TGD experience.

Rejecting Background

For many TGD people, the religious experience is inherently exclusionary not explicitly because of cultural bigotry, but because in "doing religion," one must simultaneously be "doing gender" (West & Zimmerman, 1987) as it is historically defined in scripture and understood by modern practitioners (Sumerau et al., 2019). For example, during their gender transition, Jewish trans men have struggled with the "how and when" of donning the kippah (ritual head garment) worn by other observant men within specific sects of Judaism (Strassfeld, 2010). It has been well-argued that gender is a social construct, akin to an accomplishment (West & Zimmerman, 1987), but different from other accomplishments, it needs to be continually reperformed in front of other social actors in order to hold onto the ownership of the accomplishment (Butler, 1990). Due to the prescriptive gendered rituals, totems and taboos found within many sacred scriptures, many religions inadvertently create a gender-essentialist ideal for their adherents to follow (Rich, 2023; Orme et al., 2017), an ideal that often excludes those who expand upon the traditionally limited scope of gender. By virtue of their binary-subverting relationship with gender identity, TGD individuals often fall short of concepts such as the *good Christian woman* or Islam's *Kamil* (perfect) *mu'min*, leading them to feel unable to embody being a (gendered) child of God.

Research shows that TGD exclusion varies widely across interpretations of religious scripture and are expressed to greater or lesser degrees in specific sects or denominations (Campbell et al., 2019). Key factors in determining a religious community's interpersonal and theological mistreatment and rejection of TGD individuals has been shown to be correlated with and identified by one's level of religiosity, or the degree to which religion influences their daily life. Religiosity is a mixture of spiritual fundamentalism (religious dogmatism), biblical literalism (taking scripture to be literal and not as interpretable for a modern context), and attendance rates at religious services (Campbell et al., 2019). Assessing the degree of religiosity of a client's past will help clinicians understand the depth and frequency that they were exposed to anti-trans rhetoric, teaching, and relationships. Furthermore, despite the acquisition of a secular identity and an outward rejection of a religious past, messaging around sin, damnation, and divine rejection can still linger in the psyche, causing continued harm and requiring intentional clinical space to allow for healing (Stone, 2013; Sumerau et al., 2019).

Accepting Background

Some secular TGD clients may have historically experienced mixed or even positive experiences with faith groups and spirituality (Wang et al., 2023) and nevertheless still migrated toward a secular social or theological position. Much of the academic work in the area of LGBTQ individuals in organized religion focused on the necessity for queer individuals to find reconciliation between their identities and a "contradicting" faith practice (Gibbs & Goldbach, 2015), dismissing the potential for some individuals to experience authentic, non-conflicted religious/spiritual experiences (Fuist, 2016). Wang and colleagues (2023) note that some TGD individuals have found trans-affirming faith communities and even utilize their faith in the process of "finding peace that a higher power shaped their identity intentionally" (p. 4). Furthermore, all-or-nothing thinking about religious exclusion dismisses modern trends of some religions, denominations, or specific fellowships to generate inclusivity and move past exclusionary scriptures and theologies (Kitaen & Xu, 2023). This development is most clearly demonstrated by the 2022 schism in the United Methodist Church, the United States' largest Christian denomination, which officially fissured after years of individual congregations and pastors refusing to side against queer inclusion (Johnson & Lukert, 2023). There are distinctions between religions, too, with research suggesting that Judaism can have more tolerant attitudes toward out-groups, such as gender minorities, than Christians (Ben-Lulu, 2021; Campbell et al., 2019). Similarly, Islam has gone through different epochs of supporting trans-affirming care with reassignment-affirming fatwas (Quranic legal interpretations) being delivered by leading Islamic jurists (legal scholars) in the 1980s (Zaharin & Pallotta-Chiarolli, 2020).

It is important to note that the nature of power, even hegemonic or authoritarian power within organized religion, is not inherently static or fixed. Discourse and struggle with dominant narratives within religion can serve as an essential venue for identity construction (Fuist, 2016), such as after wars and humanitarian crises demonstrated (Seul, 1999). As an example, many Cambodian survivors of the Khmer Rouge killing fields returned to Buddhism to make sense of the atrocities they experienced, deepening their connection to ritual and the quest to understand the soul (Agger, 2015). In the case of TGD persons, it is possible that faith-based exclusion and marginalization can turn them either away from or toward the soul. By maintaining an open phenomenological frame, clinicians and researchers can step back and allow secular TGD people to make space for their rejection (or acceptance) of a life of faith that can be driven by the same reasons that may drive a cisgender person (Pérez & Vallières, 2019).

Faith Questioning

A growing body of work suggests that participation in religion can promote physical and psychological health, with religiosity being associated with lower levels of depression, substance use, and suicidality (Garssen et al., 2020, Lucchetti, et al., 2021). Less discussed is how religiosity can also produce various forms of religious struggles and inflict emotional distress. Extant scholarship has conceptualized religious struggles in three domains: divine, intrapsychic, and interpersonal (Exline, 2013). For TGD individuals, these religious struggles may be exacerbated by transnegative sentiments and practices in organized religions (Exline et al., 2021). Religious struggles in the divine domain entail negative perceptions of God, which lead to anger toward God and fear of punishment. TGD individuals from religious backgrounds often express fear related to disapproval and punishment from God for defying "God's chosen sex" (or in other words, affirming their own gender identities), which is a popular narrative in conservative religions that is used against TGD communities. Conversely, some TGD individuals believe that their TGD identities are part of God's plan. While they are then less likely to fear God's admonishment, they are not immune from religious struggles that come from having to grapple with their belief that God was responsible for their TGD identities and subsequently their gender-based minority stress (Meyer, 1995).

Religious struggles concerning morals, ultimate meaning, and doubt constitute intrapsychic religious struggles (Pargament et al., 2005). Due to the transnegative messages that proliferate in organized religions, TGD individuals may carry internalized stigma toward their gender identity and experience moral religious struggles. One may also grapple with felt discrepancies between personal beliefs and religious doctrines. This gap is more pronounced for TGD individuals given the uptick in religious conservatism in the United States, which is correlated with the increase of anti-transgender laws and the general public's hostile stance toward TGD issues (Lipka & Tevington, 2022; Nagourney & Peters, 2023). Subsequently, they may begin to doubt religious teachings, which can be disruptive to their self-concept and orientation to the world (Exline et al., 2021). The controversial scholarship on the cognitive science of religion suggested that nonbelief is "unnatural" (i.e., culturally less familiar and salient), revealing the possible benefit of existential and social security that religions can provide—especially in majority religious countries such as the United States (Norenzayan & Gervais, 2013). Indeed, many TGD individuals may struggle with finding meaning or purpose in life as they embark on paths toward nonbelief (Exline et al., 2021). Simultaneously, religious exiting may be the only feasible way TGD individuals can manage these various religious struggles.

Both divine and intrapsychic religious struggles may manifest interpersonally. In fact, interpersonal religious struggles are most frequently experienced among formerly religious TGD individuals, with more than half reporting an experience of social rejection from religious communities (Exline et al., 2021). Furthermore, research indicates that religious fundamentalism is a significant predictor of prejudice against TGD people (Campbell et al., 2019) and that conceptualizing God as punitive is associated with restricting the civil rights of marginalized groups (Froese & Bader, 2008). Since a great portion of Americans are raised religious, nonbelievers may also have to disengage from their family when they exit religion (Zimmerman et al., 2015). At any stage of their path to nonbelief, a TGD individual may experience discrimination and rejection from their religious family and community members based on gender, nonbelief, or both. In their former religious communities, TGD individuals may experience invalidation and ostracization due to the rigid cis-patriarchal gender norms and gender segregation prevalent in many organized religions (Cadge, 2004). After denouncing faith, nonbelievers have reported experiencing unaffirming experiences, such as others' resisting and questioning their nonbelief (Brewster, 2014). For TGD nonbelievers, these experiences can also trigger experiences of transphobia and exacerbate interpersonal struggles.

Secular Quest for Meaning

Given these religious struggles, paths toward nonbelief can feel uncertain. Traditionally, religiosity has helped people cope with existential concerns, such as connecting to their life purpose and managing their death-related anxieties, which can promote overall psychological well-being (Arrowood et al., 2021). In a predominantly religious society, nonbelief can make it challenging to find meaning and purpose separate from religious beliefs, whether one has a former religious affiliation or not. Meaning-making may be especially hard for TGD individuals, who may hold gender-based existential doubts that cannot be quenched by religiosity and that can further increase emotional distress and a sense of isolation—especially when they exit their former religious communities (Exline et al., 2021).

This doubt can be a double-edged sword. Indeed, the ability to doubt and search for meaning has been connected to higher levels of open-mindedness and cultural tolerance (Arrowood et al., 2021). Furthermore, a quest for meaning in a "godless universe" illuminates other avenues for cultivating a purposeful life that promotes personal growth, virtuosity, and relationality (Wielenberg, 2022, p. 217). This process of self-producing meaning in life can enhance one's sense of agency, which was common for nonbelievers and did not attenuate the benefits of having self-constructed meaning compared to religious meaning (Speed et al., 2018). In other words, while doubt produced by religious struggles can incite negative emotions, it may also have potential long-term benefits by inspiring a new, more aligned set of personal significance and purpose.

It is worth adding that, while some TGD nonbelievers may continue along socially congruent lines of seeking meaning amid their disentanglement from societally dominant conceptualization of gender, some nonbelievers may choose to exist in and/or learn to tolerate varying levels of meaningless or purposeless to their lives. It is outside the context of this chapter to explore the myriad ways in which nonbelievers have absolved themselves from the burden of meaning-making. Yet given the data already presented, TGD individuals may be well positioned to challenge the social norm of meaning-making due to the already demonstrated history of living outside of society's ideologies.

Coming Out as a Nonbeliever

Holding a nonbeliever identity in the United States, a predominantly Christian nation, can be fraught with internal and interpersonal conflicts. Christian values embedded in the cultural landscape dominate the mainstream perspectives on gender and the meaning of life in ways that may marginalize TGD nonbelievers. Consequently, TGD nonbelievers face an added layer of interpersonal challenges when they "come out" as nonbelievers (Abbott & Mollen, 2018). Based on Quinn and Earnshaw's (2011) concealable stigmatized identity framework, a nonbeliever identity requires self-disclosure in the United States, where religiosity is typically assumed and expected. However, many nonbelievers choose to hide their identities to avoid potential discrimination, including negative stereotyping of atheists as immoral and deviant, pressure to pretend to be religious, social exclusion, physical threats, and danger (Brewster et al., 2016). Unfortunately, identity concealment comes at a cost, including a diminished sense of community connection and positive emotions with the nonbeliever identity, ultimately negatively impacting psychological well-being (Abbott & Mollen, 2018). It is also important to acknowledge that TGD gender identity may be a concealable stigmatized identity to many TGD individuals, particularly binary transgender people. In such cases, navigating identity disclosure and concealment becomes an extremely complicated process requiring further support.

Case Study

Beyond providing context for the unique experiences TGD nonbelievers may experience, the purpose of this chapter is to support clinicians in working with TGD nonbelievers and those negotiating new relationships with their faith systems. To that end, the latter half of this chapter is dedicated to providing readers with support for how to do so by drawing upon the authors' clinical experiences. The following case study is a de-identified example of a TGD client in the process of negotiating a new worldview.

Presenting Problem and Client Description

Rowan is a White, middle-class, assigned-female-at-birth junior at a medium-sized private Catholic university located in the Midwest region of the United States. Rowan has been surrounded by the Catholic community—first in the form of their immediate and moderately religious family, and then at university—for their entire life. At their parents' urging, Rowan chose a Catholic university so that they could continue to center their Catholic identity while in college, even though Rowan has historically held a casual relationship with Catholicism.

Rowan entered college suspecting that they may identify as nonbinary. Terrified of coming out, Rowan instead became involved in their university's branch of the Catholic

Church. Rowan self-nominated to co-lead their school's Bible study club with their boyfriend, whom they met during first-year seminar. Rowan also volunteered to clean the priest's vestments before mass each Sunday and has subsequently developed close relationships with several members of the priesthood. To their friends, family, boyfriend, and peers, Rowan uses she/her pronouns and is the poster child for a college-aged Catholic woman. However, Rowan feels like a fraud, as they have never felt fully invested in the Catholic Church and have begun to self-identify as nonbinary in private.

Without telling their friends or family, Rowan began attending their school's Queer Alliance club as a heterosexual, cisgender ally. They experienced meetings to be cliquey and felt negatively judged because of their close affiliation with certain priests who made transphobic and homophobic remarks toward students in previous years. Rowan attended a handful of times before deciding that the club was not for them.

Unsure of what to do, Rowan turned to Father Ron, their family's priest, and came out to him as nonbinary. Father Ron was warm and kind to Rowan, offering to meet regularly to support Rowan with their identity formation. However, it soon became clear to Rowan that Father Ron was using these meetings to express concern over and disapproval of Rowan's identity and to convince Rowan to "move on from this phase of life." Rowan cut off contact with Father Ron, leading their parents to become suspicious of Rowan's sudden change in attitude toward someone who has been a mentor to the family.

Following their break with Father Ron, Rowan began feeling increasingly ostracized by Catholicism and abandoned by God. They stayed up late for several nights in a row to research the Catholic Church's long and complicated history with the queer community, and the more they read, the more convinced they became that a core aspect of their identity was irreconcilable with their religion. To that end, in addition to identifying as nonbinary, Rowan began to see themselves as an agnostic.

This inner tension physically manifested when Rowan experienced a panic attack while at Sunday mass. Soon after, they scheduled an appointment at their university's counseling center. To the intake coordinator, they reported, "I don't know what to do. I don't belong anywhere." They also expressed the fear that if they were to come out as nonbinary and/or agnostic, they would lose the support of their boyfriend, their friends, and their family.

Key Considerations

The aforementioned case study is designed to not only illustrate the nuances of a young person's journey toward nonbelief, but also to foster self-reflection on how we as clinicians might react to this type of case. Rowan is seeking mental health treatment at a volatile and sensitive time in their life. They have experienced significant ruptures with the Catholic Church and the queer community. To that end, Rowan may enter into therapy understandably hesitant to invest in a new relationship. Therapy should thus focus on leveraging the therapeutic alliance (Bordin, 1979) to create an opportunity for Rowan to construct a self-perception that more fully affirms all aspects of their personhood, religious or otherwise. This work may carry its own set of challenges given that Rowan reported feeling unmoored and isolated in multiple ways. Indeed, Rowan may rely on their therapist more than the average client, particularly as they navigate the process of individuation and separation (Mahler, 1972) from Catholicism and, perhaps, from friends and family depending upon those people's reactions to Rowan's nonbinary and/or agnostic identities. As such, treatment must account for the potential of Rowan's strong transferential (Rowan responding to the clinician similarly to how they have reacted to others in their life; Klein, 1952).

Regarding the clinician themselves, it is important that Rowan's therapist examines their own biases and assumptions. Literature suggests that mental health providers bring in a slew of their own biases and assumptions into work with their clients *regardless* of the valence (positive or negative) of those biases; for instance, well-meaning clinicians might over-emphasize a person's TGD identity, while avoidant therapists might under-emphasize it by only wishing to speak about their client's queerness (Mizock & Lundquist, 2016). Either path would constitute poor clinical practice insofar as they would center the clinician's assumptions about the course of treatment over Rowan's therapeutic needs. It is, therefore, paramount that Rowan's therapist remembers that a single, universal, and coherent coming out narrative—either as it pertains to gender or religious identity—neither exists nor should be encouraged.

An additional pitfall clinicians must be on the lookout for is that of unexamined countertransferential (Tower, 1956) reactions—in other words, those in which the therapist reacts to Rowan as if Rowan were someone in the therapist's own life. Relatedly, over-eager therapists may see their role as that of a savior or, should they hold similar experiences to Rowan's, as a "wounded healer" (McBeath, 2019). One example might be of a clinician who sees a younger version of themselves in Rowan and subconsciously pushes Rowan down the same path because they found such personal meaning in it.

The therapist's potential influence over Rowan is a reflection of the power differential inherent in the therapeutic dyad of knower (therapist) and known (client), though scholars have aptly pointed to the ways this dyad is not necessarily problematic (Brown, 2007). This consideration is important from both a knowledge/expertise and positionality differential. Clinicians working with TGD populations are often in a position of power and privilege in relation to their clients due to factors of class, earning potential, and professional status (Bergkamp et al., 2023; Carpenter et al., 2020). Cisgender and heterosexual clinicians only further widen that power gap and are encouraged to bridge the power distance by socially locating their secular TGD client within Western cultural hegemony's matrix of power.

Widening the Lens

The motifs at the heart of Rowan's case can be generalized to treatment approaches to TGD nonbelievers across a variety of circumstances. Similarly to having a minority sexual orientation, TGD individuals and nonbelievers are the recipients of both prejudice and mistrust while also being unique from other forms of discrimination in that they are each potentially concealable identities (Totton et al., 2023). Thus, well-meaning post-feminists and neoliberal ideologies often assume an inherent necessity for gender and sexual minorities to disclose identities without factoring in the costs of such disclosures (Khuzwayo, 2021). Given a secular TGD client's social, socioeconomic, and geographic location, clinicians are encouraged to challenge narratives on the inherent necessity of being "out" with either or both identities. This consideration is important because for some TGD individuals, the compounding dyad of prejudice and mistrust may prove too much due to already elevated vulnerability to violence, discrimination, and stigmatization (Kade, 2021), while for others, being out with either or both identities may generate a source of personal empowerment and positive mental health outcomes (Sequeira et al., 2020; Smith, 2011).

Similar to assumptions about disclosure, clinicians who bear vicarious witness to their secular TGD client's compounding marginalization in a repressive region may be led to make non-client centered assumptions about their TGD clients' need to relocate to less social conservative, less religious, and more accepting locales. While evidence suggests that some regions of the Global North provide more sanctuary to LGBQT+ individuals than others (Nemoto et al., 2015), these assumptions may pressure TGD clients to prioritize certain aspects of themselves over others. For example, a well-intentioned clinician may assume that their secular TGD clients need to relocate out of the United States Bible Belt without taking into consideration familial, relational, political, racial, ethnic, and cultural ties that keep a secular TGD client in a less-than-ideal social and political environment (Frey et al., 2021).

Not only do these assumptions negate the potential that secular TGD individuals may have valid personal ties to discriminatory cultures, but they also make classist and regionalist assumptions that freedom of movement is equal for all (Carpenter et al., 2020). TGD individuals have been shown to suffer financially when compared to their cisgender peers (Carpenter et al., 2020). Similar to current assumptions that do not take socioeconomic class into account being made in cross-state access to abortion, lower-SES TGD individuals may be unlikely to bear the financial cost of relocation, exacerbating disparities in TGD mental health (Hermaszewska et al., 2022). Lastly, it makes assumptions that because discrimination may be less common in urban or coastal areas, secular TGD discrimination does not exist at all in these locations and is therefore inherently worth the financial and emotional expense to relocate (Arayasirikul et al., 2022).

Intersectionality

Considerations of wealth, mobility, and access speak to the importance of intersectionality, or the compounding impact holding multiple marginalized identities can have on a person (Crenshaw, 1989). In the United States, religion (Christianity) is often conflated with patriotism (Abbott et al., 2022), making secular immigrants and non-citizens doubly othered. Outsider status is magnified when secular cultural minorities are expected to use religious institutions catering to immigrants and refugees as the entrance point into work (Scribner et al., 2023, p. 148). Intersectionality also impacts the relationship between religious privilege and social class privilege. Similarly to secular ethnic minorities, the experience of working-class and low-income secularists is an understudied phenomenon, with class being a strong influence on anti-atheist stigma. Simply put, low-income secular individuals face different tensions than the rest of the secular population, such as increased class stigma and limited venues for identity disclosure (Abbott et al., 2022). Lastly, a cisgender gender identity can also play a role in freedom to express non-theistic thought (with cisgender men having more freedom), the logic of which may extend to trans women and gender-diverse individuals (Abbott et al., 2020).

The experience of secularism also varies greatly among different ethnic, cultural, and racial groups. As an example, in the introduction to his book, *Black Freethinkers: A History of African American Secularism* (2019), Christopher Cameron identifies the assumption that Black people are naturally religious and that the Black church is the de facto center of the Black community, an assumption that has historically erased Black secularism from academic inquiry. Similar assumptions have been made about Arab (Wu, 2007) and Indian (Quack, 2012) populations despite non-theism likely originating on the Indian subcontinent and playing a sizable role in Arab history and the shaping of various Arab cultures.

Clinical Takeaways

As clinicians are well-aware, no two clients are alike. With this constant in mind, the authors present several takeaways that may guide future clinical work with TGD nonbelievers.

Take What You Want and Leave the Rest

While some TGD populations have found validating communities of faith, an outsized portion of religions, scriptures, and faith groups have expressed implicit and explicit transphobic and trans-exclusionary rhetoric. In his seminal postcolonial work, *Black Skin, White Masks* (1952, p. 20), Frantz Fanon outlined a framework for how some oppressed populations are able to grasp power by internalizing the discriminatory-ethos of the oppressor. Similar to the internalization of the colonizer, the internalization of a god figure can continue to exert itself on the psyche even after a person has ended their faith (Stone, 2013). As stated above, some clinicians lacking in nuanced understanding of religion may feel inspired to impose an all-or-nothing approach to their secular TGD client's religious and spiritual pasts. Regardless of whether or not the client has had an explicit previous relationship with organized religion, the recommendation is to support TGD persons seeking their own nuanced relationship to spirituality that is free of assumption yet critically validating. This approach aligns with the 12-step motto of "take what you want, leave the rest," recognizing that 12-step programs can be religiously moored (see chapter 13). In this open framework, secular clients are encouraged to engage with and reclaim the aspects of spirituality and historical religious practice that they find helpful, while still respecting the potential for transphobic messaging to have been internalized.

Mourning the Loss of Religious Community, Approval, and Solace

Mourning the loss of valued aspects of difficult relationships is a cornerstone in supporting survivors of trauma and domestic violence (Messing et al., 2013). The difficulty in leaving such abusive relationships can mirror the difficulty in leaving coercive religious communities (Galanter, 1989). Just as has been shown in the support of survivors of abusive relationships (Fleischack et al., 2020), if the clinician sides too strongly with the TGD client's fear or hatred of their religious experience, it is possible that they will position themselves against different parts of the client who may be simultaneously missing or yearning for aspects of their former faith. Holding a dialectical approach to a client's faith journey—in other words, to see it as a rejection of certain aspects and the continued need for others—is thus crucial.

Research on the socially, economically, and psychologically adaptive aspects of religion among cisgender religious participants is abundant (Koenig, 2012). TGD-specific research has even shown religious community affiliation and church attendance sometimes decrease mortality and suicide (Ghazzawi et al., 2020; Grossman et al., 2016). Even secular TGD persons with no personal experience in a faith community are still capable of experiencing a sense of absence due to the cultural hegemonic ideal still placed on "having" a religion, which positions faith communities and religious identities as the presumptive Global North norm (Artz & Murphy, 2000). Clinicians are encouraged to strive toward a neutral and reflective stance, thereby creating space for the client to develop their own understanding without reenacting histories of coercion and paternalism (Stone, 2013). As conflicting feelings arise in the therapy, clinicians are encouraged to support clients in grieving the positive aspects of religious life while integrating them with experiences of damage and exclusion.

Naming General and Gender-Specific Religious Trauma

Winell (2011) proposed Religious Trauma Syndrome as a specific articulation of psychic trauma experienced by individuals leaving coercive and dogmatic religions. More generally, religious trauma can be defined as the "pervasive psychological damage resulting from religious messages, beliefs, and experiences" (Stone, 2013, p. 3). The construct of religious trauma is supported by intersecting near-concepts such as moral injury, soul distress, and spiritual bypass; all of which intersect on the point where spiritual coercion, clerical abuse, and authoritarianism touches the psyche (Jones et al., 2022). As of the time of this paper, there is not a manualized approach to treating religious trauma. Current recommendations include group and individual trauma therapy, psychoeducation on religion's ability to co-opt the attachment process, and education on the ability for religious trauma to make the continuance of spirituality difficult (Stone, 2013). Once the religious trauma framework is established for TGD persons, erasure, distancing, and religious-specific micro and macro aggressions can be processed like any other form of trauma (Hollier et al., 2022).

Managing Countertransference with Religiously Abused or Persecuted Persons

Clinicians, particularly those existing closer-in on the continuum toward the cultural center, have been observed manifesting a variety of perennial countertransferential concerns when working with TGD populations, including biological naturalism (Harris, 2022), concerns of over or under self-disclosing, and stirring unsettled notions of our own gender, sexuality, and privilege (Baumann et al., 2020). Similarly, when working with survivors of religious trauma, countertransferential enactments can include trying to control the session, avoiding specific topics and/or emotions, as well as a potential traumatic reopening of the clinician's own potential religious trauma (Stone, 2013). When working at the intersection of both of these avenues of marginalization and potential pain, clinicians are encouraged to examine their motivation for working with this population and to dialectically make space for their internal motivations to pull away from it. Clinicians are similarly encouraged to remember that serving as a holding space or container for traumatic affect (Anderson, 2022) can often inadvertently wound the container itself through the process of vicarious trauma (Kim et al., 2022). Lastly, even the most affirming and allied clinicians are not above (accidentally or intentionally) placing their TGD clients in the position of providing psychoeducation about their own gendered experiences (Mizock & Lundquist, 2016). Clinicians serving at this intersection will need to learn and continue to relearn how to best support this unique population.

Conclusion

Particularly in an age where conservative lawmakers are criminalizing TGD-affirming medical interventions and banning the discussion of TGD issues using thinly veiled religious justification, the dissonance between religiosity and a TGD identity may be widening. Indeed, in 2022 alone, hate crimes against TGD people rose by almost 33 percent compared to 2021 (FBI, n.d.). And with waitlists for TGD-affirming medical and psychological services in the United States ballooning to twelve to twenty-four months or longer (Dahlgren Allen et al., 2021; Savage & Bauer, 2021), it is clear that TGD people are in need of greater support. The question then becomes how we best provide it.

As clinicians, our job is two-fold: First, to educate ourselves on the unique needs and experiences of TGD nonbelievers and/or those on a faith journey; and second, to integrate this knowledge with our education on interventions, treatments, and psychological processes. As when working with clients at the intersection of any identity matrix, it is important to remember that a monolithic experience of and approach to treatment does not exist—despite the temptation to believe otherwise. There is also no such thing as a singular, "best" outcome. Indeed, as articulated above, TGD persons with both secular and religious pasts are routinely impacted by religious cultural dominance, prejudice, and stigmatization. While these factors likely impact all TGD persons to varying extents, an individual's social location can widely influence the experience and impact of marginalization. An intersectional approach is necessary in understanding the impact of secularism and religion on intersecting and diverging powers and privileges of class, race, ethnicity, and ableism are essential in socially locating an individual secular TGD person.

This truth is one that clinicians must confront, including the clinician assigned to Rowan. Rowan ended up engaging in treatment for several months, during which time they came out to select friends and to their boyfriend, most of whom were accepting. They also resigned as the co-leader of their school's Bible study group and withdrew from the duty of cleaning the priest's vestments. Throughout this time, Rowan reported varying levels of psychological distress in the forms of grief, anxiety, and depression, in addition to finding fulfillment in new forms of community outside of Catholicism (such as by attending a queer-affirming, nondenominational church). However, when confronted by their family about their decisions, Rowan promptly terminated therapy, became unresponsive to outreach attempts, renewed their extracurricular commitment to Catholicism, and resumed using she/her pronouns.

Those reading this chapter may, understandably, have complex emotional reactions to and lingering questions about Rowan's time in therapy. Abrupt terminations are seldom ideal and Rowan's therapist has had to come to terms with this lack of closure. Furthermore, while it is important to examine the course of treatment to understand why Rowan may not have felt able to continue therapy—or continue with this therapist—it is equally necessary to consider that this decision met a particular need for Rowan at a critical point in time.

Leaning on many of the strategies recommended in this chapter, Rowan's clinician can examine their own biases and assumptions about how therapy for TGD nonbelievers and/or those questioning their faith can look. Moreover, as difficult as it may be to accept, the decision to end therapy was part of Rowan's process. It would have been more harmful for Rowan's therapist to push a specific agenda onto Rowan's treatment, however well-intentioned doing so may have been.

Final Thoughts

The alarming spike in requests for TGD-affirming services and the dearth of clinicians able to provide them is an invitation to all of us to consider which roles we can and wish to play in supporting TGD nonbelievers. At the same time, we must remember that the very act of helping risks shoehorning our clients into a particular experience aligned with our personal belief systems regarding how secularism and gendered religiosity clash and intertwine. We also risk accidentally leveraging systems of power and oppression existent in any clinical relationship to push our own beliefs onto those we serve. This stance applies to any therapeutic relationship, yet it carries additional weight in the context of projecting what we believe to be the best manifestation of the intersection of TGD secularism.

That is not to say that clinicians must, should, or can embody complete neutrality—especially when there is substantial evidence suggesting that TGD-affirming medical and psychological interventions are positively correlated with mental well-being (e.g., Almazan & Keuroghlian, 2021; Dhejne et al., 2016; Fontanari et al., 2020). Rather, it is crucial for clinicians to understand what their particular TGD client needs, not what a well-intentioned, social justice-oriented clinician might *want* them to need, because while there is abundant opportunity for a more fulfilling life in integrating one's religious and gendered identities, so, too, is there unavoidable loss.

References

Abbott, D. M., & Mollen, D. (2018). Atheism as a concealable stigmatized identity: Outness, anticipated stigma, and well-being. *The Counseling Psychologist*, 46(6), 685–707. https://doi.org/10.1177/0011000018792669

Abbott, D. M., Mollen, D., Boyles, J. A., & Anaya, E. J. (2022). Hidden in plain sight: Working class and low-income atheists. *Journal of Counseling Psychology*, 69(1), 37–50. https://doi.org/10.1037/cou0000562

Abbott, D. M., Mollen, D., Mercier, C., Anaya, E. J., & Rukus, V. A. (2020). "Isn't atheism a White thing?": Centering the voices of atheists of color. *Journal of Counseling Psychology*, 67(3), 275–87. https://doi.org/10.1037/cou0000399

Agger, I. (2015). Calming the mind: Healing after mass atrocity in Cambodia. *Transcultural Psychiatry*, 52(4), 543–60. https://doi.org/10.1177/1363461514568336

Alliance Defending Freedom. (2022, August 31). *Gender dysphoria expert discusses the "science" regarding gender identity*. https://adflegal.org/article/gender-dysphoria-expert-discusses-science-regarding-gender-identity

Alliance Defending Freedom. (2024). *Parental rights*. https://adflegal.org/issues/parental-rights

Almazan, A. N., & Keuroghlian, A. S. (2021). Association between gender-affirming surgeries and mental health outcomes. *JAMA Surgery*, 156(7), 611–18. https://doi.org/10.1001/jamasurg.2021.0952

American Psychiatric Association. (2025, August 1). *Study finds long-term mental health benefits of gender-affirming surgery for transgender individuals*. https://www.psychiatry.org/patients-families/gender-dysphoria/what-is-gender-dysphoria

Anderson, J. N. (2017). Transgenderism and the Christian Church: An Overview. *Reformed Faith & Practice: The Journal of Reformed Theological Seminary*, 2(2), 51–71. https://journal.rts.edu/article/transgenderism-christian-perspective/

Andersson, P. (2022). Countertransference and therapeutic holding: Working with a perpetrator of domestic violence. *Psychodynamic Practice*, 28(3), 275–95. https://doi.org/10.1080/14753634.2022.2047101

Arayasirikul, S., Turner, C., Trujillo, D., Sicro, S. L., Scheer, S., McFarland, W., & Wilson, E. C. (2022). A global cautionary tale: Discrimination and violence against trans women worsen despite investments in public resources and improvements in health insurance access and utilization of health care. *International Journal for Equity in Health*, 21(32), 1–11. https://doi.org/10.1186/s12939-022-01632-5.

Arrowood, R. B., Vail, K. E., & Cox, C. R. (2021). The existential quest: Doubt, openness, and the exploration of religious uncertainty. *The International Journal for the Psychology of Religion*, 32(2), 89–126. https://doi.org/10.1080/10508619.2021.1902647

Artz, L., & Murphy, B. O. (2000). *Cultural hegemony in the United States.* SAGE. https://doi.org/10.4135/9781452204673

Avishai, O., Jafar, A., & Rinaldo, R. (2015). A gender lens on religion. *Gender & Society*, 29(1), 5–25. https://doi.org/10.1177/0891243214548920

AZ H.B. 1700, 56th Leg., 1st Reg. Sess. (2023, Arizona). Arizona Legislature. https://www.azleg.gov/legtext/56leg/1R/bills/SB1700S.pdf

Balmer, R. (2021, August 30). *The evangelical abortion myth: An excerpt from "Bad Faith."* Religion Dispatches. https://religiondispatches.org/the-evangelical-abortion-myth-an-excerpt-from-bad-faith/

Baumann, E. F., Ryu, D., & Harney, P. (2020). Listening to identity: Transference, countertransference, and therapist disclosure in psychotherapy with sexual and gender minority clients. *Practice Innovations*, 5(3), 246–56. https://doi.org/10.1037/pri0000132

Ben-Lulu, E. (2021). "Let us bless the twilight": Intersectionality of traditional Jewish ritual and queer pride in a reform congregation in Israel. *Journal of Homosexuality*, 68(1), 23–46. https://doi.org/10.1080/00918369.2019.1621555

Bergkamp, J., O'Leary Sloan, M., Krizizke, J., Lash, M., Trantel, N., Vaught, J., Fulmer, T., Waite, I., Martin, A. M., Scheiderer, C., & Olson, L. (2023). Pathways to the therapist paragon: A decolonial grounded theory. *Frontiers in Psychology*, 14(1), 1–13. https://doi.org/10.3389/fpsyg.2023.1185762

Bordin, E. S. (1979). The generalizability of the psychoanalytic concept of the working alliance. *Psychotherapy: Theory, Research & Practice*, 16(3), 252–60. https://doi.org/10.1037/h0085885

Brewster, M. E. (2014). *Atheists in America.* Columbia University Press.

Brewster, M. E., Hammer, J., Sawyer, J. S., Eklund, A., & Palamar, J. (2016). Perceived experiences of atheist discrimination: Instrument development and evaluation. *Journal of Counseling Psychology*, 63(5), 557–70. https://doi.org/10.1037/cou0000156

Brown, C. (2007). Situating knowledge and power in the therapeutic alliance. In Brown, C., & Augusta-Scott, T. (Eds.), *Narrative therapy: Making meaning, making lives* (pp. 3–22). SAGE. https://doi.org/10.4135/9781452225869.n1

Brown, L. S. (2007). Empathy, genuineness—and the dynamics of power: A feminist responds to Rogers. *Psychotherapy*, 44(3), 257–59. https://doi.org/10.1037/0033-3204.44.3.257

Brown v. Board of Education, 347 U.S. 483 (1954).

Butler, J. (1990). *Gender trouble: Feminism and the subversion of identity.* Routledge.

Cadge, W. (2004). Gendered religious organizations: The case of Theravada Buddhism in America. *Gender & Society*, 18(6), 777–93. https://doi.org/10.1177/0891243204268324

Cameron, C. (2019). *Black freethinkers: A history of African American secularism.* Northwestern University Press.

Campbell, M., Hinton, J. D. X., & Anderson, J. R. (2019). A systematic review of the relationship between religion and attitudes toward transgender and gender-variant people.

The International Journal of Transgenderism, 20(1), 21–38. https://doi.org/10.1080/15532739.2018.1545149

Caraves, J. (2021). Trans*formative spirituality and self-preservation in the lives of trans Latinxs. *Latino Studies*, 19(2), 207–225. https://doi.org/10.1057/s41276-021-00323-6

Carpenter, C. S., Eppink, S. T., & Gonzales, G. (2020). Transgender status, gender identity, and socioeconomic outcomes in the United States. *ILR Review*, 73(3), 573–99. https://doi.org/10.1177/0019793920902776

Chaney, C., & Patrick, L. B. (2011). The invisibility of LGBT individuals in Black mega churches: Political and social implications. *Journal of African American Studies*, 15(2), 199–217. https://doi.org/10.1007/s12111-010-9153-y

Conron, K. J., Goldberg, S. K., & O'Neill, K. K. (2020). Religiosity among LGBT adults in the US. *UCLA School of Law, Williams Institute*. https://williamsinstitute.law.ucla.edu/publications/lgbt-religiosity-us/

Crenshaw, K. (1989). Demarginalizing the intersection of race and sex: A Black feminist critique of antidiscrimination doctrine, feminist theory and antiracist politics. *University of Chicago Legal Forum*, 1(8), 139–77. https://doi.org/10.4324/9780429500480-5

Cyrus, K. (2017). Multiple minorities as multiply marginalized: Applying the minority stress theory to LGBTQ people of color. *Journal of Gay & Lesbian Mental Health*, 21(3), 194–202. https://doi.org/10.1080/19359705.2017.1320739

Dahlgren Allen, S., Tollit, M. A., McDougall, R., Eade, D., How, M., & Pang, K. C. (2021). A waitlist intervention for transgender young people and psychosocial outcomes. *Pediatrics*, 148(2), 1–10. https://doi.org/10.1542/peds.2020-042762

Darwin, H. (2020). Navigating the religious gender binary. *Sociology of Religion*, 81(2), 185–205. https://doi.org/10.1093/socrel/srz034

DeChants, J. P., Price, M. N., Nath, R., Hobaica, S., & Suffredini, K. (2023). *The mental health and well-being of Indigenous LGBTQ young people*. The Trevor Project. https://www.thetrevorproject.org/wp-content/uploads/2023/10/Research-Report-Indigenous-LGBTQ-Youth-Mental-Health-Report.pdf

Delatolla, A. (2020). Sexuality as a standard of civilization: Historicizing (homo)colonial intersections of race, gender, and class. *International Studies Quarterly*, 64(1), 148–58. https://doi.org/10.1093/isq/sqz095

Dhejne, C., Van Vlerken, R., Heylens, G., & Arcelus, J. (2016). Mental health and gender dysphoria: A review of the literature. *International Review of Psychiatry*, 28(1), 44–57. http://doi.org/10.3109/09540261.2015.1115753

Dias, E., & Graham, R. (2023, June 22). The growing religious fervor in the American right: "This is a Jesus movement." *The New York Times*. https://www.nytimes.com/2022/04/06/us/christian-right-wing-politics.html

Exline, J. J. (2013). Religious and spiritual struggles. In K. I. Pargament, J. J. Exline, & J. W. Jones (Eds.), *APA handbook of psychology, religion, and spirituality (Vol. 1): Context, theory, and research* (pp. 459–75). American Psychological Association. https://doi.org/10.1037/14045-025

Exline, J. J., Przeworski, A., Peterson, E. K., Turnamian, M. R., Stauner, N., & Uzdavines, A. (2021). Religious and spiritual struggles among transgender and gender-nonconforming adults. *Psychology of Religion and Spirituality*, 13(3), 276. https://doi.org/10.1037/rel0000404

Family Research Council. (2016, May 13). *Title IX and transgendered students.* https://www.frc.org/get.cfm?i=IF16E01
Fanon, F. (1952). *Black skin, white masks.* Grove Press.
Federal Bureau of Investigation. (n.d.) *Hate crime in the United States incident analysis.* Federal Bureau of Investigation Crime Data Explorer. https://cde.ucr.cjis.gov/LATEST/webapp/#/pages/explorer/crime/hate-crime
Fleischack, A., Macleod, C., & Böhmke, W. (2020). The conundrums of counseling women in violent intimate partner relationships in South Africa: Implications for practice. *International Journal for the Advancement of Counseling*, 42(1), 65–80. https://doi.org/10.1007/s10447-019-09384-8
Fontanari, A. M., Vilanova, F., Schneider, M. A., Chinazzo, I., Soll, B. M., Schwarz, K., Inês Rodrigues Lobato, M., & Brandelli Costa, A. (2020). Gender affirmation is associated with transgender and gender nonbinary mental health improvement. *LGBT Health*, 7(5), 237–47. https://doi.org/10.1089/lgbt.2019.0046
Frey, J. J., Hall, W. J., Goldbach, J. T., & Lanier, P. (2021). "Here in the Bible Belt, it's predominantly negative": Sexual identity stigma in the American south, 50 years after Stonewall. *Frontiers in Psychology*, 12, 804064. https://doi.org/10.3389/fpsyg.2021.804064
Froese, P., & Bader, C. (2008). Unraveling religious worldviews: The relationship between images of God and political ideology in a cross-cultural analysis. *The Sociological Quarterly*, 49(4), 689–718. https://doi.org/10.1111/j.1533-8525.2008.00132.x
Fuist, T. N. (2016). "It just always seemed like it wasn't a big deal, yet I know for some people they really struggle with it": LGBT religious identities in context. *Journal for the Scientific Study of Religion*, 55(4), 770–86. https://doi.org/10.1111/jssr.12291
Galanter, M. (1989). *Cults: Faith, healing, and coercion.* Oxford University Press.
Garssen, B., Visser, A., & Pool, G. (2020). Does spirituality or religion positively affect mental health? Meta-analysis of longitudinal studies. *The International Journal for the Psychology of Religion*, 31(1), 4–20. https://doi.org/10.1080/10508619.2020.1729570
Geonzon, J. (2021, December 17). Fox News pushes to ban two LGBTQ books, lies that they "promote pedophilia." *Media Matters.* https://www.mediamatters.org/fox-news/fox-news-pushes-lgbtq-book-bans-lies-they-promote-pedophilia
Ghazzawi, A., Suhail-Sindhu, S., Casoy, F., Libby, N., McIntosh, C. A., Adelson, S., Ashley, K., Drescher, J., Goldenberg, D., Hung, K., Lothwell, L. E., Mattson, M. R., McAfee, S. G., Schwartz, A., Tompkins, D. A., Yarbrough, E., & Barber, M. E. (2020). Religious faith and transgender identities: The Dear Abby project. *Journal of Gay & Lesbian Mental Health*, 24(2), 190–204. https://doi.org/10.1080/19359705.2019.1706682
Gibbs, J. J., & Goldbach, J. (2015). Religious conflict, sexual identity, and suicidal behaviors among LGBT young adults. *Archives of Suicide Research: Official journal of the International Academy for Suicide Research*, 19(4), 472–88. https://doi.org/10.1080/13811118.2015.1004476
Golriz, G. (2022). "I am enough": Why LGBTQ Muslim groups resist mainstreaming. *Sexuality & Culture*, 25(2), 355–76. https://doi.org/10.1007/s12119-020-09773-x
Goodyear, T., Kinitz, D. J., Dromer, E., Gesink, D., Ferlatte, O., Knight, R., & Salway, T. (2022). "They want you to kill your inner queer but somehow leave the human alive": Delineating the impacts of sexual orientation and gender identity and expression change efforts. *Journal of Sex Research*, 59(5), 599–609. https://doi.org/10.1080.00224499.2021.1910616

Grossman, A. H., Park, J. Y., & Russell, S. T. (2016). Transgender youth and suicidal behaviors: Applying the interpersonal psychological theory of suicide. *Journal of Gay & Lesbian Mental Health*, 20(4), 329–49. https://doi.org/10.1080/19359705.2016.120758

Harris A. (2022). Transgender and analytic countertransference. *Psychoanalytic Review*, 109(3), 277–286. https://doi.org/10.1521/prev.2022.109.3.277

Helminiak, D. A. (2018). Matters of religion and spirituality for transgender and gender diverse persons. In E. J. M. van den Akker, A. M. Brewster, & M. S. Allen (Eds.), *Transgender and gender diverse persons* (pp. 181–204). Routledge. https://doi.org/10.4324/9781351207119-11

Hermaszewska, S., Sweeney, A., Camminga, B., Botelle, R., Elliott, K., & Sin, J. (2022). Lived experiences of transgender forced migrants and their mental health outcomes: Systematic review and meta-ethnography. *BJPsych Open*, 8(3), 1–13. https://doi.org/10.1192/bjo.2022.51

Hollier, J., Clifton, S., & Smith-Merry, J. (2022). Mechanisms of religious trauma amongst queer people in Australia's evangelical churches. *Clinical Social Work Journal*, 50(3), 275–85. https://doi.org/10.1007/s10615-022-00839-x

HRC Foundations. (n.d.). *What does the Bible say about transgender people?* Human Rights Foundations. https://www.hrc.org/resources/what-does-the-bible-say-about-transgender-people

Hughto, J. M. W., Gunn, H. A., Rood, B. A., & Pantalone, D. W. (2020). Social and medical gender affirmation experiences are inversely associated with mental health problems in a U.S. non-probability sample of transgender adults. *Archives of Sexual Behavior*, 49(7), 2635–47. https://doi.org/10.1007/s10508-020-01655-5

Johnson, L., & Lukert, B. (2023). Science, scripture, and sexuality: The US United Methodist Church at Crossroads. *Journal of Religion and Health*, 62(4), 2711–33. https://doi.org/10.1007/s10943-023-01806-7

Jones, J. M. (2023, June 8). Social conservatism in U.S. highest in about a decade. Gallup. https://news.gallup.com/poll/506765/social-conservatism-highest-decade.aspx

Jones, T. W., Power, J., & Jones, T. M. (2022). Religious trauma and moral injury from LGBTQA+ conversion practices. *Social Science & Medicine*, 305, 115040. https://doi.org/10.1016/j.socscimed.2022.115040

Kade, T. (2021). "Hey, by the way, I'm transgender": Transgender disclosures as coming out stories in social contexts among trans men. *Socius*, 7(1), 1–12. https://doi.org/10.1177/23780231211039389

Khuzwayo Z. (2021). "Why do I need to come out if straight people don't have to?" Divergent perspectives on the necessity of self-disclosure among bisexual women. *Frontiers in Sociology*, 6(1), 1–11. https://doi.org/10.3389/fsoc.2021.665627

Kim, J., Chesworth, B., Franchino-Olsen, H., & Macy, R. J. (2022). A scoping review of vicarious trauma interventions for service providers working with people who have experienced traumatic events. *Trauma, Violence & Abuse*, 23(5), 1437–60. https://doi.org/10.1177/1524838021991310

Kindy, K. (2022, March 25). GOP lawmakers push historic wave of bills targeting rights of LGBTQ teens, children and their families. *The Washington Post*. https://www.washingtonpost.com/politics/2022/03/25/lgbtq-rights-gop-bills-dont-say-gay/

Kitaen, L., & Xu, J. (2023). Open doors: Understanding LGBTQ-affirming perspectives in church leadership. *Journal of Student Research*, 12(4), 1–8. https://doi.org/10.47611/jsrhs.v12i4.5160

Kelin, M. (1952). The origins of transference. *The International Journal of Psychoanalysis*, 33(1), 433–38.

Koenig H. G. (2012). Religion, spirituality, and health: The research and clinical implications. *ISRN Psychiatry*, 2012(1), 1–33. https://doi.org/10.5402/2012/278730

Leung, H. H. S. (2017). Our city of colours: Queer/Asian publics in transpacific Vancouver. *Inter-Asia Cultural Studies*, 18(4), 482–97. https://doi.org/10.1080/14649373.2017.1387091

Lipka, M., & Tevington, P. (2022, July 7). Attitudes about transgender issues vary widely among Christians, religious 'nones' in U.S. *Pew Research Center*. https://www.pewresearch.org/short-read/2022/07/07/attitudes-about-transgender-issues-vary-widely-among-christians-religious-nones-in-u-s/

Lucchetti, G., Koenig, H. G., & Lucchetti, A. L. G. (2021). Spirituality, religiousness, and mental health: A review of the current scientific evidence. *World Journal of Clinical Cases*, 9(26), 7620–31. https://doi.org/10.12998/wjcc.v9.i26.7620

Mahler, M. S. (1972). On the first three subphases of the separation-individuation process. *The International Journal of Psychoanalysis*, 53(1) 333–38.

McBeath, A. (2019). The motivations of psychotherapists: An in-depth survey. *Counseling and Psychotherapy Research*, 19(4), 377–87. https://doi.org/10.1002/capr.12225

Meckler, L., & Clement, S. (2023, May 6). Most Americans support anti-trans policies favored by GOP, poll shows. *The Washington Post*. https://www.washingtonpost.com/education/2023/05/05/trans-poll-gop-politics-laws/

Messing, J., Mohr, R & Durfee, A. (2013). Intimate partner violence and women's experiences of grief. *Child & Family Social Work*, 20(1), 30–39. https://doi.org/10.1111/cfs.12051

Meyer, I. H. (1995). Minority stress and mental health in gay men. *Journal of Health and Social Behavior*, 36(1), 38–56. https://doi.org/10.2307/2137286

Mizock, L., & Lundquist, C. (2016). Missteps in psychotherapy with transgender clients: Promoting gender sensitivity in counseling and psychological practice. *Psychology of Sexual Orientation and Gender Diversity*, 3(2), 148–55. https://doi.org/10.1037/sgd0000177

Morgensen, S. L. (2010). Settler homonationalism: Theorizing settler colonialism within queer modernities. GLQ: *A Journal of Lesbian and Gay Studies*, 16(1–2), 105–31. https://doi.org/10.1215/10642684-2009-015

Nagourney, A., & Peters, J. W. (2023, April 17). How a campaign against transgender rights mobilized conservatives. *The New York Times*. https://www.nytimes.com/2023/04/16/us/politics/transgender-conservative-campaign.html

Namubiru, L., & Wepukhulu, K. S. (2020, October 29). US Christian right pours more than $50m into Africa. *Open Democracy*. https://www.opendemocracy.net/en/5050/africa-us-christian-right-50m/

Nemoto, T., Cruz, T. M., Iwamoto, M., & Sakata, M. (2015). A tale of two cities: Access to care and services among African-American transgender women in Oakland and San Francisco. *LGBT Health*, 2(3), 235–42. https://doi.org/10.1089/lgbt.2014.0046

Norenzayan, A., & Gervais, W. M. (2013). The origins of religious disbelief. *Trends in Cognitive Sciences*, 17(1), 20–25. https://doi.org/10.1016/j.tics.2012.11.006

Norton, J. (2011, September 19). *Vatican says "sex-change" operation does not change person's gender*. National Catholic Reporter. https://www.ncronline.org/news/vatican-says-sex-change-operation-does-not-change-persons-gender

OK SB129, 59th Legislature. (2023).

Oliver, M. (2013). Transnational sex politics, conservative Christianity, and antigay activism in Uganda. *Studies in Social Justice*, 7(1), 83–105. https://doi.org/10.1163/2210-7975_hrd-4019-3008

Orme, L. M. N., Hall, M. E. L., Anderson, T. L., & McMartin, J. (2017). Power, sexism, and gender: Factors in biblical interpretation. *Journal of Psychology and Theology*, 45(4), 274–85. https://doi.org/10.1177/009164711704500403

Pargament, K. I., Murray-Swank, N. A., Magyar, G. M., & Ano, G. G. (2005). Spiritual struggle: A phenomenon of interest to psychology and religion. In W. R. Miller & H. D. Delaney (Eds.), *Judeo-Christian perspectives on psychology: Human nature, motivation, and change* (pp. 245–68). American Psychological Association. https://doi.org/10.1037/10859-013

Parker, K., Horowitz, J. M., & Brown, A. (2022, June 28). *Americans' complex views on gender identity and transgender issues*. Pew Research Center. https://www.pewresearch.org/social-trends/2022/06/28/americans-complex-views-on-gender-identity-and-transgender-issues/

Parks, C. (2024, February 14). Trans adults on edge as legislatures broaden focus beyond children. *The Washington Post*. https://www.washingtonpost.com/dc-md-va/2024/02/15/trans-adults-bathroom-medical-identity/

Pérez, S., & Vallières, F. (2019). How do religious people become atheists? Applying a grounded theory approach to propose a model of deconversion. *Secularism and Nonreligion*, 8(0), 1–14. https://doi.org/10.5334/snr.108

Perkins, T. (2023, July 9). US religious right pours millions into LGBTQ+ global culture war. *The Guardian*. https://www.theguardian.com/world/2023/jul/09/us-religious-right-lgbtq-global-culture-fronts

PRRI Staff. (2021, July 8). The American religious landscape in 2020. *PRRI*. https://www.prri.org/research/2020-census-of-american-religion/

Quack, J. (2012). Organised atheism in India: An overview. *Journal of Contemporary Religion*, 27(1), 67–85. https://doi.org/10.1080/13537903.2012.642729

Quinn, D. M., & Earnshaw, V. A. (2011). Understanding concealable stigmatized identities: The role of identity in psychological, physical, and behavioral outcomes. *Social Issues and Policy Review*, 5(1), 160–90. https://doi.org/10.1111/j.1751-2409.2011.01029.x

Rich, B. E. (2023). *Gender essentialism and orthodoxy: Beyond male and female*. Fordham University Press.

Robinson, C. M., & Spivey, S. E. (2019). Ungodly genders: Deconstructing ex-gay movement discourses of "transgenderism" in the US. *Social Sciences*, 8(6), 191. https://doi.org/10.3390/socsci8060191

Roughgarden, J. (2013). *Evolution's rainbow: Diversity, gender, and sexuality in nature and people*. University of California Press.

Savage, R., & Bauer, S. (2021, December 6). Trans people waiting years for gender healthcare as demand surges. Reuters. https://www.reuters.com/article/idUSKBN2IM0FP/

Schjonberg, M. F. (2017, February 8). Episcopal Church Executive Council reaffirms stand with Standing Rock. *Episcopal News Service*. https://www.episcopalnewsservice.org/2017/02/08/episcopal-church-executive-council-reaffirms-stand-with-standing-rock/
Scribner, T., Weiner, M.C., Clifton, K. (2023). Religion resettles refugees: Religion's role in integration in the United States. In E. M. Goździak, & I. Main (Eds.), *Debating religion and forced migration entanglements (politics of citizenship and migration)* (pp. 147–63). Palgrave Macmillan. https://doi.org/10.1007/978-3-031-23379-1_8
Sequeira, G. M., Ray, K. N., Miller, E., & Coulter, R. W. S. (2020). Transgender youth's disclosure of gender identity to providers outside of specialized gender centers. *The Journal of Adolescent Health: Official publication of the Society for Adolescent Medicine*, 66(6), 691–98. https://doi.org/10.1016/j.jadohealth.2019.12.010
Seul, J. R. (1999). "Ours is the way of God": Religion, identity, and intergroup conflict. *Journal of Peace Research*, 36(5), 553–69. http://www.jstor.org/stable/424533
Shine, R. (2024, March 2). Pope Francis refers to "gender ideology" as the "worst danger" today. *New Ways Ministry*. https://www.newwaysministry.org/2024/03/02/pope-francis-refers-to-gender-ideology-as-the-worst-danger-today/
Smith, G. A., Tevington, P., Nortey, J., Rotolo, M., Kallo, A., & Alper, B. A. (2024, January 24). Religious "nones" in America: Who they are and what they believe. Pew Research Center. https://www.pewresearch.org/wp-content/uploads/sites/20/2024/01/PR_2024.01.24_religious-nones_REPORT.pdf
Smith, J. M. (2011). Becoming an atheist in America: Constructing identity and meaning from the rejection of theism, *Sociology of Religion*, 72(2), 215–37. https://doi.org/10.1093/socrel/srq082
Smithers, G. (2022). *Reclaiming two-Spirits: Sexuality, spiritual renewal and sovereignty in Native America*. Beacon Press.
Speed, D., Coleman, T. J., & Langston, J. (2018). What do you mean, "What does it all mean?": Atheism, nonreligion, and life meaning. *SAGE Open*, 8(1), 1–13. https://doi.org/10.1177/2158244017754238
Stewart, K. (2022, July 5). Religious liberty used to uphold conservative religious privileges. American Bar Association. https://www.americanbar.org/groups/crsj/publications/human_rights_magazine_home/intersection-of-lgbtq-rights-and-religious-freedom/religious-liberty-used-to-uphold-conservative-religious-privileges/
Stone, A. M. (2013). Thou shalt not: Treating religious trauma and spiritual harm with combined therapy. *Group*, 37(4), 323–37. https://doi.org/10.13186/group.37.4.0323
Stop the Sexualization of Children Act, H.R.9197. (2022).
Strassfeld, M. K. (2010). Becoming a good boy: A transmasculine meditation on gendered ritual objects and the challenges of transfeminism. In N. Dzmura (Ed.), *Balancing on the Mechitza: Transgender in Jewish community* (pp. 112–19). North Atlantic Books.
Stuart, R., & Nichols, J. (2020). Transgender: A useful category of Biblical analysis? *Journal for Interdisciplinary Biblical Studies*, 1(2), 1–24. https://doi.org/10.17613/ak2n-9z27
Sumerau, J. E., Mathers, L. A. B., & Lampe, N. (2019). Learning from the religious experiences of bi+trans people. *Symbolic Interaction*, 42(2), 179–201. https://www.jstor.org/stable/26629977
Thomas, W., & Jacobs, S. E. (1999). "… And we are still here": From berdache to two-spirit people. *American Indian Culture and Research Journal*, 23(2), 91–107. https://escholarship.org/uc/item/70r4x9k2#author

Tordoff, D. M., Wanta, J. W., Collin, A., Stepney, C., Inwards-Breland, D. J., & Ahrens, K. (2022). Mental health outcomes in transgender and nonbinary youths receiving gender-affirming care. *JAMA Network*, 5(2), 1–13. https://doi.org/10.1001/jamanetworkopen.2022.0978

Totton, R. R., Rios, K., & Shogren, N. (2023). Distrusted disclosures: Deception drives anti-transgender but not anti-atheist prejudice. *Frontiers in Psychology*, 13(1), 1–15. https://doi.org/10.3389/fpsyg.2022.1006107

Tower, L. E. (1956). Countertransference. *Journal of the American Psychoanalytic Association*, 4(2), 224–55. https://doi.org/10.1177/000306515600400202

Trans Legislation Tracker. (2024, April 25). *2024 anti-trans bills tracker*. https://translegislation.com/

Trispiotis, I., & Purshouse, C. (2022). "Conversion therapy" as degrading treatment. *Oxford Journal of Legal Studies*, 42(1), 104–32. https://doi.org/10.1093/ojls/gqab024

Walker, A. T. (2022, July 23). The transgender fantasy: What I wish every pastor knew. *Desiring God*. https://www.desiringgod.org/articles/the-transgender-fantasy

Wang, J. C., McFarland, W., Arayasirikul, S., & Wilson, E. C. (2023). The association between religiosity and resilience among young trans women. *PloS one*, 18(7), e0263492. https://doi.org/10.1371/journal.pone.0263492

Wesley, D. L. (2015). Reimagining two-spirit community: Critically centering narratives of urban two-spirit youth [Master's thesis, Queen's University]. https://qspace.library.queensu.ca/server/api/core/bitstreams/7e4b3989-5774-4f26-a42f-5449214b79a3/content

West, C., & Zimmerman, D. H. (1987). Doing gender. *Gender and Society*, 1(2), 125–51. http://www.jstor.org/stable/189945

Wielenberg, E. J. (2022). Atheism and meaning in life. In A. V. Ruvinsky & J. Waterman (Eds.), *The Oxford Handbook of Meaning in Life* (pp. 216–30). Oxford University Press. https://doi.org/10.1093/oxfordhb/9780190063504.013.15

Winell, M. (2011). Religious Trauma Syndrome. *Cognitive Behavioural Therapy Today*, 39(2). https://www.journeyfree.org/rts/rts-its-time-to-recognize-it/

Wu, B. (2007). Secularism and secularization in the Arab world. *Journal of Middle Eastern and Islamic Studies (in Asia)*, 1(1), 55–65. https://doi.org/10.1080/19370679.2007.12023103

WY SF0111, 67th Leg., Reg. Sess. (2023, Wyoming). Wyoming Legislature. https://legiscan.com/WY/bill/SF0111/2023

Zaharin, A. A. M., & Pallotta-Chiarolli, M. (2020). Countering Islamic conservatism on being transgender: Clarifying Tantawi's and Khomeini's fatwas from the progressive Muslim standpoint. *International Journal of Transgender Health*, 21(3), 235–41. https://doi.org/10.1080/26895269.2020.1778238

Zimmerman, K. J., Smith, J. M., Simonson, K., & Myers, B. W. (2015). Familial relationship outcomes of coming out as an atheist. *Secularism & Nonreligion*, 4(4), 1–13. http://dx.doi.org/10.5334/snr.aw

Zoledziowski, A. (2023, March 21). "Under his wings": Leaked emails reveal an anti-trans "Holy War." *Vice News*. https://www.vice.com/en/article/leaked-emails-reveal-an-anti-trans-holy-war/

9

Leaving Religion, Leaving Patriarchy?

Carrie Bohmer and Dena M. Abbott

Chapter Outline

This chapter outlines the reasons why therapists need to be attuned to the secular/atheist worldview, and to the ways in which psychotherapy intersects with secular values, gender, and sexuality. We begin by discussing how the patriarchal structures and practices within many organized religions may drive women and femmes, including cisgender women, nonbinary, and transfeminine people, to exit religion and adopt a nonreligious worldview. We then discuss the process of becoming nonreligious and the potential unique gendered consequences of acting on this identification as a woman/femme-identified person. We then move on to demonstrate that patriarchy is not exclusive to religious organizations and highlight common ways it manifests in nonreligious communities as well, posing obstacles for nonreligious women. We conclude with suggestions for therapists working with nonreligious women, particularly in settings where nonreligion is implicitly or explicitly stigmatized. We focus on the importance of exploring nonreligious sources of values, identities, morality, and meaning, while also accounting for the possible role one's religious past plays in the shaping of their gendered selves. Validating nonreligious femme-identifying clients and helping them articulate their secular identities in relation to religious and nonreligious cultures can unlock routes toward self-actualization, resilience, and freedom.

Terminology

The psychological and sociological study of nonreligion is a relatively young field and the nomenclature frequently changes (Lee, 2015). We use the terms "nonreligious," "secular," or "nones" as umbrellas encompassing a range of identities, such as skeptics, freethinkers, agnostics, secularists, and atheists. We use "atheist" to describe individuals who reject, negate, or deny theism in all its forms (Hyman, 2007). We may also refer to nonspirituality, or the absence of belief in supernatural forces that control or guide the universe and people's lives (e.g., higher power, miracles; Cragun, 2015). Importantly, not all nonreligious people are also nonspiritual; some nonbelievers retain spirituality, but it is important to understand religion and spirituality as distinct constructs. Notably, as we discuss nonreligious communities and gender, we primarily have New Atheists in mind. New Atheists have been the most prominent and publicly visible nonreligious group over the past two decades; their atheism is marked by criticism of religion and a focus on countering religion's public presence and influence with rationality and logic (Cragun, 2015).

With regard to gender, the terms "woman," "women," and "femmes" are used throughout this chapter and are intended to be inclusive of all people who may currently identify as women and/or were assigned female at birth (AFAB) and socialized with feminine gender roles. We acknowledge these terms do not accurately describe the gender of all the nonreligious people that experience sexism and misogyny. Importantly, much of the scholarship on nonreligion centers on White, cisgender, heterosexual men, and the few studies that have broader gender diversity primarily focus on White, cisgender, and highly educated women. Thus, we attempt to infuse more nuanced and intersectional analyses and advice throughout this chapter, however, this chapter is limited by the extant scholarship on the topic.

Positionality Statement

This chapter is authored by women who share similar demographics to the women often studied in nonreligion (i.e., White, cisgender, highly educated); thus, our lived experiences may mirror that literature and inevitably influence this chapter. We acknowledge the chapter is not, and cannot be, an exhaustive guide to working with every type of nonreligious client in therapy; rather, it serves as an introduction to the relationship between patriarchy and nonreligion and how to integrate this knowledge into psychotherapy practices with nonreligious clients. People are complex as is their sociopolitical context. Systems of dominance (e.g., racism, patriarchy) result in myriad and varied experiences informed by unique constellations of marginalized and privileged identities. The nonreligious and women are not monoliths, and their experiences will vary with intrapersonal factors and their social locations. We write this chapter from the position that the United States, and therefore all systems and organizations within it, are subject to imperialist White supremacist capitalist-patriarchal structures (hooks, 2004). We will focus on patriarchy while acknowledging the interlocking and complex matrix of domination (Collins, 1990) that is operating simultaneously to create the world in which people exist.

Gender and Nonreligion

In the mid-twentieth century, those who identified with "no religion," or "nones," were overwhelmingly men (Brown, 2011). Currently in the United States, people unaffiliated with a religion are roughly evenly split between men (51 percent) and women (47 percent; Pew Research Center, 2024). Since 2009, the share of "nones" among both women and men has risen by 10 percentage points (Pew Research Center, 2019). Simultaneously, the share of women who identify as Christian has fallen by 11 points (from 80 percent to 69 percent). Among the youngest adult generational cohort, people born between 1997 and 2012 (i.e., Gen Z), 39 percent of women identify as religiously unaffiliated whereas 34 percent of Gen Z men are nonreligious. This is significant as it marks the first generation in which the gender ratio in nonreligiousness has flipped, albeit by small margins (Cox & Hammond, 2024).

Patriarchy, Misogyny, and Sexism

Patriarchy is defined as a system of social hierarchy that affords power to men and devalues women or the feminine both in ideological and concrete ways (Hunnicutt, 2009). Misogyny is "negative affective or emotional orientation towards women as a group"; sexism is "the institutionalized expression of individual misogyny (e.g., lower wages for women, lack of access to comprehensive reproductive healthcare)" (Wrisley, 2024, p. 192). These three forces, patriarchy, misogyny, and sexism, impact the way people of all genders experience the world and create a social risk for women and femmes that does not exist for men and masculine people. Of note, these systems and processes also hurt men through limiting their range of affective experience through toxic masculinity and positioning them as the superior gender thus disconnecting them from the women and femmes in their lives. In the context of nonreligion, we will explore the social and systemic costs that women/femmes face in their decisions and processes related to (non) religious affiliation.

The term patriarchy actually finds its roots in religion. The three Hebrew patriarchs—Abraham, his son Isaac, and grandson Jacob—give their title to "patriarchy": the concept that most succinctly summarizes what feminists oppose. Patriarchy is rule by men, ideologically bolstered by the claim that men and women are innately different and men are innately superior. Judaism, Christianity, and Islam have been, and mostly still are, profoundly patriarchal, both in their own organizations and in their legitimation of patriarchal social structures and cultures. Indeed, one does not have to be a feminist to recognize that religions generally treat women differentially. Looking to religious professionals and leaders offers credence to this statement. Although many religious organizations in the United States currently allow women to be ordained, few allow women to hold the highest leadership positions (Sandstrom, 2016). Of those who do allow women in these roles, few actually have had women hold these roles, suggesting that there are still patriarchal forces within even the most progressive of religious organizations.

Patriarchy in Religion

While women inhabit nonreligious culture in greater numbers than ever before, few openly declare themselves "as convinced atheists" (Mahlamäki, 2012; Scheitle et al., 2019). American women are more likely to remain in religion and less likely to remain nonreligious, when compared to their male counterparts (Kosmin et al., 2009). Of note, this difference almost disappears when education level and political affiliation are considered, such that highly educated liberal men and women are roughly equally likely to remain religious or nonreligious (Baker & Whitehead, 2016). Globally, trends are similar with women affiliating with religion at higher rates than men in most countries (Pew Research Center, 2016). Femme nonreligiousness also appears nuanced and harder to define; it ranges from indifference to outward hostility toward religion, though not necessarily spirituality, whereas male nonreligiousness tends to be more definitive and anti-theism. The cultural constraints that women operate under may explain why women are reluctant to "come out" as atheists in the United States. As Edgell et al. (2017) demonstrated, on average women face a greater social risk than men when they identify with a stigmatized group, such as atheists. Where atheism intersects with race and sexual orientation, the social penalty may be even greater for nonreligious women who are queer and/or Black, indigenous, people of color (BIPOC) as compared to their White straight counterparts (Hutchinson, 2020; Brewster, 2013).

So why is the rejection of belief by women so much more socially threatening than for men? It may be partly because it represents much more than the loss of a community member. Female noncompliance often threatens the status quo and signifies larger changes on a societal level. Leaving religion and god(s) behind is a symptom of independence. In patriarchal societies, the most prevalent in the world, women's lives have been almost universally and inescapably dictated by religions for most of recorded history. Traditionally, many religions have opposed efforts to expand the rights of women (e.g., abortion, contraception, legal protection from domestic violence), suggesting a potentially vested interest by these groups in limiting women's agency (Trzebiatowska, 2019). Further, many authors have pointed out the ways in which religious rules are stricter for women as compared to men. This creates additional pressure for women to stay religious and in religious communities. For women, atheism signifies more than just an escape from religious authority; it is bound up with nonconformism more generally. As the journey to nonbelief primarily consists of independent study and an unconventional approach to the world, the women who undertake it may feel liberated not only from religion but from a more general sense of oppression as a class (Abbott & Anaya, 2022).

For women in the United States, motherhood and the desire to be a mother is assumed and is almost a cultural imperative (Burkett, 2000), especially in the current sociopolitical context where bodily autonomy for people capable of pregnancy is being undermined daily. Although motherhood is not unique to religion and Christianity, there is no doubt the link between reproduction and religion influences people's reproductive lives, from specific religious decrees about the use of birth control methods to the Christian Bible being cited in recent legal cases to justify rulings that limit reproductive autonomy (*LePage v. The Center for Reproductive Medicine, 2024*). In the United States, there has been a steady decrease in birth rates, with many women choosing to have fewer children and delaying family building until later in their life, particularly for those with bachelor's degrees (Martinez & Daniels, 2023). Of note, this decline in birth rates is much steeper among nonreligious women as compared to their religiously affiliated counterparts (Stone, 2022), a trend that is observed over many decades and in many countries (Kolk & Saarela, 2024; Nguyen et al., 2024). These declining birth rates are insufficient for religious organizations to maintain their congregations (Stone, 2022), providing a potential vested interest in religious groups removing access to reproductive healthcare services that allow people capable of pregnancy to limit the number of pregnancies and births they have. In this way, nonreligious women pose a threat to society in that they are less reproductively useful to religious organizations, as well as the economy at large.

Often, women are seen as the carriers of culture, tasked with passing on values, morals, and traditions, and this can primarily be boiled down to the gendered ways in which US culture views parenting and all things domestic as innately feminine (Verniers & Vala, 2018). Since women are assumed to be the primary caretakers of the next generation, they are often held to a higher standard than their male counterparts (in cisgender heterosexual monogamous contexts) and, as a result, may feel more pressure to remain within religious communities or belief systems. Traditionally women have been cast in the role of moral guardians and beacons of virtue to the point of being held responsible for the honor of not only family members but of whole nations (Trzebiatowska & Bruce, 2012). Thus, when women leave religion, there are not just implications for themselves but also for those in their orbit. This perceived abandonment of the obligation to serve as a spiritual leader in their families and communities is a major driver of atheist discrimination among BIPOC women (Abbott et al., 2020). In these cases, women are seen as the cause of disruption in the family transmission of faith.

As Laurel Thatcher Ulrich (1976) noted, "well-behaved women seldom make history," while rule-breakers are remembered for challenging the status quo. But nonreligious female rule-breakers commit a double crime: against the commonly accepted rules of social conduct and against gender expectations. The consequences can be severe but potentially worth it, as a turn to atheism may put women in charge of their lives and relationship with the world around them. Many realize that leaving organized religion grants them existential autonomy and freedom to choose the life they want to live. While liberating, this realization can also induce anxiety, which inevitably comes with the freedom of choice. Embracing a stigmatized label has repercussions which are relational, such as a loss of community, family, or friendship groups, but also create the opportunity to create new, values-congruent communities with like-minded others. That said, when nonreligious women turn to atheist organizations, particularly those associated with New Atheism or predominated by men, they often find them just as patriarchal as their religious equivalents.

Patriarchy in Nonreligion

Although patriarchal structures are most readily visible and deeply ingrained in conservative and fundamentalist religions, gendered and heteronormative messaging and practices are also common in more mainstream congregations and alternative, progressive religious communities are difficult to find outside of large, urban city centers. Therefore, women and femmes from a variety of religions are exiting religion and may be in search of community. It would be tempting to assume that when women leave organized religion, they automatically leave patriarchal cultural settings, but this is not necessarily the case. Exiting religion throws up new challenges to female "nones," one of which is the search for belonging. A logical next step would be to search for like-minded people in ready-made humanist and atheist organizations. However, these communities tend to be overwhelmingly male (Langston et al., 2017) and susceptible to the dangers of patriarchy.

In 2018, the Pew Research Center created a new typology for understanding (non) religious people in the United States. Three categories emerged: the highly religious, the somewhat religious, and the nonreligious. Among the nonreligious (29 percent), there were two distinct groups—Religion Resisters and Solidly Secular (Pew Research Center, 2018). The "Religion Resisters" opposed organized religion but held spiritual beliefs; the "Solidly Secular" held virtually no religious beliefs and rejected spiritual and/or New Age beliefs. More women (55 percent) than men (45 percent) were Religion Resisters, and men outnumbered women in the Solidly Secular category (65 percent as opposed to 35 percent). Religion Resisters profess to derive the meaning of life from things like nature, family time, caring for pets, and reading, all of which might coincide with the sphere of life coded as feminine. Moreover, a majority of Religion Resisters believed in a "spiritual force" (87 percent), spiritual energy in material objects (98 percent), psychics (62 percent), and reincarnation (50 percent). About two-thirds identified with the "spiritual but not religious" label (Pew Research Center, 2018). Therefore, traditional humanist and atheist communities, which tend toward Solidly Secular, may not be the best fit for women.

This is likely due, in part, to the absence of women in the creation of such groups and potential mismatch in values for women who retain some spiritual beliefs. In short, these communities were built by men, for men.

Zuckerman and colleagues (2016) found a similar pattern in gender difference when exploring the role of personality and cognition among nonreligious people. One aspect of cognition is the "empathizing-systemizing continuum" whereby some individuals are better at reading and reacting to others' emotions, while others are more skilled at "organizing factual information and discerning patterns and logical relationships" (Zuckerman et al., 2016, p. 115). And thus, "Studies using this empathizing-systemizing continuum indicate that there is a sex difference such that, on average, men tend to use systemizing cognition, whereas women are more adept at empathizing and mentalizing (thinking about others' thoughts)" (p. 115). This is not to say that atheist women do not systematize but it does mean that, for whatever reason, predominantly male atheist communities tend to value logic, rationality, scientism, and facts over other qualities. They may devalue experiences and feelings which are less readily quantifiable, logical, or empirically testable. The devaluation of the qualities culturally coded as feminine reinforces their patriarchal structures. Given this, the key to nonreligious women successfully finding a community may lie in organizing such communities around the values which are relevant to their interests or deliberately gender-neutral and welcome the traditionally feminine.

Organized Nonbelief and Sexism

Nonreligious groups have been characterized as misogynistic and at times outwardly hostile to female members (Guenther, 2019). In the past decade the atheist movement has been plagued with accusations of misogyny, sexual harassment, and general hostility toward women (Mooney, 2011; Oppenheimer, 2014). See Box 9.1 for a brief description of "Elevatorgate," perhaps one of the most prominent examples of womens' gendered experiences in atheist spaces. Part of the issue is that many male atheists see the movement's primary goal as a critique of religion and not to be diluted by the feminist agenda female activists often bring with them (Marcotte, 2014). However, it is practically impossible to separate female atheism from its emancipatory roots. The absence of belief in God has been associated with feminism due to the historical trajectory of the women's rights movement. The fight for women's rights grew out of the sociocultural context infused with Western Christian values whereby gender norms were prescribed, reinforced, and guarded by religious institutions, which were intrinsically patriarchal. It is no wonder that the most basic form of rebellion against gender-based oppression would be a rebellion against organized religion.

The organized atheist movement is internally contradictory with regard to gender (Schnabel et al., 2016). On the one hand, surveys demonstrate that atheists are inclined to support gender equality and women's rights (Zuckerman, 2009), and nations with high percentages of atheism show greater concern for gender equality than highly religious nations (Beit-Hallahmi, 2007; Zuckerman, 2008). On the other hand, atheists can be just as patriarchal as their religious peers. Male atheists do not grow up in a cultural vacuum,

Box 9.1. "Elevatorgate": A Case Example of Patriarchy in the Atheist Community

Perhaps the most well-known case of gender discrimination within an atheist community is "Elevatorgate" which took place in 2011 at the World Atheist Convention in Dublin, Ireland. New Atheism refers to a prominent social movement that opposed the influence of religion on politics and was overtly anti-religious. The unofficial but perceived leaders of the movement were referred to as the Four Horsemen: Richard Dawkins, Sam Harris, Christopher Hitchens, and Daniel Dennett. Notably, all four are White, cisgender men. Many women were a part of the New Atheist movement and even helped shape it; however, these four men are generally credited with its growth in influence, particularly in the early 2000s.

In 2011 at the aforementioned World Atheist Convention, Rebecca Watson, a woman atheist and online content creator, presented on a panel about the challenges faced by women in atheist communities, including sexual objectification. At around 4 o'clock in the morning, after socializing with other attendees in the hotel, she was approached by a male conference attendee who invited her back to his room. Later, Watson published a video blog (vlog) about the conference that included a criticism of sexism in atheist communities using the example of this unwelcome advance to illustrate her point. Although her comment was brief and not the central topic of the vlog, members of the atheist community who disagreed with her criticism and opposed infusion of feminism into the movement were quick to respond. Most notably, Richard Dawkins responded with the "Dear Muslima" parody letter, a response to Watson trivializing her experience and encouraging her to "stop whining" and "grow a thicker skin." In particular, although Watson did not compare her experience to any other woman's, Dawkins framed his message to communicate that she, as a woman in the US, did not experience the misogyny faced by Muslim women in other parts of the world.

The consequences of this very public conflict for the New Atheist movement were far-reaching and beyond the scope of this chapter. However, as one expects in a patriarchal system, many men in the movement, including leaders, refused to acknowledge sexual misconduct, blamed victims of sexual violence, and even threatened Watson and other women's lives for suggesting sexism was present in their community. Many women departed and the movement was irreparably harmed, entrenching itself further in misogyny, racism, and xenophobia. To its detriment, New Atheism refused to acknowledge the ways nonreligion could replicate the very systems of oppression they rejected in theism.

and dominant gender norms, many of which are shaped and reinforced by religious institutions, affect their view of gender relations in private and public spaces. Moreover, while atheists reject religious justifications of sexism, they may draw on science to validate sexist assumptions. Despite their avowed support for gender equality in theory, atheists have a record of misogynistic behavior in practice, both on- and offline (Schnabel et al.,

2016; Simmons, 2020). The complexity of male atheists' attitudes to gender equality is exemplified well in a study of atheist men by Stinson and colleagues (2013). Although the participants unanimously supported gender equality and pointed to daily injustices they noticed (where women were treated as second-class citizens), they were more divided on feminism. Some saw themselves as feminist and pro-feminist and felt that atheism in its emphasis on humanism was inextricably connected to gender equality. Others, meanwhile, distanced themselves from feminism personally, claiming that it played no role in their lives (Stinson et al., 2013).

Perhaps the most apt descriptor of nonreligious people is that they are individuals, not joiners (Kosmin, 2019). Most nones are relatively free and independent—male, young, well-educated, single, and child-free (Macdonald & Clark, 2017). There is some evidence to show that the number of women among nonbelievers is growing (Hassall & Bushfield, 2014; Barna Group, 2015) but, as Langston and colleagues (2015) indicated, this may well be the result of changing leadership structures of nonreligious groups with women assuming more leadership roles, thus attracting other women. Langston's study of nonbelievers' views of nonreligion as a movement sampled overwhelmingly White (93 percent) men (61.9 percent) and women (38.1 percent). Their research demonstrated that women were just as interested as men in "politicking and officiating," though less so in proselytizing. The authors suggest that

> a female-led movement might result in noticeable differences in strategies, and thus also outcomes. It is possible that such a movement might more readily achieve social acceptance in the American public at large, or at least diminished stigma—although this in turn depends on what one thinks about the efficacy of an accommodationist strategy over an elimination strategy (p. 215).

This is not to say that a movement led by women would be rid of hostility altogether but a more tempered approach to criticism of religion may well result in a greater number of female members. As Langston and colleagues (2015) showed, a third of their female participants gave nonreligious groups' focus on attacking and criticizing religion as the primary reason for not joining them. Only 19 percent of the male respondents claimed it kept them from joining. Some commentators put the gender difference in the membership down to men's proclivity for militancy, which makes organized religion less attractive to women. This finding has resulted in efforts to make organized nonreligion more diverse through initiatives such as Women in Secularism Conferences and subgroups for African Americans within American Humanist Association (AHA) and Center for Inquiry (CFI; Kosmin, 2019).

This feminist corrective to New Atheism in all its guises offers an alternative approach to (self) knowledge, which prioritizes embodiment (e.g., issues around reproductive health and sexuality) and connection instead of cold logic and scientific evidence. Atheist groups whose values reflect women's lived experiences of the world potentially create a hospitable space for female nonbelievers. Membership in national or local secular organizations was found to be an important protective factor against depression and loneliness (Frazer et al., 2022). Moreover, a less militant and competitive approach can offer a chance for incorporating religious biographical background into a nonreligious identity through self-exploration but also maintaining relationships with religious friends, family, and community members (Schaefer, 2014), should someone desire to do so.

Supporting Women Nonbelievers in Therapy: Identity, Belonging, and Values

The following section offers insights into clinical mental health practice with women and femmes who were raised religious and who no longer believe in god(s) and/or participate in organized religion. Given the context outlined in the previous section, there are emotional, cognitive, and relational impacts for women leaving a religion that can and should be attended to therapeutically. The pressure for many women to stay in religion and in religious communities does not simply disappear when a woman begins to identify as nonreligious and/or atheist. Not only might female religious exiters have to navigate the potential shame and guilt of leaving religion that any individual may feel, but they may also have shame and guilt for the relational shifts that may follow the exiting of a religion.

In addition to the ramifications for their identities, sense of belonging, and the practical aspects of everyday life, there is plenty of evidence that nonreligious women in the southern states of the United States find it more challenging to locate a secular, rather than faith-based, therapist or counselor (Almeida, 2017). Further, in these states, women are more likely to conceal their nonreligious identity (Frost et al., 2023), making social isolation more likely. Organizations like Recovering from Religion and the Secular Therapy Project, for example, provide resources for those disaffiliating from religion, which include a directory of secular therapists. The list of common presenting concerns among nonreligious people seeking mental health treatment provided on these websites range from overcoming one's fear of hell to navigating life without religious values, finding community, and developing a sense of purpose. For women and femmes who leave organized religion in all its guises, one of the key factors appears to be the desire to escape from patriarchal structures (Abbott & Anaya, 2022).

Deciding to Leave Religion

Working with women who are considering leaving a religion is important therapeutic work. Leaving a religion is an incredibly nuanced process and should not be unequivocally suggested for all clients. There are real social and emotional costs to separating from a religion, and these must be weighed carefully with any client considering exiting religion. As Gorham (2013) suggested—as a result of their marginalized status in the United States women, and BIPOC women in particular, need to assess whether they have emotionally *and* cognitively come to a clear decision on their beliefs and have sufficient social support outside of a church community. The former may require processing of religious-based fears and/or traumas (e.g., images of hell, beliefs of punishment) and offering psychoeducation to the client that these fears and images may never be completely resolved. For psychodynamic therapists, exploring what it might mean about the client that they are considering/leaving religion can be particularly useful interventions. While exploring these questions, the therapist can identify the most painful parts of the story for the client, explore their origins, and find ways to help them heal some of this pain. Additionally, exercises from motivational interviewing that explore the pros and cons of leaving and/or staying in a religion could identify reasons that are most important to the client in their decision-making process, and therefore, inform the direction of treatment. In some cases, sexism driving clients' religious exits may constitute religious trauma (See chapter 12 of this volume for more information about working with clients with a history of religious and/or spiritual abuse.).

Exploring the client's level of involvement with a religious community may be an important step in their decision-making process. If your client is a stay-at-home parent with young children who is dependent on a partner's income and whose only friends attend her church, leaving her religion may be incredibly difficult and potentially detrimental to her well-being. For example, she may risk losing access to adult socialization and/or child care resources. Alternatively, if your client is a college-educated single woman with friends and family of various belief systems, there is a greater likelihood that she could leave her religious community without losing all of her social support. Like in a family system, clients may find themselves enmeshed with church and/or faith communities—finding it difficult to establish emotional boundaries and a strong sense of self. Bowenian family therapy (Bowen, 1993) strategies aimed at individuation may support a client developing a personal, secular worldview independent of the values of their religious community. Importantly, this individuation also supports the creation of healthy boundaries that honor the client's autonomy and encourage the maintenance of relationships with religious community members despite differences in worldviews, if so desired. Additionally, helping the client to connect to social support networks of other nonreligious women and femmes could be a beneficial treatment goal in preparation for existing religion and/or treatment termination.

Reprogramming After Religion

Many women leaving religious groups often hope to find solace and community within nonreligious organizations. Unfortunately, many of these organizations often mimic the same patriarchal structure as churches, leaving nonreligious women in similar binds to those they found themselves in within religion (Abbott & Anaya, 2022). There are many reasons this may be the case, but most compelling is that these organizations appear to be subconsciously modeled after religious organizations and congregations. The reasons for this are complex. First, we know that most people who identify as atheist also identify as cisgender men, and we know that most atheists tend to identify politically as more liberal and progressive. In the United States, these political beliefs are assumed to be inclusive, non-discriminatory, and free of bias, and there is research supporting the idea that those who see themselves as free of bias, whether racist, sexist, heterosexist, are likely to carry unexamined and harmful bias because they see themselves as the "good ones" who are fighting for others' rights (Nesbitt, 2021; Sullivan, 2014). When you add onto that an atheist or nonreligious identity, this could amplify this effect because these individuals will likely see themselves as freethinkers who are rooted in logic and data—perhaps morally superior to their religious counterparts. However, for male atheists, this is the perfect storm to carry forward patriarchal structures into nonreligious spaces. Women becoming nonreligious is a necessarily different (and less privileged) experience from that of men because of the devaluation of their gender. So, when a woman leaves a religion, she likely will take inventory of the ways that religion taught her about her gender because she experienced the teachings as oppressive, but when a man leaves a religion that showed preference to his gender and did not necessarily create dissonance between his sense of himself and the way the world saw him, he has no reason to dissect the systems of power and privilege around him because they were made for him. Thus, he carries these unexamined biases and beliefs into the nonreligious spaces and reifies them into structures and systems that continue to marginalize women. It is this political ideology, tendency to see oneself as incapable of bias and prejudice, and sense of being "more evolved" that could insulate some atheist men from seeing how they are perpetuating the same systems they disavow.

Therefore, by contrast, for nonbelieving women, transitioning away from religion can be a long and difficult process that can involve questioning everything one ever believed. For many women exiting religion and later identifying as atheist, pursuing education that challenges the teachings of their religious upbringing is often the impetus for this change (Abbott & Anaya, 2022). This process may involve a questioning of existential and spiritual beliefs, but, due to the patriarchal organization of most religions, it could also involve a questioning of the world and the way it is structured. When religion is questioned, it can create cracks in the way a person understands the self and the world around them, which can be incredibly scary and destabilizing. Importantly, many atheist women who leave religion describe embracing atheism as enhancing both their life and their sense of self (Abbott & Anaya, 2022). Part of therapy can involve helping a woman through this process to deconstruct her beliefs, values, and worldview in order to reintegrate and strengthen their sense of self. Such a process can be liberating and grounding, in turn helping to sustain mental health in the face of other life stressors.

Identity Exploration and Sense-Making

One's identity and understanding of themselves is often meaningfully connected to their well-being and mental health. Further, the belief systems that people hold can inform their identity in both helpful and harmful ways. For women who were raised with religion and exit that religion, there can be a significant loss or shift in identity that is important to acknowledge and work through therapeutically. Even if this shift is ultimately liberating, it involves a reimagining of oneself and the establishment of a personal set of values that may or may not align with their previously religious life. At the core of this struggle may lie the following questions: "Who am I without religion?," "What does it mean about me that

I left a religion?," and "Who am I now that I don't have a religious identity?" It is within these questions that mental health professionals need to be especially aware of their own worldview and biases. Below are self-reflective questions for counselors to ask themselves in order to take an inventory of their beliefs about (non)religion and women:

1) What does it mean to me to be (non)religious and/or (non)spiritual? How does my gender influence my experience as a (non)religious and/or (non)spiritual person?
2) What images come to mind when I think of a nonreligious woman? How might these images inform how I would approach working with nonreligious femmes?
3) What have I heard about nonreligious women and femmes within
   - **a** my professional training?
   - **b** my personal social network?
   - **c** in the news and/or media?
   - **d** How might these messages inform my work with nonreligious women?
4) What comes to mind when I think about a woman being nonreligious? How, if at all, does that change depending on her race, sexuality, relationship status, and/or whether she has children?

Helping women make sense of themselves during and after exiting religion is important work for promoting well-being. Exploring, openly and nonjudgmentally, how they understand themselves at any point within their nonreligious journey is essential, and therapists need to be aware of how their responses to their clients could either hinder or support this exploration. A therapist with a positive bias toward nonreligious women may feel pulled to reframe the client's sense-making with positive affirmations of nonreligion, ultimately keeping the client from being able to fully explore the ways in which they are understanding themselves as a nonreligious person, both positively and negatively. For example, a clinician who is staunchly nonreligious/atheist may respond dismissively to a client's grappling with the things they enjoyed about their religion, akin to a friend saying, "You're too good for him anyway," after someone ends a romantic relationship and is sitting with the dialectic of love and pain a relationship can hold. Clients may feel cautious to share with the therapist some of their more complicated feelings or pro-religion opinions. By not allowing for the exploration of the full range of possible emotions related to leaving a religion, the client will likely feel invalidated and ashamed for how they are feeling, which is not growth-fostering. Below is an exchange between a therapist and client that offers examples of unhelpful and helpful responses to a client grappling with their sense of self following a religious exit.

Client: *I am really struggling with all the things I feel like I am losing since leaving the church. I miss my bible study group, the way I felt after leaving certain services, and how my church connected me to nonprofits in my community. I know I also felt really bad after some services and bible studies because of the way we talked about certain topics, but I can't help but miss some parts.*

Unhelpful therapist response: *Yeah, I hear that, but remember what we talked about last session-about all the bad things about your church? Perhaps focusing on that list will help you stop missing those things.*

Helpful therapist response: *Yeah, I hear that. You are feeling torn between the things you gained from your church/religion and the ways it hurt you. I know that we talked about the difficulties you had with it last session, and I just want you to know that it is okay to miss certain things as well. This isn't a clearcut process and I am here. I also am hearing that a lot of what you miss is related to community and connection. Would talking more about how to get those needs met outside of a church be helpful?*

Further, a counselor with a negative bias toward nonreligious women may also do harm by asking questions or making statements that communicate judgment of her decision, and this also keeps her from fully exploring her sense of self. For example, misinformation about the relationship between religion and health (see chapter 5) may lead therapists to unduly warn clients of the potential risks of disaffiliation. Thus, regardless of your own beliefs, biases, and understandings of nonreligiousness and women, allowing clients to fully explore their beliefs, or absence thereof, as they relate to their (non)religious identities will create the space in which they can come to understand themselves and their worldviews in a more full and nuanced way. Here are some particularly helpful questions and areas to explore that may support women in understanding their identities after exiting religion:

1) What does it mean about you that you left (or are considering leaving) your religion? What would it mean about you if you stayed within your religion?
2) What does it mean to/for you that you left (or are considering leaving) your religion? What would it mean to/for you if you stayed within your religion?
3) What did religion teach you about what it means to be a woman, if anything? What parts of this understanding of femininity do you feel in/congruent with?

Belonging

A sense of belonging and social support are some of the strongest protective factors against negative mental health outcomes (Harandi et al., 2017; Moeller et al., 2020; Wang et al., 2018). Many nonreligious women have to reorganize and integrate their new understanding of themselves intrapersonally, or within themselves, and, interpersonally, or within their relationships with others. For some, their social support and community were comprised almost exclusively of church and/or faith group members, and the loss of this is something that must be acknowledged and explored. For others, their social supports were diversified enough before becoming nonreligious that they can still feel a sense of belonging with others. Importantly, it is not just proximity to others (e.g., spending time with others) that facilitates belonging, but also feeling *understood* and *affirmed* by others. Some clients may retain large social networks but conceal their nonreligiousness or be met with anti-atheism within those networks in ways that are painful and disconnecting. Therefore, in either case, there may be a loss of, or decrease in, belongingness that is worth exploring therapeutically. Below is an example exchange between a therapist and client that shows an example of an unhelpful and helpful response to a client grappling with this.

Client: *I just don't know where I belong anymore. I used to know who my people were and where I fit into my community. Ever since I stopped believing in God and going to church, I don't know how I fit into the world. My old friends still have their weekly lunch, but I don't feel like I should go anymore because we don't have this religion in common anymore. I tried out one of those atheist groups you shared with me last week, but I don't know if I fit there either.*

Unhelpful therapist response: *Well, making new friends is always hard. Keep going back to that group I told you about, and I am sure in a few weeks, you will feel right at home! How about we practice some icebreaker questions that you can use next time at the group?*

Helpful therapist response: *Yeah, that's really tough. You miss your friends and maybe the routine that going to a weekly lunch gave you, and it feels like this new group doesn't really compare. That is a really understandable way to feel. Change is hard, even when it is what is best for us. I know the group I sent you the info for can sometimes be mostly men attending, was that the case?*

(Client nods)

A lot of women joining the nonreligious communities feel like you do. You are not only changing your belief system but your social network in a lot of ways. How does it feel to be one of few women in a group rather than being surrounded by women as you were in your lunch group?

Additionally, as reviewed earlier in this chapter, even communities that are nonreligious are not always immune to patriarchal structures and sexism. Thus, if connecting a client to these communities, discussing this reality and processing how this may impact her sense of belongingness is important. In some cases, these communities may be reminiscent of the religious institution that the woman left and thus could be especially harmful to her. In your area, there may be women-only and/or queer nonreligious communities that could be a good fit for your clients' need for belongingness and social support. Digital affinity groups, too, may be safe and connecting spaces, particularly for those in geographic locations where secular organizations are few or nonexistent and/or where nonreligious communities do not include people with whom they share other social locations. Most importantly, having a frank discussion about the options your client may or may not have for connecting with social support is important throughout her journey of leaving a religion so that she can make informed decisions along the way. If you are a therapist who has many clients who are nonreligious, it may be worthwhile for you to gather a list of local and/or online organizations and/or communities that newly nonreligious women can join if they are feeling alienated after leaving a religion.

Resources:

1) Secular Coalition for America
2) American Atheists
3) Unitarian Universalist Association
4) Sunday Assembly

Values

Values are, at their core, what is important to someone. People gain their values through many avenues, including religion. Thus, when a woman is leaving a religion, exploring her current and past values can help her understand herself without religion. This exploration can be done through more structured exploration of values and/or through more informal conversations. In Acceptance and Commitment Therapy (ACT; Harris, 2019), exploring and understanding one's values is a central intervention that allows people to have a gauge on with what actions, behaviors, and experiences they want to engage. For a more formal exercise, a counselor may have a set of cards with a range of values written on each and ask their client to sort them according to the values that are most important, least important, and neutral to them in the interest of narrowing the list to a handful of "core" values. For women exiting religion, doing this exercise first from the perspective of the previous religion can be useful for you both to gain understanding of the values they are reevaluating or might feel expected to value. The central guiding question for this exercise can be "What values did your religion suggest/endorse/teach for women?" Following this step, engage in a process dialogue about what it was like to engage in the exercise and any takeaways the client may have about their former values.

Next, have the client repeat the sorting for her personal values, paying particular attention to moments she feels compelled to identify a value as important due to expectations rooted in religion. Discuss and process any similarities and/or differences between the lists generated in steps one and two. For some, this exercise may offer greater resolve with their decision to become nonreligious by seeing discrepancies between their personal values and incongruent religiously based values that led to them exiting religion. For others, this exercise may offer a nuanced understanding of how one's religious experience may have positively impacted them and their sense of self. For example, if the client identified kindness and generosity as positive values her previous religion purported, and she also ranks these values high for herself personally, she might discover some gratitude for her former faith even if it no longer serves a positive purpose in her life. As the therapist, you can help her process these similarities; in fact, highlighting similarities could help protect the client from shame and regret related to their previous religious involvement. For another client who personally values inclusivity and openness, and perceived her religion as devaluing these things in favor of judgment and hierarchy, this exercise can help validate her decision, should she feel shame or guilt for exiting religion or question the accuracy of her experience. Below are examples of helpful and unhelpful therapist responses to a client processing this values-clarification exercise.

Client: *This exercise was really interesting and has me reflecting on my values a lot. I never realized how many of my core values like open-mindedness and unconventionality did not align with my previous faith until now. I mean, I guess I knew on some level, but this just laid it all out there for me. But I also am seeing that some of my values actually were aligned with that faith, like service to others and spirituality. That makes me wonder if I made the wrong choice leaving.*

Unhelpful Therapist Response: *Yeah, it's tough when we realize we aren't living out our values, but open-mindedness and unconventionality are your top two values, so I think that's a sign that you made the right choice. We can't have it all, and remember all the reasons you left!*

Helpful Response: *That is a tough question to sit with. It can be really challenging to realize ways that our lives aren't currently aligning with our values. I don't think this necessarily means you made a wrong choice. What are some ways to live out the values of serving others and spirituality now that you are nonreligious?*

Conclusion

Women and femmes may find religious exiting to be liberating and an opportunity to build personal worldviews and communities that better reflect their values and offer some protection from the negative impact of patriarchy. Therefore, practitioners assisting clients through disaffiliation or other forms of exiting religion can use it as a growth-fostering catalyst with the potential to enhance mental health. Importantly, clinicians should attend to the gendered nature of their clients' transition to or identification with nonbelief, including unique strengths and challenges. Organized nonbelief may be a source of connection, and therefore a common suggestion for clients; however, clinicians should be aware of the pervasive nature of structural oppression, in this case patriarchy and the many systems of dominance that may intersect with it (e.g., gendered racism), and be prepared to offer support if clients are disappointed with the replication of subordination in nonreligious spaces and/or need alternative forms of community.

References

Abbott, D. M., & Anaya, E. J. (2022). "Breaking free": A grounded theory study of atheist women in the United States. *Psychology of Women Quarterly*, 46(4), 501–17. https://doi.org/10.1177/03616843221115338

Abbott, D. M., Mollen, D., Mercier, C., Anaya, E. J., & Rukus, V. A. (2020). "Isn't atheism a White thing?": Centering the voices of atheists of color. *Journal of Counseling Psychology*, 67(3), 275. https://doi.org/10.1037/cou0000399

Almeida, A. (2017, March). The atheists struggling to find therapists in the Bible Belt. The Atlantic. https://www.theatlantic.com/health/archive/2017/03/secular-therapy-in-the-south/520914/

Baker, J. O., & Whitehead, A. L. (2016). Gendering (non)religion: Politics, education, and gender gaps in secularity in the United States. *Social Forces*, 94(4), 1623–45. https://doi.org/10.1093/sf/sov119

Barna Group. (2015, March 24). (2015). State of atheism in America. https://www.barna.com/research/2015-state-of-atheism-in-america/

Beit-Hallahmi, B. (2007). Atheism: A psychological profile. In M. Martin (Ed.), *The Cambridge companion to atheism*(pp. 300–317). Cambridge University Press. https://doi.org/10.1017/CCOL0521842700.019

Bowen, M. (1993). *Family therapy in clinical practice*. Jason Aronson, Inc.

Brewster, M. E. (2013). Atheism, gender, and sexuality. In S. Bullivant & M. Ruse (Eds.), *The Oxford handbook of atheism* (pp. 511–24). Oxford University Press. https://doi.org/10.1093/oxfordhb/9780199644650.013.006

Brown, C. (2011). The people of no religion: The demographics of secularisation in the English-speaking world since c.1900. *Archiv für Sozialgeschichte*, 51, 37–61.

Burkett, E. (2000). *The baby boon: How family-friendly America cheats the childless*. Simon & Schuster.

Collins, P. H. (1990). Black feminist thought in the matrix of domination. *Black Feminist Thought: Knowledge, Consciousness, and the Politics of Empowerment*, 138, 221–38.

Cox, D. A. & Hammond, K.E. (2024, April 4). Young women are leaving church in unprecedented numbers. Survey Center on American Life. https://www.americansurveycenter.org/newsletter/young-women-are-leaving-church-in-unprecedented-numbers/

Cragun, R. (2015). Who are the new atheists? In L. G. Beaman & S. Tomlins (Eds.), *Atheist identities—Spaces and social contexts* (pp. 195–211). Springer. https://doi.org/10.1007/978-3-319-09602-5_12

Edgell, P., Frost, J., & Stewart, E. (2017). From existential to social understandings of risk: Examining gender differences in nonreligion. *Social Currents*, 4(6), 556–74. https://doi.org/10.1177/2329496516686619

Frazer, S., El-Shafei, A., Gill, A. M. (2022). Nonreligious women in America: A brief from the US secular survey. American Atheists and Secular Women. *Annual Review of the Sociology of Religion: Sociology of Atheism*, 7, 75–97. https://www.secularsurvey.org/nonreligiouswomen

Frost, J., Scheitle, C. P., Ecklund, E. H. (2023) Patterns of perceived hostility and identity concealment among self-identified atheists. *Social Forces*, 101(3), 1580–605. https://doi.org/10.1093/sf/soab165

Gorham, C. R. M. (2013). *The ebony exodus project: Why some black women are walking out on religion—and others should too*. Pitchstone Publishing.

Guenther, K. M. (2019, January). Secular sexism: The persistence of gender inequality in the US New Atheist Movement. *Women's Studies International Forum*, 72, 47–55. Pergamon. https://doi.org/10.1016/j.wsif.2018.11.007

Harandi, T. F., Taghinasab, M. M., & Nayeri, T. D. (2017). The correlation of social support with mental health: A meta-analysis. *Electronic physician*, 9(9), 5212. https://doi.org/10.19082/5212

Harris, R. (2019). *ACT made simple* (2nd ed.). New Harbinger Publications.

Hassall, C., & Bushfield, I. (2014). Increasing diversity in emerging non-religious communities. *Secularism and Nonreligion*, 3, Art. 7. https://doi.org/10.5334/snr.as

hooks, b. (2004). *We real cool: Black men and masculinity*. Psychology Press. https://doi.org/10.4324/9780203642207

Hunnicutt, G. (2009). Varieties of patriarchy and violence against women: Resurrecting "patriarchy" as a theoretical tool. *Violence Against Women*, 15(5), 553–73. https://doi.org/10.1177/1077801208331246

Hutchinson, S. (2020). Intersectional politics among atheists and humanists of color. In G. Yukich & P. Edgell (Eds.), *Religion is raced: Understanding American religion in the twenty-first century* (pp. 58–73). https://doi.org/10.18574/nyu/9781479838271.003.0006

Hyman, G. (2007). Atheism in modern history. In M. Martin (Ed.), *The Cambridge companion to atheism* (pp. 27–46). Cambridge University Press.

Kolk, M., & Saarela, J. (2024). Religion and fertility: A longitudinal register study examining differences by sex, parity, partner's religion, and religious conversion in Finland. *European Journal of Population*, 40(9), 1–25. https://doi.org/10.1007/s10680-023-09693-0

Kosmin, B., (2019, October 22). Converting the nones: Why an aware Homo Secularis is paramount. *The Humanist*. https://thehumanist.com/magazine/november-december-2019/features/converting-the-nones-why-an-aware-homo-secularis-is-paramount/

Kosmin, B. A., Keysar, A., Cragun, R. T., & Navarro-Rivera, J. (2009). American nones: The profile of the no religion population. Institute for the Study of Secularism in Society and Culture. https://www.ryantcragun.com/american-nones-the-profile-of-the-no-religion-population/

Langston, J., Hammer, J., & Cragun, R. T. (2015). Atheism looking in: On the goals and strategies of organized nonbelief. *Science, Religion and Culture*, 2(3), 70–85. https://doi.org/10.17582/journal.src/2015/2.3.70.85

Langston, J., Hammer, J., Cragun, R., & Sikes, M. E. (2017). Inside the minds and movement of America's nonbelievers: Organizational functions, (non)participation, and attitudes toward religion. In R. T. Cragun, C. Manning, & L. L. Fazzino (Eds.), *Organized secularism in the United States: New directions in research* (pp. 191–219). De Gruyter.

Lee, L. (2015). *Recognizing the non-religious: Reimagining the secular.* Oxford University Press. https://doi.org/10.1093/acprof:oso/9780198736844.001.0001

LePage v. The Center for Reproductive Medicine, P.C. SC-2022-0515. (2024)

Mahlamäki, T. (2012). Religion and atheism from a gender perspective. *Approaching Religion*, 2(1), 58–65. https://doi.org/10.30664/ar.67492

Martinez, G. M., & Daniels, K. (2023). Fertility of men and women aged 15–49 in the United States: National Survey of Family Growth, 2015–2019. https://doi.org/10.15620/cdc:122080

Macdonald, S., & Clarke, B. P. (2017). *Leaving christianity: Changing allegiances in Canada since 1945* (Vol. 2). McGill-Queen's Press-MQUP.

Marcotte, A. (2014, October 3). Atheism's shocking woman problem: What's behind the misogyny of Richard Dawkins and Sam Harris? Salon. Retrieved from https://www.salon.com/2014/10/03/new_atheisms_troubling_misogyny_the_pompous_sexism_of_richard_dawkins_and_sam_harris_partner/

Moeller, R. W., Seehuus, M., & Peisch, V. (2020). Emotional intelligence, belongingness, and mental health in college students. *Frontiers in Psychology*, 11. https://doi.org/10.3389/fpsyg.2020.00093

Mooney, C. (2011). The future of irreligion, part 2: A conversation with Barry A. Kosmin. *Free Inquiry*, 31(8), 44.

Nesbitt, G. B. (2021). *Being somebody and black besides.* University of Chicago Press. https://doi.org/10.7208/chicago/9780226716831.001.0001

Nguyen, Y. T. H., Dang, T. N. H., Sukontamarn, P., & Teerawichitchainan, B. (2024). Religious affiliation and fertility in Vietnam: Exploring desire for additional children and actual fertility. *Socius*, 10. https://doi.org/10.1177/23780231241244598

Oppenheimer, M. (2014, September 12). ,Will sexism bring down the atheist movement? Buzzfeed. Retrieved from https://www.buzzfeed.com/markoppenheimer/will-misogyny-bring-down-the-atheist-movement?utm_term=.sknBwgn6Q#.gcnENg7nw

Pew Research Center. (2016). The gender gap in religion around the world. https://www.pewresearch.org/religion/2016/03/22/the-gender-gap-in-religion-around-the-world/

Pew Research Center. (2018). The religious typology. https://www.pewresearch.org/religion/2018/08/29/the-religious-typology/

Pew Research Center. (2019). In U.S., decline of Christianity continues at rapid pace. https://www.pewresearch.org/religion/2019/10/17/in-u-s-decline-of-christianity-continues-at-rapid-pace/

Pew Research Center. (2024). Religious 'nones' in America: Who they are and what they believe. https://www.pewresearch.org/religion/2024/01/24/who-are-the-nones-how-are-they-defined/

Sandstrom, A. (2016). Women relatively rare in top positions of religious leadership. Pew Research Center. https://www.pewresearch.org/short-reads/2016/03/02/women-relatively-rare-in-top-positions-of-religious-leadership/

Schaefer, D. O. (2014). Embodied disbelief: Poststructural feminist atheism. *Hypatia*, 29(2), 371–87. https://doi.org/10.1111/hypa.12039

Scheitle, C. P., Corcoran, K. E., & Hudnall, E. B. (2019). Adopting a stigmatized label: Social determinants of identifying as an atheist beyond disbelief. *Social Forces*, 97(4), 1731–56. https://doi.org/10.1093/sf/soy084

Schnabel, L., Facciani, M., Sincoff-Yedid, A., & Fazzino, L. (2016). Gender and atheism: Paradoxes, Contradictions, and an Agenda for future research. *Annual Review of the Sociology of Religion: Sociology of Atheism*, 7, 75–97. https://doi.org/10.1163/9789004319301_006

Simmons, J. (2020). Feminist women's attitudes towards feminist men in the Canadian atheist movement. *Religion and Gender*, 10(2), 182–201. https://doi.org/10.1163/18785417-01002002

Stinson, R., Goodman, K. M., Bermingham, C., & Rasheed Ali, S. (2013). Do atheism and feminism go hand-in-hand?: A qualitative investigation of atheist men's perspectives about gender equality. *Secularism and Nonreligion*, 2, 39–60. https://doi.org/10.5334/snr.ak

Stone, L. (2022, August 8). American's growing religious-secular fertility divide. Institute for Family Studies. https://ifstudies.org/blog/americas-growing-religious-secular-fertility-divide

Sullivan, S. (2014). *Good white people: The problem with middle-class white anti-racism*. State University of New York Press. https://doi.org/10.1515/9781438451701

Trzebiatowska, M. (2019). "Atheism is not the problem. The problem is being a woman." Atheist women and reasonable feminism. *Journal of Gender Studies*, 28(4), 475–87. https://doi.org/10.1080/09589236.2018.1523053

Trzebiatowska, M., & Bruce, S. (2012). *Why are women more religious than men?* Oxford University Press. https://doi.org/10.1093/acprof:oso/9780199608102.001.0001

Ulrich, L. T. (1976). Virtuous women found: New England ministerial literature, 1668–1735. *American Quarterly*, 28(1), 20–40. https://doi.org/10.2307/2712475

Verniers, C., & Vala, J. (2018). Correction: Justifying gender discrimination in the workplace: The mediating role of motherhood myths. *Plos One*, 13(7), e0201150. https://doi.org/10.1371/journal.pone.0201150

Wang, J., Mann, F., Lloyd-Evans, B., Ma, R., & Johnson, S. (2018). Associations between loneliness and perceived social support and outcomes of mental health problems: a systematic review. *BMC Psychiatry*, 18, 1–16. https://doi.org/10.1186/s12888-018-1736-5

Wrisley, S. P. (2024). Feminist theory and the problem of misogyny. *Feminist Theory*, 24(2), 188–207. https://doi.org/10.1177/14647001211039365

Zuckerman, P. (2008). *Society without god: What the least religious nations can tell us about contentment*. NYU Press.

Zuckerman, P. (2009). Atheism, secularity, and well-being: How the findings of social science counter negative stereotypes and assumptions. *Sociology Compass*, 3(6), 949–71. https://doi.org/10.1111/j.1751-9020.2009.00247.x

Zuckerman, P., Galen, L. W., & Pasquale, F. L. (2016). *The nonreligious: Understanding secular people and societies*. Oxford University Press. https://doi.org/10.1093/acprof:oso/9780199924950.001.0001

10

Sexuality and Secularity

The Influence of Purity Culture and Faith

Debra Mollen and Ginny Maril

Chapter Outline

In the last three decades, the percentage of US Americans who are Christian has been decreasing, with 64 percent of people identifying as Christian and 30 percent unaffiliated in a recent poll (Pew Center, 2022). If the current trend of people identifying less with Christianity and more with no religion continues, experts predict unaffiliated US Americans will reach a statistical majority by 2070 (Pew Center, 2022). Although renouncing one's Christian identity, particularly one's affiliation with fundamentalist sects, can initially be challenging (Krause & Pargament, 2017), most researchers have found apostates—those who leave their former religion—enjoy improved well-being, increased autonomy, greater freedom, better self-esteem, and enhanced self-worth (Nica, 2020; Streib, 2021).

Traditionally and currently, many faith traditions promote purity as a virtue, especially sexual purity. Purity culture is "a term often used for the evangelical movement that promote[s] a biblical view of purity by discouraging dating and promoting sexual abstinence before marriage" (Natarajan et al., 2022, p. 5). Those who advocate purity culture beliefs from a Christian perspective call for strict adherence to religious scriptures, particularly biblical tenets that venerate abstinence from engaging in sexual relationships until (heterosexual) marriage (Natarajan et al., 2022). Notably, purity culture perpetuates racist ideas that reify white body supremacy while denigrating

Black women, particularly by advancing the Jezebel and mammy tropes (Schultz, 2021). Moreover, purity culture emboldens "rape-culture discourse, sex-shaming messages, body dysphoria, spousal abuse, sex-and-gender based violence as well as coercion," which disproportionately harms people marginalized by race/ethnicity, gender, and sexual orientation (Schultz, 2021, p. 16).

Those who advance the messages of purity culture most typically support abstinence-only based sex education, which is replete with scientific inaccuracies, scare tactics, gendered and racist stereotypes that reinforce (White) girls' and women's passivity, and anti-gay messages. Moreover, abstinence-only sex education, also referred to as abstinence only until marriage (AOUM), is demonstrably ineffective, with those who receive it unlikely to delay sexual intercourse and less likely to use contraception when they have sex (Fahs, 2010; Santelli et al., 2017).

Mental health practitioners should understand the power and influence of religion, particularly among groups that espouse purity culture teachings, in influencing their clients' (mis)understanding and experiences with sexuality and reproduction. Moreover, given the centrality of evangelical Christianity in promulgating purity culture, therapists ought to consider how secular clients may be especially alienated from and confused by the confluence of sexuality and purity. In this chapter, we review the literature on religion and its influence on adherents' experiences with sex, explore the impact of purity culture on sex, consider means for decolonizing and reclaiming sex, and delineate the clinical considerations therapists can employ to serve their clients. In the second part of the chapter, we share a case example, designed to show the ways that secularity can provide an avenue to embrace sex-positive attitudes and advance wellness, including resources for therapists.

Religion's Influence on Sexuality

Proponents of many faith traditions, particularly Christianity, promote conventional, conservative ideals regarding sexuality. Runkel (1998) provided a useful primer about some key tenets that inform Christianity's views, particularly through a lens of asceticism, the practice of stringent self-denial that proscribes all practices of indulgence, including corporeal gratification. Through this lens, celibacy is especially valorized, most notably for unmarried people, and sex for non-procreative reasons is chastised. Further, abstaining from sex until (heterosexual) marriage is believed to solidify one's worth, faith, and purity (Estrada, 2021).

In practice, however, practicing celibacy until marriage, as emphasized by proponents of abstinence-only sex education, can introduce confusion about self-worth, faith, and purity. Several researchers have examined the impacts of the AOUM approach to sex education. Results have revealed individuals feeling disconnected from their bodies, insecure about their sexuality, lacking in knowledge about sex, taking responsibility for others' behaviors, experiencing shame for not living up to standards set forth by God

(Gregoire et al., 2021; Klein, 2018; Lemke, 2017; Martin et al., 2017), and having post-traumatic stress-like symptoms for some (Bolz-Weber, 2019). In the United States, thirty states require schools to emphasize the importance of abstinence outside of marriage in sex education, indicating that these concerns are likely quite prevalent throughout the country and across demographics (SIECUS, 2022). Moreover, Christianity has traditionally relied on strict biblical interpretations that call for the subjugation of women to men, most notably through heterosexual marriage, such that women learn to defer to their husbands and prioritize men's needs and pleasure over their own. As Runkel incisively surmised, "Christian sexual suppression is an institutionalized, self-fulfilling prophecy; it offers reduction for the anxiety and guilt that it causes" (1998, p. 118). Students from secular families may find AOUM curricula particularly unrelatable, confusing, and nonsensical. Moreover, they may be marginalized by AOUM lessons with covert or direct messages centered in Christianity.

Scholars have examined the role of religion on sexual attitudes and behaviors, finding widespread support for the relationship between conservative religious beliefs and pejorative views about sexuality, especially regarding any expression or practice outside of procreative, heterosexual sex. Knowing about sex itself can be condemnable. In a study of Saudi American Muslim women, for example, researchers found that participants believed that single women had no need to understand issues related to sex and reproduction and in fact, that unfamiliarity with sexuality was evidence of their own purity (Alomair et al., 2022). Conventional views of religion inform ideas about gender. In one study, researchers studied 340 women who attended a private evangelical university and found that having traditional, conservative religious beliefs was positively related to embracing traditional gender roles, such that participants who espoused more conventional Christian beliefs were less likely to have career aspirations, voiced more shame about their bodies, and endorsed more sexist beliefs (Eliason et al., 2017). Prina and Schatz-Stevens (2020) surveyed nearly 400 adults from the United States and Italy, finding that religiosity predicted both sexist attitudes and rape myth acceptance in both countries while Owens and colleagues (2020) found, among a group of ninety-nine Christian women and men, a positive association between the endorsement of purity culture and rape myths, as well as being more likely to mislabel rape as consensual sex.

The obligation of women to have sex with their husbands provides another example of a problematic script. This duty to engage in sex is typically communicated in conjunction with the belief that women are unlikely to enjoy sex even once married. This belief conveys that a woman's physical and/or emotional needs are less important than the requirements of obligation to her husband (Estrada, 2021). This script likewise infers that it is the wife's responsibility to fulfill her husband's sexual needs in order to prevent him from straying sexually. Gregoire et al. (2021) identified that Christian-identified women who endorsed belief in this script were 79 percent more likely to have sex with their husbands out of obligation than their secular counterparts. The author discovered other significant correlations with this script including body mistrust, sexual shame, sexual dissatisfaction, and sexual dysfunction. One particularly troubling implication of the findings was the increased likelihood of believing a woman is the gatekeeper of male sexual advances, further perpetuating the myth that problematically misascribes the responsibility of rape and assault on the survivor.

Religious beliefs also correlate with ideas about sexual morality, wellness, and behaviors. In one study of 713 women and men, researchers found that the stronger participants' certainty of their belief in god's existence, the more likely they were to perceive their own internet pornography use as addictive, likely because of religious teachings that regard pornography as sinful (Bradley et al., 2016). The researchers also found that perceiving oneself as being addicted to pornography was predictably related to experiencing psychological distress. In another study, researchers examined beliefs about supernatural evil (i.e., the devil) among 1,721 adults and found that beliefs regarding supernatural evil was related to endorsing conservative views on sexuality, particularly views on abortion, homosexuality, pre- and extramarital sex, and pornography use (Baker et al., 2020). The authors found that it was the presence of belief in supernatural evil that was most compelling, beyond merely identifying as religious.

Because sexual health outcomes tend to be worse in marginalized communities, whose members' access to sexual and reproductive education and healthcare is poor compared to majority group members, research on the role of religion among marginalized group members is striking. Thorpe et al. (2021), for example, surveyed 1,426 Black female adolescents and found that as the importance of religion in their lives increased, so did their feelings of sexual guilt. The researchers found that those adolescent girls who identified as more religious reported delaying sexual activity and had decreased expectations for sexual pleasure. Among a group of 255 African American highly religious churchgoers participating in an HIV education and screening project, Hawes and Berkley-Patton (2014) found considerable evidence of sexual risk taking, including low consistent condom use and acknowledging having had sex while using drugs or alcohol. Thorpe and their colleagues (2023) studied 242 Black women regarding the messages they had received about masturbation and found that many recalled receiving explicitly negative messages from Christianity. Pejorative messages around masturbation included its sinfulness, ungodliness, and disgust, which the participants internalized as shameful. In another study, Piper and their colleagues (2020) interviewed forty-two women who were active members in African American churches in a large urban area. They found that their church leaders condemned women who experienced pregnancy outside of marriage and that those who came from religious families faced harsher messages around the importance of remaining abstinent. The authors surmised that the attitudes participants' religious communities conveyed made it difficult for women to be sexually assertive, with many having experienced unwanted sexual contact and engaging in more sexually risky behaviors in adolescence.

Religious leaders and adherents, particularly from conservative traditions, have had a long-standing conflict between their faith's tenets and same-gender sexual relationships. Most often, identifying as lesbian, gay, bisexual, or queer (LGBQ) in traditional Christian communities has yielded considerable distress, especially for younger people, which necessitates a complex process of confronting and reconciling anti-gay bias. Levy and Harr (2018) interviewed seventeen bisexual and pansexual adults who grew up Christian and found that most were taught that being LGBQ was a sin. Their process of resolving the conflict between their sexuality and religion involved experiencing dissonance, accessing resources, reaching a turning point, accepting themselves and coming out, and eventually living authentically and unapologetically. To cope with the initial dissonance they experienced, some participants adapted their religious beliefs to be more congruent with their sexual identities while others left their religious communities altogether. In a study of more than 1,200 LGBTIQA+ Australian students, Jones (2023) found that those who attended religious schools were more likely to hear anti-LGBTIQA+ messages from educators and staff, experience efforts to change their sexual orientation and gender identity, and had worse outcomes, such as feeling shunned and ostracized from school activities, being reported to others, assigned worse grades, and being punished.

In another study with 1,128 LGBQ Mormons and former Mormons, Lefevor et al. (2019) found that those who continued to identify as Mormon reported more depression and less well-being and flourishing than those who had left the church. Unsurprisingly, participants with higher degrees of internalized homonegativity reported higher degrees of anxiety and depression and less life satisfaction. By contrast, those who embraced sexuality as healthy reported less disgust and better psychological outcomes than their peers. Those who experienced more guilt associated with using pornography, who were less likely to see masturbation as permissible, and more likely to see sex as dirty reported worse psychological well-being.

Researchers have likewise examined attitudes toward marriage equality and the role that religion serves in shaping beliefs. Anderson and colleagues (2021), for example, surveyed more than two hundred people, including Christians and nonbelievers. They found that Christians were more likely to demonstrate sexual prejudice and reject marriage equality compared to nonbeliever participants, particularly when examining the role of religious fundamentalism and intrinsic religiosity.

Whether indicative of a bias toward studying religiousness or because of the ubiquity of people identifying as religious, far less research has been conducted regarding atheism/secularity and its relationship to sexuality. We found two notable exceptions. The first was Brewster et al.'s (2021) study of 234 sexual minority atheists. Among their sample, the author found that participants' perceptions of their families' religiosity was inversely related to their experience of familial support. The sexual minority atheists whose families were more religious were also more likely to experience psychological distress and less likely to report higher levels of life satisfaction. The second was Abbott and Anaya's (2022) study of atheist women in the United States. The researchers found that participants, who by virtue of their atheism were sometimes regarded by others as sexually immoral, also found liberation from the constraints of religion, which may provide the impetus for pursuing sexual liberation more specifically.

Taken together, researchers have generally found that religion, especially fundamentalist and/or evangelical Christian and Muslim faith denominations, exacts a deleterious toll on its adherents' sexuality. Among these impacts are the tendency to see pornography use as addictive, the cultivation of sexual prejudice and rejection of marriage equality efforts, the encouragement of sexual passivity among women, and guilt and shame, particularly toward any sexual expression outside heterosexual, procreative sex.

Purity Culture's Influence

The early 2000s saw a rise in purity culture that included rites of passage such as young people making purity pledges in which they publicly promise to abstain from engaging in sexual activity until (heterosexual) marriage and wearing purity rings. These ceremonies often involve fathers and daughters, though other members of the family can be present and involved. Scholars have recognized that pledges and the ceremony surrounding them had the opportunity to involve memorable, potentially more nuanced conversations about sex that included both positive and negative aspects (Manning, 2014; Rosenbaum, 2009). An earlier study revealed that while those who wore purity rings were more likely to delay their first sexual experience, they were also less likely to practice safer sex when they did engage in sexual behavior (Bruckner & Bearman, 2005).

Manning's (2014) qualitative study examining family discourses about purity pledges identified varying perspectives within the family regarding sexual behavior. Pop culture and media were a significant part of the discourse. For children, daughters specifically, they recognized their parents were confused about media representations of sex and the potential impacts on adolescents. Parents tended to underestimate the extent of their children's media savvy and their discourses, which varied by parents' gender, differed from their children's. Mothers were primarily concerned about pregnancy and resulting repercussions. Fathers' discourses focused on the negative influences of media, fear of boys aggressing against their daughters, the presumed innocence and naiveté of their daughters, and the value of wearing purity rings as a warning to ward off boys.

There are quite a few biases and problematic assumptions encapsulated in the literature. Those surveyed, including parents and the proponents of AOUM and purity culture, often perpetuate pronatalism, the tethering of one's worth to procreation, and heteronormativity. The beliefs undergirding pronatalism and heteronormativity include not only the assumption that relationships are dyadic, made up of one man and one woman who are cisgender and heterosexual, but also that such couples necessarily have children who themselves are cisgender, heterosexual, and will want to have children. Presumptions of heterosexuality are both myopic and often perpetuate traditional gender roles, which is limiting and most often oppressive.

By further examining Manning's (2014) results, we made note of racist overtones, as well. One common discourse of fathers was the idea that the media can make boys sexually aggressive toward girls. The fathers cited television shows, movies, and rap music as contributing factors. No other musical genre was cited, though there are certainly examples in most genres of popular music that include misogyny and perpetuate rape myths. Purity culture, then, creates fertile ground for the problematic advancement of pejorative views of sexuality embedded at the intersection of racism, cisgenderism, pronatalism, sexism, and heterosexism (Schultz, 2021). Psychologists and other mental health workers are subsequently tasked with helping their clients identify and excavate the harms inherent in traditional faith-based messages that juxtapose sex and shame. Nonreligious people raised with faith, particularly Christianity, may still bear the religious residue of purity culture and benefit from support in unlearning unhealthy sexual messages.

Reclaiming Healthy Sexuality

Given the extent of traditional conservative faith groups' influence on sexuality, historically and currently, efforts to combat destructive messaging by reclaiming a healthier perspective have been gradual. Notably, women of color have advanced some especially positive alternatives to purity culture. Mental healthcare workers are also likewise uniquely situated to help their clients adopt a more critical consciousness around harmful internalized messages, replacing them with a more empowered, emboldened approach to sexuality.

In their study of nine women of color, Natarajan et al. (2022) found that a catalyst for their liberation was often a change or life transition that ushered in new understandings about the racist messages undergirding purity culture. Part of their healing involved problematizing whiteness as the default in understanding the extent of purity culture's harm. The women were better able to see the extent to which the internalization of harmful purity culture messages took a toll on their mental health and denounced the racist ideals inherent in purity culture beliefs. They cultivated healthier relationships with their bodies, identities, and ideals about sex. Thorpe and colleagues (2023) similarly stressed the importance of Black women in particular pursuing sexual exploration and sex-positive, feminist spaces in an effort to reclaim what many Christian churches had instilled.

Some scholars have provided suggestions to those impacted by purity culture to reclaim a healthy right to their sexuality. These can be adapted by those who work with both religious and secular clients in the provision of psychological care. Schultz, for example, noted the importance of reinterpreting scripture for those who continue to identify with a faith, dismantling heterosexual marriage as the best option for everyone, and the importance of centralizing people as "sexual agents who deserve love, pleasure, and intimacy" (2021, p. 38). Dinse and colleagues (2023) offered a more empowering religious perspective on sexuality including normalizing discussing sex openly, reclaiming sex as a gift, and examining and challenging traditional ideas about gender that many Christian congregations perpetrate. For mental health practitioners who work with secular clients, we advocate exploring messages about sexuality and encouraging the claiming of healthy, enthusiastic, pleasure-focused sex. It is important to remember that even secular clients may struggle with embracing sex positivity given the ubiquity of purity culture, although we caution readers from assuming that secular clients have internalized purity culture tenets.

Case Example

This case example represents a composite of common presenting concerns and experiences of clients spanning a decade of the authors' clinical practice. It is not our intention to represent an actual specific therapy client. We have changed details to ensure we are not inadvertently identifying any single client.

Radha is a thirty-eight-year-old queer, biracial woman who uses she/they pronouns. To honor the client's gender identities, we intentionally use both pronouns when discussing them and their case. Radha initially presented to therapy due to a recurrence of major depressive disorder. The client noted a recent relocation to the Southern United States to be closer to her partner's family who could help provide care for their three-year-old child while she and her partner worked. At the time Radha sought therapy, they and their lesbian-identified partner (she/her) had been partnered for approximately eight years. Their partner was a White woman the same age as Radha. In looking for a therapist, Radha deliberately sought out someone queer-identified since this was an important part of their identity, and they began work with a lesbian-identified woman about fifteen years her senior in private practice.

Radha's primary complaint was that her partner's desire for sex far outweighed their own. This problem had persisted since the early years of their partnership with the client reporting that desire discrepancy was the only topic about which they argued. Other than this ongoing source of conflict, Radha noted each was satisfied in the relationship. The client described herself as "broken" when it came to sex. Rarely had they found pleasure in sex with their partner and often noted she felt "obligated" to engage in physical intimacy. She was clear to share there was no coercion nor pressure from her partner to engage when they did not want to. From Radha's description, however, they never wanted to be sexual with their partner. Radha's hope for therapy was to change their desire for sex with their partner.

There were two notable aspects of Radha's development that emerged early in therapy. When exploring their history, they shared that they had grown up in an Evangelical Christian church whose messaging included the importance of remaining sexually abstinent until pursuing a heterosexual marriage and having children. This mandate was symbolized via purity ceremonies where children were required to pledge to God and their family their promise to abstain from sex until they were married. Radha participated in one such ceremony, which they now recognized was a "convenient" way to disguise their sexual orientation. They shared that it was easier for them to dissuade and rebuff male suitors "with a flash of [their] ring" that they wore to symbolize their intentions to abstain from sex. The ring further offered a convenient excuse of why she declined physical intimacy with men and an easy way to end a romantic relationship. She shared that telling others that she was ending a relationship because her boyfriend was pressuring her for sex was never questioned by her parents or friends.

A second significant event that impacted their feelings about sex was a sexual assault they survived when the client was seventeen. After this assault, she began having sex with partners of various genders, almost exclusively when using alcohol. After they experienced a flashback during sex with one of these partners, she met with a therapist who diagnosed and treated her for post-traumatic stress disorder. While she believed that she had successfully processed their trauma in therapy, she also knew that it would never be completely resolved. She wondered aloud with her new therapist if she might be asexual (a person who either does not feel sexual attraction or does not want to have sexual relationships; notably, asexuality occurs on a spectrum reflecting varying degrees of sexual attraction (Asexual Visibility and Education Network, n.d.). She felt frustrated that she could not know "the truth" about her romantic and sexual orientations because of the pervasive influences of the messages of the church and of her assault.

Radha's initial goal for therapy was to discern her relationship with sex so that she could more fully engage with her partner and provide the intimacy her partner sought. As the therapeutic work continued, it became clear that disentangling problematic messaging about sex would be a critical piece of this process. With guidance from their therapist, Radha revisited early messaging that their body was bad and, in fact, did not exist for nor belong to themself. Their virginity was to be protected at all costs and only shared with the one heterosexual cisgender man whom she would eventually marry and with whom she would have children.

When Radha was assaulted, this narrative was upended. She believed she no longer had the value of her "virginity" to demonstrate her worth. She elected not to share the fact of her assault with anyone for reasons relating to self-blame, embarrassment, and shame. Though she would not hear and become familiar with the phrase *rape myth* for many years, she had been profoundly impacted by the internalization of these beliefs (see Figure 10.1 for examples of rape myths). Though cognitively able to recognize that in no world should she have been raped, she could not shake that it was her fault for "putting [her]self in the position in the first place." Radha's way of thinking reflected many years of hearing and internalizing rape myths. She shared, "I was somewhere I should not have been, drinking things I shouldn't have been drinking, and just left myself open to it." She internalized that the assault was, to an extent, her fault. She had not followed the rules of avoiding rape, and she believed she suffered the consequences. Eventually, she confided in her partner after they had been together for several years. Her partner responded with compassion and empathy and encouraged Radha to seek care, while remaining frustrated by the lack of change in their sexual relationship.

After Radha's intake appointment, consistent with her approach with all her clients, the therapist engaged in a sustained period of reflection and identified several points to guide her work with her client. It was clear that she would need to stay mindful and attentive to her own experience of religion and how that might be impacting her approach to the care of this client. Radha's experiences with religion were not dissimilar from the therapist's. The therapist was also a queer-identified person who had grown up in a family and church with high religious control. She had spent time in therapy of her own to untangle what she could of the messaging she received. While their shared experience with religion could serve as an advantage in connecting with her client's experience, she also recognized that there was risk of overidentification. From the therapist's experience, she knew the potential for overidentification could lead to an inability for her to work as effectively as she typically did. She recalled that overidentification often resulted in her imposing more direction than would have been therapeutically indicated about topics about which she felt passionately or in moving too quickly to providing the solutions that had worked for her without allowing the client the appropriate time and space to process their own experiences.

The therapist recognized that when she found herself reflecting on a specific client or situation outside of work, as she had felt pulled to do with Radha, it was usually a good

RAPE MYTHS

"Women lie about rape when they regret having sex or want to get revenge"

Most people tell the truth about rape. Only 2–4% are false reports, which is similar to other crimes. Most people do NOT want to report sexual violence. In fact, only 6% of sexual assaults in Canada are ever reported to the police and only 1–2% of date sexual assaults.

"Most rapes are committed by strangers in dark, secluded places".

Most [73%] of sexual assaults are perpetrated by someone the victim knows. Most [80%]occur in someone's home or residence.

"Sexual assault does not happen in same-sex relationships"

Statistics indicate that sexual assault happens just as frequently in same-sex relationships as it does in heterosexual relationships.

"Being accused of rape will ruin a man's reputation"

Most [73%] of sexual assaults are perpetrated by someone the victim knows. Most [80%] occur in someone's home or residence. Only 12% of sexual assault cases make it to trial and only 0.3% are found guilty. Many people in society continue to blame the victims.

"Women who want to want to avoid sexual assault should dress properly and should not get too drunk at parties"

How a person dresses does not affect their chances of sexual assault. while drunk women may be targeted by perpetrators, the responsibility to stop rape should not be put on women's shoulders alone. As a community, we are responsible for each other's safety.

"Men have right to sex if they have paid for drinks, if the other person is their partner/spouse, or if they have been "led on"

No one has the right to sex when the other partner has not consented

"If both people were drunk it can't be sexual assault"

It is rare that two people are experiencing exactly the same level of intoxication at the same time. Usually one person is less intoxicated than the other. A less drunk person still has the responsibility to make sure their very drunk friend doesn't drive. similarly. the less drunk person has the responsibility to make sure their person has a responsibility to make sure their partner is not too intoxicated to consent.

Figure 10.1 Rape Myths. Credit to St. Francis Xavier University.

indication she needed to seek consultation. She did this in two ways. First, she shared the case in consultation with her work partners. This practice was particularly helpful when reflecting on areas of similarity and difference between her and her client. The therapist, a White woman, recognized she did not and could not fully understand the lived experience of a biracial person. Through consulting the research on the experiences of biracial people, seeking guidance from her professional peers, and having conversations in therapy, the therapist was better able to temper her assumptions and help Radha decipher the gendered-racial messages they had internalized.

The therapist's exploration of the scholarship helped her understand the pervasive sexual double standards that often emerge among Asian and Asian American people (Guo, 2019) and the importance of parental messages, themselves typically quite gendered, around abstinence among Asian Americans (Trinh & Kim, 2020). While refraining from assuming Radha's experiences were necessarily representative of those she read about, the therapist was able to use these as a backdrop for helping Radha explore the ways they were impacted by cultural messages about sex.

Through their work together, the therapist learned that Radha's father worked as a petroleum engineer, and they often had lived abroad. Her US American-born father met her mother when living temporarily in India, and Radha, who identified as white and South Asian Indian, held dual citizenship. Her identity as a biracial, South Asian nonbinary person was particularly salient and brought additional nuance to their experience. In sessions, Radha reflected on the frequency with which she was exoticized by people she knew, as well as by strangers. She shared that her darker skin tone combined with Western features, including light eyes, drew unwanted attention. Her appearance also resulted in fetishization, which manifested in unsolicited comments from strangers as well as partners. She provided a number of examples when a sexual partner requested behaviors she experienced as demeaning and nonconsensual.

Further, while Radha and the therapist were both from high-control religions, they grew up in different religious traditions. The therapist learned that her client held hurtful stereotypes about the therapist's own church, which raised the therapist's defensiveness. While she noted the work consultation was helpful, insofar as her colleagues were supportive, she recognized that it was reigniting some feelings from her own childhood. Accordingly, the therapist decided to discuss her thoughts and feelings with her personal therapist so that she could more explicitly share concerns and experiences that she did not want to discuss with her coworkers.

Course of Treatment

Of note, Radha's goal at intake was to feel the desire to be sexually intimate with her partner. The therapist recognized there were a number of steps to take prior to this goal. She began with a detailed treatment plan (see Table 10.1).

Fava and Fortenberry (2021) noted the necessity of employing trauma-informed therapy, particularly in their work with clients with sexual trauma histories. They suggested focusing on helping clients enhance their sexual well-being, sexual health, and sexual pleasure. In consideration of Radha's history of sexual assault, her therapist knew that any approach she took would need to be trauma-informed and grounded in principles such as safety, trust, transparency, collaboration and mutuality, and empowerment (Fava & Fortenberry, 2021). Providing trauma-informed care was achieved throughout therapy by supporting Radha's autonomy for their own sexual behavior, avoiding judgment of what they shared

Table 10.1 Conceptualizing and Treatment Planning

Conceptualization	
Messages regarding purity culture, in combination with a sexual assault, contributed to Radha's current symptom presentation including avoidance of sexual intimacy with her partner, dissatisfaction and disconnection with her body, and heightened experiences of guilt and shame	
Treatment Plan for Radha	
Primary Concern/ Diagnostics	• Low to no desire for sex • Major Depressive Disorder • Persistent Depressive Disorder (rule out) • Post-Traumatic Stress Disorder (rule out)
Goal	• Short term: Identify and clarify current diagnostics • Long term: Determine the extent to which the client desires to engage in sexual activity and reduce depressive and trauma symptoms
Objective	• Connect the client with things that bring physical pleasure • Increase the client's ability to communicate with their partner about sexual intimacy
Planned Interventions/ Modalities of Therapy	• Referral to primary care physician to identify any potential organic cause for current symptoms • Referral to psychiatrist to evaluate any perimenopausal influence and discuss medication adjustment • Referral to trauma-informed yoga group to assist in reconnecting their body and mind • Cognitive and behavioral intervention to address thoughts and behaviors that impact her connection to pleasure including dismantling distortions about sex • Affective interventions to explore Radha's feelings about their body, sexuality, and capacity for and entitlement to pleasure • Somatic intervention (e.g., resourcing and bilateral stimulation) to reduce trauma symptoms • Enhance critical consciousness around the internalization of purity culture and rape myths (See Figure 10.1)
Anticipated number of sessions or timeline of care	• Initial course of 12 sessions

with the therapist, empowering her to make her own sexual decisions, and maintaining a collaborative therapeutic environment in which power differentials were acknowledged and minimized.

Throughout Radha's treatment, consent played a critical role in the therapeutic relationship, as well as their relationship at home. Their therapist recognized the import of trauma-informed care in Radha's case and emphasized a collaborative relationship of ongoing consent. Radha's religious background was characterized by unidirectional demands of belief and behavior. Tasks were prescribed to her such as not engaging in sexual activity with anyone other than their husband lest there be negative consequences

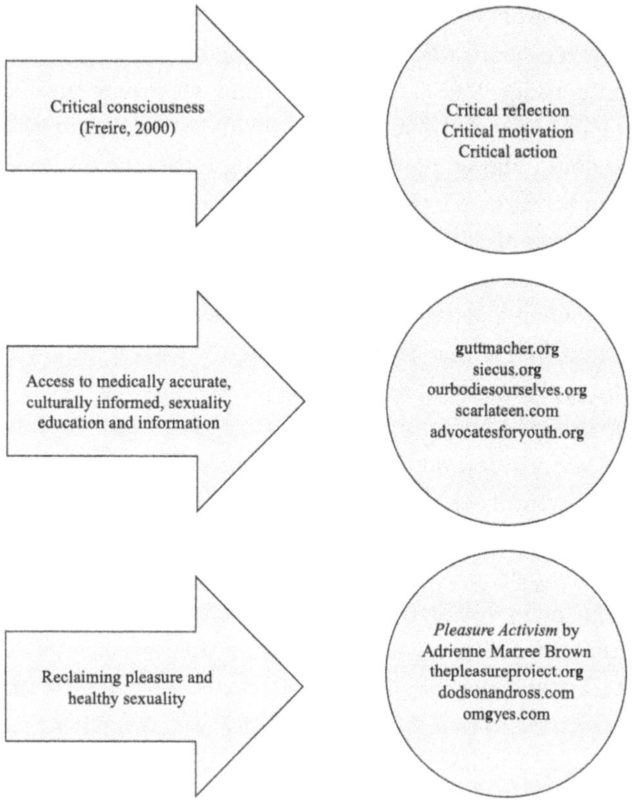

Figure 10.2 Strategies and Resources for Sex-Positive Psychotherapy.

up to and including damnation. The therapist did not want to recreate a paternalistic, prescriptive relationship whereby she instructed the client what to do. She instead fostered Radha's volition and autonomy by countering Radha's tendency to ask for advice with exploratory questions of how Radha might handle things as well as process comments about Radha's tendency to look to the therapist for directive advice as well as clarification of what was right and what was wrong.

The therapist initiated an early intervention in treatment to increase Radha's exposure to touch that she knew would not lead to any form of sexual activity. In one session, Radha shared that she enjoyed receiving professional massages and did so regularly. She also reflected that she often would "just lay there" and not provide feedback if she became uncomfortable with the pressure or specific massage techniques employed during the session. Her reaction during these moments was to freeze and sometimes dissociate. Radha and the therapist agreed that before her next massage, they would speak with the massage therapist about her reluctance to provide feedback. The therapist also taught Radha a grounding exercise she could use when she started to dissociate during a massage. Before their next massage, Radha told their massage therapist about their reluctance to be forthcoming when they were uncomfortable during their massages. The massage therapist responded with compassion and together they agreed that Radha would offer a physical gesture (i.e., raising their hand) when they identified an unmet need to address.

During the next massage, Radha raised their hand when they felt uncomfortable, and her massage therapist stopped the massage to invite Radha's feedback. Radha was able to initiate both feedback and employ the grounding technique her therapist taught her, which allowed them to relax even more during those sessions. This technique constituted trauma-informed behavioral intervention. Radha and their therapist together identified a cognitive component. In conversation, Radha expressed that she "needed" to receive massage because of ongoing pain she experienced. She had been sure to explain that her insurance had covered it for a time. The therapist inquired about the possibility of enjoying massage as something that brought her physical pleasure, asking, "What would happen if you scheduled a massage just because it felt good?" The therapist continued to encourage the client to reduce her justifications of these experiences and open herself to experiencing something that was physically enjoyable without being sexual.

After three sessions of staying present in her body during massage, Radha decided to try connecting with her partner in a similar way. After they shared with their partner what they had been practicing in therapy, they engaged in mutual cuddling and massage. Radha also engaged in grounding exercises when necessary. After this attempt, Radha asked their partner for feedback. Their partner shared that she also enjoyed the time and felt more connected. Radha's partner asked something she felt was troubling that Radha brought back to the next session. Radha's partner had noted that when she approached Radha for any kind of sexual activity, Radha often responded in what her partner termed "baby talk." Exploring this in therapy brought up quite a bit of shame and embarrassment for Radha. The therapist took time to help Radha work through those feelings while ensuring she was employing a judgment-free approach. Eventually, Radha recognized that her tendency to speak in an infantilized manner was another way she avoided sex. She recognized that because babies are not considered sexual and should not be approached for sex, she had been staving off invitations to be sexual with her partner. She had unconsciously been responding in a childlike manner to make herself less attractive to her partner, similarly to how she hoped her purity ring would signal others to leave her alone. With that awareness and her increased mindfulness practice, Radha found it easier to approach sex as an adult and in her typical voice.

For the first several years of their relationship, Radha's partner had bragged to others about the quality, amount, and frequency of their sex life. While this made Radha feel uncomfortable, she most often responded by nodding and smiling. She recognized that this felt like what she was supposed to do. She also recognized that the more they had sex with her partner when she did not want to, the more resentment built up in her. She reflected on how silenced she felt because she could not discuss this experience with anyone. Though they were not of *traditional* gender, internalized traditional gender roles had seeped into their relationship. By not declining sex over the years, they had begun to associate all sex as something they did not want to do. Their body began expressing it by automatically recoiling from their partner's touch, which their partner could not help but take personally.

She also took it personally when Radha would have flashbacks of her assault when they were together.

A combination of fetishization, dissociation, and people pleasing culminated in a core event that spurred Radha to therapy. In order to ensure her partner enjoyed themselves, Radha would "put on a show." This performative approach to their sexual relationship involved a striptease dance while wearing a sari. When dancing for her partner, Radha found it critical to "become a completely different person." She shared that it actually felt good to be in the body of someone who was confident in their sexuality, but that it was wholly an act and something to which she did not authentically connect. Her vocalizations during sex were informed by pornography she had watched from which she had learned how people, women in particular, were "supposed" to sound during sex. While she felt more in control, she did not experience any sexual pleasure from the interaction. Indeed, once when she was bottoming (on the receiving end of a sexual encounter), she began crying. Upon reflection, they shared that her body was for others and not for herself. When the therapist asked if she had ever been sexual with someone who helped her feel like her body was for herself, she was able to identify two people she had been with, although neither was their current partner.

The therapist helped Radha explore what it was about those partners that helped her feel safe to experience pleasure. They shared a memory from their twenties when they were involved with a heterosexual couple. She spent time with them separately and together and had sex with them separately and together. She felt like this was a safe relationship to be in because she was "the guest star." She could move in and out of the relationship as she felt comfortable. There was always someone else to focus on. The couple was, "kind, settled, and caring." They cared for Radha and appreciated what she brought into their relationship. When they were with them, they were able to relax into the time and truly enjoy the exploration. It was playful, kind, and authentic. There was no expectation of sex and there was always consent. Despite feeling "so happy with them," Radha withdrew from this relationship because, having internalized early messages about heterosexuality and mononormativity, she knew it was "not okay." Growing up, she had been taught that there were two discrete sexes and genders and that relationships were for one man and one woman; they had already "ruined that" by not being a man or a woman. She knew that having multiple partners would have been completely unacceptable to her friends, family, and broader society. With that understanding, she painfully withdrew from the relationship, which meant terminating contact from the only people she had ever felt sexually safe with. She reflected that perhaps because there was no blueprint for a three-person relationship that she knew of, they each formed their own approach. There was not baggage connected to how it was "supposed to be" precisely because it was not "supposed to be."

In their work together, the therapist often drew attention to the language Radha used and hypothesized its relation to her religious socialization. For example, they frequently described themselves as "ruined," "broken," "disgusting," and "embarrassing." The therapist encouraged the client to notice when they were using these or similar words and to replace them with more affirming language. Radha had a hard time adjusting them for herself so the therapist drew from the work of mindful self-compassion and encouraged them to speak to themself as they might a friend. Together they identified a close friend whom Radha loved very much. She was instructed to think about how that conversation might go if her friend was sharing this with her. Radha said, "I would *never* call them ruined or disgusting! They were just having fun and exploring!" The therapist encouraged Radha to shift that language to "I am not ruined or disgusting! I was just having fun and exploring!" in the same tone she would have used to support her friend.

Another frequent topic of therapy was Radha's self-named "the me double standard." This phrase referred to her expansive generosity toward, compassion for, and acceptance of others while she expected perfection and rigidity from herself. She judged herself harshly for the same behaviors she accepted and even admired in others. For example, she had had a friend who grew up in the same church and was now in a same-sex marriage with a child. The couple had an open relationship when they were apart from each other. Radha was enthusiastic and nonjudgmental about the couple's relationship; she loved to hear stories about her friend's adventures. However, when she thought about partnering outside of her relationship, they could not break out of the confines of monogamy and exhibited intense distress and self-judgment.

There were many early messages that Radha needed untangled in her work. The therapist employed a multi-pronged approach that proved most effective. Underlying the entirety of the work was trauma-informed and sex-positive care, especially around pacing, consent, and nonjudgment. Cognitive behavioral therapy served to challenge Radha to shift thought patterns, change the words she used, and incorporate copious amounts of self-compassion. Further, behavioral intervention that included nonsexual intimate touch via an adapted fear hierarchy was helpful. Somatic work was incorporated not only in the massage example above, but also in Radha's participation in a trauma-informed yoga therapy group. The therapist also taught Radha resourcing techniques and employed the use of bilateral stimulation to reduce distress related to several targets related to their sexual assault. The therapist taught and encouraged Radha to use mindfulness and self-compassion work as well to help her stay in her body when engaged in any sort of touch. Finally, Radha explored self-forgiveness for how harsh she had been toward herself with the gentle guidance of her therapist.

Radha spent their formative decades internalizing beliefs about purity and the ways their worth was intertwined with those beliefs. With her value tied directly to her sexual experiences and performance, she internalized purity culture and rape culture to deleterious effect as an adult. By engaging in therapy with a sex-positive, trauma-informed provider, she was able to untangle those internalizations and increase her awareness of how messages of purity impacted various aspects of her life. By increasing Radha's power and autonomy in various situations, she began to experience confidence and self-efficacy across domains. In addressing damaging messages and bolstering their ability to clearly consent and withdraw consent, she challenged herself to be present in her body for massage, physical movement, and sex. While these internalized messages persist even after awareness is brought to them, Radha completed therapy with a greater understanding and greater compassion for the person who grew up believing things she no longer believed.

Conclusion

In this chapter, we have examined the scholarship on the relationship between religion and sexuality with a particular focus on how traditional faith messages can undermine healthy experiences with sexuality. Most often, these religious messages are introduced and cemented in childhood and reinforced through media, education, and culture, which can make untethering them especially challenging. Accordingly, we presented a fictitious case example in which a therapist works with a client with a complex history of hearing and internalizing sex-negative ethnically and religiously based messages, a sexual assault, and the concomitant resultant trauma they endured. We offered specific suggestions for adopting a sex-positive, trauma-informed approach to working with clients who present to therapy with pejorative misunderstandings about sex, gender, and relationships.

References

Abbott, D. M., & Anaya, E. J. (2022). "Breaking free": A qualitative theory study of atheist women in the United States. *Psychology of Women Quarterly*, 46(4), 501–17. https://doi.org/10.1177/03616843221115338

Alomair, N., Alagell, S., Davies, N., & Bailey, J. V. (2022). Barriers to sexual and reproductive wellbeing among Saudi women: A qualitative study. *Sexuality Research and Social Policy*, 19(6), 860–69. https://doi.org/10.1007/s13178-021-00616-4

Anderson, J. R., Ashford, L. J., Prakash, P., & Gerace, A. (2021). The role of religion in explaining the relationship between sexual prejudice and the rejection of marriage equality. *Psychology & Sexuality*, 13(3), 610–27. https://doi.org/10.1080/19419899.2021.1900346

Asexual Visibility and Education Network (n.d.). https://www.asexuality.org/

Baker, J. O., Molle, A., & Bader, C. D. (2020). The flesh and the devil: Belief in religious evil and views of sexual morality. *Review of Religious Research*, 62(1), 133–51. https://doi.org/10.1007/s13644-020-00403-4

Bolz-Weber, N. (2019). *SHAMELESS: A sexual reformation*. Canterbury.

Bradley, D. F., Grubbs, J. B., Uzdavines, A., Exline, J. J., & Pargament, K. I. (2016). Perceived addiction to internet pornography among religious believers and nonbelievers. *Sexual Addiction & Compulsivity*, 23(2–3), 225–43. http://doi.org/10.1080/10720162.2016.1162237

Brewster, M., Velez, B., Sawyer, J., Motulsky, W., Chan, A., & Kim, V. (2021). Family religiosity, support, and psychological well-being for sexual minority atheist individuals. *Psychology of Religion and Spirituality*, 13(3), 266–75. https://doi.org/10.1037/rel0000356

Brown, A. M. (2019). *Pleasure activism: The politics of feeling good*. AK Press.

Bruckner, H., & Bearman, P. (2005). After the promise: The STD consequences of adolescent virginity pledges. *Journal of Adolescent Health*, 36(4), 271–78. https://doi.org/10.1016/j.jadohealth.2005.01.005

Dinse, L., Adams, M., Vietta, C., Smith, A., Wilson, L., & Harris, S. (2023). A transformative approach to authentic sexuality. *Social Work & Christianity*, 50(2), 149–63. https://nacsw.org/Publications/SWC/SWC50_2.pdf

Eliason, K. D., Hall, M. E. L., Anderson, T., & Willingham, M. (2017). Where gender and religion meet: Differentiating gender role ideology and religious beliefs about gender. *Journal of Psychology and Christianity*, 36(1), 3–15.

Estrada, L. L. (2021). Clinical considerations of the evangelical purity movement's impact on female sexuality. *Journal of Sex & Marital Therapy*, 48(2), 121–32. https://doi.org/10.1080/0092623X.2021.1977445

Fahs, B. (2010). Daddy's little girls: On the perils of chastity clubs, purity balls, and ritualized abstinence. *Frontiers: A Journal of Women's Studies*, 31(3), 116–42. https://doi.org/10.5250/fronjwomestud.31.3.0116

Fava, N. M., & Fortenberry, J. D. (2021). Trauma-informed sex-positive approaches to sexual pleasure. *International Journal of Sexual Health*, 33(4), 537–49. https://doi.org/10.1080/19317611.2021.1961965

Gregoire, S. W., Lindenbach, R. G., & Sawatsky, J. (2021). *The great sex rescue: The lies you've been taught and how to recover what god intended*. Baker Books.

Guo, Y. (2019). Sexual double standards in white and Asian Americans: Ethnicity, gender, and acculturation. *Sexuality & Culture*, 23, 57–95. https://doi.org/10.1007/s12119-018-9543-1

Hawes, S. M., & Berkley-Patton, J. Y. (2014). Religiosity and risky sexual behaviors among an African American church-based population. *Journal of Religion and Health*, 53(2), 469–82. https://doi.org/10.1007/s10943-012-9651-4

Jones, T. (2023). Religious freedom and LGBTIQA+ students. *Sexuality Research and Social Policy*, 20(6–7), 1133–51. https://doi.org/10.1007/s13178-022-00785-w

Klein, L. K. (2018). *Pure: Inside the religious movement that shamed a generation of young women and how we broke free*. Touchstone.

Krause, N., & Pargament, K. I. (2017). Losing my religion: Exploring the relationship between a decline in faith and a positive affect. *Applied Research Quality Life*, 12(4), 885–901. https://doi.org/10.1007/s11482-016-9495-2

Lefevor, G. T., Blaber, I. P., Huffman, C. E., Schow, R. L., Beckstead, A. L., Raynes, M., & Rosik, C. H. (2019). The role of religiousness and beliefs about sexuality in well-being among sexual minority Mormons. *Psychology of Religion and Spirituality*, 12(4), 460–70. http://doi.org/10.1037/rel0000261

Lemke, R. (2017). *The scarlet virgins: When sex replaces salvation*. Anatole Publishing.

Levy, D. L., & Harr, J. (2018). "I never felt like there was a place for me": Experiences of bisexual and pansexual individuals with a Christian upbringing. *Journal of Bisexuality*, 18(2), 186–205. https://doi.org/10.1080/15299716.2018.1431169

Manning, J. (2014). Exploring family discourses about purity pledges: Connecting relationships and popular culture. *Qualitative Research Reports in Communication*, 15(1), 92–99. https://doi.org/10.1080/17459435.2014.955597

Martin, N., Baralt, L., & Garrido-Ortega, C. (2017). What's religion got to do with it? Exploring college students' sexual and reproductive health knowledge and awareness of sexual and reproductive health services in relation to their gender and religiosity. *Journal of Religious Health*, 57(5), 1856–75. https://doi.org/10.1007/s10943-017-0432-y

Natarajan, M., Wilkins-Yel, K. G., Sista, A., Anantharaman, A., & Seils, N. (2022). Decolonizing purity culture: Gendered racism and White idealization in evangelical Christianity. *Psychology of Women Quarterly*, 46(3), 316–36. https://doi.org/10.1177/03616843221091116

Nica, A. A. (2020). Leaving my religion: How ex-fundamentalists reconstruct identity related to well-being. *Journal of Religion and Health*, 59(1), 2120–34. https://doi.org/10.1007/s10943-019-00975-8

Owens, B. C., Hall, M. E. L., & Anderson, T. L. (2020). The relationship between purity culture and rape myth acceptance. *Journal of Psychology and Theology*, 49(4), 405–18. https://doi.org/10.1177/0091647120974992

Pew Research Center. (2022). Modeling the future of religion in America. https://www.pewresearch.org/religion/wp-content/uploads/sites/7/2022/09/US-Religious-Projections_FOR-PRODUCTION-9.13.22.pdf

Piper, K. N., Fuller, T. J., Ayers, A. A., Lambert, D. N., Sales, J. M., & Wingood, G. M. (2020). A qualitative exploration of religion, gender norms, and sexual decision-making within African American faith-based communities. *Sex Roles*, 82(3–4), 189–205. https://doi.org/10.1007/s11199-019-01047-7

Prina, F., & Schatz-Stevens, J. N. (2020). Sexism and rape myth acceptance: The impact of culture, education, and religiosity. *Psychological Reports*, 123(3), 929–51. https://doi.org/10.1177/0033294119826896

Rosenbaum, J. E. (2009). Patient teenagers? A comparison of the sexual behavior of virginity pledgers and matched nonpledgers. *Pediatrics*, 123(1), 110–20. https://doi.org/10.1542/peds.2008-0407

Runkel, G. (1998). Sexual morality of Christianity. *Journal of Sex & Marital Therapy*, 24(2), 103–22. https://doi.org/10.1080/00926239808404924

Santelli, J. S., Kantor, L. M., Grilo, S. A., Speizer, I. S., Lindberg, L. D., Heitel, J., Schalet, A. T., Lyon, M. E., Mason-Jones, A. J., McGovern, T., Heck, C. J., Rogers, J., & Ott, M. A. (2017). Abstinence-only-until-marriage: An updated review of U.S. policies and programs and their impact. *Journal of Adolescent Health*, 61(3), 273–80. http://doi.org/10.1016/j.jadohealth.2017.05.031

Schultz, O. J. (2021). Purity culture's racist fruit: Centering the voices of black womanists and feminists in the deconstruction of purity culture. *Journal of the School of Religious Studies*, 49(2021), 1–47. https://doi.org/10.26443/arc.v49i.292

The SIECUS State Profiles 2019/2020—the state of sex ed. SIECUS. (2022). https://siecus.org/state-profiles-2019-2020//.

Streib, H. (2021). Leaving religion: Deconversion. *Current Opinion in Psychology*, 40, 139–44. https://doi.org/10.1016/j.copsyc.2020.09.007

Thorpe, S., Peterson, R. L., Malone, N., Coleman, M. N., Annett, J., & Hargons, C. N. (2023). From sin to sexual self-awareness: Black women's reflection on lifetime masturbation messages. *Archives of Sexual Behavior*, 42(4), 1403–15. https://doi.org/10.1007/s10508-022-02473-7

Thorpe, S., Tanner, A. E., Nichols, T. R., Kuperberg, A., & Foh, E. P. (2021). Black female adolescents' sexuality: Pleasure expectancies, sexual guilt, and age of sexual debut. *American Journal of Sexuality Education*, 16(2), 199–220. https://doi.org/10.1080/15546128.2021.1892005

Trinh, S. L., & Kim, J. L. (2020). The correlates of sexual experience and reasons for abstinence among Asian Americans. *Cultural Diversity and Ethnic Minority Psychology*, 27(1), 82–94. https://doi.org/10.1037/cdp0000350

11

Counseling Nonreligious Clients Experiencing Grief

Jacob S. Sawyer

Chapter Outline

While the number of atheists and other religiously unaffiliated individuals in the United States has grown significantly over the past several decades (Pew Research Center, 2024), there have been few studies specifically related to grief and bereavement in these samples. A review of social science scholarship from 2001–2012 found only one article specifically related to grief, loss, and bereavement for atheist individuals (Brewster et al., 2014). Though research in this area appears to have increased somewhat since Brewster and colleagues' 2014 publication, the nonreligious have still received relatively little attention from social science researchers.

Much of what is known about grief and belief consists of research conducted with predominantly religious samples, with hypotheses that were predominantly religious in nature. Many might assume that religious belief would be helpful, or in some cases, even essential, for effective coping during bereavement. The research paints a more complex picture, however, with researchers noting that religion "can be a source of distress as well as a source of solutions in coping" (Pargament et al., 1998, p.721). In terms of primary methods of religious coping, one study from the 1980s found that putting trust and faith in God, prayer, and perceptions of help and strength from God were the top forms utilized by religious individuals (Koenig et al., 1988). It does appear that some of these methods can be comforting and adaptive during bereavement. For instance, others have found that religious belief can be helpful for grief when it allows the bereaved to make sense of or find meaning in the loss, provides a sense of comfort due to the belief in life after death, and provides for additional opportunities for social support from other churchgoers (Chapple et al., 2011). Alternatively, there are elements of religious belief that appear to be unhelpful during bereavement. Individuals are more likely to have negative experiences during bereavement if they believe that death was a punishment by God, God did not hear their prayers, or if the bereaved feels anger toward God (Chapple et al., 2011; Exline et al., 2011).

It is important to note that while certain elements of religious coping can be genuinely helpful for religious individuals, there is no evidence suggesting that atheist people are at a disadvantage during bereavement because they are not utilizing these religious coping methods. In addition to religious or spiritual perspectives, the meaning-making process during bereavement can also take place from more of a general philosophical perspective (Neimeyer, 2019), which will likely resonate more with nonreligious people. As Greta Christina (2015) noted in the book *Comforting Thoughts About Death That Have Nothing to Do with God*,

> Atheists, on the other hand, have *had* to come up with ways of dealing with death, more or less on our own. Like anyone who rejects the dominant culture, and who rejects the default answers to hard questions that get spoon-fed to us by this culture, we've had to come up with our own answers. The same way that LGBT people are forced to think about sexuality and gender; the same way that vegetarians are forced to think about the ethics of food . . . atheists are forced to think about death, and what kind of value life might have when it's brief and finite (pp. 42–43).

Current Theories About Grief and Bereavement

One theory that has received significant research attention in recent years is the Dual Process Model of coping with bereavement (DPM) developed by Stroebe and Schut (1999, 2010, 2015). Importantly, the DPM highlights the nonlinear nature of grief. The DPM also emphasizes the importance of grieving *dosage*, where periods devoid of active grief-related coping are recognized as important for the bereaved.

The initial DPM (Stroebe & Schut, 1999) included three primary elements: loss-oriented coping, restoration-oriented coping, and the oscillation between loss-oriented and restoration-oriented coping methods. Loss-oriented coping processes include aspects related to historical conceptions of grief work (e.g., emotional expression and processing of loss), intrusion of grief, breaking bonds/ties/relocation, and denial/avoidance of restoration changes. Restoration-oriented processes include attending to life changes, doing new things, distraction from grief, denial/avoidance of grief, and new roles/identities/relationships. A key component of the DMP involves the flexible use of both coping styles. That is, the *oscillation* between loss-oriented and restoration-oriented coping is associated with adaptive coping.

The DPM makes sense as we consider the different coping needs for each individual based on their own unique circumstances during bereavement. While some individuals might not need to engage in intensive forms of emotional expression or other forms of what was traditionally considered "grief work" (Bonanno, 2004), some individuals might find it helpful to spend more time engaged in emotionally processing loss. After a period of time spent engaging in loss-oriented coping, which again will vary in time frame based on the unique needs of each bereaved individual, one might then shift to activities not related to emotionally reacting to the loss. Subsequent studies have found that the bereaved often spend more time engaged in loss-oriented coping earlier in bereavement, and more time in restoration-oriented coping later on (Stroebe & Schut, 2010).

A revision to the original DPM highlighted the importance of appraisal processes via meaning reconstruction, noting that "how a person feels and reacts on becoming bereaved is dependent on the meaning that is assigned to the loss" (Stroebe & Schut, 2001, p. 56). An additional revision to the original DPM illustrated how the oscillation between loss-oriented and restoration-oriented processes occur at the individual and family levels (Stroebe & Schut, 2015). For instance, each reaction toward grief was considered from the individual level (e.g., "accept reality of loss") and family level (e.g., "family acceptance of reality of loss"). A systematic review of the DPM from its inception in 1999 to 2016 found that the model is an accurate representation of how people often grieve, and that interventions that utilize DPM coping methods can be more effective than other forms of grief therapy (Fiore, 2021).

Psychoeducation about grief responses illustrated by the DPM might be especially useful for nonreligious individuals during bereavement, particularly those who value rationality and the scientific method. As noted previously, the effectiveness of interventions utilizing the DPM framework has been empirically supported (e.g., Fiore, 2021). Furthermore, many nonreligious individuals will likely resonate with the active coping processes highlighted by the DPM. For instance, grief work, or the emotional expression of grief responses, is included as a coping method that might be helpful for some, but it is not considered mandatory for adaptive coping during bereavement. This differs from the historical emphasis on emotional expression and catharsis, and the belief that the lack of emotionally working through one's grief is indicative of a pathological response (Wortman & Silver, 1989). The DPM instead highlights the importance of active coping processes in the restoration-orientation category of coping.

Grief as a Potential Disorder

The concept of *complicated grief*, or severe and prolonged grief response, has been examined by researchers since the 1990s (O'Connor, 2019; Shear, 2015). Prolonged Grief Disorder (PGD) is a controversial new addition to the Diagnostic and Statistical Manual of Mental Disorders, 5th Edition, Text Revision (DSM-5-TR). See Table 11.1 for the full diagnostic criteria of Prolonged Grief Disorder.

While scholars have outlined numerous criticisms for the inclusion of grief as a diagnosable mental disorder (Bergsmark & Ramsing, 2023; Eisma, 2023), the experience of complicated or prolonged grief reactions after the death of a loved one has been extensively documented by researchers. The percentage of bereaved individuals who go on to develop complicated grief reactions is typically around 10 percent of the US population (Lundorff et al., 2017; Rosner et al., 2021; Prigerson et al., 2022). This percentage can increase to close to 50 percent when the death is potentially traumatic or unnatural, such as in cases of sudden and violent deaths (Djelantik et al., 2020; Kristensen et al., 2012).

Identifying who may or may not benefit from therapy or counseling services specifically targeting grief responses is an essential task for mental health professionals. One assessment tool that is validated for screening the presence of PGD is the Prolonged Grief Disorder Revised Scale (PG-13-R), developed by Prigerson and colleagues (2021). The first two scale items identify whether the respondent has lost someone significant and the number of months since the person died. From there, the PG-13-R includes ten items specifically related to the diagnostic criteria of PGD in the DSM-5-TR (e.g., "Do you feel yourself longing or yearning for the person who died?"). Finally, respondents indicate whether they are experiencing symptoms that cause significant impairment in social, occupational, or other important areas of functioning (Prigerson et al., 2021). See Figure 11.1 for the full assessment tool provided with permission from the authors.

For those who do meet criteria for PGD, there are a variety of evidence-based treatment modalities that are recommended by researchers and clinicians specifically for treatment of PGD symptoms. One of the primary methods of treating PGD was developed and evaluated by M. Katherine Shear, who is the founding director of the Center for Prolonged Grief at Columbia University's School of Social Work. While the Center for Prolonged Grief offers trainings for a structured sixteen-week, evidence-based approach to working with individuals diagnosed with PGD (Center for Prolonged Grief, 2023), Iglewicz and colleagues (2019) noted that bereaved clients can be helped by using the general principles and goals of evidence-based complicated grief treatment. The seven core themes of complicated grief therapy include understanding and accepting grief, managing emotional pain, thinking about the future, strengthening ongoing relationships, telling the story of the death, living with reminders, and connecting to memories (Iglewicz et al., 2019). Importantly, these evidence-based treatment modalities do not assume the presence or necessity of religious belief in order to utilize adaptive coping skills during bereavement.

Table 11.1 Prolonged Grief Disorder

A. The death, at least 12 months ago, of a person who was closed to the bereaved individual (for children and adolescents, at least 6 months ago).	
B. Since the death, the development of a persistent grief response characterized by one or both of the following symptoms, which have been present most days to a clinically significant degree. In addition, the symptom(s) has occurred nearly every day for at least the last month:	1. Intense yearning or longing. 2. Preoccupation with thoughts or memories of the deceased person (in children and adolescents, preoccupation may focus on the circumstances of the death).
C. Since the death, at least three of the following symptoms have been present most days to a clinically significant degree. In addition, the symptoms have occurred nearly every day for at least the last month:	1. Identity disruption (e.g., feeling as though part of oneself has died) since the death. 2. Marked sense of disbelief about the death. 3. Avoidance of reminders that the person is dead (in children and adolescents, may be characterized by efforts to avoid reminders). 4. Intense emotional pain (e.g., anger, bitterness, sorrow) related to the death. 5. Difficulty reintegrating into one's relationships and activities after the death (e.g., problems engaging with friends, pursuing interests, or planning for the future). 6. Emotional numbness (absence or marked reduction of emotional experience) as a result of the death. 7. Feeling that life is meaningless as a result of the death. 8. Intense loneliness as a result of the death.
D. The disturbance causes clinically significant distress or impairment in social, occupational, or other important areas of functioning.	
E. The duration and severity of the bereavement reaction clearly exceed expected social, cultural, or religious norms for the individual's culture and context.	
F. The symptoms are not better explained by another mental disorder, such as major depressive disorder or posttraumatic stress disorder, and are not attributable to the physiological effects of a substance (e.g., medication, alcohol) or another medical condition.	

(American Psychiatric Association [APA], 2022)

1. Have you lost someone significant to you? ○ Yes ○ No

2. How many months has it been since your significant other died? ☐ Months

For each item below, please indicate how you currently feel

Since the death, or as a result of the death...	Not at all	Slightly	Somewhat	Quite a bit	Overwhelmingly
3. Do you feel yourself longing or yearning for the person who died?	○	○	○	○	○
4. Do you have trouble doing the things you normally do because you are thinking so much about the person who died?	○	○	○	○	○
5. Do you feel confused about your role in life or feel like you don't know who you are anymore (ie, feeling like that a part of you has died)?	○	○	○	○	○
6. Do you have trouble believing that the person who died is really gone?	○	○	○	○	○
7. Do you avoid reminders that the person who died is really gone?	○	○	○	○	○
8. Do you feel emotional pain (eg, anger, bitterness, sorrow) related to the death?	○	○	○	○	○
9. Do you feel that you have trouble re-engaging in life (eg, problems engaging with friends, pursuing interests, planning for the future)?	○	○	○	○	○
10. Do you feel emotionally numb or detached from others?	○	○	○	○	○
11. Do you feel that life is meaningless without the person who died?	○	○	○	○	○
12. Do you feel alone or lonely without the deceased?	○	○	○	○	○

13. Have the symptoms above caused significant impairment in social, occupational, or other important areas of functioning? ○ Yes ○ No

Figure 11.1 Prolonged Grief Disorder Revised Scale (PG-13-R), (Prigerson et al., 2021).

Factors Related to Nonreligious Grief and Bereavement

The majority of individuals manage to cope effectively after experiencing a potentially traumatic event (Bonanno, 2004), and this is true of bereaved individuals as well. An Australian study examining bereavement risk and support needs found that around 58 percent of the sample were at low risk of PGD, around 35 percent were at moderate risk, and around 6 percent were at high risk (Aoun et al., 2015). Overall risk level corresponds to the types of support required during bereavement. For those at low risk of developing PGD, support from family and friends can be most helpful. Those at moderate risk can sometimes benefit from additional supports beyond family and friends. Community supports such as peer-led grief groups might be beneficial for this group. Those at high risk for PGD are most likely to benefit from specialized treatment from a qualified mental health professional.

Additional research supports the assertion that informal sources of support are typically the most helpful during bereavement. In another study of 678 bereaved individuals, about 90 percent reported that family and friends were very helpful or quite helpful during bereavement (Aoun et al., 2018). Specifically, family and friends were identified as helpful sources of emotional support, practical assistance (e.g., providing food and transportation), and allowed for the bereaved to feel a sense of belonging. For this particular group, formal sources of support, such as psychiatrists, bereavement support groups, and social workers, were used the least and rated as the least helpful. The authors of this study noted that "early, particularly unrequested, referrals to a counselor have the potential to problematise grief and compromise the support that could be offered by existing networks" (Aoun et al., 2015, p. 1385).

While nonreligious individuals would not be at higher risk for grief-related distress compared to religious individuals simply based on an absence of religious beliefs or belief in a higher power, nonreligious people might experience some unique stressors during bereavement that are worthy of clinical attention. For instance, religious individuals could be more likely to have sources of community or other social supports that are consistent with their belief systems related to loss. Post-loss rituals might take place at a church or other religious setting with messages that might not resonate with the nonreligious (e.g., the deceased is in a better place now, everything happens for a reason, etc.). If a nonreligious person is part of a highly religious family or community, they might not have the same opportunities to receive the informal sources of support that researchers have identified as helpful for the majority of individuals during bereavement (Aoun et al., 2015).

The lack of support during bereavement that is specifically related to a nonreligious identity can result in disenfranchised grief. According to Kenneth Doka (1989), disenfranchised grief is "the grief that persons experience that is not or cannot be openly acknowledged, publicly mourned, or socially supported" (p. 4). Researchers have identified several categories of disenfranchised grief (e.g., Corr, 1999; Doka, 1989). One is when the *relationship* is not recognized. This can include situations where the deceased was a friend, colleague, in-law, ex-lover, or someone with whom the bereaved was engaged in an extramarital affair. Another category includes instances when the *loss* is not recognized. This can include instances of perinatal loss, abortions, loss of limbs or overall health, suicide, or, as noted by Cordaro (2012) death of a pet. A third category includes instances where the *griever* is not recognized. For instance, children, elderly, and individuals with intellectual disabilities can be more likely to experience disenfranchised grief due to assumptions that they do not experience grief in the same way as the average adult.

Nonreligious individuals also run the risk of experiencing disenfranchised grief if their beliefs and/or experiences related to grief and loss are not validated. As noted previously, this might include, but is not limited to, post-death rituals that are religious in nature or messages about the deceased that are at odds with the bereaved individual's beliefs (e.g., the deceased is in a better place or they will see the deceased again one day in the afterlife). In support of the notion that nonreligious individuals are at risk of experiencing disenfranchised grief, one study found that experiences of anti-atheist discrimination was significantly related to complicated grief reactions and psychological distress for atheist individuals during bereavement (Sawyer, 2022).

Certain demographic factors can increase the risk of disenfranchisement. Although any given region might be more or less religious, recent survey findings broken down at the state level suggests that people are least likely to describe themselves as atheist, agnostic, or nothing in particular in the US South (e.g., Alabama, Georgia, Louisiana, etc.) and in North and South Dakota (Burge, 2023). Mental health professionals working with nonreligious individuals living in these areas should be mindful of the risks for disenfranchised grief reactions if bereaved clients are unable to access social or community supports that validate their beliefs.

In order to highlight challenges during bereavement related to bias and stigma, Tashel Bordere (2014, 2016) coined the term *suffocated grief* to describe experiences where grief and mourning responses are penalized. Suffocated grief experiences include penalties for "violation of rituals and rules (e.g., social, political, and religious) around grief and mourning" (Bordere, 2017, p. 10). A growing body of research indicates that atheists of color often experience unique forms of anti-atheist discrimination in ways that could result in additional stress during bereavement. For instance, Abbott and colleagues (2020) found that atheists of color often describe the experience of violating cultural expectations of religiosity in their racial/ethnic groups, which could result in a loss of support or alienation from their racial/ethnic communities. In their sample, expectations of religiosity were especially pronounced in women (Abbott et al., 2020). Another study by Howard and colleagues (2023) found that Black atheists often experienced general anti-atheist bias, along with racial identity denial (i.e., Black atheists were perceived as less Black than non-atheists). Thus, in the context of bereavement, atheists and nonreligious People of Color are especially susceptible to disenfranchised and suffocated grief experiences.

Competence in Counseling Nonreligious Clients Experiencing Bereavement

Counselors beginning treatment with bereaved clients should be aware of some common assumptions that can limit the effectiveness of grief counseling, or even cause harm to the client. First and foremost, counselors should be aware that nonreligious and atheist individuals do not lack the ability to engage in meaning making processes during bereavement, they just go about it in a different way than their religious counterparts. A study on end-of-life preferences in atheist individuals found that the most common themes were a desire to find meaning in their lives, to maintain connections with friends and family, and to continue to experience and enjoy the natural world (Smith-Stoner, 2007). The prominent atheist Richard Dawkins (2006) suggested that the beliefs of nonreligious and atheist individuals allow for explanation, guidance, consolation, and inspiration in ways similar to religious beliefs, just without the context of the supernatural.

Some evidence suggests that the protective nature of belief is curvilinear. That is, individuals who express greater certainty in their belief, or nonbelief, might experience less distress in some circumstances compared to those who are uncertain about their beliefs in religion or a higher power (Galen & Kloet, 2011). This seems to be the case in several studies examining belief and death anxiety. For example, one study found that certainty of belief or nonbelief predicted more effective coping for older individuals (Wilkinson & Coleman, 2010), while another found that certainty of nonbelief in a sample of atheists was related to lower levels of death anxiety and higher levels of death acceptance (Sawyer et al., 2021). Additionally, other recent research in a sample of atheist people found that feelings of emptiness and meaninglessness were related to higher levels of psychological distress and complicated grief reactions during bereavement (Sawyer, 2022). Though meaning making might look different for nonreligious individuals, counselors should not avoid the exploration of more naturalistic meaning making processes or personal nonreligious spiritual beliefs that could be helpful for coping during bereavement.

Counselors would also benefit from assessing, and in many cases, increasing their overall levels of competency in working with bereaved clients. Breen and colleagues (2022) suggested that a *grief literacy* is necessary so that individuals "recognize and acknowledge grief from non-death losses, and pet deaths, and not rank those losses vis-à-vis human death loss" (p. 428). Additionally, grief literacy focuses on the different styles of grieving that are influenced by gender, race, and culture. In order to promote a grief literate society, Breen and colleagues (2022) suggested that grief education should be part of the educational curricula starting at the junior level.

Several studies have found that many counselors feel that they have not had sufficient coursework in their clinical training to address grief-related issues, and they may be likely to rely on their own experiences with grief or outdated theories in their clinical work with bereaved clients (Blueford et al., 2021; Jankauskaite et al., 2021, Ober et al., 2012; Servaty-Seib & Taub, 2010). One pervasive myth related to grief and bereavement is Elisabeth Kübler-Ross's stage theory of grief (1969). According to this model of grief, the bereaved progress through a series of five stages including *denial*, *anger*, *bargaining*, *depression*, and ultimately, *acceptance*. The idea of a linear, stage model of grief appears often in the mainstream lexicon, and is often referenced in American college and university textbooks (Corr, 2020). A recent study on how stages of grief are portrayed on the internet found that a majority of English and Dutch websites related to grief included information about a stage model of grief (Avis et al., 2021).

The widespread and incorrect assumption that grief progresses through distinct stages is found among the general public and mental health professionals. One survey found that 46 percent of a sample of mental health professionals believed that the process of grief progresses through a predictable series of stages, starting with denial and ending with acceptance, while 68 percent of the general public endorsed this same belief (Sawyer et al., 2021). See Table 11.2 for a summary of common myths. Another survey in a sample of 964 mental health professionals found that "only 330 (34.2%) of the clinicians were deemed knowledgeable; 462 (47.9%) were questionable; and 172 (17.9%) were misinformed,

Table 11.2 Bereavement Beliefs

Statement	Mental Health Professionals	General Public
1. The process of grief can be expected to progress through a predictable series of stages, starting with denial and ending with acceptance.	Definitely True: 8% Probably True: 38% **Probably False: 15%** **Definitely False: 39%**	Definitely True: 30% Probably True: 38% **Probably False: 13%** **Definitely False: 18%**
2. People are more likely to show signs of resilience rather than long-term grief responses after experiencing the death of a loved one.	**Definitely True: 15%** **Probably True: 59%** Probably False: 20% Definitely False: 7%	**Definitely True: 10%** **Probably True: 46%** Probably False: 34% Definitely False: 10%
3. Older people are usually more anxious about death than younger people.	Definitely True: 3% Probably True: 26% **Probably False: 51%** **Definitely False: 20%**	Definitely True: 14% Probably True: 32% **Probably False: 42%** **Definitely False: 12%**
4. About 20%–30% of people who have experienced the death of a loved one will experience intense yearning, longing, or emotional pain, frequent preoccupying thoughts and memories of the deceased person, a feeling of disbelief or an inability to accept the loss, and difficulty imagining a meaningful future without the deceased person.	Definitely True: 13% Probably True: 72% **Probably False: 13%** **Definitely False: 2%**	Definitely True: 37% Probably True: 56% **Probably False: 7%** **Definitely False: 0%**
5. People who do not become depressed after the death of a loved one are probably denying their true feelings.	Definitely True: 0% Probably True: 8% **Probably False: 41%** **Definitely False: 51%**	Definitely True: 4% Probably True: 27% **Probably False: 44%** **Definitely False: 26%**
6. Approximately 25%–30% of college students have experienced the death of someone within the past year.	**Definitely True: 3%** **Probably True: 64%** Probably False: 33% Definitely False: 0%	**Definitely True: 15%** **Probably True: 70%** Probably False: 14% Definitely False: 1%
7. Most people develop a mental disorder after the death of a loved one.	Definitely True: 2% Probably True: 0% **Probably False: 20%** **Definitely False: 79%**	Definitely True: 3% Probably True: 21% **Probably False: 50%** **Definitely False: 25%**
8. Responses to grief are typically consistent even when considering cultural differences.	Definitely True: 3% Probably True: 21% **Probably False: 43%** **Definitely False: 33%**	Definitely True: 4% Probably True: 50% **Probably False: 30%** **Definitely False: 15%**
9. It is typically more helpful for people to "move on" with their lives rather than think about memories of the deceased.	Definitely True: 2% Probably True: 12% **Probably False: 41%** **Definitely False: 45%**	Definitely True: 5% Probably True: 32% **Probably False: 41%** **Definitely False: 21%**

Statement	Mental Health Professionals	General Public
10. Most people need professional help to cope with grief.	Definitely True: 0% Probably True: 8% **Probably False: 38%** **Definitely False: 54%**	Definitely True: 5% Probably True: 34% **Probably False: 48%** **Definitely False: 11%**
11. Bereaved children and adolescents do not grieve as deeply as adults.	Definitely True: 0% Probably True: 0% **Probably False: 18%** **Definitely False: 82%**	Definitely True: 3% Probably True: 20% **Probably False: 35%** **Definitely False: 40%**
12. Experts typically recommend that children should be protected from the pain and suffering that death creates.	Definitely True: 0% Probably True: 3% **Probably False: 43%** **Definitely False: 54%**	Definitely True: 7% Probably True: 29% **Probably False: 40%** **Definitely False: 23%**

Note. Bold ratings in the mental health professional and general public response sections are considered to have support from prior research.

(Sawyer et al., 2021) Reprinted with author approval.

continuing to use Kubler-Ross' stage theory for grief" (McCoyd et al., 2023, p. 1). These findings are concerning given that prominent grief researchers have noted that "stage theory should be discarded by all concerned (including bereaved persons themselves); at best, it should be relegated to the realms of history" (Stroebe et al., 2017, p. 456).

While taking steps to increase grief literacy and other grief-related competencies is important for mental health professionals, increasing grief literacy in the form of psychoeducation could also be beneficial for bereaved individuals. There are some coping methods that seem to be more effective than others during bereavement (e.g., those outlined in the Dual Process Model of Bereavement), but there is no one right way to grieve. Those who believe some of the common myths about bereavement (e.g., there are linear stages of grief, or the majority of people develop a mental disorder after the death of a loved one) could experience heightened distress. Recent empirical findings support this. In a sample of bereaved US college students, the belief that people who do not become depressed after the death of a loved one are denying their true feelings was associated with higher levels of complicated grief reactions (Sawyer, 2024).

Mental health professionals can help bereaved clients by validating their reactions during bereavement and correcting some of these common myths. This can help to address some challenges that the bereaved sometimes experience, such as a fear that they are grieving incorrectly, their emotions are not valid, or they are "going crazy" (Doka, 2016, p. 4; Pinheiro et al., 2022). Researchers have also noted that laypeople often believe that maladaptive grief responses are typical (McLean et al., 2022). This is at odds with findings indicating that only around 10 percent of bereaved individuals go on to develop PGD, and most people are resilient during times of significant stress (Bonanno, 2004; Lundorff et al., 2017; Rosner et al., 2021; Prigerson et al., 2022). Nonreligious clients will likely appreciate the inclusion of scientific and evidence-based findings as part of the counseling process.

Counselors and other mental health professionals should also strive to increase their understanding of the experiences of atheist and other nonreligious clients. Historically, the experiences of the nonreligious, nonbelieving, and nonspiritual have not been considered to be salient multicultural factors among mental health professionals (Bishop, 2018; D'Andrea & Sprenger, 2007). This has a number of implications. As D'Andrea and Sprenger (2007) noted, "when clients have no belief in heaven, a better place, or life in the hereafter, the counselor, particularly one who does not share the nonbelief, faces the challenge of not only understanding the most personal and hidden motivations for life itself but creating interventions that are at once respectful and effective" (p. 155). In addition to learning more about the experiences of the nonreligious, counselors should also be prepared to examine their assumptions, biases, and countertransference reactions toward nonreligious clients.

Applying Theory to Practice

The Case of Vanessa—Background

Vanessa is a twenty-year-old Black woman, born and raised in the southern United States, who has experienced chronic distress and sadness after the sudden death of her partner of three years, Ann, due to suicide just over a year ago. Vanessa reported that she initially experienced a sense of "shock" and "numbness" during the initial few weeks after Ann's death, which is a time she describes as "being on autopilot." Vanessa is currently a junior at a large state flagship university in the southern United States, where she is worried about her recent academic performance. Her university is not religiously affiliated. She noted that she has always been a "great student," but she had several instances last semester where she lost a significant number of points due to submitting her coursework after the due date, and she had lower exam scores compared to what she is used to. She indicated that she has a very hard time concentrating, and that she frequently wonders, "What is the point of life if we all die in the end?"

She initially sought counseling services with a therapist that she described as a "terrible fit." Specifically, Vanessa reported that her previous therapist wanted to explore what she would say once she was reunited with Ann in heaven. Since her previous counselor would often bring up her own religious beliefs, Vanessa had not disclosed that Ann was her partner rather than a close friend. Vanessa feels that there are few, if any, people she can talk to about her ongoing distress after Ann's death. She indicated that her family are Southern Baptists, while Vanessa describes herself as "agnostic" and "definitely not religious, but maybe spiritual."

Assessment and Other Clinical Considerations

Several elements of Vanessa's experience with grief put her at a higher risk for complicated grief reactions and Prolonged Grief Disorder. Before we interpret any clinically significant symptoms that Vanessa is experiencing, we will need to examine the cultural context of her current concerns. Vanessa is a twenty-year-old Black woman from the southern United States, where religiosity is high. This is reflected in her experiences of invalidation from a prior counselor who attempted to address Vanessa's concerns from a religious perspective. This ineffective treatment approach might have been a result of an assumption that Vanessa was also religious, given her identity as a Black woman from the South, or from the belief that a religious perspective on grief and bereavement would be the most effective method of addressing her concerns regardless of Vanessa's personal beliefs. Additionally, the ubiquity of religious belief in Vanessa's current family and friend network puts her at risk of social isolation, along with disenfranchised and suffocated grief experiences.

In this case, there are multiple ways where Vanessa's grief might be disenfranchised. There is a high risk for disenfranchisement due to the *relationship* not being recognized. This seems to be true in Vanessa's case, as she did not feel comfortable disclosing her same-sex relationship with her previous counselor. It would be important to identify what, if any, social supports are present for Vanessa to openly discuss her relationship with Ann in a way that is not stigmatized, invalidated, or regarded as sinful. In cases of suicide, there is a higher risk of disenfranchisement due to the *loss* not being recognized. Researchers have found that the risk for complicated grief reactions are higher for those experiencing the death of a loved one due to suicide compared to natural death, though many mourners feel that they are unable to talk about loss due to suicide because of the stigma surrounding this form of loss (de Groot et al., 2006; Tal Young et al., 2012). Suicide might also be regarded as sinful or shameful in religious communities (Tal Young et al., 2012), further raising the risk for isolation. Vanessa's loss also runs the risk for disenfranchisement due to the *griever* not being recognized. As a nonreligious person in a highly religious region of the United States, she may have to take some additional steps to seek out social supports beyond her current social network of family and friends in order to openly discuss her reactions to Ann's death in ways that can be validated without the risk of receiving religious platitudes about death and loss.

In addition to numerous risks for disenfranchised grief, counselors should also be mindful of risks for suffocated grief that Vanessa might experience. As noted previously, suffocated grief occurs when bereaved individuals are penalized for violating social rituals and rules. She might experience situations where she feels forced to engage in prayer or other religious ritual in opposition of her personal beliefs in order to not stir up trouble. Researchers have noted that nonreligious identity concealment and being pressured to pass as religious can be related to psychological distress (Abbott & Mollen, 2018; Brewster et al., 2016). Counselors should be prepared to acknowledge and validate Vanessa's personal beliefs about grief and bereavement, while maintaining an awareness of the real risks that she could face by being outspoken about her beliefs with religious friends and family members.

As a college student, Vanessa is one of many who will experience the loss of a loved one prior to graduation. Researchers have found that around 60 percent of college students had experienced the death of a friend or family member by the time they finished college (Cox et al., 2015), and several studies have found that around 40 percent to 50 percent of college students have experienced the death of a friend or family member within the past two years (Balk et al., 2010; Cousins et al., 2017). Others have noted that bereaved college students are likely to face academic challenges as a result of emotional distress and additional secondary stressors such as missing class and falling behind on coursework (Servaty-Seib & Taub, 2010). This appears to be a clinically significant factor for Vanessa's bereavement, as she noted increased difficulties with concentration and submitting coursework on time after Ann's death.

Developmentally, Vanessa is currently in the emerging adulthood stage. Arnett (2000) developed the theory of emerging adulthood to describe "a distinct period demographically, subjectively, and in terms of identity exploration" (p. 469) between adolescence and young adulthood. Importantly, the concept of emerging adulthood applies to cultures that promote independence and self-exploration (e.g., the traditional college-age years in US culture). The typical range used to describe the emerging adulthood stage is from ages eighteen to twenty-nine (Arnett et al., 2014). Worldview evaluation and development is a major aspect of this developmental stage as part of one's overall exploration of identity. One's religious beliefs are also often critically examined at this time. One study on a sample of college students found that, on average, overall religiousness and service attendance decreased during emerging adulthood, while spirituality increased (Koenig, 2015). As a result, this developmental stage has a number of challenges and opportunities for meaning-making interventions. Spiritual but nonreligious clients like Vanessa would likely benefit from further examining their beliefs about death and grief with a qualified mental health professional. It is important to reiterate that Vanessa's absence of religious belief should not be conflated with a lack of meaning-making or other coping strategies. In fact, counselors can explore how for some, and particularly some women of color, adopting nonreligious and/or atheist identities can be experienced as a form of liberation (Abbott & Anaya, 2022). This framework can allow counselors to approach their work with clients like Vanessa from a strengths-based orientation.

There are likely additional supports that Vanessa can utilize as a college student even though she is located in a predominately religious region of the United States. As a student at a large public university that is not religiously affiliated, there may be opportunities to interact with campus clubs or other organizations specifically related to secular identities. One such organization with chapters across colleges in the United States is the Secular Student Alliance. According to information posted on the Secular Student Alliance web page, the organization is dedicated to empowering secular students to express their identities, build community, promote secular values, and engage in lifelong activism (Secular Student Alliance, n.d.). Another off-campus resource could include the Black Nonbelievers organization. As of 2024, the Black Nonbelievers organization is active in seven major US cities (including cities in the southern United States) and provides opportunities for education, scholarship support, and community events (Black Nonbelievers, 2024).

While these organizations would not be a space for Vanessa to necessarily process her emotional reactions to grief, this could be a helpful resource for social support while addressing her grief in counseling. Vanessa will also likely have access to counseling services through her university counseling center. There may be opportunities for group counseling with a focus on grief and bereavement through this resource.

Addressing Primary Elements of This Case Example Using the Seven Core Themes of Complicated Grief Therapy

The following suggestions are based on the seven core themes of grief. See the article by Iglewicz and colleagues (2019) for additional information and examples of how to utilize the seven core themes of grief in counseling.

Understanding and Accepting Grief

A primary element early on in the counseling process includes assisting the client in understanding their unique grief responses. People may feel a number of strong emotions during bereavement. While people often acknowledge feelings such as sadness and yearning during bereavement, people may be less likely, or at least, less comfortable at times, to acknowledge feelings of anger or even relief after the death of a loved one. The early stage of counseling should allow for clients to freely express and explore their emotions. The counselor can play an important role during this time by validating emotions that are expressed and providing psychoeducation on typical grief responses. This can include a discussion on common emotions experienced during bereavement, along with factors that might lead to more prolonged grief responses. A grief literate counselor can also assist the client by countering myths that the client might hold (see Table 11.2 for a summary of common myths).

In Vanessa's case, a counselor might acknowledge that it is not uncommon for college students to experience additional academic challenges after the loss of a loved one, and that death as a result of suicide can be especially painful. It would also be important for counselors to acknowledge the existential concerns that Vanessa is facing. The question of what the point of life is if we all die in the end is a big one that humans have struggled with for thousands of years. Thankfully, counselors do not need to have an answer for that, but they should be prepared to help Vanessa explore what her answer might be, while reinforcing the fact that this question can be examined without the context of religious belief.

Managing Emotional Pain

Distressing emotions are common during bereavement, and grief is a natural response to loss. Accepting, rather than pushing away feelings that arise can help the bereaved better understand where their emotional responses are coming from. Iglewicz and colleagues (2019) recommend that grieving clients should

> take just 5 minutes at the end of each day to think back over their day, identify a time when their grief was at its highest, rate its intensity on a scale of 1–10 and make a note about what was happening at the time. This is repeated for the lowest grief of the day and patients are then asked for an overall rating for the day. At the next session, patient and therapist briefly discuss just one day when the grief was highest for the week and one day when grief was lowest (p. 95).

Experiencing the death of a partner due to suicide can be especially painful. Vanessa might benefit from thinking of the intensity of her grief as a reflection of the intensity of love she felt toward Ann. The DPM underscores the importance of "dosage" with grief (Stroebe & Schut, 1999). That is, one cannot be expected to function adaptively if consumed by the emotional and cognitive pain of the loss. Vanessa would likely benefit from exploring other restoration-oriented tasks, such as doing new things, finding other ways to distract herself from grief, or even avoid feelings of grief at times. It can be helpful for the bereaved to have spaces where the focus is not solely on the loss they have experienced. This can be easier said than done at times, and an evaluation of depressive symptomatology (e.g., anhedonia, sleep disturbance, etc.) should also be addressed, if needed.

Vanessa's experience of growing up in a Southern Baptist family will also likely shape her experiences with grief related to suicide. Researchers have noted that suicide deaths have the potential to be especially stigmatized in religious communities (Lehmann, et al., 2021; Potter, 2021). This raises Vanessa's risk for disenfranchised grief reactions due to potentially limited sources of social support and internalized shame about the suicide death.

Thinking About the Future

The restoration-oriented aspects of the DPM include the tasks of taking on new roles, identities, and relationships. This can be explored with clients by having them consider what they want their future to look like and what kind of goals they may have going forward. Clients may have a hard time thinking about the future if they are experiencing prolonged grief, as one of the DSM-5-TR criteria for PGD includes difficulty with reintegration with life after death. Individuals might describe a sense of being stuck in their grief (Iglewicz et al., 2019). The specifics of how one addresses their thoughts about the future will of course differ from person to person, but a discussion about goals can be helpful in identifying what type of future the client desires.

Vanessa could benefit from identifying her remaining goals as a college student. She may benefit from the structure of the academic year where she has the opportunity to focus on tasks related to coursework and other extracurricular events, even if she currently experiences difficulties with focus and motivation. This is another area where education about the DPM can be helpful. Clients may find it validating to know that it is okay to think about the future and their life without the physical presence of their deceased loved one.

Strengthening Ongoing Relationships

Researchers have noted that informal social supports (i.e., friends and family members) are often identified as the most helpful types of support during bereavement. For Vanessa, it might be possible for her to find some way to receive support from friends and family, though this might be complicated by unhelpful religious messaging. This is a situation where secular student groups (e.g., Secular Student Alliance) or grief-focused group counseling could be especially helpful.

Telling the Story of the Death

It can be helpful for bereaved individuals to share their story about the death of the deceased loved one throughout the counseling process. Bereaved individuals may receive messages from others that they should "move on" from their grief or that they should avoid talking about the death. Additionally, others can often feel uncomfortable talking with the bereaved about their grief and loss. The retelling of the story can be emotionally intense, especially at the beginning of treatment. These overwhelming feelings may diminish over time as the client builds the capacity for emotion regulation while discussing the loss.

Bereavement due to suicide can elicit strong emotions in the bereaved, along with challenges in making meaning of the death. Vanessa described a sense of numbness early on in her bereavement, followed by chronic distress and sadness. A counselor could assist Vanessa in telling her story by asking about what took place as she first heard about Ann's death and allowing Vanessa to slowly add details throughout subsequent counseling sessions. Counselors would need to utilize their clinical judgment in determining how much of the story of the death to explore at any one session.

Living with Reminders

The bereaved will encounter numerous reminders about the deceased as they continue living. While painful, it can be helpful to engage with, rather than avoid situations that remind the bereaved of the deceased. Counselors can assist bereaved clients in the complex emotions that are often evoked by memories, where clients can feel simultaneously happy and sad about the reminders. Vanessa and Ann were together as partners for three years. There would certainly be plenty of reminders to explore in this case.

Connecting to Memories

Nonphysical connections to the deceased continue in the form of memories during bereavement. Contrary to the idea of some form of end stage or "closure" for bereavement, it is normal to continue to maintain an emotional bond with the deceased. Researchers call this ongoing relationship *continuing bonds*, which is based on Bowlby's (1969, 1973, 1980) attachment theory. Counselors can encourage clients to share memories throughout their work. In the same way that Vanessa will have numerous reminders of Ann throughout their three-year partnership, she will also have many memories that can be recalled throughout her time in counseling.

Additional Considerations for Counselors Working with Bereaved Nonreligious Clients

- Examine your own reactions to death and loss
    - What meaning making strategies have you used to address the question of what happens after we die?
    - What thoughts and feelings come up for you when you interact with people who have beliefs about death and the afterlife that differ from your own?
    - How have you dealt with your own experiences of death and loss?
- Increase grief literacy by becoming familiar with current theories related to grief
    - Two common theoretical models in use today include the Dual Process Model of Grief (Stroebe & Schut, 1999, 2010, 2015) and meaning making processes (see Neimeyer et al., 2019 for a review). Additional information can be found at https://www.portlandinstitute.org/
    - Additional information, along with extensively researched and validated treatment modalities can be found at the Center for Prolonged Grief web page (https://prolongedgrief.columbia.edu/).
- Assess whether bereaved clients meet criteria for Prolonged Grief Disorder
    - Specialized assessment tools are publicly available for this. One such tool, the PG-13-R, can be found in Figure 11.1.

References

Abbott, D. M., & Anaya, E. J. (2022). "Breaking free": a grounded theory study of atheist women in the United States. *Psychology of Women Quarterly*, 46(4), 501–17. https://doi.org/10.1177/03616843221115338

Abbott, D. M., & Mollen, D. (2018). Atheism as a concealable stigmatized identity: Outness, anticipated stigma, and well-being. *The Counseling Psychologist*, 46(6), 685–707. https://doi.org/10.1177/0011000018792669

Abbott, D. M., Mollen, D., Mercier, C., Anaya, E. J., & Rukus, V. A. (2020). "Isn't atheism a white thing?": Centering the voices of atheists of color. *Journal of Counseling Psychology*, 67(3), 275–87. https://doi.org/10.1037/cou0000399

American Psychiatric Association. (2022). *Diagnostic and statistical manual of mental disorders* (5th ed., text rev.). https://doi.org/10.1176/appi.books.9780890425787

Aoun, S. M., Breen, L. J., Howting, D. A., Rumbold, B., McNamara, B., & Hegney, D. (2015). Who needs bereavement support? A population based survey of bereavement risk and support need. *PLOS ONE*, 10(3), 1–14. https://doi.org/10.1371/journal.pone.0121101

Aoun, S. M., Breen, L. J., White, I., Rumbold, B., & Kellehear, A. (2018). What sources of bereavement support are perceived helpful by bereaved people and why? Empirical evidence for the compassionate communities approach. *Palliative Medicine*, 32(8), 1378–88. https://doi.org/10.1177/0269216318774995

Arnett, J. J. (2000). Emerging adulthood: A theory of development from the late teens through the twenties. *American Psychologist*, 55(5), 469–80. https://doi.org/10.1037//0003-066x.55.5.469

Arnett, J. J., Žukauskienė, R., & Sugimura, K. (2014). The new life stage of emerging adulthood at ages 18–29 years: Implications for mental health. *The Lancet Psychiatry*, 1(7), 569–76. https://doi.org/10.1016/s2215-0366(14)00080-7

Avis, K. A., Stroebe, M., & Schut, H. (2021). Stages of grief portrayed on the internet: A systematic analysis and critical appraisal. *Frontiers in Psychology*, 12, 1–11. https://doi.org/10.3389/fpsyg.2021.772696

Balk, D. E., Walker, A. C., & Baker, A. (2010). Prevalence and severity of college student bereavement examined in a randomly selected sample. *Death Studies*, 34(5), 459–68. https://doi.org/10.1080/07481180903251810

Bergsmark, L. P., & Ramsing, F. (2023). Which considerations are lost when debating the prolonged grief disorder diagnosis? *Theory & Psychology*, 33(6), 856–72. https://doi.org/10.1177/09593543231172193

Bishop, B. (2018). Advocating for atheist clients in the counseling profession. *Counseling and Values*, 63(1), 17–30. https://doi.org/10.1002/cvj.12070

Black Nonbelievers (2024). https://blacknonbelievers.org/

Blueford, J. M., Diambra, J. F., & Wheat, L. S. (2021). Counselor preparedness to counsel grieving clients: Insights and implications. *Death Studies*, 46(10), 2413–23. https://doi.org/10.1080/07481187.2021.1956644

Bonanno, G. A. (2004). Loss, trauma, and human resilience: Have we underestimated the human capacity to thrive after extremely aversive events? *American Psychologist*, 59(1), 20–28. https://doi.org/10.1037/0003-066x.59.1.20

Bordere, T. (2014). Adolescents and homicide. In K. Doka & A. Tucci (Eds.), *Helping adolescents cope with loss* (pp. 161–81). Hospice Foundation of America.

Bordere, T. (2017). Disenfranchisement and ambiguity in the face of loss: The suffocated grief of sexual assault survivors. *Family Relations*, 66(1), 29–45. https://doi.org/10.1111/fare.12231

Bordere, T. C. (2016). Social justice conceptualizations in grief and loss. In D. Harris & T. C. Bordere (Eds.), *Handbook of social justice in loss and grief: Exploring diversity, equity, and inclusion* (pp. 9–20). Routledge.

Bowlby, J. (1969). Attachment and loss, Vol. I: Attachment. Basic Books.

Bowlby, J. (1973). Attachment and loss, Vol. 2: Separation. Basic Books.

Bowlby, J. (1980). Attachment and loss, Vol. 3: Loss, sadness and depression. Basic Books.

Breen, L. J., Kawashima, D., Joy, K., Cadell, S., Roth, D., Chow, A., & Macdonald, M. E. (2022). Grief literacy: A call to action for compassionate communities. *Death Studies*, 46(2), 425–33. https://doi.org/10.1080/07481187.2020.1739780

Brewster, M. E., Hammer, J., Sawyer, J. S., Eklund, A., & Palamar, J. (2016). Perceived experiences of atheist discrimination: Instrument development and evaluation. *Journal of Counseling Psychology*, 63(5), 557–70. https://doi.org/10.1037/cou0000156

Brewster, M. E., Robinson, M. A., Sandil, R., Esposito, J., & Geiger, E. (2014). Arrantly absent. *The Counseling Psychologist*, 42(5), 628–63. https://doi.org/10.1177/0011000014528051

Burge, R. (2023, October 19). *Which states are the least religious? Which are the most?* Graphs about religion. https://www.graphsaboutreligion.com/p/which-states-are-the-least-religious

The Center for Prolonged Grief (2023). *Prolonged Grief Treatment*. https://prolongedgrief.columbia.edu/prolonged-grief-treatment/

Chapple, A., Swift, C., & Ziebland, S. (2011). The role of spirituality and religion for those bereaved due to a traumatic death. *Mortality*, 16(1), 1–19. https://doi.org/10.1080/13576275.2011.535998

Christina, G. (2015). *Comforting thoughts about death that have nothing to do with god.* Pitchstone Publishing.

Cordaro, M. (2012). Pet loss and disenfranchised grief: Implications for mental health counseling practice. *Journal of Mental Health Counseling*, 34(4), 283–94. https://doi.org/10.17744/mehc.34.4.41q0248450t98072

Corr, C. A. (1999). Enhancing the concept of disenfranchised grief. *OMEGA—Journal of Death and Dying*, 38(1), 1–20. https://doi.org/10.2190/ld26-42a6-1eav-3mdn

Corr, C. A. (2018). Elisabeth Kübler-Ross and the "Five stages" model in a sampling of recent American textbooks. *OMEGA—Journal of Death and Dying*, 82(2), 294–322. https://doi.org/10.1177/0030222818809766

Cousins, C., Servaty-Seib, H., & Lockman, J. (2017). College student adjustment and coping for bereaved and nonbereaved college students. *OMEGA—Journal of Death and Dying*, 74(4), 386–409. https://doi.org/10.1037/e563502014-001

Cox, B. E., Dean, J. G., & Kowalski, R. (2015). Hidden trauma, quiet drama: The prominence and consequence of complicated grief among college students. *Journal of College Student Development*, 56(3), 280–85. https://doi.org/10.1353/csd.2015.0030

D'Andrea, L. M., & Sprenger, J. (2007). Atheism and Nonspirituality as diversity issues in counseling. *Counseling and Values*, 51(2), 149–58. https://doi.org/10.1002/j.2161-007x.2007.tb00072.x

Dawkins, R. (2006). *The god delusion*. Harper Collins.

De Groot, M., De Keijser, J., & Neeleman, J. (2006). Grief shortly after suicide and natural death: A comparative study among spouses and first-degree relatives. *Suicide and Life Threatening Behavior*, 36(4), 418–31. https://doi.org/10.1521/suli.2006.36.4.418

Djelantik, A., Smid, G. E., Mroz, A., Kleber, R. J., & Boelen, P. A. (2020). The prevalence of prolonged grief disorder in bereaved individuals following unnatural losses: Systematic review and meta regression analysis. *Journal of Affective Disorders*, 265, 146–56. https://doi.org/10.1016/j.jad.2020.01.034

Doka, K. J. (1989). *Disenfranchised grief: Recognizing hidden sorrow*. Lexington Books.

Doka, K. J. (2016). *Grief is a journey: Finding your path through loss*. Atria Books.

Eisma, M. C. (2023). Prolonged grief disorder in ICD-11 and *DSM*-5-TR: Challenges and controversies. *Australian & New Zealand Journal of Psychiatry*, 57(7), 944–51. https://doi.org/10.1177/00048674231154206

Exline, J. J., Park, C. L., Smyth, J. M., & Carey, M. P. (2011). Anger toward god: Social cognitive predictors, prevalence, and links with adjustment to bereavement and cancer. *Journal of Personality and Social Psychology*, 100(1), 129–48. https://doi.org/10.1037/a0021716

Fiore, J. (2021). A systematic review of the dual process model of coping with bereavement (1999–2016). *OMEGA—Journal of Death and Dying*, 84(2), 414–58. https://doi.org/10.1177/0030222819893139

Galen, L. W., & Kloet, J. D. (2011). Mental well-being in the religious and the non-religious: Evidence for a curvilinear relationship. *Mental Health, Religion & Culture*, 14(7), 673–89. https://doi.org/10.1080/13674676.2010.510829

Howard, S., Kennedy, K. C., & Vine, K. T. (2023). "You don't believe in god? You ain't Black": Identifying as atheist elicits identity denial from Black ingroup members. *Cultural Diversity & Ethnic Minority Psychology*, 29(2), 202–7. https://doi.org/10.1037/cdp0000397

Iglewicz, A., Shear, M. K., Reynolds, C. F., Simon, N., Lebowitz, B., & Zisook, S. (2019). Complicated grief therapy for clinicians: An evidence-based protocol for mental health practice. *Depression and Anxiety*, 37(1), 90–98. https://doi.org/10.1002/da.22965

Jankauskaite, G., O'Brien, K. M., & Yang, N. (2021). Assessing knowledge and predicting grief counseling skills among University counseling center therapists. *The Counseling Psychologist*, 49(3), 458–84. https://doi.org/10.1177/0011000020983525

Koenig, H. G. (2015). Religion, spirituality, and health: A review and update. *Advances in Mind Body Medicine*, 29(3), 19–26.

Koenig, H. G., George, L. K., & Siegler, I. C. (1988). The use of religion and other emotion-regulating coping strategies among older adults. *The Gerontologist*, 28(3), 303–10. https://doi.org/10.1093/geront/28.3.303

Kristensen, P., Weisæth, L., & Heir, T. (2012). Bereavement and mental health after sudden and violent losses: A review. *Psychiatry: Interpersonal and Biological Processes*, 75(1), 76–97. https://doi.org/10.1521/psyc.2012.75.1.76

Kübler-Ross, E. (1969). *On death and dying*. Macmillan.

Lehmann, C. S., Leung, C. A., Miller, I., & Girguis, S. M. (2021). An action research framework for religion and the stigma of suicide. *Religions*, 12(802), 1–32. https://doi.org/10.3390/rel12100802

Lundorff, M., Holmgren, H., Zachariae, R., Farver-Vestergaard, I., & O'Connor, M. (2017). Prevalence of prolonged grief disorder in adult bereavement: A systematic review and meta-analysis. *Journal of Affective Disorders*, 212, 138–49. https://doi.org/10.1016/j.jad.2017.01.030

McCoyd, J. L., Goldblatt Hyatt, E., Hennessy, K., & Akincigil, A. (2023). Revising ruling discourses: The griefwork evidence-to-practice gap and the mental health workforce. *Death Studies*, 47(10), 1136–45. https://doi.org/10.1080/07481187.2023.2171159

McLean, E., Singer, J., Laurita, E., Kahler, J., Levin, C., & Papa, A. (2022). Perception of grief responses: Are maladaptive grief responses and the stages of grief considered *normal*? *Death Studies*, 46(6), 1414–23. https://doi.org/10.1080/07481187.2021.1983890

Neimeyer, R. A. (2019). Meaning reconstruction in bereavement: Development of a research program. *Death Studies*, 43(2), 79–91. https://doi.org/10.1080/07481187.2018.1456620

Ober, A. M., Granello, D. H., & Wheaton, J. E. (2012). Grief counseling: An investigation of counselors' training, experience, and competencies. *Journal of Counseling & Development*, 90(2), 150–59. https://doi.org/10.1111/j.1556-6676.2012.00020.x

O'Connor, M. (2019). Grief: A brief history of research on how body, mind, and brain adapt. *Psychosomatic Medicine*, 81(8), 731–38. https://doi.org/10.1097/psy.0000000000000717

Pargament, K. I., Smith, B. W., Koenig, H. G., & Perez, L. (1998). Patterns of positive and negative religious coping with major life stressors. *Journal for the Scientific Study of Religion*, 37(4), 710–24. https://doi.org/10.2307/1388152

Pew Research Center (2024). Religious "nones" in America: Who they are and what they believe. https://www.pewresearch.org/religion/2024/01/24/religious-nones-in-america-who-they-are-and-what-they-believe/

Pinheiro, P., Gonçalves, M. M., Nogueira, D., Pereira, R., Basto, I., Alves, D., & Salgado, J. (2022). Emotional processing during the therapy for complicated grief. *Psychotherapy Research*, 32(5), 678–93. https://doi.org/10.1080/10503307.2021.1985183

Potter, J. (2021). Is suicide the unforgivable sin? Understanding suicide, stigma, and salvation through two Christian perspectives. *Religions*, 12(987), 1–19. https://doi.org/10.3390/rel12110987

Prigerson, H. G., Boelen, P. A., Xu, J., Smith, K. V., & Maciejewski, P. K. (2021). Validation of the new DSM-5-TR criteria for prolonged grief disorder and the PG-13-Revised (PG-13-R) scale. *World Psychiatry*, 20(1), 96–106. https://doi.org/10.1002/wps.20823

Prigerson, H. G., Shear, M. K., & Reynolds, C. F. (2022). Prolonged grief disorder diagnostic criteria—Helping those with maladaptive grief responses. *JAMA Psychiatry*, 79(4), 277–78. https://doi.org/10.1001/jamapsychiatry.2021.4201

Rosner, R., Comtesse, H., Vogel, A., & Doering, B. K. (2021). Prevalence of prolonged grief disorder. *Journal of Affective Disorders*, 287, 301–7. https://doi.org/10.1016/j.jad.2021.03.058

Sawyer, J. S. (2022). Bereavement outcomes for atheist individuals: The role of spirituality, discrimination, and meaning. *OMEGA—Journal of Death and Dying*, 86(2), 395–412. https://doi.org/10.1177/0030222820974536

Sawyer, J. S. (2024). Grief and bereavement beliefs and their associations with death anxiety and complicated grief in a U.S. college student sample. *Death Studies*. Advance online publication. https://doi.org/10.1080/07481187.2024.2349933

Sawyer, J. S., Brewster, M. E., & Ertl, M. M. (2021). Death anxiety and death acceptance in atheists and other nonbelievers. *Death Studies*, 45(6), 459–68. https://doi.org/10.1080/07481187.2019.1648339

Sawyer, J. S., Wilner, L. L., & Ertl, M. M. (2022). Grief and bereavement beliefs among U. S. mental health professionals and the general public. *Death Studies*, 46(10), 2346–53. https://doi.org/10.1080/07481187.2021.1944399

Secular Student Alliance. (n.d.). About us. https://secularstudents.org/about-us/#mission

Servaty-Seib, H. L., & Taub, D. J. (2010). Bereavement and college students: The role of counseling psychology. *The Counseling Psychologist*, 38(7), 947–75. https://doi.org/10.1177/0011000010366485

Shear, M. K. (2015). Complicated grief. *New England Journal of Medicine*, 372(2), 153–60. https://doi.org/10.1056/nejmcp1315618

Smith-Stoner, M. (2007). End-of-life preferences for atheists. *Journal of Palliative Medicine*, 10(4), 923–28. https://doi.org/10.1089/jpm.2006.0197

Stroebe, M., & Schut, H. (1999). The dual process model of coping with bereavement: Rationale and description. *Death Studies*, 23(3), 197–224. https://doi.org/10.1080/074811899201046

Stroebe, M., & Schut, H. (2010). The dual process model of coping with bereavement: A decade later. *OMEGA—Journal of Death and Dying*, 61(4), 269–71. https://doi.org/10.2190/om.61.4.a
Stroebe, M., & Schut, H. (2015). Family matters in bereavement. *Perspectives on Psychological Science*, 10(6), 873–79. https://doi.org/10.1177/1745691615598517
Stroebe, M., Schut, H., & Boerner, K. (2017). Cautioning health-care professionals: Bereaved persons are misguided through the stages of grief. *OMEGA—Journal of Death and Dying*, 74(4), 455–73. https://doi.org/10.1177/0030222817691870
Stroebe, M. S., & Schut, H. (2001). Meaning making in the dual process model of coping with bereavement. In R. A. Neimeyer (Ed.), *Meaning reconstruction & the experience of loss* (pp. 55–73). American Psychological Association. https://doi.org/10.1037/10397-003
Tal Young, I., Iglewicz, A., Glorioso, D., Lanouette, N., Seay, K., Ilapakurti, M., & Zisook, S. (2012). Suicide bereavement and complicated grief. *Dialogues in Clinical Neuroscience*, 14(2), 177–86. https://doi.org/10.31887/dcns.2012.14.2/iyoung
Wilkinson, P. J., & Coleman, P. G. (2010). Strong beliefs and coping in old age: A case-based comparison of atheism and religious faith. *Ageing and Society*, 30(2), 337–61. https://doi.org/10.1017/s0144686x09990353
Wortman, C. B., & Silver, R. C. (1989). The myths of coping with loss. *Journal of Consulting and Clinical Psychology*, 57(3), 349–57. https://doi.org/10.1037//0022-006x.57.3.349

12

Spiritual Abuse and Religious Trauma Among Nonbelievers

Patrick T. Meyer

Chapter Outline

"When trust is lost, traumatized people feel that they belong more to the dead than to the living." (Herman, 2015, p. 52)

It has long been understood that religious communities can inflict psychological distress on their members through abusive acts and harmful messages (Blue, 1993). Much of the research literature in the social sciences, however, has focused on the benefits of religiousness (Moreira-Almeida et al., 2006) or framed negative mental health outcomes among nonreligious people (Hayward et al., 2016) as a result of their nonbelief as opposed to the most robust source: being negatively perceived by others (Weber et al., 2012). Scholarly interest in exploring the impact of adverse religious experiences on psychological well-being has increased significantly from the 1990s to the present. Nonreligious patients may utilize psychotherapy to help process feelings attached to their adverse religious experiences and explore how to make sense of their nonreligious identity in light of their traumatic experiences. It is the responsibility of mental health professionals to provide culturally responsive services to nonreligious patients from a trauma-informed framework that honors their religious journey and affirms their nonreligious identity.

This chapter reviews the typical concerns of survivors of spiritual abuse and aims to help mental health professionals feel more equipped to work with this population. I begin by providing an overview of the common symptoms of religious trauma and the various forms of abuse that can occur within religious communities. In the following section, I detail how adverse religious experiences serve as a potential pathway to nonbelief. Additionally, I explore how nonreligious patients in the United States may experience retraumatization given the omnipresence and privileged status of Christianity and the stigma associated with nonreligiousness (Blumenfeld et al., 2008; Swan & Heesacker, 2012). In the final section, I provide recommendations to help mental health professionals guide their nonreligious patients in the process of healing from religious trauma from a psychodynamic and trauma-informed perspective.

My Social Positionality: Influences on This Chapter

> Each and every one of us has the capacity to be an oppressor. I want to encourage each and every one of us to interrogate how we might be an oppressor and how we might be able to become liberators for ourselves and for each other.
>
> —Laverne Cox

I am a White, gay, nonbinary, able-bodied person living on the land of the Ponca, Omaha, Winnebago, Dakota, and Oto Peoples in Lincoln, Nebraska as a doctoral student in counseling psychology at the University of Nebraska-Lincoln. I was raised in a White, middle-class, suburban community on the land of the Cherokee. This community was embedded in cisheteronormativity, hegemonic Christianity, and White supremacy. I have grown up in a community that normalizes religiousness, specifically Evangelicalism, and oppresses nonreligious people. I have privileges on the basis of my citizenship, race, body size, ability status, and education. I was raised Catholic and currently identify as spiritual but not religious. Though I no longer consider myself religious, I have not personally experienced religious and/or spiritual trauma or abuse. I was drawn to this area of research after being exposed to narratives of religious trauma in popular media, including books and reality television shows. As a queer nonreligious person living in a conservative Midwestern state, I believe I may experience discrimination yet acknowledge that the privileges I hold onto protect me from the most severe forms of marginalization. I share these facets of myself in an effort to illuminate my perspective of the world around me and the lens I bring to scholarly work. Although I write with the intention to uplift marginalized voices, I am cognizant of how my biases and lived experiences influence this process.

The Nature of Religious and Spiritual Trauma

Key Terms and Definitions

Spiritual abuse, also known as *religious abuse*, is a relatively new term utilized to describe abuse that is directly influenced by a religious and/or spiritual (R/S) person, setting, or context. It is a term that began being utilized in the United States (Johnson & VanVonderen, 1991) and eventually gained traction in other countries. Scholars have struggled to reach a consensus on a singular definition of spiritual abuse that captures the variety of ways one can come to experience this phenomenon, but Oakley et al. (2024, p. 190) proposed the following definition based on the emerging literature:

> Spiritual abuse is a form of emotional and psychological abuse characterized by a systematic pattern of coercive and controlling behavior in a religious context or with a religious rationale. This context includes religious or spiritual institutions, places of education, and homes in which there is a religious, spiritual, or faith belief. Spiritual abuse can have a deeply damaging impact on those who experience it and can be experienced in a variety of different relationships.

The term *religious trauma* is often utilized to convey the psychological impact of adverse religious experiences. Stone (2013) defines religious trauma as "pervasive psychological damage resulting from religious messages, beliefs, and experiences" (p. 324). Although these definitions may not fully capture the essence of all cases of R/S abuse/trauma, they will be utilized for the purposes of this chapter.

Types of Spiritual Abuse

Individuals can experience spiritual abuse in a variety of settings and contexts. Though most scholarly inquiry regarding spiritual abuse began with people in new or high demand religious movements, known colloquially as cults, it can also occur in mainstream religions. In a recent systematic review, Ellis et al. (2022) discovered three core themes of R/S abuse: (1) misuse of power, (2) psychological harm, and (3) spiritual harm. Even though R/S abuse takes many forms, there is likely some connection with these concepts in most cases. In the following sections, the literature on spiritual abuse is organized into three sections based on Swindle's (2017) types of R/S abuse: (1) abuse perpetrated by religious leadership, (2) abuse perpetrated by a religious group, and (3) abuse with a religious component.

Abuse Perpetrated by Religious Leadership

Given that an imbalance of power often lays the foundation for abusive dynamics, perhaps it is unsurprising that many cases of spiritual abuse include a perpetrator who is a religious leader (e.g., pastor, priest, rabbi, imam). Ward (2011) found that many religious leaders who perpetrate spiritual abuse have charming personalities with narcissistic tendencies that aid them in manipulating people. In many religious traditions, leaders are assumed to be in close proximity with a higher power whereas some groups view their leaders as god(s) themselves. Perhaps the most well-documented form of abuse within this category is sexual abuse perpetrated by a religious leader, often targeting a vulnerable population, such as youth (Raine & Kent, 2019). In 2024, the Catholic Archdiocese of Los Angeles agreed to pay $880 million to 1,353 victims, primarily minors, of sexual abuse perpetrated by over three hundred priests in the Catholic Church. In addition to the harm inflicted by the abusive acts, religious institutions have also been criticized for systematically protecting abusers by engaging in coverups, conducting dodgy investigations, and transferring abusers to different institutions despite allegations and/or evidence. This process often leaves survivors feeling silenced and ignored by institutions that claim to foster their spiritual well-being. Additionally, members of high demand religious movements have reported that their leaders required obedience and questioning or refusing to engage in certain behaviors resulted in being cut off from receiving special rituals, such as blessings and healings (Lucas, 2003). Super and Jacobson (2011) reinforce the idea that abuse perpetrated by leaders often involves the withholding of support and affirmation as opposed to the direct infliction of harm, such as threatening to oust an LGBT (lesbian, gay, bisexual, transgender) member if they do not conceal their sexual orientation or gender identity. Individuals who have experienced abuse by religious leaders showed similar depressive and anxiety symptoms as those who were abused by parents (Stevens et al., 2019). This form of spiritual abuse may lead survivors to experience feelings of fear and distrust of individuals they perceive as holding authority or power, including mental health professionals.

Abuse Perpetrated by a Religious Group

Spiritual abuse can also be perpetrated by other members of the religious community. This category of abuse encompasses acts perpetrated by all lay members of a religious community, including family members, friends, and partners. Most of the previous literature examining this form of abuse has explored how religious communities represent a microcosm of society at large and especially target those from marginalized communities. Nadal (2018) asserted that frequent exposure to microaggressions can be traumatic in and of itself, meaning subtle and common messages promoted in religious and spiritual communities that convey hostile or derogatory attitudes may lead to religious trauma. For example, members of the LGBT community report experiencing frequent microaggressions within their religious communities (e.g., "We all have crosses to bear, this is just yours.") and have often been othered in these spaces (Lomash et al., 2019). Dehan and Levi (2009) explored spiritual abuse among ultraorthodox Jewish women and discovered that they received harmful and misogynistic messages from their husbands. One participant reported being told that their prayer was worthless on the basis of her gender, whereas another described experiencing rape during her menstrual period when sexual intercourse during this timeframe is forbidden in Jewish law. Many abusive religious communities isolate members from individuals outside of the community, meaning people experiencing this form of abuse may be unaware of the abnormality of these dynamics due to the lack of healthy, meaningful, and egalitarian relationships. This insularity commonly seen in cases of spiritual abuse likely has the potential to have significant influence over survivors' self-concepts and interpersonal relations. In a psychotherapeutic setting, this form of spiritual abuse may result in transference wherein the patient unconsciously expects the therapist to inflict harm as their religious community did.

Abuse with a Religious Component

Survivors of spiritual abuse may have experienced abuse with an explicit R/S component. This form of spiritual abuse involves the direct connection of religious texts or beliefs to the specific act of abuse. Religious texts and beliefs have been utilized to justify racism (Fletcher, 2017), slavery (Whitford, 2016), sexism (Dehan & Levi, 2009), heterosexism (Barrett-Fox, 2016), transphobia (Blyth & McRae, 2018), domestic violence (Childress et al., 2023), and child sexual abuse (Raine & Kent, 2019). In addition to experiencing the abuse, the survivor is often made aware of the religious justification behind the action (Swindle, 2017). Some survivors of spiritual abuse report that religious ideology was interpreted in a unique way or misused to justify actions (Oakley et al., 2024), whereas people within fundamentalist communities may report literal passages being used to justify abusive acts. This often leaves survivors feeling spiritually disempowered, because resisting this form of abuse inevitably coincides with betraying one's belief system.

Though these three categories outlined by Swindle (2017) serve as a framework for understanding the various forms of spiritual abuse, many experiences may fall into multiple types or beyond these categories entirely. Mental health professionals should aim to listen for religious and spiritual themes in the stories of survivors, as spiritual abuse may only emerge once their patients discuss another form of abuse (e.g., physical, sexual, psychological) first. These categories also may assist practitioners in case conceptualization. Perhaps a survivor who experienced abuse perpetrated by religious leadership struggles with a prevailing sense of powerlessness. It is possible that a patient who experienced abuse by their religious family experiences a lack of belongingness.

Symptoms of Religious Trauma

Dr. Marlene Winell (2011) is credited with coining the term *religious trauma syndrome* after working with Christian Fundamentalists who were experiencing trauma symptoms after leaving their religious community. Religious trauma encapsulates the psychological challenges people experience after adverse religious experiences. Individuals experiencing this phenomenon often experience internalized stigma, shattered assumptions, an altered worldview, and loss of social support (Yates & Snodgrass, 2019). Common symptoms associated with religious trauma syndrome outlined by Winell (2011) are listed in Figure 12.1.

To help illuminate the unique and painful nature of this phenomenon, Figure 12.2 includes a selection of quotes from people who have experienced religious trauma (Winell, 2011).

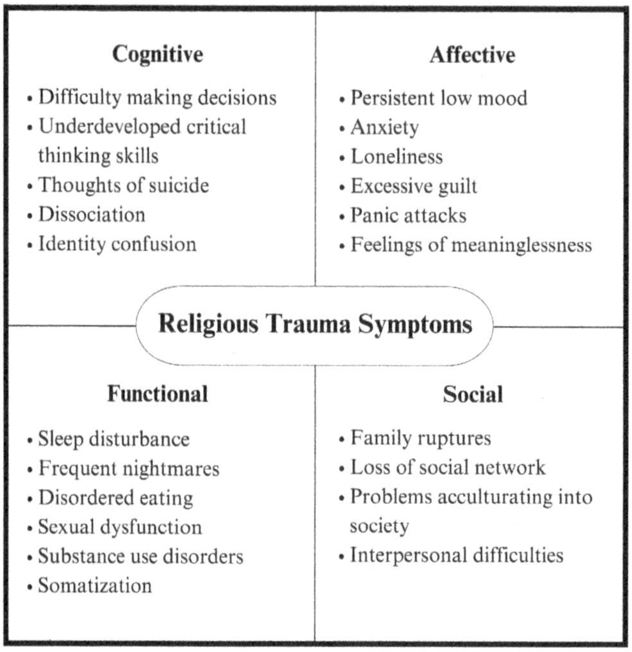

Figure 12.1 Symptoms of Religious Trauma.

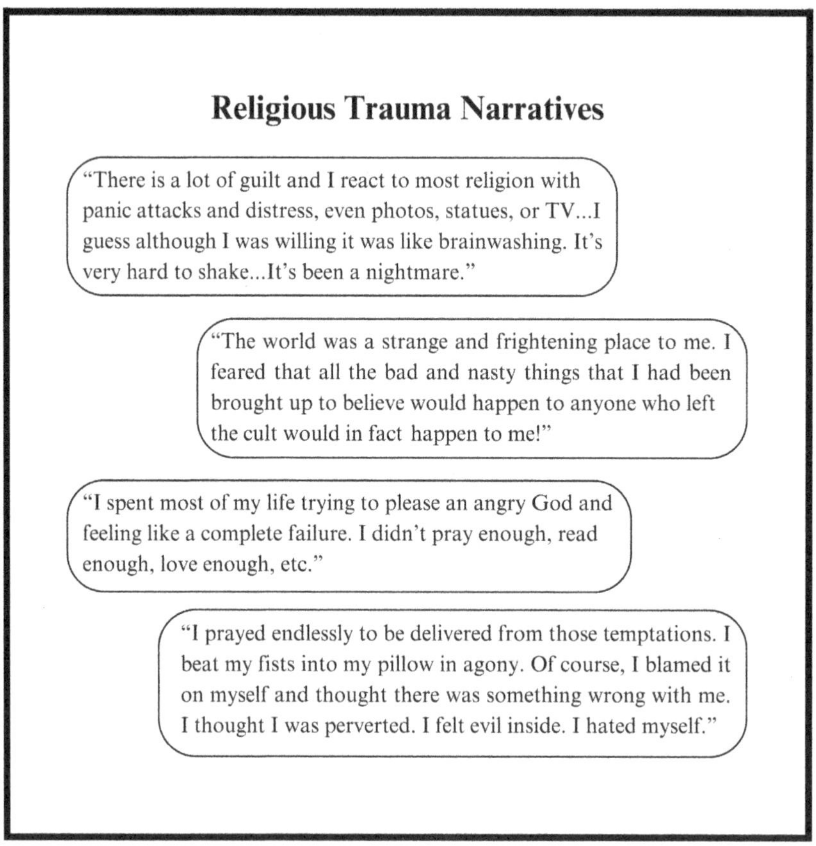

Figure 12.2 Narratives of Religious Trauma.

Religious Trauma Among Nonbelievers

One of the various implications of religious trauma that has been explored is changes in R/S identity following adverse religious experiences. Though many people utilize religious coping (e.g., prayer, religious support groups) and report that their traumatic experiences have strengthened their faith (de Castella & Simmonds, 2013), others indicate that their adverse religious experiences led them to leave organized religion altogether and adopt a nonreligious identity (e.g., atheist, agnostic, secular humanist) (Lee & Gubi, 2019). In the following section, I detail how adverse religious experiences serve as a pathway to nonbelief for some survivors. Additionally, I explore how nonbelievers may be uniquely impacted by religious trauma given the stigmatization of nonbelief. Finally, I describe how nonbelievers in the United States navigate living in a society dominated by Christianity and how this population may be at risk for retraumatization.

A Pathway to Nonbelief

People come to not believe in the existence of god(s) through a variety of pathways, including secular socialization and skepticism of religious beliefs (LeDrew, 2013). One of the potential routes to nonbelief is a change in worldview and belief system following an adverse religious experience. Previous research has examined how the experience of spiritual abuse influenced the R/S identities of survivors. Although existing literature suggests that most people arrive at nonbelief due to the perceived irrelevance of religion in their lives, a portion of people do adopt a nonbelieving worldview due to religious trauma (Sheard, 2014). In a study examining adults who experienced childhood sexual abuse in the Roman Catholic Church, only around a third of the sample (*n* = 38) reported believing in a religion or a belief system as adults (Pereda & Segura, 2021). The researchers discovered that about three-quarters of the sample reported never attending religious ceremonies and just under half of the sample (44.8 percent) reported that experiencing sexual abuse as a child by leaders in the Catholic Church had an extreme or considerable impact on their belief in God. In a similar study, only one out of 25 participants who experienced childhood sexual abuse perpetrated by priests in the Catholic Church identified as a Catholic as an adult and a majority of the sample were religiously unaffiliated (Mart, 2004).

It is worth noting that many survivors of spiritual abuse considered themselves deeply religious at one point in their lives and arriving at a nonbelieving worldview was a long and tumultuous journey. In light of their adverse religious experiences, many individuals report that they feel betrayed by god. God has been described by some survivors as "rejecting, arbitrary, unreasonable, uncaring, mean-spirited, and sometimes hateful" (Yates & Snodgrass, 2019, p. 259). For some people, religion provides an organized and cohesive framework that assists them in making meaning of their lives (Manuti et al., 2016), yet survivors of spiritual abuse often choose not to turn to religious beliefs or communities in order to protect their psychological well-being (Yates & Snodgrass, 2019). Some survivors may focus on creating a personal spirituality through activities that benefit their sense of self and personal well-being (e.g., spending time in nature, yoga) in a way that feels freer and safer than organized religion (Beagan & Hattie, 2015).

One theory that serves as a roadmap to understanding nonbelief after experiencing spiritual abuse is shattered assumptions theory. Shattered assumptions theory posits that traumatic events can dramatically alter one's self-concept and personal worldview (Janoff-Bulman, 2010). Individuals across the lifespan hold onto assumptions, often existing unconsciously, that can become shaken or shattered following traumatic events. Theorists assert that the following three core assumptions are vulnerable to being shattered after a traumatic event:

- The world is benevolent.
- The world is meaningful.
- The self is worthy.

In cases of religious trauma, the individual may experience the shattering of the following assumptions:

- God loves me.
- My religious leader will protect me.
- I will spend eternity with my family.

Survivors of spiritual abuse may find it challenging to integrate their adverse religious experience(s) with an assumptive worldview that includes R/S (Yates & Snodgrass, 2019). The traumatic nature of such experiences potentially dissuades some survivors from organized religion, personal spirituality, or belief in a god(s). Though most people report no change in religious beliefs following traumatic events, a significant portion of those who endorse PTSD (post-traumatic stress disorder) symptoms experience a decrease in religious belief (Leo et al., 2021). When the traumatic event is directly associated with R/S, adverse religious experiences serve as a viable pathway to nonbelief.

A Bird Without a Nest?

A common challenge reported by nonbelievers is the lack of community among secular people and the loneliness that accompanies being a nonreligious person in a predominately religious country (Abbott et al., 2020). Despite an increase in identifying as nonreligious in the United States (Pew Research Center, 2024), the lack of political representation and coalition-building among nonbelievers prevents collective action that benefits nonreligious populations. Consistent social interaction is associated with psychological well-being and people who belong to religious communities often get this through services and religious celebrations. Though many organizations (e.g., American Atheists) exist to help nonbelievers connect with one another (potentially with the intention of getting the psychosocial benefits of consistent social interaction without the belief element), people with adverse religious experiences have reported that these spaces are only somewhat helpful (Lee & Gubi, 2019). Nonbelievers who have adverse religious experiences often do not feel fully understood by religious or secular people. Interactions with religious people are often accompanied by proselytizing and judgment. Despite sharing a nonreligious identity, survivors may sense that they are distinct from nonbelievers who do not have a deep and painful experience of religion. Some survivors may feel like outsiders in these spaces since they once held onto R/S beliefs. Additionally, survivors of spiritual abuse who hold marginalized identities (e.g., women, LGBTQ+ people, people of color) may find that most secular spaces primarily consist of people with significant social privilege (e.g., White, cisgender, heterosexual men with post-secondary education) and feel othered or not adequately represented (Abbott et al., 2020; Guenther, 2019). Survivors of spiritual abuse may find it more beneficial to seek out groups and communities that specifically focus on deconversion and religious trauma, as opposed to secularism more broadly (Lee & Gubi, 2019).

Retraumatization Among Survivors in the United States

Even though educators often spread the message that the United States was founded on (non)religious diversity and the country represents a "melting pot" where different religions unite in their quest for freedom, scholars have identified the privileged status held by Christianity in the United States. The Establishment Clause of the First Amendment of the US Constitution (U.S. Const. amend. I) prohibits the government from "establishing" a religion. Though this theoretically serves to ensure the separation of church and state, there are many examples that point to the dominance of Christianity in virtually all aspects of US society. For example, state and federal holidays often coincide with Christian holidays, and elected officials in the United States overwhelmingly identify as Christian. Despite the US population becoming more secular in recent years (Pew Research Center, 2024), Christian privilege still operates on interpersonal and systemic levels.

The normalization of belief, specifically Christianity, in the United States motivates many nonbelievers to engage in activism. For survivors of religious trauma, in addition to Christian dominance representing a social justice issue, it may threaten their psychological well-being. Survivors of spiritual abuse report experiencing psychological distress (e.g., panic attacks) and physical reactions (e.g., vomiting) when confronted with R/S symbolism, such as churches or prayer (Tobin, 2019; Yates & Snodgrass, 2019). What does that mean for a survivor of spiritual abuse whose polling place is a local church? What is it like for a person experiencing religious trauma to hear their elected representative advocate for Christian nationalism? Though these represent opportunities for advocacy and activism among nonbelievers in the United States, the embeddedness of religiousness into the fabric of US society may negatively influence the health and well-being of survivors of spiritual abuse.

Trauma-Informed Care for Nonbelievers with Religious and Spiritual Trauma

Mental health professionals working with nonreligious patients with religious and spiritual trauma should consider utilizing a trauma-informed perspective. Trauma-informed care is a framework psychotherapists utilize with survivors of trauma that aims to critically consider how trauma impacts nearly every aspect of the psychotherapy process. This approach encourages mental health professionals to go beyond the one-size-fits-all approach to psychotherapy and instead seeks to honor the unique experiences of the patient while also considering their sociocultural context. Trauma-informed care is guided by six principles: (1) safety, (2) trustworthiness and transparency, (3) peer support, (4) collaboration, (5) empowerment and choice, and (6) attention to sociocultural issues (Substance Abuse and Mental Health Services Administration, 2023). In the following section, I will provide clinical recommendations related to each of these principles for mental health professionals to utilize when working with this population. These recommendations are grounded in the existing literature on religious trauma, spiritual abuse, and psychotherapy with nonreligious patients. A case vignette will be utilized to help bridge the gap from theoretical considerations to clinical practice.

Case Vignette

Violet (fictional patient) is a forty-five-year-old White, bisexual, cisgender woman who uses she/her pronouns. She was raised in a conservative Western state by her biological parents who were active members of the Church of Jesus Christ of Latter-day Saints. Violet remembers going to church every Sunday during her childhood and adolescence and religion was integrated into nearly every facet of her family life (e.g., family prayers, religious holidays). She reported truly believing in God and found many aspects of her religious community to be fulfilling (e.g., volunteering with other church members). After graduating high school, Violet went on a mission, a volunteer service trip, for one-and-a-half years in South America. While she was on her mission, Violet noticed that her attitude toward her faith shifted. Though Violet enjoyed her personal relationship with God, she felt uncomfortable proselytizing and felt like she was imposing her own values onto others. She kept these feelings to herself and after she returned from her mission, she began her post-secondary education. Around this time, Violet began to realize her attraction to people of multiple genders. Growing up, Violet was encouraged to establish a heterosexual nuclear family and was informed that members of the LGBTQ community who "acted" on their attractions would not be with their families in the afterlife. Over the next few years, Violet got married to a cisgender man, had children, remained an active member of the church, and continued to conceal her sexual orientation. At the age of forty-two, Violet filed for divorce due to frequent conflicts in her marriage. During the divorce process, Violet disclosed that her husband's disgust related to her bisexual identity was one source of conflict in their marriage to another member of her church, and quickly noticed that her social support network within her local community dissolved. She received stares at the grocery store, was ignored at weekly worship services, and noticed that her children stopped receiving invites to social gatherings and birthday parties. After a few months of being ostracized, she stopped attending religious services and noticed she experienced frequent nightmares and caught herself during the day feeling afraid of "going to hell." Violet began psychotherapy four years after the divorce and presented with feelings of guilt, loneliness, and meaninglessness. After the divorce was finalized and her family heard about her bisexual identity from members of the church, Violet reported that her relationship with her parents became significantly more strained. Violet currently identifies as agnostic and stated she has no intention of returning to organized religion.

In the following sections, I provide trauma-informed suggestions for mental health professionals working with survivors of spiritual abuse, using Violet's case as a way to illuminate how interventions and guidelines can inform the process of psychotherapy.

Safety

One of the key features of the trauma-informed approach is an emphasis on the mental health professional creating an environment that fosters physical, psychological, and emotional safety (Ginicola et al., 2017). Though psychotherapy is often branded as a "safe space" where patients explore some of the most deep and painful aspects of their lives, survivors of spiritual abuse may find it challenging to perceive the psychotherapy process as safe. Patients experiencing hypervigilance may feel on edge and continually search for potential threats during psychotherapy sessions. Clinicians play an active role in laying the foundation where safety can be fostered. Psychodynamic psychotherapists often point to the importance of the therapeutic frame in promoting psychological safety. The therapeutic frame refers to fixed elements (e.g., setting, time, and session fee) of psychotherapy that lay the groundwork for meaningful work. From this theoretical perspective, the more secure the boundaries of psychotherapy are, the more free the patient feels to explore painful thoughts and feelings (Gray, 2013).

It is recommended that clinicians be transparent about the boundaries and rules of psychotherapy and continually attend to holding the frame throughout the treatment process, such as beginning and ending sessions on time. This consistency and reliability on behalf of the mental health professional may assist a survivor of spiritual abuse who may have previously experienced a lot of inconsistency, chaos, and violation of boundaries to feel safer in sessions. When working with nonreligious patients, practitioners should maintain an open and curious stance toward their nonreligious identity and their religious experience. Patients should repeatedly be invited to share their feelings regarding these areas of their lives, as these topics are often avoided in US society. Through repeated attempts to have the patient "join" the exploration process, a therapeutic alliance can form which ideally carries a sense of safety.

Practical Suggestions for Violet's Case:

- During the intake session ask Violet, "What would help you feel safe with me?" If her response is possible and reasonable, make an active effort to help her feel safe.
- Do not display religious items in the therapy office. These items could instill fear in survivors of religious trauma and signal that they cannot be fully vulnerable in the space.
- After the intake session, allow Violet to begin dialogue at the beginning of each session. Though she may find the silence to be initially uncomfortable, it conveys respect and grants her the agency to determine what to bring to the therapeutic space. Additionally, it serves as a reminder of the stark difference between meaningful psychotherapy and social banter.

Trustworthiness and Transparency

Related to a sense of relational safety is the ability of the survivor of spiritual abuse to trust their mental health professional. Although many mental health professionals aspire to have an egalitarian therapeutic relationship with their patients, practitioners do represent authority figures with inherent privileges. Patients who have experienced spiritual abuse perpetrated by religious leadership may be justifiably hesitant to be completely honest, open, and vulnerable with a mental health professional. It is recommended that mental health professionals meet patients where they are and normalize feelings of discomfort in the context of psychotherapy. Though trauma-informed practitioners aspire to develop therapeutic relationships full of trust and transparency, these aspirations may not be as important as attuning to the patient's subjective experience. Some mental health professionals may find it helpful to bring attention to the unique nature of psychotherapy and how it is significantly different from nearly all other forms of social interaction. Establishing trust with patients who have experienced spiritual abuse may take time and it may be beneficial to honor the patient's pace and autonomy to decide for themselves if and when the mental health professional is a trustworthy person. If applicable, mental health professionals may consider openly stating that the patient is participating in secular psychotherapy, as opposed to religious-based counseling, in an effort to alleviate any fear that they are being treated from a R/S perspective. Although opinions on therapist self-disclosure vary drastically across theoretical orientations, nonreligious mental health professionals may consider sharing their nonreligious identity with the patient to aid in establishing rapport and alleviate anxieties about being judged by a religious healthcare provider.

Practical Suggestions for Violet's Case:

- Bring attention to the elephant in the room. Openly discuss that you are a stranger to the patient and acknowledge how strange and one-sided psychotherapy often is. Normalize feelings of unease and discomfort, and choose to sit with these feelings as opposed to offering remarks such as "This is a safe space."

- Discuss with Violet parallels that might be occurring between what is currently happening in the therapeutic relationship and what happened during the conversation with her friend during the divorce process. Does she feel like the therapist will betray her? How do past experiences of honesty and vulnerability influence the here and now?
- If nonreligious: Consider sharing your nonreligious identity if clinically appropriate. How does Violet feel about this? Acknowledge differences between nonreligious identities (e.g., atheist versus agnostic), if applicable.
- If formerly religious: Consider sharing your former faith if clinically appropriate. This may help Violet feel understood, given your knowledge of religious beliefs, practices, and expectations.
- If religious: Consider sharing your religious identity if clinically appropriate. Discuss with Violet how she feels about this cultural difference. Does she think this will impact the therapeutic relationship?

Peer Support

As discussed earlier in the chapter, many nonbelievers experience loneliness and social isolation. Survivors of spiritual abuse may have experienced the loss of their support network within their religious community. One of the key ways trauma-informed practitioners can help patients with a history of adverse religious experiences is to support them in connecting with other individuals with similar lived experiences. For patients who are exploring their nonreligious identity, the practitioner could provide them with resources on local and online groups and organizations dedicated to fostering social connections among nonreligious people (e.g., American Atheists). For patients who are seeking to connect with others who experience religious trauma, the mental health professional could connect them with groups that focus on supporting others with adverse religious experiences (e.g., Reclamation Collective support groups). See Figure 12.3 for a list of websites and media that could be helpful to patients.

Though the therapeutic relationship differs from other social interactions in significant and meaningful ways, one of the intended effects of developing a strong therapeutic alliance is to provide the patient with a corrective emotional experience that leads to healthy and fulfilling relationships with other individuals (Bridges, 2006). Survivors of spiritual abuse have often experienced relationships where there was a persistent focus on performance, power, and obedience (Ward, 2011), so a therapeutic relationship with a trauma-informed clinician could allow them to expand their awareness of what relationships with relational depth and mutual respect feel like.

Practical Suggestions for Violet's Case:

- Provide Violet with resources on local and online groups dedicated to connecting with others experiencing religious trauma.
- Explore with Violet what kind of relationships she desires. What does she value in friendships? In relationships? How does she feel about the therapeutic relationship?
- Discuss how Violet feels about losing her support network at church. What was it like for these relationships to change once she was outed?

Religious Trauma Resources

- Reclamation Collective serves as a community for individuals who have experienced adverse religious experiences. They offer a list of providers specializing in religious trauma, support groups, and workshops. Visit the Reclamation Collective website: https://www.reclamationcollective.com/
- Watch Deconstructing My Religion (2018), a short documentary special that showcases narratives of religious trauma
- Recovering from Religion offers peer support (phone call, chat) for individuals experiencing religious doubts or adverse religious experiences. Their mission is to connect people with resources and support to help them live after experiencing a faith crisis. Visit the Recovering from Religion website: https://www.recoveringfromreligion.org/
- The Secular Therapy Project aims to help patients connect with secular mental health professionals who provide mental health services from a secular perspective. Visit the Secular Therapy Project website: https://www.seculartherapy.org/

Figure 12.3 Resources for Patients with Religious Trauma.

Collaboration

Another important feature of trauma-informed clinical work is the importance of collaboration in the process of psychotherapy. From a trauma-informed perspective, mental health professionals have expertise in psychological theories and supporting the process of psychological change whereas patients are the experts of their lived experiences. For survivors of spiritual abuse, a mental health professional valuing their own perspective and input may represent a novel experience. People with adverse religious experiences may have been accustomed to hierarchical relationships where they were told what to do instead of being invited to share their own personal thoughts and feelings. It is quite possible patients with a history of spiritual abuse have never felt fully seen or heard by another person before, which speaks to the potential impact mental health professionals can have in working with this population. Mental health professionals can make it clear that discussions about R/S are welcome in the therapy space (Magaldi-Dopman & Park-Taylor, 2010). Practitioners may consider inviting patients to be active participants in creating their treatment plans (Zaeske et al., 2024). This invitation signals that their input is valued and ensures that there is alignment between patient and therapist on the overarching goals and objectives of psychotherapy. Nonreligious patients report that mental health professionals have recommended religious coping strategies, including prayer and attending church services, despite informing their provider of their nonreligious identity (Byrne et al., 2021). Though efforts to provide such coping strategies likely come with good intentions, psychotherapy with nonreligious patients with religious trauma should aim to examine the therapeutic relationship and break the patient free from maladaptive ways of relating. Rushing to provide patients with a skill or strategy may only reenact patterns of relating with religious family members or religious leaders, whereas openly exploring their thoughts and feelings can open them up to new ways of being.

Practical Suggestions for Violet's Case:

- Involve Violet in the process of creating a treatment plan. How often does she want psychotherapy sessions? What are her goals for psychotherapy? How will she know when she has reached these goals?
- Encourage Violet to share her experience of psychotherapy and what, if anything, she's finding beneficial. The therapeutic relationship can be seen as a vehicle to explore her expectations, wishes, and desires.

Empowerment and Choice

One of the hallmarks of trauma-informed care is empowering patients to make independent choices (SAMSHA, 2023). Though having the freedom to make choices for oneself presents patients with the opportunity to direct their path in life, existentialists frequently point out that acknowledging this freedom is a challenging task. In their religious communities, patients who have experienced spiritual abuse may have had limited access to freedom. Survivors of spiritual abuse may have been raised in religious families, meaning even the decision to become religious was not granted to them. Members of this population may have also been forced to attend religious services, engage in prayer, and only associate with people within their religious community.

Though nonbelievers may have left their religious community, patients may, paradoxically, experience challenges in adjusting to living with fewer restrictions. Making decisions without the guidance of religious leadership may be accompanied by feelings of guilt, so mental health professionals, in most cases, must resist giving their patients direct advice. Though patients may seek advice from their mental health professionals, it may be particularly important when working with this population to emphasize their ability to make choices and take personal responsibility.

Yates and Snodgrass (2019) encouraged clinicians to openly speak with patients about the meaning they attach to their traumatic experiences and how they feel about labels such as spiritual abuse and religious trauma. Additionally, Ginicola et al. (2017) urged practitioners to have explicit discussions about the power differential in the therapeutic relationship and encourage the patient to give feedback about the therapy process. Hopefully, patients eventually embrace the freedom to actively explore how they make sense of their nonreligious identity and/or adverse religious experiences as opposed to looking to the mental health professional for an answer.

Practical Suggestions for Violet's Case:

- Discuss with Violet how she feels about terms like spiritual abuse and religious trauma. Does she see them as congruent with her experience? Are these words that speak to what she's endured? Do they feel pathologizing?
- Encourage Violet to choose what she wants to assign meaning to and clarify what she truly values.
- Generally, do not give advice. This may be temporarily frustrating for Violet because she's experiencing distress, but trauma-informed therapy is more focused on helping patients reach their own conclusions.

Attention to Sociocultural Issues

Trauma-informed care also encourages mental health professionals to critically consider how social and cultural factors influence the patient's presenting problems as well as the therapeutic relationship. In cases of religious trauma among nonbelievers, mental health professionals should affirm the nonreligious identity of the patient while also acknowledging the role R/S may have had on their life at one time. Additionally, although the patient may have personally distanced themselves from religion, their existence in a country with Christian dominance likely sparks a variety of feelings. Efforts to bring these feelings to consciousness may reduce intrapsychic conflict and provide the space to reconcile differences between their personal identity and pervasive cultural norms.

Trauma-informed mental health professionals are tasked with the challenging balance between cultural competence and cultural humility. On one hand, practitioners must possess a baseline understanding of R/S issues and nonreligious identity. On the other hand, mental health professionals must have an openness to learn about the patient's unique lived experience and display a willingness to enter their world and discuss cultural topics (Stubbe, 2020). Though discussions about R/S are likely to emerge when interacting with patients who experience religious trauma, mental health professionals may also consider the various social identities the patient holds and how this may have influenced their R/S journey. For example, a Black patient who attended a predominately White church and experienced racism from the pastor must grapple with the intersection of spiritual abuse and racism.

In addition to displaying a willingness to explore the sociocultural aspects of the patient's world, mental health professionals must also explore how they as cultural beings influence the psychotherapy process. I encourage readers to read, reflect on, and journal answers to the following questions:

- How is my perspective on religion influenced by historical and familial events?
- How do I understand harm inflicted on individuals and communities in the name of religion?
- How would it feel to be in a religious community that communicates messages that you are somehow less than others, wrong, or bad?

- Can you imagine how it feels when religious people and groups you have come to love exclude you?

Mental health professionals may also find it helpful to explore their own relationship with R/S through exercises, such as spiritual genograms (Yates & Snodgrass, 2019). Though psychotherapists can never reach a state of total neutrality, they can become more aware of how their biases, assumptions, and lived experiences arise in their clinical work. Increasing this awareness may help them become more effective when working with survivors of spiritual abuse.

Practical Suggestions for Violet's Case:

- Encourage Violet to verbalize what being agnostic means to her.
- Explore how Violet feels about her bisexual identity. Is this influenced by her R/S journey? What was it like for her to conceal it for most of her adult life? What is it like for her to be a divorcée in this community?
- Discuss with Violet how she feels about your social identities as her mental health professional. Does she feel understood?

Closing the Case

Violet's exploratory psychotherapy grounded in trauma-informed principles will continue with her mental health professional. When Violet presented to psychotherapy, she struggled to make meaning and felt abandoned by the community she was raised in. She was experiencing unresolved conflicts related to her spiritual abuse perpetrated by a religious group and her sexual orientation. Psychotherapy will ideally provide Violet with the opportunity to construct a more secure sense of self including her nonreligious identity. She can utilize the therapeutic relationship as a laboratory to experiment with new ways of being, ideally empowering her to form more meaningful relationships that are not contingent on her religiousness or presumed heterosexuality. A trauma-informed psychotherapist can also help Violet explore her hesitancy to hide her feelings and needs from others, by acknowledging the origins of such behaviors, empathizing with what this tendency once provided her, and challenging her to be more direct. Through entering an authentic encounter with a mental health professional, Violet can work through her religious trauma and develop a freer way of being in the world as a nonreligious person.

Conclusion

In this chapter, I provided an overview of religious and spiritual trauma, in hopes to shed light on the overlooked phenomenon that significantly impacts the lives of many patients. I also detailed how nonreligious patients in the United States may be uniquely impacted by religious and spiritual trauma, given the presence of hegemonic Christianity.

Finally, I offered recommendations from existential, psychodynamic, and trauma-informed perspectives to help mental health professionals feel more equipped to work with nonreligious patients experiencing religious and spiritual trauma. My call to mental health professionals is to engage in culturally responsive clinical work that honors the existence of difficult and painful religious experiences while also holding hope in our interactions with nonreligious patients who can go on to live meaningful lives in a more equitable world.

References

Abbott, D. M., Mollen, D., Mercier, C., Anaya, E. J., & Rukus, V. A. (2020). "Isn't atheism a White thing?": Centering the voices of atheists of color. *Journal of Counseling Psychology*, 67(3), 275–87. https://doi.org/10.1037/cou0000399

Barrett-Fox, R. (2016). *God hates: Westboro Baptist Church, American nationalism, and the religious right*. University Press of Kansas.

Beagan, B. L., & Hattie, B. (2015). LGBTQ experiences with religion and spirituality: Occupational transition and adaptation. *Journal of Occupational Science*, 22(4), 459–76. https://doi.org/10.1080/14427591.2014.953670

Blue, K. M. (1993). *Healing spiritual abuse: How to break free from bad church experiences*. InterVarsity Press.

Blumenfeld, W. J., Joshi, K. Y., & Fairchild, E. E. (2008). *Investigating Christian privilege and religious oppression in the United States*. Brill Academic Pub.

Blyth, C., & McRae, P. (2018). "Death by a thousand paper cuts": Transphobia, symbolic violence, and conservative Christian discourse. In C. Blyth, E. Colgan, & K. B. Edwards (Eds.), *Rape culture, gender violence, and religion: Interdisciplinary perspectives* (pp. 111–33). Springer International Publishing. https://doi.org/10.1007/978-3-319-72224-5_7

Bridges, M. R. (2006). Activating the corrective emotional experience. *Journal of Clinical Psychology*, 62(5), 551–68. https://doi.org/10.1002/jclp.20248

Byrne, J. S., Lack, C. W., & Taylor, K. J. (2021). Experiences of the non-religious in psychotherapy: Implications for clinical practice and therapist education. *Secular Studies*, 3(2), 187–205. https://doi.org/10.1163/25892525-bja10023

CBS News (2018, December). *Deconstructing my religion* [Video]. CBS News. https://www.cbsnews.com/video/deconstructing-my-religion/

Childress, S., Shrestha, N., Kenensarieva, K., Urbaeva, J., & Schrag, R. V. (2023). The role of culture in the justification and perpetuation of domestic violence: The perspectives of service providers in Kyrgyzstan. *Violence Against Women*, 30(5), 1198–225. https://doi.org/10.1177/10778012231186814

de Castella, R., & Simmonds, J. G. (2013). "There's a deeper level of meaning as to what suffering's all about": Experiences of religious and spiritual growth following trauma. *Mental Health, Religion & Culture*, 16(5), 536–56. https://doi.org/10.1080/13674676.2012.702738

Dehan, N., & Levi, Z. (2009). Spiritual abuse: An additional dimension of abuse experienced by abused haredi (ultraorthodox) Jewish wives. *Violence Against Women*, 15(11), 1294–1310. https://doi.org/10.1177/1077801209347619

Ellis, H. M., Hook, J. N., Zuniga, S., Hodge, A. S., Ford, K. M., Davis, D. E., & Van Tongeren, D. R. (2022). Religious/spiritual abuse and trauma: A systematic review of the empirical literature. *Spirituality in Clinical Practice*, 9(4), 213–31. https://doi.org/10.1037/scp0000301

Fletcher, J. H. (2017). *The sin of White supremacy: Christianity, racism, and religious diversity in America*. Orbis.

Ginicola, M. M., Filmore, J. M., & Stokes, M. (2017). Working with LGBTQI+ clients who have experienced religious and spiritual abuse using a trauma-informed approach. In M. M. Ginicola, C. Smith, & J. M. Filmore (Eds.), *Affirmative Counseling With LGBTQI+ People* (pp. 329–42). John Wiley & Sons, Ltd. https://doi.org/10.1002/9781119375517.ch24

Gray, A. (2013). *An introduction to the therapeutic frame*. Routledge. https://doi.org/10.4324/9781315882185

Guenther, K. M. (2019). Secular sexism: The persistence of gender inequality in the US New Atheist Movement. *Women's Studies International Forum*, 72(2), 47–55. https://doi.org/10.1016/j.wsif.2018.11.007

Hayward, R. D., Krause, N., Ironson, G., Hill, P. C., & Emmons, R. (2016). Health and well-being among the non-religious: atheists, agnostics, and no preference compared with religious group members. *Journal of Religion and Health*, 55(3), 1024–37. https://doi.org/10.1007/s10943-015-0179-2

Herman, J. (2015). *Trauma and recovery: The aftermath of violence—from domestic abuse to political terror*. Basic Books.

Janoff-Bulman, R. (2010). *Shattered assumptions*. Simon & Schuster.

Johnson, D. R., & VanVonderen, J. (1991). *The subtle power of spiritual abuse*. Bethany House Pub.

LeDrew, S. (2013). Discovering atheism: Heterogeneity in trajectories to atheist identity and activism. *Sociology of Religion*, 74(4), 431–53. https://doi.org/10.1093/socrel/srt014

Lee, K. A., & Gubi, P. M. (2019). Breaking up with Jesus: A phenomenological exploration of the experience of deconversion from an Evangelical Christian faith to Atheism. *Mental Health, Religion & Culture*, 22(2), 171–84. https://doi.org/10.1080/13674676.2019.1623767

Leo, D., Izadikhah, Z., Fein, E. C., & Forooshani, S. A. (2021). The effect of trauma on religious beliefs: A structured literature review and meta-analysis. *Trauma, Violence, & Abuse*, 22(1), 161–75. https://doi.org/10.1177/1524838019834076

Lomash, E. F., Brown, T. D., & Paz Galupo, M. (2019). "A whole bunch of love the sinner hate the sin": LGBTQ microaggressions experienced in religious and spiritual context. *Journal of Homosexuality*, 66(10), 1495–511. https://doi.org/10.1080/00918369.2018.1542204

Lucas, P. C. (2003). Spiritual harm in new religions: Reflection on interviews with former members of NRMs. *Cultic Studies Review*, 2(1), 30–37.

Magaldi-Dopman, D., & Park-Taylor, J. (2010). Sacred adolescence: Practical suggestions for psychologists working with adolescents' religious and spiritual identity. *Professional Psychology: Research and Practice*, 41(5), 382–90. https://doi.org/10.1037/a0020941

Manuti, A., Scardigno, R., & Mininni, G. (2016). Me, myself, and God: Religion as a psychocultural resource of meaning in later life. *Culture & Psychology*, 22(1), 3–34. https://doi.org/10.1177/1354067X14551294

Mart, E. G. (2004). Victims of abuse by priests: Some preliminary observations. *Pastoral Psychology*, 52(6), 465–72. https://doi.org/10.1023/B:PASP.0000031524.23793.bf

Moreira-Almeida, A., Lotufo Neto, F., & Koenig, H. G. (2006). Religiousness and mental health: A review. *Brazilian Journal of Psychiatry*, 28, 242–50. https://doi.org/10.1590/S1516-44462006005000006

Nadal, K. L. (2018). *Microaggressions and traumatic stress: Theory, research, and clinical treatment*. American Psychological Association. https://doi.org/10.1037/0000073-000

Oakley, L., Kinmond, K., & Blundell, P. (2024). Responding well to Spiritual Abuse: Practice implications for counselling and psychotherapy. *British Journal of Guidance & Counselling*, 52(2), 189–206. https://doi.org/10.1080/03069885.2023.2283883

Pereda, N., & Segura, A. (2021). Child sexual abuse within the Roman Catholic Church in Spain: A descriptive study of abuse characteristics, victims' faith, and spirituality. *Psychology of Violence*, 11(5), 488–96. https://doi.org/10.1037/vio0000390

Pew Research Center. (2024). Religious "nones" in America: Who they are and what they believe. https://www.pewresearch.org/religion/2024/01/24/religious-nones-in-america-who-they-are-and-what-they-believe/

Raine, S., & Kent, S. A. (2019). The grooming of children for sexual abuse in religious settings: Unique characteristics and select case studies. *Aggression and Violent Behavior*, 48, 180–89. https://doi.org/10.1016/j.avb.2019.08.017

Sheard, M. (2014). Ninety-eight atheists: Atheism among the non-elite in twentieth century Britain. *Secularism and Nonreligion*, 3(0), 1–66. https://doi.org/10.5334/snr.ar

Stevens, J. M., Arzoumanian, M. A., Greenbaum, B., Schwab, B. M., & Dalenberg, C. J. (2019). Relationship of abuse by religious authorities to depression, religiosity, and child physical abuse history in a college sample. *Psychological Trauma: Theory, Research, Practice, and Policy*, 11(3), 292–99. https://doi.org/10.1037/tra0000421

Stone, A. M. (2013). Thou shalt not: Treating religious trauma and spiritual harm with combined therapy. *Group*, 37(4), 323–37. https://doi.org/10.13186/group.37.4.0323

Stubbe, D. E. (2020). Practicing cultural competence and cultural humility in the care of diverse patients. *FOCUS*, 18(1), 49–51. https://doi.org/10.1176/appi.focus.20190041

Substance Abuse and Mental Health Services Administration. (2023). Practical guide for implementing a trauma-informed approach. https://store.samhsa.gov/sites/default/files/pep23-06-05-005.pdf

Super, J. T., & Jacobson, L. (2011). Religious abuse: implications for counseling lesbian, gay, bisexual, and transgender individuals. *Journal of LGBT Issues in Counseling*, 5(3–4), 180–96. https://doi.org/10.1080/15538605.2011.632739

Swan, L. K., & Heesacker, M. (2012). Anti-atheist bias in the United States: Testing two critical assumptions. *Secularism and Nonreligion*, 1, 32–42. https://doi.org/10.5334/snr.ac

Swindle, P. J. (2017). A twisting of the sacred: The lived experience of religious abuse (Publication No. 10264116). [Doctoral dissertation, The University of North Carolina at Greensboro.] Proquest Dissertation and Theses Global. https://www.proquest.com/docview/1927630238/abstract/BE62E9BF76C413FPQ/1

Tobin, T. W. (2019). Religious faith in the unjust meantime: The spiritual violence of clergy sexual abuse. *Feminist Philosophy Quarterly*, 5(2), 1–29. https://doi.org/10.5206/fpq/2019.2.7290

U.S. Const. amend. I

Ward, D. J. (2011). The lived experience of spiritual abuse. *Mental Health, Religion & Culture*, 14(9), 899–915. https://doi.org/10.1080/13674676.2010.536206

Weber, S. R., Pargament, K. I., Kunik, M. E., Lomax, J. W., & Stanley, M. A. (2012). Psychological distress among religious nonbelievers: A systematic review. *Journal of Religion and Health*, 51(1), 72–86. https://doi.org/10.1007/s10943-011-9541-1

Whitford, D. M. (2016). *The curse of Ham in the early modern era: The Bible and the justifications for slavery*. Routledge. https://doi.org/10.4324/9781315240367

Winell, M. (2011, May). Religious trauma syndrome: It's time to recognise it. *CBT Today*, 39(2), 16–18.

Yates, J., & Snodgrass, J. L. (2019). The religious locations of LGBTQ+ survivors: Survivors of Christian nonsexual spiritual abuse. In J. L. Snodgrass (Ed.), *Navigating Religious Difference in Spiritual Care and Counseling* (Vol. 2, pp. 251–80). Claremont Press. https://doi.org/10.2307/j.ctvwrm4c3.18

Zaeske, L. M., Dye, A. R., Spadoni, S., Strothkamp, R., Kane, M. L., Ridgway, K., Dugan, A. J., Patterson, T. P., McEathron, S. R., & Cole, B. P. (2024). Addressing harm from adverse religious/spiritual experiences in psychotherapy: A scoping review. *Practice Innovations*, 9(1), 1–18. https://doi.org/10.1037/pri0000237.

13

Secularity and Substance Use Treatment

Teagan M. Wilson

Chapter Outline

To understand substance use and evaluate current treatment options for substance use disorders, it is critical to recognize the interplay of substance use and mental health specifically in the context of cultural religious dominance and related discrimination and stigma against nonreligious individuals. Given that discrimination negatively impacts mental health (Meyer, 2003; Pascoe & Smart Richman, 2009; Paradies, 2006) and that mental health and substance use frequently go hand in hand (Flynn & Brown, 2008; Watkins et al., 2001), it is important to be cognizant of how religious discrimination within substance use treatment settings may negatively impact nonreligious clients. Likewise, such awareness can help clinicians and researchers develop and recommend more culturally appropriate treatments for nonreligious individuals who experience substance use disorders (SUDs).

The importance of understanding SUDs and their treatment in the United States (US) has become increasingly imperative as drug overdose deaths increased between

2001 and 2021 (Spencer et al., 2022) driven, in part, by an increase in opioid addiction. Opioid-related deaths were the cause of 70.6 percent of all drug overdose deaths in 2019 and 81.8 percent of all drug overdose deaths in 2022 (Centers for Disease Control and Prevention, 2023; 2024b). In particular, substance use substantially increased during the early years of the COVID-19 pandemic as people were socially isolated and used substances to cope with depressive and anxious symptoms, as well as unemployment and other stressors (Roberts et al., 2021). People who engaged in substance use were, and still are, at a greater risk for developing COVID-19 and increased risk of complications from COVID-19, among other health risks that correlate with substance use (Mellos & Paparrigopoulos, 2022). Substance misuse can negatively impact an individual's nutrition and sleep quality, increase risk for experiencing violence or trauma, increase risk of contracting communicable diseases like HIV and hepatitis C, and increase pregnancy and birth complications for those carrying pregnancies (U.S. Department of Health and Human Services (HHS), Office of the Surgeon General 2016).

The American Psychological Association defines addiction as "a state of psychological and/or physical dependence on the use of drugs or other substances, such as alcohol, or on activities or behaviors . . . such as sex, exercise, and gambling" (American Psychological Association, n.d.). Currently, the *Diagnostic and Statistical Manual of Mental Disorders* (DSM-5) has four general groups of symptoms within Criterion A associated with SUDs including impaired control over use of the substance, social impairment, risky behaviors, and pharmacological criteria (American Psychiatric Association, 2022). Clinicians are able to specify the severity as mild (2–3 symptoms), moderate (4–5 symptoms), or severe (6 or more symptoms) (American Psychiatric Association, 2022). While the DSM-5 does not use the term "addiction" diagnostically, other organizations and individuals still use it when discussing substance use. The switch from using the term "addiction" to "substance use disorder" was intentional and meant to replace a stigmatized, and less defined, phrase with something more neutral (American Psychiatric Association, 2022).

Trends in Substance Use

Although substance use and substance use disorders (SUDs) are more common among men, the gender gap in SUDs is shrinking as the prevalence of substance use is increasing in women (McHugh et al., 2018). Men are more likely to drink alcohol compared to women but also engage in binge drinking (four drinks in one sitting for women, five drinks in one sitting for men) at higher rates than women (Centers for Disease Control and Prevention, 2025). Compared to women, men are more likely to engage in illicit drug use (including marijuana as it is still criminalized at the federal level) but women may be more susceptible to relapse in recovery (National Institute on Drug Abuse, 2022). Overall, men have higher rates of substance use across age demographics and most substances with the exception that girls and women aged 12 to 20 years use alcohol and binge drink at a higher rate than boys and men of the same age and high school girls are more likely to misuse prescribed opiates compared to high school boys (National Institute on Drug Abuse, 2022; Jones et al., 2020).

Most government reported statistics on substance use focus on gender as a binary and thus miss important data about the trends of substance use and overdoses for sexual and gender minority (SGM) individuals. The Trevor Project found that LGBTQ youth were more likely than their straight and cisgender high school counterparts to engage in alcohol or marijuana use and LGBTQ youth who did engage in substance use were more likely to experience a suicide attempt (Trevor Project, 2022). Those who experience SGM-related victimization are also at an increased risk of hazardous drug and alcohol use, which further indicates that substances may be used as a coping mechanism for those who experience distal stressors (Hinds et al., 2024).

Substance use disorders often co-occur with other psychiatric disorders, referred to as dual diagnosis. Research specifically around dual diagnoses is relatively new, beginning in 1990, as the comorbidity of two diagnoses was a reason to exclude this group from previous research (Adan & Benaiges, 2016). Therefore, much historical SUD treatment does not account for potential comorbidity despite over one third, 36.5 percent, of adults with a substance use disorder meeting criteria for another mental health diagnosis (Jegede et al., 2022). In turn, even mental health professionals working outside of primary SUD treatment are likely to see clients with comorbid substance use concerns.

Given the increase in substance use overdoses and deaths, it is important for mental health professionals to continue working to understand how to best support those with SUDs. Religion and spirituality have long played an integral part in addiction treatment and support in the United States (Weinandy & Grubbs, 2021). Although there is evidence of addiction and attempts to treat addictions that trace back centuries (Nathan et al., 2016), classification of addiction began in the nineteenth century (Robinson & Adinoff, 2016), and our modern medical approach to treatment began in the 1950s when the American Psychiatric Association first recognized alcoholism and drug addiction in *DSM*-1 (Robinson & Adinoff, 2016). Alcoholics Anonymous (AA) was founded in 1935 by Bill Wilson and Bob Smith, which helped popularize the belief that alcoholism was a disease (Kurtz, 2002).

History of Substance Use

Humans have long engaged in substance use in order to derive positive feelings and euphoria. Opium can be traced back to 5000 BCE in present day Turkey, and later to Greece, Rome, and the Middle East where it was used to treat pain, physical ailments, and induce feelings of pleasure (Presley & Lindsley, 2018; Olsen, 2022). Cannabis can also be traced back millennia and has been used for a variety of reasons, including inflammation, antibiotic, tranquilizer, and pain reliever among other uses (Zuardi, 2006). While there were many medical uses for cannabis, the first recreational uses can be traced back to 2700 BCE when the Chinese ingested the substance for fun (Earleywine, 2002).

Around 7000 BCE humans began making alcoholic beverages, though it is likely that humans consumed alcohol through fermented fruits long before that (Phillips, 2014). Although alcohol had nutritional and medicinal uses, like as an anesthetic, its consumption was also closely tied to religious and spiritual beliefs (Mäkela, 1983). Alcohol has been associated with a variety of religions over centuries and played important roles symbolic to each respective religion. Different religions have had varied outlooks on substances; some viewed substances as neutral or a way to be closer to their god(s) whereas other religions viewed substances as something to be avoided. While these views have changed and the legality of some substances impacts their consumption, religious influence on substance use and addiction is still felt in modern society.

Impact of Substance Use on Individuals, Families, and Communities

Substance use has important implications for both the individual and society. Historically, the criminalization of drugs has racist and religious roots. The criminalization of specific drugs in the United States can be traced back to xenophobia and racism associated with erroneous, stereotypical relationships between groups of people and certain substances. For example, marijuana began to be targeted by legislation in the southwest United States as its use became associated with Mexicans and the concurrent growing Mexican immigrant population at the time (Johnstad, 2023). Johnstad (2023) also noted that substances that had not been part of European culture were seen as illicit whereas substances engrained in European history, like alcohol, were not seen as illicit. That said, religion did come to influence even the legality of alcohol during the Prohibition era. Society has slowly shifted from viewing substance use and addiction as a criminal justice problem to viewing it as a public health problem. This shift comes, in part, from increased public awareness of addiction and reduced stigma, which helped the public understand addiction as a treatable disorder rather than a criminal offense (Volkow et al., 2017).

The impact of substance use on communities can show up in lost productivity at work, increased strain on health care systems, and disrupted job continuity among those with SUDs. The Centers for Disease Control and Prevention (CDC) reported that alcohol use alone cost the United States $249 billion in 2010, the most recent year of data available (Centers for Disease Control and Prevention, 2024a). The *Surgeon General's Report on Alcohol, Drugs, and Health* estimated that substance use and substance use disorders cost the United States $442 billion annually due to lost productivity, health care costs, and criminal justice costs (U.S. Department of Health and Human Services [HHS], Office of the Surgeon General 2016). While communities and the economy as a whole face significant impacts of addiction, individuals and families are left coping with the direct impact of addiction.

The impact of substance use on families varies depending on who in the family struggles with addiction. For example, the impact of a child with an SUD will impact the family unit differently from a parent with an SUD. Substance use can impact family dynamics, attachment styles, family income, abuse and neglect, as well as legal concerns (Lander et al., 2013). Children of a parent with an SUD are also at increased risk of developing an SUD themselves as well as experiencing higher rates of mental health concerns, academic underachievement, and behavioral concerns (Velleman & Templeton, 2016).

History of Religiosity and Substance Use

Religion has also long played a role in how society views people with substance use disorders, characterizing addiction as morally bad, or a sign someone has strayed from god (Lyons et al., 2013). Even the Prohibition era in the 1920s and 1930s stemmed from a religious belief that people should fully abstain from alcohol use, which was sinful (Weinandy & Grubbs, 2021). This movement began in Protestant churches in the United States that first encouraged moderation but later advocated successfully for governments to prohibit alcohol. Through successfully integrating religious beliefs and values into US law, Protestant Christians wielded influence and, in turn, religious morality became part of American policy (Locke, 2021).

The goal of the Prohibition movement was to protect individuals and society from the consequences of alcohol use; however, it also forced a religious interpretation of morality on the public. Addiction was primarily viewed as a moral issue and a choice in the first half of the 1900s (Pickard, 2017). Assigning morality to substance use, specifically considering individuals with SUDs as lacking in their religiosity, impacted the care and treatment available to individuals with SUDs. Traits like selfishness and laziness were ascribed to individuals with SUDs, addiction was seen as a character flaw, and blame was placed on individuals for their addiction, which validated society's harsh treatment toward substance users (Pickard, 2017).

In the mid-twentieth century, the medical and health professions community began to shift to a disease model of addiction and/or biopsychosocial models. The disease model of addiction emphasizes the idea that addiction is a chronic condition that often results from changes in brain functioning and acknowledges the influence of biological and genetic factors. The disease model of addiction helped shift attitudes about the immorality of addiction to an understanding that those with addictions were deserving of treatment and respect (Blume et al., 2013). In 1977, a biopsychosocial model also emerged and was integrated into conceptual models of addiction, acknowledging sociocultural, biological, and genetic factors as contributors to a person's health. This model includes a biological/medical component; however, it does not prioritize the biological as more significant than other components including psychological and environmental impacts that are also factors in addiction and should be considered in the treatment of SUDs (Skewes & Gonzalez, 2013).

Over time, and specifically since the early 2000s, the number of people who identify as nonreligious has risen, with 16 percent to 23 percent of adults in the United States identifying as nonreligious and a higher percentage (33 percent) of adults thirty years old or younger, identifying as nonreligious (Sahker, 2016). Mental health practice has a history of secularly based treatment, and separation between clinical practice and religion. By contrast, religiosity, specifically Christianity, has deep roots in the history of substance use treatment and addiction (Brewster et al., 2014). Treatment for addiction is situated at a unique intersection between mental health treatment and religion as AA was founded years before the DSM recognized addiction as a disorder. At that time, it was categorized as a "personality disturbance" and viewed as antisocial behavior (Norko & Fitch, 2014). With a rise in the number of individuals who identify as nonreligious, it is necessary to understand the role of religion and spirituality in SUD treatment and how secular treatment options may better align with nonreligious worldviews.

Previous studies of religiosity, substance use, and recovery have typically used measures that assume participants endorse some level of religiosity or spirituality, where participants are not able to endorse absolutely zero belief in god (Tonigan et al., 2002). Given the number of adults who identify as nonreligious, including atheists, agnostics, and those who identify their religion as "nothing in particular," is increasing (see chapter 2 of this volume), it is necessary that measures of substance use accurately capture the identities and attitudes of participants.

Treatment for SUDs

Minnesota Model

One of the most common addiction treatment models is the Minnesota Model (MM) which combines the disease model with spiritually based Alcoholics Anonymous (Blume et al., 2013). Because the disease model positions addiction as "incurable," treatment centers based in MM looked to other sources outside of the medical community and saw success within AA groups. Accordingly, they integrated AA's 12-step program into their own treatment model with the intention to strike a more balanced, holistic approach to addiction and substance use (Blume et al., 2013). It is common practice for inpatient addiction treatment programs to follow the Minnesota Model. Currently, treatment centers still heavily rely on religion and spirituality as a component of treatment with 65 percent of treatment centers in the United States integrating the 12-step program from Alcoholics Anonymous into their programs for substance use (Brooks & McHenry, 2023). Given the emphasis on spirituality in this model, it is unclear the degree to which such treatment is effective with nonreligious patients.

Alcoholics Anonymous

Alcoholics Anonymous is a mutual aid fellowship that uses an abstinence based approach to recovery from alcohol. The founders created the 12-step program within AA and the organization emphasizes anonymity in meetings. Alcoholics Anonymous describes its organization as "spiritual" rather than "religious" and a large component of groups and the twelve steps are rooted in faith in a higher power. Research has consistently demonstrated that AA and integrating spirituality components into treatment programs for substance use can be beneficial for participants who identify as religious (Krentzman, 2008). This aligns with other research around religiosity, which shows that religious individuals can experience positive effects from religiosity but atheists, or those who do not believe in god(s), experience negative impacts on health when they engage in high levels of religiosity due to an incongruence with their atheistic worldview (Speed & Fowler, 2016).

Attending AA has been found to be associated with increased abstinence and reduced drinking; however, nonreligious individuals are less likely to attend AA groups and its effectiveness with this group is unclear (Tonigan et al., 2002). Nonreligious individuals are often expected by treatment programs or the courts that mandate their treatment to integrate themselves into AA groups and spiritual components of substance use treatment though it may be to their detriment. In fact, incongruence with the spiritual components of AA or disbelief in god are reasons individuals have stopped attending AA meetings (Kelly et al., 2010). As research continues to frame religiosity as a strength in recovery (and hence implies nonreligion is a barrier), it is logical that AA continues to be seen as the gold standard for community support groups and a viable part of treatment that can be integrated into mental health programs.

Other 12-Step Programs

Many other 12-step programs and fellowships have been structured based on AA including Narcotics Anonymous (NA) and Gamblers Anonymous (GA). Fellowships inspired by AA may change terminology to fit the behavior or substance of concern for members but maintain a focus on a higher power and sometimes even use the "Big Book," a foundational AA text. While these other 12-step groups focus on a range of concerns from other substances to behaviors like clutter, gambling, or co-dependence, they are subject to similar critique as AA as they deem it necessary to admit powerlessness over their problem and surrender control to god or another higher power (Dossett, 2013).

The Problem with Current Models

Practitioner Bias

Given the criminalization of substance use in the United States, the criminal justice system is often involved in decisions about the treatment of individuals with substance use disorders. Attending AA groups can often be a requirement either of probation and parole, or outpatient treatment programs (Hibbard & Sheidow, 2024). This results in many individuals being forced into religion-based organizations when secular alternatives are not available. For example, in 2007, parole officers required Barry Hazle to participate in

AA as approved secular options were not available and when Hazle, who identified as an atheist, refused to participate he was arrested and returned to prison for a hundred days due to violating his parole (Grudzina, 2016). Although the US Court of Appeals, Ninth Circuit ruled in favor of Hazle under the First Amendment, this is an all-too-common situation for nonbelievers in the criminal justice system given how intertwined AA, and as a result spirituality, is with treatment programs. When substance use treatment is mandated by the criminal justice system and nonreligious programs are not available, it harms nonreligious people's recovery as they are forced to integrate into a religious program. This can be detrimental to their progress in recovery as inability to fully integrate is viewed negatively by other members and mentors.

Given that a majority of inpatient treatment programs follow the Minnesota Model, which is heavily influenced by AA, the perception of the role of religion is important to understand. Novotná and colleagues (2013) found that employees of substance use treatment centers were biased toward their lived experiences over evidence-based research. As many counselors and employees of substance use treatment centers have direct personal or family experience(s) with addiction, many cited AA as beneficial to their or their loved ones' recovery. This poses a problem for nonreligious individuals who may not benefit from including AA in their recovery if counselors are biased toward the belief that AA is a necessary component of recovery. When service providers had lived experiences with 12-step models for addiction, they were also more likely to use a 12-step model in their provision of treatment and less likely to use other treatment options including relapse prevention medication, contingency management, and motivational interviewing techniques (Novotná et al., 2013). When counselors or treatment managers make decisions based on their own lived experiences, they negate the fact that clients have diverse needs and may not recognize when other treatment options are more appropriate.

Incongruent Values

Even though many clinicians, treatment programs, and the criminal justice system recommend or require AA for individuals with substance use concerns, the religious component of AA seems to be a barrier for many people. Laudet (2003) found that the religious component of AA groups was viewed as an obstacle to engagement by over half of the clinicians and half of the clients that took part in a study of attitudes toward 12-step programs to identify obstacles to participation. In fact, participants who attended AA reported they dropped out shortly after first attendance due to the focus on spirituality, powerlessness, and a higher power (Laudet, 2003).

Although Alcoholics Anonymous describes its organization as spiritual, the book *Alcoholics Anonymous*, colloquially known as the "Big Book," explicitly states that atheists and agnostics must find a power greater than themselves (Alcoholics Anonymous, 2001). A core belief of AA is that sobriety cannot be achieved without giving up control to god (or a higher power), which inherently contradicts nonreligiousness and a core component of atheism, the rejection and/or absence of belief in god (Alcoholics Anonymous, 2001; Brewster et al., 2014). This then implies that nonbelievers will not be able to recover without adopting some level of spirituality, or belief in the supernatural, and believing in something "bigger" than themselves.

There is an expectation that nonreligious individuals can adapt to the spiritual component of substance use treatment often being told that god can be anything, "even a doorknob" (Thatcher, 2011). However, this is just another example of atheists being told to create meaning even though for some nonbelievers creating meaning or power outside themselves does not align with their worldview or values. Nonreligiousness in AA is often viewed as a barrier to sobriety and without finding a higher power, participants are viewed as unable to "work the program" (Munro, 2019). With limited, or often no other options, members of AA have described ways they tried to incorporate god into their nonbelief with one member stating,

> I spent decades trying to get God. I mean, I tried so many different ways to bring God into my life. . . . They would say make anything your higher power, it can be your lightbulb. So, I would lay in bed and look at the lightbulb trying to imagine a higher power. . . . I just kept trying and trying and never getting any feeling that it was working. Ever. (Munro, 2019, p. 202)

Social Support Challenges

Proponents of AA argue that fellowship, communication, and support from others is a significant, positive aspect of recovery (Laudet et al., 2003). Indeed, (non)religious studies support the notion that community and belongingness are healthy and drive well-being among religious and nonreligious people alike (Galen, 2015). Although the United States is an overwhelmingly individualistic society, the need for social support is paramount in building physical and mental wellness (Laudet et al., 2006). Specifically with individuals with SUDs, increased social support is correlated with less substance use and lower levels of social support is predictive of relapse (Nikmanesh et al., 2017). The positive benefits of social support are also found among individuals with other mental health diagnoses. This is especially relevant to individuals with dual diagnoses of SUDs and other mental illnesses, where overall well-being and quality of life are important aspects of recovery (Laudet et al., 2006).

When AA, and programs that integrate or follow AA structure into their treatment like the Minnesota Model, do not recognize or encourage other ways to find that community, nonreligious individuals face continued barriers to their recovery. A central aspect of AA groups and treatment programs is creating social support, finding a sense of belonging among similar others, and fighting isolation that often accompanies addiction (Wallace, 2012). However, when nonreligious individuals attend AA or spirituality is integrated into their treatment, they often face decisions around whether or not to disclose their nonreligious identity and may not find belonging among peers because they feel out of place. The inability to live authentically can lead to feelings of disconnection from others, hopelessness, and despair, all consequences that would work against an individual's journey toward recovery and the purpose AA is supposed to serve (Menzies & Davidson, 2002).

Atheism as a Stigmatized Identity

Atheism and nonreligiousness is a concealable stigmatized identity (CSI), so individuals who identify as nonreligious can choose if and when to disclose this identity to others. Atheism is perceived negatively in the United States, with atheists facing discrimination and being ascribed negative characteristics like immorality, untrustworthiness, and anger (Abbott & Mollen, 2018). Not only do atheists face health consequences from anti-atheist discrimination, the concealment of an identity is also a contributor to negative physical and mental wellness (Abbott & Mollen, 2018; Brewster et al., 2016). When an identity, like atheism, is concealable, individuals have to consider factors like anticipated stigma and others' responses to their disclosure. Those with CSIs, like atheism, may be more likely to conceal that identity if they perceive more bias toward them (Abbott & Mollen, 2018). This is likely a common scenario for nonreligious individuals in spiritual settings, especially when that spirituality is tied to their perceived ability to pursue and maintain recovery. Quinn and colleagues (2014) found that anticipated stigma and salience of the CSI were predictive of higher distress levels. With 40 percent of Americans in one survey indicating negative attitudes toward atheists, it is not surprising that nonreligious individuals are weary about how disclosing their identity will impact them or their interactions with others. This same study also found that higher general factor scores on the Measure of Atheist Discrimination Experiences (MADE) was associated with loneliness and psychological distress (Brewster et al., 2016).

In the context of treatment programs that center spirituality, nonreligion becomes a central aspect of one's identity as the absence of belief is directly related to their ability to participate fully and authentically in treatment. The decision to disclose a nonreligious identity may feel risky when someone attends AA groups or spirituality is a part of their treatment as they do not know the response they will receive from others or if it may impact the successful completion of their program. Munro (2019) reported that participants who resisted the religious/spiritual components of AA reported experiences of being told their disbelief in god or a higher power was just their reluctance to quit drinking and relapses were viewed as evidence the individual needed to accept god. In the same study, participants reported feelings of self-doubt as they began to second guess their own commitment to recovery as a result of being told their nonreligiousness was a symptom of their addiction.

Given that a core aspect of AA is the creation of community with other members, Munro (2019) found that nonreligious members of AA reported being unsure if they could share their difficulties with the "higher power" aspect of AA as it may isolate them from the rest of the group. Participants noted that when they shared their struggle with other AA members, those members used it as an opportunity to share how they themselves were only able to achieve sobriety with the help of a higher power or by "finding God" (Munro, 2019), thus invalidating their challenge.

One of the major negative stereotypes attributed to atheists is immorality, that because a person does not believe in a god(s), they are inherently immoral, and through this lack of a moral compass, atheists are perceived as more likely to engage in immoral acts like substance use (Brewster et al., 2016). This belief directly aligns with the belief in SUD treatment programs and AA that one must find a higher power in order to achieve sobriety or refusal to incorporate spirituality into an individual's personal treatment is seen as resistance to treatment (Munro, 2019). This pressure to be seen as compliant with treatment and engaged in sobriety leads to pressure to pass as religious, a common experience among nonreligious people (Brewster et al., 2016). While these are messages that atheists may receive in any context, there is increased pressure to conform to religious standards in substance use treatment as there often are not secular alternatives. AA continuously states that its groups are not religious, they are spiritual, and treatment programs will advertise that they have a spiritual rather than religious component to their programs. However, this is meant to be inclusive of a multitude of religions not inclusive of nonreligiousness (Laudet, 2003). When atheists are coerced or feel forced to "go along" with integrating god or a higher power into their treatment, that is an explicit experience of discrimination due to their nonreligiousness.

Research continues to focus on religion as a protective factor in substance use treatment, erroneously suggesting that the absence of religion is a deficit to well-being (Speed et al., 2018; Weinandy & Grubbs, 2021). It is unsurprising, then, that when health providers, and society, view nonreligion as a deficit rather than a valid worldview, there is pressure for everyone, including the nonreligious, to participate in the spiritual components of substance use treatment. From this deficit-focused approach, there is an assumption that something is lacking in atheists' lives, for example, assuming that atheists with avoidant attachment in childhood continue this attachment style with god (Caldwell-Harris et al., 2011). Research on SUDs and treatment tends to attribute improved well-being, mental health, and prosocial behaviors to religiosity and frame religion as being beneficial to recovery (Munro, 2019), much like broader research on religion and health (see chapter 5 of this volume). This type of research, without including the unique strengths of nonreligion or secular treatment approaches, reiterates to health professionals and the general public that religion is a necessary component of recovery. However, it is important for the field to begin to shift toward a strengths-based perspective when working with nonreligious folks who bring their own positive attributes to the table.

A Multicultural and Strengths-Based View of Nonreligion

Although atheism and nonbelief have historically been viewed through a deficit lens and face continued marginalization in the United States (Bishop, 2018), nonreligion also leads to the development of positive attributes that facilitate health and well-being. Compared to religious people, research on strengths among nonreligious people is minimal and often compares nonreligious people with religious people rather than centering the nonreligious experience (Hayward et al., 2016). However, emerging evidence suggests atheists possess a multitude of strengths and positive characteristics including feelings of authenticity and liberation, being open-minded, feminist, independent, introverted, and nondogmatic (Abbott & Santiago, 2023; Brewster et al., 2014). The discrimination and stereotypes faced by atheists in US culture combined with an absence of science focused on nonreligious mental health significantly impacts the type of care available to nonreligious people and the ability of healthcare professionals to capitalize on their unique strengths.

It is important that mental health professionals make available alternative therapeutic treatment options for nonreligious clients. Therapists are in a unique position to advocate for more appropriate treatment that aligns with clients' beliefs and practice cultural competence in the therapeutic space. Even though a higher percentage of therapists identify as nonreligious as compared to the general population, there is still work to be done on understanding best practices for nonreligious clients (Mintert et al., 2020). Research around multicultural competence in psychotherapy training and practice has historically focused on diversity across religions and is not inclusive of nonreligion (Abbott, 2021).

In building multicultural competence, therapists can work to better understand how belief systems impact their personal worldview and respond with interventions that do not impose religion or spirituality on nonreligious clients. Competency in working with nonreligious clients includes honoring differences without making generalizations about how nonreligion impacts the client's belief systems (D'Andrea & Sprenger, 2007). D'Andrea and Sprenger (2007) asserted it is also important to validate experiences of nonreligious people including experiences of discrimination and feelings of isolation due to their nonreligion. Given isolation and discrimination arise when engaged in SUD treatment that does not align with one's worldview, mental health professionals in treatment settings that utilize spiritually based interventions could specifically validate identified incongruence between care clients receive and their worldview. Counselors should also integrate the concept of personal autonomy into the therapy; this can include empowerment, self-determination, and personal choice rather than imposing meaning (D'Andrea & Sprenger, 2007).

Alternatives to Alcoholics Anonymous

SMART Recovery

Other treatment options for nonreligious clients that do not require relinquishing control to or finding a higher power are available, though less frequently utilized as compared to AA/12-step models. Self-Management and Recovery Training (SMART Recovery) is a program that is explicitly nonreligious and an alternative to Alcoholics Anonymous and other programs that integrate a 12-step program. Principles of SMART Recovery include self-management, or positioning the client as in charge of their own behaviors, mutual support, emphasizing connecting with and learning from peers, and choice to establish their own goals (SMART Recovery International, 2024). SMART Recovery uses evidence-based practices including cognitive behavioral therapy (CBT) and motivational interviewing (Horvath & Yeterian, 2012).

SMART Recovery groups are led by trained facilitators (rather than volunteers with lived experience), though facilitators may or may not have lived experience in addition to their training. SMART Recovery groups follow the same general structure of AA with check in, group discussion, donations, and review lasting about ninety minutes in total. The CBT aspect of SMART Recovery groups is utilized to build motivation to change behaviors, learn to cope with urges and cravings, manage thoughts, feelings, and behaviors, and learn to live a balanced life (Horvath & Velten, 2000). Whereas AA focuses on alcohol use, SMART Recovery is inclusive of all substance use concerns as well as behavioral addictions like gambling (Kelly et al., 2024). As individuals who participate in these groups are in charge of setting their own individual goals, members do not have to be working toward abstinence but can choose to work toward reduction of their use or behavior (e.g., harm reduction; Kelly et al., 2024).

Individuals who have an internal locus of control, or the sense that they have control over the outcome of events in their life, may be more drawn to SMART Recovery, compared to 12-step programs where there is an external locus of control (e.g., higher power). SMART Recovery emphasizes the principle that individuals can learn tools and skills to manage their addiction and have an active, rather than passive, part in their own recovery (Horvath & Yeterian, 2012). Nonreligious people tend to have stronger analytic thinking rather than more intuitive cognitive processes (Ståhl & van Prooijen, 2021). This pull toward analytic thinking among atheists may be a good foundation to build on using evidence-based therapy. As nonreligious people tend to align more with concepts of empowerment, self-determination, and personal choice, this active role in SMART Recovery programs may be more aligned with the worldviews of nonreligious people compared to the more passive stance of 12-step programs (D'Andrea & Sprenger, 2007; Horvath & Yeterian, 2012). Given that the spiritual component of AA groups is a factor in people never attending and early attrition, the self-empowerment aspect of SMART Recovery may be a more appealing alternative for those looking for mutual aid groups in their community.

AA groups and treatment programs that integrate the 12-step program are so widely recommended because they have been shown to be effective in a multitude of studies (Fiorentine, 1999; Kelly et al., 2020; Winters et al., 2000). Although they may be effective for those who find spirituality to be an important component of their recovery, it is important to continue to research their efficacy with nonreligious participants as well as the efficacy of other secular programs to ensure nonreligious individuals have options that align with their beliefs. In early study, SMART Recovery has been shown to be effective in participants being able to maintain recovery; though longitudinal studies are still in exploratory stages, these results suggest that secular options can provide the same benefits as spiritual programs (Kelly et al., 2023).

Although most research that is conducted on mutual help groups focuses almost entirely on spiritual groups, understanding the role secular groups can have in society is important in showing the need to broaden research perspectives. SMART Recovery in Australia was shown to reduce reconviction rates among those who participated in the programs, although the study did not examine effects it had on substance use (Kelly et al., 2023). While more comprehensive research needs to be conducted on the efficacy of SMART Recovery to ensure best practice is being implemented, participants and facilitators have reported aspects of the group they find helpful. Kelly and colleagues (2017) found that both participants and facilitators of SMART Recovery groups found the interactive experience of the group, building tools and strategies to cope with SUD, and focus on the present as the most helpful components of the groups. By incorporating these aspects into the program, there is a focus on building participants' strengths and being able to work with a wide range of addiction concerns (Kelly et al., 2017). This same study found that while participants were satisfied with the program overall, there was also desire for an increase of, and update to, tools for participants.

LifeRing

LifeRing Secular Recovery, a peer-run, secular nonprofit that holds meetings across the country and online, differs from other 12-step programs in that it does not use mentors, but rather focuses on peer connection and the individual being their own expert; it focuses on the present moment rather than harm that has been caused in the past, unlike AA's requirement that participants make amends for past wrongs (LifeRing, 2024). Like SMART Recovery, LifeRing is not just for alcohol use concerns and is a secular organization. Importantly, though the program is secular, it is appropriate for nonreligous and religious participants and 40 percent of Lifering's members attend religious services. LifeRing was founded in 1997 and along with other mutual support groups outside of AA, attendance has grown in the last twenty years with 75 percent of attendance for these groups occurring since 2000 (Bergman et al., 2024). While AA is still one of the most attended groups and, due to its long-standing history, one of the first to be recommended to those with SUDs, in a 2010 survey, 34 percent of individuals who identified themselves as previously having misused alcohol reported they had attended a mutual support group that was not AA (Zemore et al., 2017). This suggests there is demand for more groups outside of AA, including secularly based groups using evidence-based practices.

Many of these modalities can be adapted for use in individual therapy and/or group therapy; however, peer-to-peer interaction is an important component of substance use treatment and secular options are vital to ensuring nonreligious individuals have access to groups that align with their nonbelief systems and, potentially, include members with similar values and/or nonbelief. Mutual help groups provide the opportunity for shared lived experiences, building social support, and structure. Mutual support groups also tend to offer flexibility and accessibility in the sense that they can occur in person or virtually, are held at various times of day, and are often free of cost (Kelly et al., 2024). Individuals attend these groups for a variety of reasons like mentorship, structure, and learning coping skills; however, many cite the community and the interactive features of these groups as a reason for continued attendance (Laudet, 2003). These mutual support groups are often vital parts of community care that help increase access to support while reducing health care costs for communities and individuals (Kelly et al., 2024; Laudet, 2003); practitioners and others involved in SUD treatment should consider nonreligious alternatives to AA as options for mutual support groups.

Alternative Approaches to SUDs Treatment

Secularly based therapies incorporating behavioral interventions have also been found to be effective in working with SUDs including Acceptance and Commitment Therapy (ACT), Cognitive Behavioral Therapy (CBT), and Dialectical Behavioral Therapy (DBT). Distressing thoughts and somatic feelings can be factors that lead to an individual using substances but may also be consequences following substance use. A goal of contextual CBT approaches is to work with individuals on how they relate to these thoughts and feelings rather than changing the thoughts and feelings themselves. In particular ACT and DBT focus on how the function of a particular behavior (like using substances) serves an individual and the context in which these behaviors occur (Stotts & Northrup, 2015).

Dialectical Behavior Therapy

Dialectical behavior therapy (DBT) was created by Marsha Linehan and originally used for treatment of individuals with borderline personality disorder (BPD). Since then, it has been expanded for use with a range of mental health concerns including SUDs. Although DBT has not been widely studied as a form of substance use treatment, the foci on how emotional dysregulation impacts dysfunctional behaviors and building adaptive skills to decrease dysregulation is a cogent fit for working with people with SUDs (Cavicchioli et al., 2020). Likewise, DBT skills like mindfulness, emotional regulation, and distress tolerance are useful to promote recovery in substance use populations (Cavicchioli et al., 2020). There is emerging evidence that DBT can be effective for treating SUDs in women in the United States and may be useful in addressing substance misuse as well as other clinical concerns, indicating that more research is needed to understand if DBT is a viable option for populations beyond women in the United States (Haktanır & Callender, 2020; Zamboni et a., 2021; Cavicchioli et al., 2020).

Acceptance and Commitment Therapy

The overarching goal of ACT is to build psychological flexibility in the interest of increasing individuals' ability to be in the present moment and engage in behaviors that are more aligned with their values and goals (Osaji et al., 2020). This focus on a values-oriented life is what guides behavior change rather than working to eliminate substance use behaviors that are often used by individuals as a means of avoidance. By utilizing techniques like mindfulness in ACT, individuals can work to become more aware of triggers, cravings, and impulsive behaviors and see them in a nonjudgmental way that facilitates values-congruence (Stotts & Northrup, 2015). Given that ACT can be used with other psychological concerns, this is also an approach that would be appropriate for individuals with dual diagnoses such as depression, anxiety, or other disorders that often accompany SUDs (Lee et al., 2015).

Other Cognitive Behavioral Therapies

Whereas ACT focuses more on the context and function of a behavior, CBT works to change thoughts and emotions in the interest of behavior change (Zamboni et al., 2021). CBT looks at substance use as a behavior that is reinforced and influenced by social and environmental factors (Boness et al., 2023). In using CBT with SUDs, individuals work to learn and identify their triggers and engage in healthier responses to triggers or cravings (Volkow, 2020). An advantage of CBT is that, though it has been found to be useful in treating substance use concerns by itself, it also offers flexibility in that it can be used in combination with other types of therapy or support (McHugh et al., 2010).

A specific component of cognitive-behavioral therapies that has been found effective in working with SUDs is skills training. Individuals with SUDs often struggle with communication and coping skills that can negatively impact support for their recovery as well as their ability to refuse substances. Communication skills help individuals with SUDs create stronger relationships which, in turn, aid in support for recovery (McHugh et al., 2010). Through practicing these skills in therapy, clients often increase confidence in their ability to maintain sobriety. Likewise, CBT-based emotional regulation skills are another subset of skills that have been shown to be beneficial in substance use treatments. Emotional regulation is the ability to be aware of and understand emotions, control behavior while experiencing emotions, engage in strategies to regulate emotions, and accept that experiencing emotional distress is part of living a meaningful life (Weiss et al., 2022). Many individuals may use substances as a means of regulating their emotions, as they receive short term positive reinforcement as the substance alleviates distressing feelings. Through developing skills that aid in emotional regulation like exercise, reaching out to support systems, and engaging in activities, individuals have a set of goal-directed and enjoyable alternatives to engaging in substance use (McHugh et al., 2010).

Seeking Safety is one program that integrates the concepts of CBT in a unique way for individuals who have experienced trauma and substance use. The name comes from the idea that safety is the first priority of treatment and includes safety from substances, abuse, friends who use substances, and other self-destructive behaviors (Najavits, 2006). This intersection of mental health needs is pertinent to treatment modalities as the prevalence of post traumatic stress disorder (PTSD) among those in substance use treatment ranges from 26 percent to 43 percent (Hien et al., 2021). While some modalities will address one concern first, Seeking Safety addresses both PTSD and SUDs together through an integrated model (Najavits, 2006). Seeking Safety consists of twenty-five topics in four distinct sections that include cognitive, behavioral, interpersonal, and case management, where there is a focus on the present and building up an assortment of coping skills

(Najavits, 2004). Seeking Safety is designed to be language accessible to clients and, while there is structure to the program, there is also flexibility to adapt to clients' unique needs (Najavits, 2006). Seeking Safety has been shown to be effective across genders, in group and individual format, and in a variety of settings including outpatient, community mental health, and prison (Najavits, 2004). Given that trauma can be a precursor to substance use and/or co-occur with substance use, Seeking Safety could be a unique way to address a multitude of client needs within a single modality.

Motivational Interviewing

Given that substance use treatment programs can be compulsory for some individuals, readiness for change can vary widely between clients. Change is possible when there is dissonance between a client's current substance use and related life circumstances and their desired state of being (Miller et al., 2003). Motivational interviewing is a therapeutic approach that can help people build intrinsic motivation to change (Carroll et al., 2006) as low readiness for change is often a barrier to engaging in treatment (Miller et al., 2003). Working through the Stages of Change Model is one way to identify readiness for change based on a client's behavior. People can move sequentially through these stages but it is common for individuals to move back and forth and not in any particular order as they progress through SUDs treatment.

There are four stages that make up this model, *precontemplation*, *contemplation*, *preparation*, and *action*; two additional stages, *maintenance* and *relapse* are often included. Motivational interviewing was found to be more helpful than skills-based counseling for clients who were heavy drinkers in the precontemplative and contemplative stages indicating that motivation for change could be a significant factor in determining which substance use treatment is the best fit for a client (Heather et al., 1996; Miller et al., 2003). Assessing readiness is also a preferable choice to one-size-fits-all approaches. Understanding clients' unique attributes, including readiness for change and their worldview, are important factors to consider when considering SUD treatment options.

Conclusion

While research on mutual support groups other than AA is lacking, it is important that researchers and mental health professionals work to provide appropriate care for clients including understanding best practices for nonreligious individuals in substance use treatment. Historically, substance use treatment, especially inpatient substance use programs, integrates spirituality into their provision of care (Brooks & McHenry, 2023). This creates a space that is incongruent with many nonreligious clients' nonbelief while reinforcing, implicitly or explicitly, that recovery from substance use is not possible without a god or higher power (Munro, 2019). Incorporating spirituality can be beneficial for clients who identify as such, but it is detrimental to nonreligious clients, as well as a cited reason individuals discontinue their attendance in mutual support groups (Krentzman, 2008; Laudet, 2003). Nonreligious clients deserve to have their nonbelief honored and recognized and receive care that is not a direct contradiction to personal values. Creating and supporting secular treatment options, for any individual to utilize, is an important aspect of the counseling field and advocating for client care.

Nonreligious individuals possess a set of strengths not often recognized in research or clinical settings (Bishop, 2018; Abbott & Santiago, 2023; Brewster et al., 2014). Providing treatment that capitalizes on those strengths rather than seeing secularity as a character defect is an important component of multicultural care. Researchers and therapists are in a unique position to be advocates for those with marginalized identities and can continue to do so through developing a set of resources that can be used for nonreligious clients. While nonreligious individuals are not homogenous and should be recognized in the unique ways they may identify with their nonbelief there is a necessity to continue expanding resources and treatment options that can be utilized by this group (D'Andrea & Sprenger, 2007). Evidence-based practices are a core part of therapy and continuing to include nonreligious individuals in substance use research as well as exploring the efficacy of treatment options that do not integrate AA, 12-step programs, or spirituality is vital to ensuring evidence-based treatments are accessible to all people. Care for clients takes place not only on an individual level but also on a systemic level where mental health professionals are able to engage in the social advocacy part of their role to ensure clients have access to care that is not discriminatory toward their nonbelief and/or nonspirituality.

References

Abbott, D. M. (2021). Psychotherapy with nonreligious clients: A relational-cultural approach. *Professional Psychology, Research and Practice*, 52(5), 470–6. https://doi.org/10.1037/pro0000392

Abbott, D. M., & Mollen, D. (2018). Atheism as a concealable stigmatized identity: Outness, anticipated stigma, and well-being. *The Counseling Psychologist*, 46(6), 685–707. https://doi.org/10.1177/0011000018792669

Abbott, D. M., & Santiago, H. J. (2023). Rural atheists in the United States: A critical grounded theory investigation. *Journal of Counseling Psychology*, 70(4), 377. https://doi.org/10.1037/cou0000671

Adan, A., & Benaiges, I. (2016). Comorbidity between substance use disorder and severe mental illness: Dual diagnosis. In V. Preedy (Eds)., *Neuropathology of Drug Addictions and Substance Misuse* (Vol. 3). (pp. 258–68). Elsevier Inc. https://doi.org/10.1016/B978-0-12-800634-4.00026-3

Alcoholics Anonymous (AA). (2001). *Alcoholics Anonymous: The story of how thousands of men and women have recovered from alcoholism* (4th ed.). Alcoholics Anonymous World Services.

American Psychiatric Association. (2022). *Diagnostic and statistical manual of mental disorders* (5th ed., text rev.). https://psychiatryonline.org/doi/book/10.1176/appi.books.9780890425787

American Psychological Association. (n.d.) Addiction. In *APA dictionary of psychology*. https://dictionary.apa.org/addiction

Bergman, B. G., Greene, M. C., Zemore, S. E., & Kelly, J. F. (2024). Prevalence and correlates of 12-step and second-wave mutual-help attendance in a nationally representative US sample. *Alcohol, Clinical & Experimental Research*, 48(3), 545–55. https://doi.org/10.1111/acer.15268

Bishop, B. (2018). Advocating for atheist clients in the counseling profession. *Counseling and Values*, 63(1), 17–30. https://doi.org/10.1002/cvj.12070

Blume, A. W., Rudisill, D. M., Hendricks, S., & Santoya, N. (2013). Disease model. In P. M. Miller (Eds.), *Principles of Addiction* (Vol. 1). (pp. 71–76). Elsevier Inc. https://doi.org/10.1016/B978-0-12-398336-7.00007-3

Boness, C. L., Votaw, V. R., Schwebel, F. J., Moniz-Lewis, D. I. K., McHugh, R. K., & Witkiewitz, K. (2023). An evaluation of cognitive behavioral therapy for substance use disorders: A systematic review and application of the Society of Clinical Psychology criteria for empirically supported treatments. *Clinical Psychology*, 30(2), 129–42. https://doi.org/10.1037/cps0000131

Brewster, M. E., Hammer, J., Sawyer, J. S., Eklund, A., & Palamar, J. (2016). Perceived experiences of atheist discrimination: Instrument development and evaluation. *Journal of Counseling Psychology*, 63(5), 557–70. https://doi.org/10.1037/cou0000156

Brewster, M. E., Robinson, M. A., Sandil, R., Esposito, J., & Geiger, E. (2014). Arrantly absent: Atheism in psychological science from 2001 to 2012. *The Counseling Psychologist*, 42(5), 628–63. https://doi.org/10.1177/0011000014528051

Brooks, F., & McHenry, B. (2023). *A contemporary approach to substance use disorders and addiction counseling*. John Wiley & Sons.

Caldwell-Harris, C. L., Wilson, A. L., LoTempio, E., & Beit-Hallahmi, B. (2011). Exploring the atheist personality: well-being, awe, and magical thinking in atheists, Buddhists, and Christians. *Mental Health, Religion & Culture*, 14(7), 659–72. https://doi.org/10.1080/13674676.2010.509847

Carroll, K. M., Ball, S. A., Nich, C., Martino, S., Frankforter, T. L., Farentinos, C., Kunkel, L. E., Mikulich-Gilbertson, S. K., Morgenstern, J., Obert, J. L., Polcin, D., Snead, N., & Woody, G. E. (2006). Motivational interviewing to improve treatment engagement and outcome in individuals seeking treatment for substance abuse: A multisite effectiveness study. *Drug and Alcohol Dependence*, 81(3), 301–12. https://doi.org/10.1016/j.drugalcdep.2005.08.002

Cavicchioli, M., Ramella, P., Vassena, G., Simone, G., Prudenziati, F., Sirtori, F., Movalli, M., & Maffei, C. (2020). Dialectical behaviour therapy skills training for the treatment of addictive behaviours among individuals with alcohol use disorder: the effect of emotion regulation and experiential avoidance. *The American Journal of Drug and Alcohol Abuse*, 46(3), 368–84. https://doi.org/10.1080/00952990.2020.1712411

Centers for Disease Control and Prevention. (2023, June). Drug overdose deaths. https://www.cdc.gov/nchs/hus/topics/drug-overdose-deaths.htm#print

Centers for Disease Control and Prevention. (2024a, August 6). Data on excessive alcohol use. https://www.cdc.gov/alcohol/excessive-drinking-data/index.html

Centers for Disease Control and Prevention. (2024b, August 23). SUDORS dashboard: Fatal drug overdose data. https://www.cdc.gov/overdose-prevention/data-research/facts-stats/sudors-dashboard-fatal-overdose-data.html

Centers for Disease Control and Prevention. (2025, January 14). Alcohol use and your health. https://www.cdc.gov/alcohol/about-alcohol-use/index.html

D'Andrea, L. M., & Sprenger, J. (2007). Atheism and nonspirituality as diversity issues in counseling. *Counseling and Values*, 51(2), 149–58. https://doi.org/10.1002/j.2161-007X.2007.tb00072.x

Dossett, W. (2013). Addiction, spirituality and 12-step programmes. *International Social Work*, 56(3), 369–83. https://doi.org/10.1177/0020872813475689

Earleywine, M. (2002). *Understanding marijuana: A new look at the scientific evidence*. Oxford University Press.

Fiorentine, R. (1999). After drug treatment: Are 12-Step programs effective in maintaining abstinence? *The American Journal of Drug and Alcohol Abuse*, 25(1), 93–116. https://doi.org/10.1081/ADA-100101848

Flynn, P. M., & Brown, B. S. (2008). Co-occurring disorders in substance abuse treatment: Issues and prospects. *Journal of Substance Abuse Treatment*, 34(1), 36–47. https://doi.org/10.1016/j.jsat.2006.11.013

Galen, L. (2015). Atheism, wellbeing, and the wager: Why not believing in God (with others) is good for you. *Science, Religion and Culture*, 2(3), 54–69. https://doi.org/10.17582/journal.src/2015/2.3.54.69

Grudzina, P. (2016). Secular dissent: Protecting non-believers from coercive religious parole programs. *The Journal of Criminal Law & Criminology*, 106(3), 565–92.

Haktanır, A., & Callender, K. A. (2020). Meta-analysis of dialectical behavior therapy (DBT) for treating substance use. *Research on Education and Psychology* 4 [Special issue], 74–87.

Hayward, R. D., Krause, N., Ironson, G., Hill, P. C., & Emmons, R. (2016). Health and well-being among the non-religious: Atheists, agnostics, and no preference compared with religious group members. *Journal of Religion and Health*, 55(3), 1024–37. https://doi.org/10.1007/s10943-015-0179-2

Heather, N., Rollnick, S., Bell, A., & Richmond, R. (1996). Effects of brief counselling among male heavy drinkers identified on general hospital wards. *Drug and Alcohol Review*, 15(1), 29–38. https://doi.org/10.1080/09595239600185641

Hibbard, P. F., & Sheidow, A. J. (2024). Cooperation vs. affiliation: An exploratory qualitative study of Alcoholics Anonymous' position within the recovery ecosystem. *Journal of Addictive Diseases*, 42(2), 103–11. https://doi.org/10.1080/10550887.2022.2149233

Hien, D. A., López-Castro, T., Fitzpatrick, S., Ruglass, L. M., Fertuck, E. A., & Melara, R. (2021). A unifying translational framework to advance treatment research for comorbid PTSD and substance use disorders. *Neuroscience and Biobehavioral Reviews*, 127, 779–94. https://doi.org/10.1016/j.neubiorev.2021.05.022

Hinds, Z., Herbitter, C., Bryant, W. T., Newberger, N. G., & Livingston, N. A. (2024). Hazardous substance use among sexual and gender minority adults: A deeper look into distal minority stressors. *Psychology of Sexual Orientation and Gender Diversity*, 11(1), 105–12. https://doi.org/10.1037/sgd0000583

Horvath, A. T., & Velten, E. (2000). Smart Recovery: Addiction recovery support from a cognitive-behavioral perspective. *Journal of Rational-Emotive and Cognitive-Behavior Therapy*, 18(3), 181–91. https://doi.org/10.1023/A:1007831005098

Horvath, A. T., & Yeterian, J. (2012). SMART Recovery: Self-empowering, science-based addiction recovery support. *Journal of Groups in Addiction & Recovery*, 7(2–4), 102–17. https://doi.org/10.1080/1556035X.2012.705651

Jegede, O., Rhee, T. G., Stefanovics, E. A., Zhou, B., & Rosenheck, R. A. (2022). Rates and correlates of dual diagnosis among adults with psychiatric and substance use disorders in a nationally representative U.S. sample. *Psychiatry Research*, 315, 114720. https://doi.org/10.1016/j.psychres.2022.114720

Johnstad, P. G. (2023). Racial and religious motives for drug criminalization. *Drug Science, Policy and Law*, 9, 1–17. https://doi.org/10.1177/20503245231198526

Jones, C. M., Clayton, H. B., Deputy, N. P., Roehler, D. R., Ko, J. Y., Esser, M. B., Brookmeyer, K. A., & Hertz, M. F. (2020). Prescription opioid misuse and use of alcohol and other substances among high school students - Youth Risk Behavior Survey, United States, 2019. *MMWR. Morbidity and Mortality Weekly Report*, 69(1), 38–46. https://doi.org/10.15585/mmwr.su6901a5

Kelly, J. F., Humphreys, K., & Ferri, M. (2020). Alcoholics Anonymous and other 12-step programs for alcohol use disorder. *The Cochrane Database of Systematic Reviews*, 3(3), CD012880. https://doi.org/10.1002/14651858.CD012880.pub2

Kelly, J. F., Kahler, C. W., & Humphreys, K. (2010). Assessing why substance use disorder patients drop out from or refuse to attend 12-step mutual-help groups: The "REASONS" questionnaire. *Addiction Research & Theory*, 18(3), 316–25. https://doi.org/10.3109/16066350903254775

Kelly, J. F., Levy, S., & Matlack, M. (2024). A systematic qualitative study investigating why individuals attend, and what they like, dislike, and find most helpful about, smart recovery, alcoholics anonymous, both, or neither. *Journal of Substance Use and Addiction Treatment*, 161, 209337. https://doi.org/10.1016/j.josat.2024.209337

Kelly, J. F., Levy, S. A., & Hoeppner, B. B. (2023). An investigation of SMART Recovery: protocol for a longitudinal cohort study of individuals making a new recovery attempt from alcohol use disorder. *BMJ Open*, 13(2), e066898. https://doi.org/10.1136/bmjopen-2022-066898

Kelly, P. J., Raftery, D., Deane, F. P., Baker, A. L., Hunt, D., & Shakeshaft, A. (2017). From both sides: Participant and facilitator perceptions of SMART Recovery groups. *Drug and Alcohol Review*, 36(3), 325–32. https://doi.org/10.1111/dar.12416

Krentzman, A. R. (2008). The evidence base for the effectiveness of Alcoholics Anonymous: Implications for social work practice. *Journal of Social Work Practice in the Addictions*, 7(4), 27–48. https://doi.org/10.1300/J160v07n04_03

Kurtz, E. (2002). Alcoholics Anonymous and the disease concept of alcoholism. *Alcoholism Treatment Quarterly*, 20(3–4), 5–39. https://doi.org/10.1300/J020v20n03_02

Lander, L., Howsare, J., & Byrne, M. (2013). The impact of substance use disorders on families and children: From theory to practice. *Social Work in Public Health*, 28(3–4), 194–205. https://doi.org/10.1080/19371918.2013.759005

Laudet, A. B. (2003). Attitudes and beliefs about 12-step groups among addiction treatment clients and clinicians: Toward identifying obstacles to participation. *Substance Use & Misuse*, 38(14), 2017–47. https://doi.org/10.1081/JA-120025124

Laudet, A. B., Magura, S., Vogel, H. S., & Knight, E. L. (2003). Participation in 12-step-based fellowships among dually-diagnosed persons. *Alcoholism Treatment Quarterly*, 21(2), 19–39. https://doi.org/10.1300/J020v21n02_02

Laudet, A. B., Morgen, K., & White, W. L. (2006). The role of social supports, spirituality, religiousness, life meaning and affiliation with 12-step fellowships in quality of life satisfaction among individuals in recovery from alcohol and drug problems. *Alcoholism Treatment Quarterly*, 24(1–2), 33–73. https://doi.org/10.1300/J020v24n01_04

Lee, E. B., An, W., Levin, M. E., & Twohig, M. P. (2015). An initial meta-analysis of Acceptance and Commitment Therapy for treating substance use disorders. *Drug and Alcohol Dependence*, 155, 1–7. https://doi.org/10.1016/j.drugalcdep.2015.08.004

LifeRing. (2024, May 5). About LifeRing. https://lifering.org/lifering-recovery-menu/

Locke, J. L. (2021). The prohibition crusade and American moral politics. In *A Companion to American Religious History* (pp. 252–64). https://doi.org/10.1002/9781119583707.ch19

Lyons, G. C., Deane, F. P., & Kelly, P. J. (2013). Faith-based substance abuse programs. In P. M. Miller (Ed.)., *Interventions for Addiction: Comprehensive Addictive Behaviors and Disorders* (Vol. 3). (pp. 147–54). Elsevier Inc.

Mäkela, K. (1983). The uses of alcohol and their cultural regulation. *Acta Sociologica*, 26(1), 21–31. https://doi.org/10.1177/000169938302600102

McHugh, R. K., Hearon, B. A., & Otto, M. W. (2010). Cognitive behavioral therapy for substance use disorders. *The Psychiatric Clinics of North America*, 33(3), 511–25. https://doi.org/10.1016/j.psc.2010.04.012

McHugh, R. K., Votaw, V. R., Sugarman, D. E., & Greenfield, S. F. (2018). Sex and gender differences in substance use disorders. *Clinical Psychology Review*, 66, 12–23. https://doi.org/10.1016/j.cpr.2017.10.012

Mellos, E., & Paparrigopoulos, T. (2022). Substance use during the COVID-19 pandemic: What is really happening? *Psychiatrike Psychiatriki*, 33(1), 17–20. https://doi.org/10.22365/jpsych.2022.072

Menzies, D., & Davidson, B. (2002). Authenticity and belonging: The experience of being known in the group. *Group Analysis*, 35(1), 43–55. https://doi.org/10.1177/053331602400934016

Meyer, I. H. (2003). Prejudice, social stress, and mental health in lesbian, gay, and bisexual populations: Conceptual issues and research evidence. *Psychological Bulletin*, 129(5), 674–97. https://doi.org/10.1037/0033-2909.129.5.674

Miller, W. R., Yahne, C. E., & Tonigan, J. S. (2003). Motivational interviewing in drug abuse services: A randomized trial. *Journal of Consulting and Clinical Psychology*, 71(4), 754–63. https://doi.org/10.1037/0022-006X.71.4.754

Mintert, J., Tran, A. G. T. T., & Kurpius, S. (2020). Religious and/or spiritual social justice advocacy: Guidance from the multicultural and social justice counseling competencies. *Counseling and Values*, 65(1), 2–14. https://doi.org/10.1002/cvj.12119

Munro, Z. A. (2019). Introducing the non-religious in Alcoholics Anonymous. *Implicit Religion*, 22(2), 194–214. https://doi.org/10.1558/imre.37683

Najavits, L. M. (2004). Treatment of posttraumatic stress disorder and substance abuse: Clinical guidelines for implementing seeking safety therapy. *Alcoholism Treatment Quarterly*, 22(1), 43–62. https://doi.org/10.1300/J020v22n01_04

Najavits, L. M. (2006). Seeking safety: Therapy for posttraumatic stress disorder and substance use disorder. In V. M. Follette & J. I. Ruzek (Eds.), *Cognitive-behavioral therapies for trauma* (2nd ed., pp. 228–57). The Guilford Press.

Nathan, P. E., Conrad, M., & Skinstad, A. H. (2016). History of the concept of addiction. *Annual Review of Clinical Psychology*, 12, 29–51. https://doi.org/10.1146/annurev-clinpsy-021815-093546

National Institute on Drug Abuse. 2022, May 4. Sex and Gender Differences in Substance Use. https://nida.nih.gov/publications/research-reports/substance-use-in-women/sex-gender-differences-in-substance-use

Nikmanesh, Z., Baluchi, M. H., & Motlagh, A. A. P. (2017). The role of self-efficacy beliefs and social support on prediction of addiction relapse. *International Journal of High Risk Behaviors and Addiction*, 6(1), e21209. https://doi.org/10.5812/ijhrba.21209

Norko, M. A., & Fitch, W. L. (2014). DSM-5 and substance use disorders: Clinicolegal implications. *The Journal of the American Academy of Psychiatry and the Law*, 42(4), 443–52.

Novotná, G., Dobbins, M., Jack, S. M., Sword, W., Niccols, A., Brooks, S., & Henderson, J. (2013). The influence of lived experience with addiction and recovery on practice-related decisions among professionals working in addiction agencies serving women. *Drugs: Education, Prevention & Policy*, 20(2), 140–48. https://doi.org/10.3109/09687637.2012.714015

Olsen, Y. (2022). What is addiction? History, terminology, and core concepts. *Medical Clinics*, 106(1), 1–12. https://doi.org/10.1016/j.mcna.2021.08.001

Osaji, J., Ojimba, C., & Ahmed, S. (2020). The use of Acceptance and Commitment Therapy in substance use disorders: A review of literature. *Journal of Clinical Medicine Research*, 12(10), 629–33. https://doi.org/10.14740/jocmr4311

Paradies, Y. (2006). A systematic review of empirical research on self-reported racism and health. *International Journal of Epidemiology*, 35(4), 888–901. https://doi.org/10.1093/ije/dyl056

Pascoe, E. A., & Smart Richman, L. (2009). Perceived discrimination and health: A meta-analytic review. *Psychological Bulletin*, 135(4), 531–54. http://dx.doi.org/10.1037/a0016059

Phillips, R. (2014). *Alcohol: A history*. UNC Press Books.

Pickard, H. (2017). Responsibility without blame for addiction. *Neuroethics*, 10(1), 169–80. https://doi.org/10.1007/s12152-016-9295-2

Presley, C. C., & Lindsley, C. W. (2018). DARK classics in chemical neuroscience: Opium, a historical perspective. *ACS Chemical Neuroscience*, 9(10), 2503–18. https://doi.org/10.1021/acschemneuro.8b00459

Quinn, D. M., Williams, M. K., Quintana, F., Gaskins, J. L., Overstreet, N. M., Pishori, A., Earnshaw, V. A., Perez, G., & Chaudoir, S. R. (2014). Examining effects of anticipated stigma, centrality, salience, internalization, and outness on psychological distress for people with concealable stigmatized identities. *PloS One*, 9(5), e96977. https://doi.org/10.1371/journal.pone.0096977

Roberts, A., Rogers, J., Mason, R., Siriwardena, A. N., Hogue, T., Whitley, G. A., & Law, G. R. (2021). Alcohol and other substance use during the COVID-19 pandemic: A systematic review. *Drug and Alcohol Dependence*, 229(Pt A), 109150. https://doi.org/10.1016/j.drugalcdep.2021.109150

Robinson, S. M., & Adinoff, B. (2016). The classification of substance use disorders: Historical, contextual, and conceptual considerations. *Behavioral Sciences*, 6(3), 18. https://doi.org/10.3390/bs6030018

Sahker, E. (2016). Therapy with the nonreligious: Ethical and clinical considerations. *Professional Psychology, Research and Practice*, 47(4), 295–302. https://doi.org/10.1037/pro0000087

Skewes, M., & Gonzalez, V. (2013). The biopsychosocial model of addiction. In P. M. Miller (Ed.), *Comprehensive Addictive Behaviors and Disorders* (Vol. 1). (pp. 61–70). Elsevier Inc. https://doi.org/10.1016/B978-0-12-398336-7.00006-1

SMART Recovery International. (2024). What is SMART Recovery. https://smartrecovery.org/what-is-smart-recovery

Speed, D., Coleman, T. J., & Langston, J. (2018). What do you mean, "What does it all mean?" Atheism, nonreligion, and life meaning. *SAGE Open*, 8(1), 215824401775423. https://doi.org/10.1177/2158244017754238

Speed, D., & Fowler, K. (2016). What's God got to do with it? How religiosity predicts atheists' health. *Journal of Religion and Health*, 55(1), 296–308. https://doi.org/10.1007/s10943-015-0083-9

Spencer M. R., Miniño, A. M., Warner, M. (2022). Drug overdose deaths in the United States, 2001–2021. NCHS Data Brief, no 457. National Center for Health Statistics. https://dx.doi.org/10.15620/cdc:122556

Ståhl, T., & van Prooijen, J.W. (2021). Analytic atheism: Valuing epistemic rationality strengthens the association between analytic thinking and religious disbelief. *Personality and Individual Differences*, 179, 110914. https://doi.org/10.1016/j.paid.2021.110914

Stotts, A. L., & Northrup, T. F. (2015). The promise of third-wave behavioral therapies in the treatment of substance use disorders. *Current Opinion in Psychology*, 2, 75–81. https://doi.org/10.1016/j.copsyc.2014.12.028

Thatcher, M. S. (2011). Negotiating the tension between the discourses of Christianity and spiritual pluralism in Alcoholics Anonymous. *Journal of Applied Communication Research*, 39(4), 389–405. https://doi.org/10.1080/00909882.2011.608694

The Trevor Project. (2022). Substance use and suicide risk among LGBTQ youth. https://www.thetrevorproject.org/research-briefs/substance-use-and-suicide-risk-among-lgbtq-youth-jan-2022/

Tonigan, J. S., Miller, W. R., & Schermer, C. (2002). Atheists, agnostics and Alcoholics Anonymous. *Journal of Studies on Alcohol*, 63(5), 534–541. https://doi.org/10.15288/jsa.2002.63.534

U.S. Department of Health and Human Services (HHS), Office of the Surgeon General. (2016) *Facing addiction in America: The Surgeon General's report on alcohol, drugs, and health.* https://www.ncbi.nlm.nih.gov/books/NBK424857/pdf/Bookshelf_NBK424857.pdf

Velleman, R., & Templeton, L. J. (2016). Impact of parents' substance misuse on children: An update. *BJPsych Advances*, 22(2), 108–17. https://doi.org/10.1192/apt.bp.114.014449

Volkow, N. D. (2020). Personalizing the treatment of substance use disorders. *The American Journal of Psychiatry*, 177(2), 113–16. https://doi.org/10.1176/appi.ajp.2019.19121284

Volkow, N. D., Poznyak, V., Saxena, S., & Gerra, G. (2017). Drug use disorders: Impact of a public health rather than a criminal justice approach. *World Psychiatry*, 16(2), 213–14. https://doi.org/10.1002/wps.20428

Wallace, J. (2012). Theory of 12-step-oriented treatment. In S. T. Walters & F. Rotgers (Eds.), *Treating substance abuse: Theory and technique* (3rd ed., pp. 167–90). The Guilford Press.

Watkins, K. E., Burnam, A., Kung, F. Y., & Paddock, S. (2001). A national survey of care for persons with co-occurring mental and substance use disorders. *Psychiatric Services*, 52(8), 1062–68. https://doi.org/10.1176/appi.ps.52.8.1062

Weinandy, J. T. G., & Grubbs, J. B. (2021). Religious and spiritual beliefs and attitudes towards addiction and addiction treatment: A scoping review. *Addictive Behaviors Reports*, 14, 100393. https://doi.org/10.1016/j.abrep.2021.100393

Weiss, N. H., Kiefer, R., Goncharenko, S., Raudales, A. M., Forkus, S. R., Schick, M. R., & Contractor, A. A. (2022). Emotion regulation and substance use: A meta-analysis. *Drug and Alcohol Dependence*, 230, 109131. https://doi.org/10.1016/j.drugalcdep.2021.109131

Winters, K. C., Stinchfield, R. D., Opland, E., Weller, C., & Latimer, W. W. (2000). The effectiveness of the Minnesota Model approach in the treatment of adolescent drug abusers. *Addiction*, 95(4), 601–12. https://doi.org/10.1046/j.1360-0443.2000.95460111.x

Zamboni, L., Centoni, F., Fusina, F., Mantovani, E., Rubino, F., Lugoboni, F., & Federico, A. (2021). The effectiveness of cognitive behavioral therapy techniques for the treatment of substance use disorders: A narrative review of evidence. *The Journal of Nervous and Mental Disease*, 209(11), 835–45. https://doi.org/10.1097/NMD.0000000000001381

Zemore, S. E., Kaskutas, L. A., Mericle, A., & Hemberg, J. (2017). Comparison of 12-Step groups to mutual help alternatives for AUD in a large, national study: Differences in membership characteristics and group participation, cohesion, and satisfaction. *Journal of Substance Abuse Treatment*, 73, 16–26. https://doi.org/10.1016/j.jsat.2016.10.004

Zuardi, A. W. (2006). History of cannabis as a medicine: A review. *Brazilian Journal of Psychiatry*, 28(2), 153–57. https://doi.org/10.1590/S1516-44462006000200015

14

Conclusion

Promoting Mental Health Among Nonbelievers: Revisiting Lessons and Future Directions

Dena M. Abbott

Chapter Outline

Part of our multicultural training as clinicians involves the acknowledgment that most of us belong to at least one dominant social group and/or have been socialized in contexts that privilege dominant groups (Sue et al., 2022). For example, White clinicians must be aware of the ways they bring White culture to treatment and all clinicians should remain vigilant about the ways in which being socialized in White supremacy culture (Okun, 1999) impacts the services they provide. In preparing clinicians to work in culturally responsive ways, relatively less emphasis is placed on religiousness and hegemonic religion as compared to other diversity factors. Therefore, an important lesson I hope you, the reader, will take from this book is the imperative to avoid the assumption that, because mental health treatment is secularly based, religion and its norms and messages do not find their way into the therapy space. In particular, I hope you will be thoughtful about the ways in which, when it is intentionally or unintentionally infused in psychotherapy, religion influences the therapeutic alliance, treatment progress, and mental health of nonbelieving clients. You may also adapt your preferred interventions or choose alternative approaches in order to better align services with your nonreligious clients' worldviews and values.

Anti-Deficit Focused Intervention

Although we may wish to have more clients come to us for psychotherapy as a preventive measure, many people seek mental health services as a result of distress. Therefore, it is imperative to develop skills in supporting nonreligious clients with presenting concerns directly related to their nonreligiousness (e.g., navigating religious doubt, discrimination) and to approach any other presenting concerns, even when not directly connected to their nonreligiousness, in a culturally responsive manner that honors their experiences and worldviews. That said, deficit-focused scholarship and frameworks are a problem in psychological science (Márquez-Magaña, 2024) and place responsibility on the individual rather than the oppressive systems that contribute to or cause their distress. As outlined in this text, many of the challenges faced by nonbelievers in the United States can be traced back to the influence of structural Christian dominance. Accordingly, we must ground our work in how the health of individuals we treat is a function of these systems and target our interventions at the structural level (Wilcox et al., 2024).

Advocacy as Intervention

Religion, and Christianity specifically, have often been invoked by policymakers as the rationale for the legislation they introduce, despite the Establishment Clause of the Constitution colloquially known as "separation of church and state." Christianity is increasingly being explicitly drawn upon by people with power as central to US American life. At the 2025 National Prayer Breakfast, President Donald Trump (2025) stated, "We have to bring religion back. We have to bring it back much stronger." Later, he added, "I really believe you can't be happy without religion, without that belief." Shortly after, he established a task force via executive order for eradicating anti-Christian bias (Exec. Order No. 14,202, 2025). These strong messages about the importance of religion, including for health, and threats of repercussions for those who critique Christianity are potentially harmful to nonbelievers, especially those for whom their nonreligiousness is a central and/or salient part of their identity as this group reports higher awareness of Christian privilege as compared to those with lower identity centrality (Brewster et al., in press).

Clinicians can, therefore, take steps to combat these messages in the interest of their nonreligious clients, sharing knowledge that challenges misinformation. One strategy is the use of public scholarship, or dissemination of information outside of traditional academic routes like journals and conferences. Clinicians can publish opinion pieces (i.e., op-eds), engage with media (e.g., podcasts), and create content on social media that extends the reach of our expertise to the general public (Alexander, 2024). We can also engage in public policy advocacy, wherein we interface with our legislators through phone calls, emails, public written comments, and testimonies. This form of advocacy is critical in promoting social change (Alexander & Allo, 2021). Often, advocacy for nonbelievers involves simultaneous advocacy for other groups and issues relevant to our work as mental health professionals. For example, anti-transgender legislation, like bans on gender-affirming care, are propelled by conservative Christian organizations that use religious beliefs as justification for regulating bodies (Crasnow, 2021). We can ground our opposition in secular human and sexual rights frameworks (World Association for Sexual Health [WAS], 2014) and leverage our expertise about gender diversity and the relationship between transphobic rhetoric and transgender health to discourage anti-transgender legislation and, ideally, shape health-promoting policy.

Activism, too, is an important driver of social change in which we, clinicians, may take part and that benefits the public we serve. Activism involves campaigning for causes (Alexander & Allo, 2021) and might include participation in public demonstrations (Nadal, 2017) or civil disobedience (Flynn et al., 2021). Some mental health professionals are trained to engage in political neutrality, but I assert doing so abandons our values, violates our ethical obligations to our clients, and disregards the reality that the personal is political. Of course, there are real and important considerations to make with regard to our activism, including ethics and professional boundaries; however, there are ways to responsibly engage in activism that are congruent with our roles as mental health professionals (see Nadal, 2017 for a review). Clinicians looking to support the rights and health of nonreligious people, therefore, might find opportunities to partner with organizations engaged in activism promoting (non)religious freedom, like the Freedom from Religion Foundation, American Atheists, or the American Civil Liberties Union.

Celebrating Strengths

Client-centered advocacy is also essential. Although it may not as directly address the structural problems that catalyze distress for our clients, supporting them in exploring issues of power and marginalization, making space to hear their stories, and helping them advocate for themselves also constitutes advocacy (Alexander & Allo, 2021). One way to engage in this micro-level advocacy and avoid a deficit-focus is to center the strengths that accompany a nonreligious orientation. French and colleagues (2019) conceptualized a psychological framework of radical healing that facilitates an anti-deficit approach to counseling. Developed for communities of color and, specifically, coping with racial trauma, radical healing positions justice as central to healing, promotes liberation, and emphasizes strengths-focused interventions.

The primary elements of radical healing are critical consciousness, radical hope, strength and resistance, cultural authenticity and self-knowledge, and collectivism, all of which capitalize on the strengths of clients (French et al., 2019). For clients who are marginalized, therapists may engage in advocacy on their behalf or support clients in building their own activist identity; however, therapists can also help clients reframe resistance against oppression to include more individually focused strategies like living a life full of joy. Resistance can, in turn, foster hope for a healthier personal and collective future. Again, this framework was developed with people of the global majority (i.e., people of color) in mind. However, the White Christian Nationalism that drives hegemonic religion in the

United States and, by extension, the oppression of nonbelievers, is inherently imbued with racist beliefs and practices (Butler, 2021). Therefore, the application of radical healing in psychotherapy is useful with individual nonbelieving clients and serves to help disrupt a system that perpetuates racial inequities.

In my own scholarship, numerous strengths of a nonreligious worldview emerged on which clinicians might capitalize in psychotherapy. Across studies comprised of diverse subgroups of nonbelievers (e.g., women, people of color), a sense of liberation was repeatedly cited as a primary benefit, particularly among people who had exited religion. Participants reported feeling free to construct values outside of the constraints of religious dogma (Abbott & Anaya, 2022). Given that values congruence is a critical component of health (Kashdan & Rottenberg, 2010), this ability to act in alignment with a personally constructed set of values represents a strength. Other common benefits of their nonreligion cited by participants were open-mindedness, political awakenings, development of like-minded community, and promotion of their mental health (Abbott et al., 2020; Abbott & Santiago, 2023).

Expanding on the Contributions in This Book

The authors of the chapters in this text offer excellent evidence-based information about nonbelievers as it relates to mental health care. Below, I highlight a few of the topics discussed earlier in the book and offer additional context and implications for clinical practice.

Secularization Trends in the United States

It is worth mentioning that there is scholarship that challenges the notion of secularization in the United States. Levin and colleagues (2022) rightly point out that a large majority of people categorized as religious "nones" are, in fact, believers in a higher power despite reporting no religious affiliation. Using General Social Survey data, a sizable proportion of religious nones believe in heaven and/or hell or engage in religious service attendance or prayer. Espinosa (2023) made a similar argument that the secularization of Latine people may be overstated. Atheists, by contrast, report these beliefs and activities at much lower rates (Levin et al., 2022). In my own scholarship (see Abbott & Mollen, 2018; Abbott et al., 2020), I try to emphasize that atheists represent a minority within the religiously unaffiliated and likely have a distinct experience.

In this text, we focus on the experiences of nonbelievers, broadly defined, which would exclude religiously unaffiliated people with belief. However, it is a difficult task to determine what types of belief(s) constitute religiousness and which do not. For example, is belief in a higher power nonreligious whereas belief in the Christian god is religious? What types of higher powers represent nonreligious spirituality rather than religiousness? In clinical practice, the operationalization of terms is less important than the individual's experience. So, ask questions. When a client says they have no religion, probe about what that means for them rather than assuming atheism. Get curious about the catalyzing factors for exiting religion, even when belief in a higher power is retained. It is just as important to avoid assuming nonreligiousness and nonspirituality as it is to avoid assumptions of religiousness.

Nones and Dones: Religious Exiting

The development of nonreligiousness, particularly among religious *dones*, may be misunderstood as a linear process (Smith, 2011; LeDrew, 2013). Some dones move through stages of questioning and trying on different (non)religions and worldviews during and after their process of religious exiting, a sequence of events that ends with the adoption of a congruent nonreligious identity. The time frame during which this process takes place is highly variable. For some, this might take years or even decades. For others, an epiphany about their faith results in an abrupt change that may only take days or weeks (Abbott et al., 2020).

Clinicians may also keep in mind that for many clients, nonreligion may be an end point in their exploration. For others, it may only be a stop along the way to some other place. For example, some religious *nones* become religious later in life, particularly if they marry. Notably, the frequency with which people raised without religion later become religious is much less likely in earlier generational cohorts than in later cohorts (Merino, 2012; Wilkins-Laflamme, 2020). Although nonreligion can provide a strong foundation from which nonbelievers can make sense of life events (e.g., birth of children, death of loved one), those same events could spur an otherwise firmly nonbelieving person to return to a period of (non)religious questioning. Therefore, nonreligious identity exploration is fluid and complex (Smith, 2011; LeDrew, 2013), similar to other forms of identity development (e.g., sexuality, gender). Clinicians can make room for clients to engage in dialectical thinking, or walking the middle path, in which two opposing or contradictory things can simultaneously be true (Shea, 2021). For example, a nonbeliever may have a history of religious trauma and also find comfort in religiously based ways of understanding the world or activities (e.g., listening to gospel music). If their thinking is concrete, guilt may arise from continued engagement in a system that harmed them. Dialectical thinking allows them to hold that elements of the same system that caused them immense pain can also bring joy and peace, and these opposing affective experiences are both valid.

Nonreligion, Well-Being, and Mental Health

An important reminder with regard to nonreligion and health literature is that although well-being may be lower and psychological distress may be higher during periods of questioning (Galen & Kloet, 2011), it does not make such a phase of life pathological. People experience many uncertain times in their lives with regard to work, relationships, and identities that temporarily compromise their health and well-being. Therefore, there is no need to act with a greater sense of urgency to resolve (non)religious uncertainty than any other period of uncertainty in clients' lives. Consider how you might approach working with a client who was questioning their sexual or romantic orientation. You would likely allow them to set the pace for their exploration, moving through periods of more and less certainty about their attraction and experimenting with different labels and behaviors. It is typical for people experiencing religious doubt and/or interested in establishing a personally defined (non)religion, too, to experiment with labels or different (non)religions and vacillate between belief and nonbelief.

In these processes of determining what one believes or does not believe and what identifiers fit their worldview best, people are often navigating decision-making about disclosure and/or concealment of their nonbelief. As with other identities that can be hidden and are stigmatized, there are health benefits to disclosure as it can facilitate authenticity and belonging (Meidlinger & Hope, 2014), and concealment is associated with negative health outcomes (Camacho et al., 2020). It is, therefore, tempting as a clinician to encourage clients to disclose their nonbelief to others. However, in studies of people who experienced interpersonal violence (IPV), disclosure of IPV is harmful when met with non-affirming reactions (Dworkin et al., 2019) and some people with concealable stigmatized identities may benefit from being strategic about to whom and in what settings they are "out" (Orne, 2011). For atheists, in particular, in addition to the emotional and relational risks of coming out as a nonbeliever, some atheists in rural parts of the US experience intimidation and fear for their physical safety (Abbott & Santiago, 2023). Clinicians can promote the health of their nonbelieving clients by assisting them in making thoughtful decisions about disclosure that take into account all the potential risks and honor their individual risk tolerance.

Disclosure and concealment decisions are one element of minority stress, or added and potentially chronic stress associated with navigating the world with marginalized cultural positionalities (Brooks, 1981; Meyer, 2003). Minority stress is associated with negative mental health outcomes among atheists (Abbott & Mollen, 2018; Brewster et al., 2016). Importantly, emerging evidence suggests social safety may be a better predictor of allostatic load, or the cumulative effects of stress on the body, than minority stress (Diamond & Alley, 2022). Social connection, belongingness, inclusion, recognition, and protection may buffer the negative impact of oppression, in this case, anti-atheist discrimination, on health. Therefore, clinicians may assist clients in forming and sustaining affirming communities, whether small and informal or relatively large and more structured (e.g., Black Nonbelievers, Ex-Muslims of North America).

Diverse Groups of Nonbelievers

In this text, in addition to broad suggestions for working with nonreligious clients, authors discuss the unique considerations clinicians might make when working with nonbelievers with other marginalized social locations. Specifically, we focused on Black, indigenous, and people of color (BIPOC), LGBTQ+, and women and femme nonbelievers, as these groups have the largest bodies of scholarship relative to other cultural positionalities. As such, there are many groups of nonbelievers that deserve deeper examination and are not thoroughly discussed in this book. Likewise, the intersectionality (Crenshaw, 1989) of nonreligiousness and other social identities is a critical area of consideration for clinicians (Moradi & Grzanka, 2017).

Emerging evidence suggests low-income and working class nonreligious people may face unique challenges, such as increased need for concealment due to precarity of disclosure at work and less of a sense of connection to a larger community of nonbelievers (Abbott et al., 2022). Similarly, rural nonbelievers (Abbott & Santiago, 2023) and nonbelievers in the South (Frost et al., 2023) are more cautious with regard to outness in order to feel a sense of control over their emotional and physical safety living in predominantly religious communities. Geography, therefore, appears to play a significant role in nonbelievers' comfort with public nonreligiousness; and, it also influences their sense of connection and community and the frequency with which they encounter anti-atheist discrimination.

In the hundreds of hours I have spent in qualitative interviews with nonbelievers, two common patterns emerge with regard to their geographic location. First, the more religious the region of the United States in which they reside, the more challenging finding other nonbelievers, or believers who affirm their nonbelief, becomes. The other common theme is that nonbelievers living in the northeast and western United States describe lower religiousness in their communities. They draw a contrast between their lives in these regions and moving to or visiting places like the midwestern or southern United States where religious imagery is more prevalent (e.g., religious billboards, "churches on every street"). In addition to nonreligious people in less religious parts of the country perceiving lower risk and experiencing fewer instances of anti-atheist discrimination, it also seems to make their nonreligiousness a much less salient and/or central aspect of their sense of self.

Due to the prevalence of Christianity in the United States, like broader nonreligion scholarship, studies of particular demographic groups of nonbelievers are predominated by people socialized as or around Christians. A significant limitation of the current evidence base for clinical practice with nonreligious people is the dearth of scholarship of nonbelievers from non-Christian faith backgrounds. In a forthcoming qualitative study of ex-Muslim nonbelievers in the United States, my collaborators and I found the continued influence of Islam on participants' lives was experienced as a saliently oppressive system whereas Christian supremacy was rarely mentioned. This may suggest that nonbelievers struggle most with their former faith or the faith of their families and communities, even if a more culturally dominant faith is a more powerful social force. These represent just a few examples of the differential experiences of nonbelievers when research drills down into the nuances. Therefore, clinicians working with nonreligious clients should probe about other elements and social locations (e.g., former faith, geography) that may lead to experiences that are novel or discrepant as compared to what is currently known or documented in academic literature.

Conclusion

Although the increase in religiously unaffiliated US Americans appears to have stabilized at 28 percent of the population as of 2024, atheists and agnostics increased slightly (3.1 percent to 5 percent and 4 percent to 6 percent, respectively) since the last large-scale religious landscape survey in 2014 (Pew Research, 2015; 2025). In other words, the proportion of the unaffiliated who are nonreligious, without belief in a higher power, continues to rise. Over the same time frame and particularly since 2025, the infusion of Christianity into US politics and, in turn, culture has deepened.

As such, it is critical that mental health services adapt to be culturally responsive to nonreligious people, including the potential influence of religious and Christian hegemony on their health and well-being. This book provides an introduction to and summary of the existing scholarship that informs such culturally responsive practice with nonreligious clients, outlining opportunities for intervention at the individual and structural levels.

References

Abbott, D. M., & Anaya, E. J. (2022). "Breaking free": A grounded theory study of atheist women in the United States. *Psychology of Women Quarterly*, 46(4), 501–17. https://doi.org/10.1177/03616843221115338

Abbott, D. M., & Mollen, D. (2018). Atheism as a concealable stigmatized identity: Outness, anticipated stigma, and well-being. *The Counseling Psychologist*, 46(6), 685–707. https://doi.org/10.1177/0011000018792669

Abbott, D. M., Mollen, D., Boyles, J., & Anaya, E. J. (2022). Hidden in plain sight: Low-income and working-class atheists. *Journal of Counseling Psychology*, 69(1), 37–50. https://doi.org/10.1037/cou0000562

Abbott, D. M., Mollen, D., Mercier, C., Anaya, E. J., Rukus, V. A. (2020). "Isn't atheism a White thing?": Centering the voices of atheists of color. *Journal of Counseling Psychology*, 67(3), 275–87. https://doi.org/10.1037/cou0000399

Abbott, D. M., & Santiago, H. (2023). Rural atheists in the US: A critical grounded theory investigation. *Journal of Counseling Psychology*, 70(4), 377–87. https://psycnet.apa.org/record/2023-65885-001

Alexander, A. A. (2024). Off the shelf and into the community: Advocacy and public scholarship. *American Journal of Orthopsychiatry*, 95(4), 421–26. https://doi.org/10.1037/ort0000800

Alexander, A. A., & Allo, H. (2021). Building a climate for advocacy training in professional psychology. *The Counseling Psychologist*, 49(7), 1070–89. https://doi.org/10.1177/00110000211027973

Brewster, M. E., Abbott, D. M., Velez, B., Kim, V., Meyer, P. T., & Culver, R. (In press). Unpacking the varieties of nonbelief within US-based marginalized populations. *Secularism and Nonreligion*.

Brewster, M. E., Hammer, J., Sawyer, J. S., Eklund, A., & Palamar, J. (2016). Perceived experiences of atheist discrimination: Instrument development and evaluation. *Journal of Counseling Psychology*, 63(5), 557–70. https://doi.org/10.1037/cou0000156

Brooks, V. R. (1981). *Minority stress and lesbian women*. Lexington Books.

Butler, A. (2021). *White evangelical racism: The politics of morality in America*. University of North Carolina Press.

Camacho, G., Reinka, M. A., & Quinn, D. M. (2020). Disclosure and concealment of stigmatized identities. *Current Opinion in Psychology*, 31, 28–32. https://doi.org/10.1016/j.copsyc.2019.07.031

Crasnow, S. J. (2021). The legacy of "gender ideology": Anti-trans legislation and conservative Christianity's ongoing influence on U.S. law. *Religion and Gender*, 11, 67–71. https://doi.org/10.1163/18785417-01101005

Crenshaw, K. W. (1989). Demarginalizing the intersection of race and sex: A Black feminist critique of antidiscrimination doctrine, feminist theory, and antiracist politics. *University of Chicago Legal Forum*, 140, 139–67.

Diamond, L. M., & Alley, J. (2022). Rethinking minority stress: A social safety perspective on the health effects of stigma in sexually-diverse and gender-diverse populations. *Neuroscience & Biobehavioral Reviews*, 138, 104720. https://doi.org/10.1016/j.neubiorev.2022.104720

Dworkin, E. R., Brill, C. D., & Ullman, S. E. (2019). Social reactions to disclosure of interpersonal violence and psychopathology: A systematic review and meta-analysis. *Clinical Psychology Review*, 72, 101750. https://doi.org/10.1016/j.cpr.2019.101750

Espinosa, G. (2023). Nones, no religious preference, no religion and the misclassification of Latino religious identity. *Religions*, 14(3), 420–41. https://doi.org/10.3390/rel14030420

Exec. Order No. 14,202, 3. C. F. R. (2025). https://www.federalregister.gov/documents/2025/02/12/2025-02611/eradicating-anti-christian-bias

Flynn, A. W. P., Domínguez, Jr., S., Jordan, R. A. S., Dyer, R. L., & Young, E. I. (2021). When the political is professional: Civil disobedience in psychology. *American Psychologist*, 76(8), 1217–31. https://doi.org/10.1037/amp0000867

French, B. H., Lewis, J. A., Mosley, D. V., Adames, H. Y., Chaves-Dueñas, N. Y., Chen, G. A., & Neville, H. A. (2019). Toward a psychological framework of radical healing in communities of color. *The Counseling Psychologist*, 48(1), 14–46. https://doi.org/10.1177/0011000019843506

Frost, J., Ecklund, E. H., & Scheitle, C. P. (2023). Patterns of perceived hostility and identity concealment among self-identified atheists. *Social Forces*, 101(3), 1580–605. https://doi.org/10.1093/sf/soab165

Galen, L. W., & Kloet, J. D. (2011). Mental well-being in the religious and the non-religious: Evidence for a curvilinear relationship. *Mental Health, Religion, & Culture*, 14(7), 673–89. https://doi.org/10.1080/13674676.2010.510829

Kashdan, T. B., & Rottenberg, J. (2010). Psychological flexibility as a fundamental aspect of health. *Clinical Psychology Review*, 30(7), 865–78. https://doi.org/10.1016/j.cpr.2010.03.001

LeDrew, S. (2013). Discovering atheism: Heterogeneity in trajectories to atheist identity and activism. *Sociology of Religion*, 74(4), 431–53. https://doi.org/10.1093/socrel/srt014

Levin, J., Bradshaw, M., Johnson, B. R., & Stark, R. (2022). Are religious "nones" really not religious?: Revisiting Glenn, three decades later. *Interdisciplinary Journal of Research on Religion*, 18(7), 1–29. https://www.baylorisr.org/religious-nones-really-not-religious/

Márquez-Magaña, L. (2024). Anti-deficit is anti-racist and transformative. *Patterns*, 5(3), 100934. https://doi.org/10.1016/j.patter.2024.100934

Meidlinger, P. C., & Hope, D. A. (2014). Differentiating disclosure and concealment in measurement of outness for sexual minorities: The Nebraska Outness Scale. *Psychology of Sexual Orientation and Gender Diversity*, 1(4), 489–97. https://doi.org/10.1037/sgd0000080

Merino, S. M. (2012). Irreligious socialization? The adult religious preferences of individuals raised with no religion. *Secularism and Nonreligion*, 1, 1–16. https://doi.org/10.5334/snr.aa

Meyer, I. H. (2003). Prejudice, social stress, and mental health in lesbian, gay, and bisexual populations: Conceptual issues and research evidence. *Psychological Bulletin*, 129(5), 674–97. https://doi.org/10.1037/0033-2909.129.5.674

Moradi, B., & Grzanka, P. R. (2017). Using intersectionality responsibly: Toward critical epistemology, structural analysis, an social justice activism. *Journal of Counseling Psychology*, 64(5), 500–513. https://doi.org/10.1037/cou0000203

Nadal, K. L. (2017). "Let's get in formation": On becoming a psychologist-activist in the 21st century. *American Psychologist*, 72(9), 935–46. https://doi.org/10.1037/amp0000212

Okun, T. (1999). White supremacy culture. https://www.whitesupremacyculture.info/uploads/4/3/5/7/43579015/okun_-_white_sup_culture_2020.pdf

Orne, J. (2011). "You will always have to 'out' yourself": Reconsidering coming out through strategic outness. *Sexualities*, 14(6), 681–703. https://doi.org/10.1177/1363460711420462

Pew Research Center. (2015). America's changing religious landscape. https://www.pewresearch.org/religion/2015/05/12/americas-changing-religious-landscape

Pew Research Center. (2025). Religious landscape study. https://www.pewresearch.org/religious-landscape-study/

Shea, L-M. (2021). The courage to be: Using DBT skills to choose who to be in uncertainty. *Journal of Humanistic Psychology*, 61(2), 260–74. https://doi.org/10.1177/0022167820950887

Smith, J. M. (2011). Becoming an atheist in America: Constructing identity and meaning from the rejection of theism. *Sociology of Religion*, 72, 215–37. https://doi.org/10.1093/socrel/srq082

Sue, D. W., Sue, D., Neville, H. A., & Smith, L. (2022). *Counseling the culturally diverse: Theory and practice* (9th ed.). Wiley.

Trump, D. J. (2025, February 6). Remarks at the National Prayer Breakfast [Transcript]. https://www.presidency.ucsb.edu/documents/remarks-the-national-prayer-breakfast-37

Wilcox, M. M., Peréz-Rojas, A. E., Marks, L. R., Reynolds, A. L., Suh, H. N., Flores, L. Y., McCubbin, L. D., Wilkins-Yel, K. G., & Miller, M. J. (2024). Structural competencies: Re-grounding counseling psychology in antiracist and decolonial praxis. *The Counseling Psychologist*, 52(4), 650–91. https://doi.org/10.1177/00110000241231029

Wilkins-Laflamme, S. (2020). Like parent, like millennial: Inherited and switched (non) religion among young adults in the U.S. and Canada. *Journal of Religion and Demography*, 7(1), 123–49. https://doi.org/10.1163/2589742X-12347103

World Association for Sexual Health. (2014). *WAS declaration on sexual rights*. https://www.worldsexualhealth.net/was-declaration-on-sexual-rights

Index